THE
Common Core

Teaching Students in Grades 6–12 to Meet the Reading Standards

Maureen McLaughlin
Brenda J. Overturf

THE COLLEGE AND CAREER READINESS ANCHOR STANDARDS IN ACTION

INTERNATIONAL
Reading Association
800 BARKSDALE ROAD, PO BOX 8139
NEWARK, DE 19714-8139, USA
www.reading.org

The International Reading Association attempts, through its publications, to provide a forum for a wide spectrum of opinions on reading. This policy permits divergent viewpoints without implying the endorsement of the Association.

Executive Editor, Publications   Shannon Fortner
Acquisitions Manager   Tori Mello Bachman
Managing Editors   Christina M. Lambert and Susanne Viscarra
Editorial Associate   Wendy Logan
Creative Services/Production Manager   Anette Schuetz
Design and Composition Associate   Lisa Kochel

Art   Cover Design, Lise Holliker Dykes; Cover and Interior Photography, Maureen McLaughlin; Cover Graphic, antishock and 578foot at Shutterstock

Library of Congress Cataloging-in-Publication Data

McLaughlin, Maureen.
  The common core : teaching students in grades 6-12 to meet the reading standards / Maureen McLaughlin, Brenda J. Overturf.
      pages ; cm
  Includes bibliographical references and index.
  ISBN 978-0-87207-706-5
  1. Language arts (Secondary)--Curricula--United States--States. 2. Language arts (Secondary)--Standards--United States--States. I. Overturf, Brenda J. II. Title.
  LB1631.M3953 2013
  428.0071'2--dc23
                                                                        2013003902

Suggested APA Reference
McLaughlin, M., & Overturf, B.J. (2013). *The Common Core: Teaching students in grades 6–12 to meet the Reading Standards.* Newark, DE: International Reading Association.

For Ryan Brake and all middle school and high school students
in the age of the Common Core
—MM

To my first teachers, Paul and Nancy Scott
—BJO

Contents

About the Authors   vii

Preface   ix

PART I   1
The Evolution of the Common Core State Standards

CHAPTER 1   7
How Can Teachers Effectively Use the Standards?

CHAPTER 2   17
Assessment and the Common Core

CHAPTER 3   30
Implementation of the Common Core Standards

CHAPTER 4   42
English Learners, Students With Disabilities, Gifted and Talented Learners, and the Common Core

CHAPTER 5   53
Reshaping Curriculum to Accommodate the Common Core and the Teaching of Reading

CHAPTER 6   64
Disciplinary Literacy

PART II   73
Teaching the Common Core State Standards for Reading

CHAPTER 7   77

CCR Reading Anchor Standard 1: Reading Closely and Citing Textual Evidence

CHAPTER 8   95

CCR Reading Anchor Standard 2: Determining Central Ideas and Themes

CHAPTER 9   110

CCR Reading Anchor Standard 3: Individual, Event, and Idea Development

CHAPTER 10   124

CCR Reading Anchor Standard 4: Meanings of Words and Phrases

CHAPTER 11   145

CCR Reading Anchor Standard 5: Structure of Texts

CHAPTER 12   160

CCR Reading Anchor Standard 6: Point of View

CHAPTER 13   174

CCR Reading Anchor Standard 7: Diverse Media and Formats

CHAPTER 14   188

CCR Reading Anchor Standard 8: Claims, Reasons, and Evidence

CHAPTER 15   200

CCR Reading Anchor Standard 9: Compare/Contrast Themes and Topics

CHAPTER 16   213

CCR Reading Anchor Standard 10: Text Complexity

Future Directions   227

Index   229

About the Authors

Maureen McLaughlin is a professor of reading education at East Stroudsburg University of Pennsylvania in East Stroudsburg, Pennsylvania, USA. She earned her doctorate at Boston University in reading and language development. Prior to her tenure at East Stroudsburg University, Maureen spent 15 years as a classroom teacher, reading specialist, and department chair in a public school system.

Maureen was a member of the Board of Directors of the International Reading Association from 2005 to 2008, and she will serve as the IRA president in 2013–2014. She was the recipient of IRA's Jerry Johns Outstanding Teacher Educator in Reading Award in 2010. The author of numerous publications about the teaching of reading, reading comprehension, content area literacies, and the Common Core State Standards, Maureen recently published the second editions of *Guided Comprehension in the Primary Grades* and *Guided Comprehension in Grades 3–8* (coauthored with Mary Beth Allen), and in spring 2012, she published *Guided Comprehension for English Learners*. She also wrote *Content Area Reading: Teaching and Learning in an Age of Multiple Literacies* (Allyn & Bacon, 2010). Maureen is currently working on multiple Common Core publications. A frequent speaker at international, national, and state conferences, Maureen is a consultant to schools and universities throughout the world.

Brenda J. Overturf served as a 2009–2012 member of the International Reading Association Board of Directors. While on the Association's board, she chaired a Common Core State Standards Task Force, and she continues as chair of the IRA Common Core Standards Committee.

Brenda began her career as a classroom teacher, teaching 18 years at the elementary and middle school levels. She then served as the Jefferson County Public Schools (Louisville, Kentucky, USA) district reading coordinator for six years, where she led professional development, program design, standards implementation, curriculum alignment, and assessment systems for K–12 districtwide literacy development. In 2005, she entered a partnership with the University of Louisville to head the graduate program in reading education, where she designed and taught K–12 literacy courses, chaired committees, provided leadership for literacy grants and programs, and worked on state literacy task forces and initiatives. Brenda was the director of the University of Louisville Kentucky Reading Project site for K–5 teachers, as well as a partner in a Kentucky Striving Readers grant for adolescent literacy development. She is also past president of the Kentucky Reading Association.

Brenda earned her doctorate with a specialty in literacy education from the University of Louisville. She is a consultant to schools and universities and a conference speaker focused on student literacy achievement. Brenda recently coauthored *Word Nerds: Teaching All Students to Learn and Love Vocabulary* (Stenhouse, 2013). She is currently working on additional publications about the Common Core Standards.

Preface

As literacy professionals, we find ourselves in the midst of the Common Core revolution. This transformation has occurred in what might be described as a whirlwind. As a result, we find ourselves wondering, How do the College and Career Readiness (CCR) Anchor Standards for Reading differ from the Common Core State Standards for Reading? How are the Standards structured? What do the Standards mean? What do various grade levels require? and How can we teach to help our students achieve the Standards? In this book, we respond to these queries and more as we explore the Common Core from its inception to its implementation.

The Common Core: Teaching Students in Grades 6–12 to Meet the Reading Standards is designed to provide essential knowledge not only about the Standards but also about the literacy practices needed to achieve them. The book is divided into two sections. Part I provides information ranging from the inception of the Standards to their assessment, implementation, and effects on curriculum. Chapter 1 details how to effectively use the Standards, and Chapter 2 focuses on both formative assessment and the instruments being developed by the Common Core assessment consortia. Implementing the Standards is delineated in Chapter 3, and the needs of special populations of students (English learners, students with disabilities, and gifted and talented learners) are addressed in Chapter 4. The curricular implications of the Standards are explored in Chapter 5, and disciplinary literacy is the focus of Chapter 6.

The College and Career Readiness Anchor Standards for Reading are the foundation of Part II, which contains Chapters 7–16. Each chapter is dedicated to one of the CCR Anchor Standards. The structure of these chapters focuses on these essential questions:

- What does the anchor standard mean?
- How do the Common Core Standards build to the CCR Reading Anchor Standards?
- What literacy skills and strategies support the Reading Standards?
- How can we teach the Reading Standards to ensure that our students achieve?
- How do we integrate 21st-century skills with the Common Core Standards?
- How can we integrate other ELA Standards with the Reading Standards?
- What does the teaching of the CCR Anchor Standards look like in today's classrooms?

The book concludes with a hopeful glance at future directions, as the Common Core reaches full implementation. Classroom examples permeate Chapters 7–16. Teachers names used throughout the book are pseudonyms.

The Common Core: Teaching Students in Grades 6–12 to Meet the Reading Standards is designed to be a focused and easily accessed comprehensive resource for classroom teachers, staff developers, reading specialists, curriculum coordinators, school administrators, and teacher educators. It contains everything necessary to successfully teach the Common Core from grades 6 through 12.

Acknowledgments

As always, there are many people to thank for making this book possible. We express our appreciation to all who contributed to the manuscript's development as well as all who enhanced the quality of our lives during the research and writing process. We thank them for their insight, their understanding, and their support.

We are particularly grateful to the following people:

- All the teachers who contributed to this book, especially Tracy Reidinger
- Betsy Kettle
- Latricia Bronger
- Roland O'Daniel
- Stroudsburg Area School District, Pennsylvania
- Dr. Mary Ann Matras, Chairperson, Department of Mathematics, East Stroudsburg University of Pennsylvania
- Our colleagues and our students
- Our families and friends
- Shannon Fortner, Executive Editor of Publications, International Reading Association
- Tori Bachman, Acquisitions Manager, International Reading Association

Finally, we thank you, our readers, for joining us in our quest to discover meaningful ways to successfully teach our students to achieve the Common Core State Standards.

—MM and BJO

PART I

The Evolution of the Common Core State Standards

Adoption of the Common Core State Standards (CCSS) is one of the most ambitious educational plans ever to be implemented in the United States. Carrying out this plan is a challenge faced by every educator in every state that has adopted the CCSS. Questions abound. Answers are often elusive. In this volume, we respond to queries ranging from how the Standards emerged to exactly what each standard means and the multifaceted nature of effective professional development, implementation, and assessment.

We begin in this Part I introduction by posing and responding to six key questions about the development of the CCSS:

1. How did the Common Core State Standards emerge?

2. What is the goal of the Common Core State Standards Initiative?

3. What are the ELA College and Career Readiness Anchor Standards?

4. What are the Common Core State Standards?

5. How can the Appendixes in the Common Core State Standards document serve as resources?

6. How are the Common Core K–12 English Language Arts Standards organized?

How Did the Common Core State Standards Emerge?

Although more than 90% of states and territories are currently committed to the implementation of the Standards, it is important to note that the CCSS movement did not emerge overnight. Its roots can be traced to a national standards movement that began in the 1990s, when the U.S. government began to collect evidence that students were not performing as well as expected when compared with their international counterparts. Then, federal discussion around national standards diminished for several reasons. One explanation was that in the United States, education is a right of the state. Few states were inclined to allow the federal government to decide what their students should know and be able to do. A second difficulty arose in determining which standards the students should be required to meet. Disagreements over topics and instructional methods to be included in a set of national standards became the fodder for heated discussions in Washington, DC, as well as among educational organizations. As a result, national discussions quickly dwindled, and each state created its own set of standards. This was an ambitious move that led to varied, state-by-state expectations for students. Some students thrived. Others did not.

As time passed, the world continued to change, and students became more mobile. In 2006, ACT (formerly American College Testing) published *Reading Between the Lines: What the ACT Reveals About College Readiness in Reading*, a document that focused on steps for improving the reading skills of students attending our nation's high schools. New job skills began to emerge, and the United States experienced increased global competition. In 2008, a policy publication from ACT released data that showed that fewer than 2 in 10 eighth graders were on target to be ready for college-level work by the time they graduated from high school. The National Governors Association Center for Best Practices (NGA Center) and the Council of Chief State School Officers (CCSSO) collaborated to develop a state-led initiative that established a set of common standards in English language arts and mathematics to enable students to become college and career ready. The NGA Center and the CCSSO developed the Standards at the request of their members and with substantial encouragement and support from philanthropies, such as the Bill & Melinda Gates Foundation. The group began with a set of college and career readiness standards, which were drafted by a committee representing various education entities. The College and Career Readiness (CCR) Standards were released in draft form in September 2009. After feedback from states, organizations, and the public, the K–12 English Language Arts and Mathematics Common Core State Standards, based on the CCR Standards, were published in June 2010. It was also in 2010 that the federal Race to the Top grant program required state applicants to adopt a common set of standards. This gave many states considerable incentive to adopt the CCSS immediately.

What Is the Goal of the Common Core State Standards Initiative?

The Common Core State Standards Initiative adopted the ACT (2008) definition of college and career readiness, which is the "acquisition of the knowledge and skills a student needs to enroll and succeed in credit-bearing, first-year courses at a postsecondary institution, such as a two- or four-year college, trade school, or technical school...not needing to take remedial courses in college" (p. 1). The goal of the K–12 Common Core State Standards Initiative is for every student in the United States to be college and career ready by the end of high school. The Standards for English Language Arts and Literacy in History/Social Studies, Science, and Technical Subjects, as well as Mathematics, were created to ensure that students are prepared to meet the challenges of college and their future careers. *A First Look at the Common Core and College and Career Readiness*, an ACT (2010) publication using longitudinal college and career readiness data to estimate student performance on the Common Core Standards, reported that we are far from this goal.

What Are the ELA College and Career Readiness Anchor Standards?

As noted in the Common Core State Standards for English Language Arts (NGA Center & CCSSO, 2010), "The CCR standards anchor the document and define general, cross-disciplinary literacy expectations that must be met for students to be prepared to enter college and workforce training programs ready to succeed" (p. 4). The College and Career Readiness Anchor Standards are the foundation of the Common Core State Standards Initiative. In fact, the CCSS are organized according to the CCR Standards.

In the CCSS document, students who are college and career ready are characterized as being able to do the following:

- They demonstrate independence.
- They build strong content knowledge.
- They respond to the varying demands of audience, task, purpose, and discipline.
- They comprehend as well as critique.
- They value evidence.
- They use technology and digital media strategically and capably.
- They come to understand other perspectives and cultures. (NGA Center & CCSSO, 2010, p. 7)

What Are the Common Core State Standards?

The CCSS are comprised of multiple characteristics. According to the Common Core State Standards Initiative (2010), the Standards

- Are aligned with college and work expectations;
- Are clear, understandable and consistent;
- Include rigorous content and application of knowledge through high-order skills;
- Build upon strengths and lessons of current state standards;
- Are informed by other top performing countries, so that all students are prepared to succeed in our global economy and society; and
- Are evidence-based. (para. 4)

How Can the Appendixes in the Common Core State Standards Document Serve as Resources?

There are three ELA appendixes included in the CCSS document. The information in the first, Appendix A, focuses on research supporting key elements of the Standards and provides a glossary of key terms. Text exemplars and sample performance tasks are offered in Appendix B, and examples of student writing are presented in Appendix C.

Each of the appendixes is designed to further inform educators' use of the CCSS. For example, a rationale for standards focusing on text complexity, as well as a three-part model for measuring text complexity, is provided in Appendix A. In Appendix B, example texts, designated by type and grade level, are followed by a short list of performance tasks. Following each student writing sample in Appendix C, a list of annotations, or comments, about the student's writing is provided. This serves as a model for teachers seeking to respond to similar types of writing in their classrooms.

How Are the Common Core K–12 English Language Arts Standards Organized?

The K–12 Common Core State Standards are based on the College and Career Readiness Anchor Standards, which describe what students should know and be able to do by the time they enter college or the workplace after high school graduation. Backward mapping is then used in the K–12 Standards to describe what all students should know and be able to do at each grade level. Each standard is an end-of-grade expectation, beginning at kindergarten and advancing in a staircase of complexity to the conclusion of the 12th grade.

The CCR Anchor Standards for English Language Arts and Literacy in History/Social Studies, Science, and Technical Subjects are organized into

- 10 Reading Standards

- 10 Writing Standards

- 6 Speaking and Listening Standards

- 6 Language Standards (This includes two standards on conventions of standard English, one on knowledge of language, and three on vocabulary acquisition and use.)

The K–12 ELA Standards are organized according to the College and Career Readiness clusters: key ideas and details, craft and structure, integration of knowledge and ideas, and range of reading and level of text complexity. The Reading Standards encompass the substrands Literature (K–12), Informational Text (K–12), and Foundational Skills (K–5 only). In this volume, we focus on the Reading Standards for grades 6–12. In the Overview of Common Core State Standards for Grade 6–12 English Language Arts chart, we delineate how the CCR Anchor Standards relate to the CCSS.

To date, almost all of the U.S. states and territories have adopted the Common Core Standards. Participating states are allowed to add up to 15% of their own content to the CCSS. For example, they might choose to expand the Standards to include a pre-K level or add information about reading comprehension strategies. Unfortunately, at this point, most states have added little content and made few, if any, changes.

In Chapter 1, we continue our discussion of the CCSS by focusing on the effective use of both the CCR Anchor Standards and the CCSS. In the remainder of Part I, we explore formative and summative assessment in Chapter 2; implementing the Common Core in Chapter 3; concerns about English learners, students with disabilities, and gifted and talented learners in Chapter 4; curricular issues in Chapter 5; and disciplinary literacy in Chapter 6.

Overview of Common Core State Standards for Grade 6–12 English Language Arts

Standards Strand	Substrand	CCR Anchor Standards Cluster	Focus of Each Standard
Reading	Literature	• Key Ideas and Details	1. Citing textual evidence; analysis of text
			2. Determining themes or central ideas; summarizing
			3. Story elements
		• Craft and Structure	4. Meanings of words and phrases
			5. Narrative text structure
			6. Point of view
		• Integration of Knowledge and Ideas	7. Multiple versions of texts
			8. Not applicable to literature
			9. Comparing and contrasting texts and elements
		• Range of Reading and Level of Text Complexity	10. Reading grade-level literature
	Informational Text	• Key Ideas and Details	1. Citing textual evidence; analysis of text
			2. Central ideas and analysis of their development
			3. Connections and interactions among individuals, events, ideas, and concepts
		• Craft and Structure	4. Meanings of words and phrases
			5. Informational text structure and idea organization
			6. Point of view or purpose
		• Integration of Knowledge and Ideas	7. Information in diverse media and formats
			8. Analyzing arguments and reasoning
			9. Analyzing various themes and topics
		• Range of Reading and Level of Text Complexity	10. Reading grade-level informational text
Writing		• Text Types and Purposes	1. Arguments to support claims
			2. Informative/explanatory texts
			3. Narrative texts
		• Production and Distribution of Writing	4. Development and organization
			5. Revising and editing
			6. Use of technology
		• Research to Build and Present Knowledge	7. Short and extended research projects
			8. Gathering information from varied sources; paraphrasing and citing correctly
			9. Evidence to support analysis, reflection, and research
		• Range of Writing	10. Extended time frames, varied purposes
Speaking and Listening		• Comprehension and Collaboration	1. Collaborative conversations
			2. Multimedia sources of information
			3. Delineating speaker's arguments and claims
		• Presentation of Knowledge and Ideas	4. Speaker's arguments and claims
			5. Multimedia presentations
			6. Adapting speech to purpose and context
Language		• Conventions of Standard English	1. Standard English grammar and usage
			2. Capitalization, punctuation, spelling
		• Knowledge of Language	3. Knowledge of language and conventions
		• Vocabulary Acquisition and Use	4. Unknown and multiple-meaning words and phrases
			5. Figurative language, word relationships, and nuances in meaning
			6. Academic and domain-specific words and phrases

Note. CCR = College and Career Readiness. Adapted from "The Common Core: Insights Into the K–5 Standards," by M. McLaughlin and B.J. Overturf, 2012, *The Reading Teacher, 66*(2), pp. 156–157.

ESSENTIAL RESOURCES

- Common Core State Standards and Appendixes: www.corestandards.org/the-standards

- Appendix A: Research Supporting Key Elements of the Standards and Glossary of Key Terms: www.corestandards.org/assets/Appendix_A.pdf

- Appendix B: Text Exemplars and Sample Performance Tasks: www.corestandards.org/assets/Appendix_B.pdf

- Appendix C: Samples of Student Writing: www.corestandards.org/assets/Appendix_C.pdf

References

ACT. (2006). *Reading between the lines: What the ACT reveals about college readiness in reading.* Iowa City, IA: Author.

ACT. (2008). *The forgotten middle: Ensuring that all students are on target for college and career readiness before high school.* Iowa City, IA: Author. Retrieved May 31, 2012, from www.act.org/research/policymakers/pdf/ForgottenMiddle.pdf

ACT. (2010). *A first look at the Common Core and college and career readiness.* Iowa City, IA: Author. Retrieved May 31, 2012, from www.act.org/commoncore/pdf/FirstLook.pdf

Common Core State Standards Initiative. (2010). *About the Standards.* Washington, DC: National Governors Association Center for Best Practices & Council of Chief State School Officers. Retrieved March 4, 2013, from www.corestandards.org/about-the-standards

McLaughlin, M., & Overturf, B.J. (2012). The Common Core: Insights into the K–5 Standards. *The Reading Teacher, 66*(2), 153–164. doi:10.1002/TRTR.01115

National Governors Association Center for Best Practices & Council of Chief State School Officers. (2010). *Common Core State Standards for English language arts and literacy in history/social studies, science, and technical subjects.* Washington, DC: Authors. Retrieved August 3, 2012, from www.corestandards.org/assets/CCSSI_ELA%20Standards.pdf

CHAPTER 1

How Can Teachers Effectively Use the Standards?

The Common Core State Standards (CCSS) are the focus of educators in more than 90% of the states, as well as in U.S. territories, such as the U.S. Virgin Islands. This unexpected connection between educators and the Standards has resulted in a communal effort to use the Standards effectively. The movement has an energy about it that appears to be fueled by the need to know everything possible about the Common Core.

As participants in this undertaking, teachers are wondering about numerous aspects of the multifaceted Standards. How the College and Career Readiness (CCR) Anchor Standards support the English Language Arts Standards is a prime example of this. Others include the need to know how to align the Standards with teaching strategies and how to assess students as they engage with the Common Core.

In this chapter, we address teachers' needs. We explore how we, as educators, can effectively use the CCSS with our students. We share our thinking by responding to the following questions:

- How can we use the College and Career Readiness Anchor Standards to gain an overview of the expectations of the CCSS?
- How should we read the Common Core State Standards?
- How can we align the content of the Standards with viable teaching strategies?
- How should we assess students when using the CCSS?
- How should we plan to teach the English Language Arts CCSS?
- What can we do differently to help our students achieve?

How Can We Use the College and Career Readiness Anchor Standards to Gain an Overview of the Expectations of the CCSS?

Because the Common Core State Standards are multifaceted, using them is a complex task. To begin, the College and Career Readiness Anchor Standards provide a foundation for the CCSS. These Anchor Standards are what students should know and be able to do by the end of 12th grade to succeed in college and the workplace. The CCSS are organized according to the CCR Anchor Standards. The

Table 1.1 Overview of the Common Core State Standards

English Language Arts and Literacy in History/Social Studies, Science, and Technical Subjects	Mathematics
Reading • Literature: K–12 • Informational Text: K–12 • Foundational Skills: K–5 Writing: K–12 Speaking and Listening: K–12 Language: K–12 • Conventions • Vocabulary Literacy in History/Social Studies: 6–12 Literacy in Science and Technical Subjects: 6–12	Mathematical Practice: K–12 (same for every grade level) Mathematical Content: K–8 and High School

CCR Standards are the broader, more general anchors; the CCSS are the more specific benchmarks that underpin each anchor. The grade-specific Common Core State Standards connect to the CCR Standards as benchmarks of what students in each grade level, K–12, should know and be able to do to meet the CCR Standards by the time they graduate from high school. As represented in Table 1.1, the K–12 Common Core State Standards are divided into two general categories: English language arts and mathematics. (The CCSS in their entirety are available online at www.corestandards.org.)

The College Career and Readiness (CCR) Anchor Standards delineate what students must know and be able to do when they graduate from high school. In the English Language Arts Standards, there are four strands of CCR Anchor Standards: Reading, Writing, Speaking and Listening, and Language. Understanding the substance of each CCR Anchor Standard helps us clarify the content of the Common Core State Standards as a whole. For example, the CCR Anchor Standards for Reading are organized into four clusters: Key Ideas and Details, Craft and Structure, Integration of Knowledge and Ideas, and Range of Reading and Level of Text Complexity. Table 1.2 features an overview of the CCR Anchor Standards for Reading.

How Should We Read the Common Core State Standards?

The CCSS are organized by grade level to correspond with the categories of the CCR Anchor Standards. This structure allows teachers to read the Standards both vertically and horizontally.

The designations for the strands of the English Language Arts standards are

RL—Reading Literature

RI—Reading Informational Text

RF—Reading Foundational Skills

W—Writing

SL—Speaking and Listening

L—Language

Further, each standard has an assigned code that describes the strand, grade level, and standard number. For example, the designation RI.8.3 means **R**eading **I**nformational Text, Grade **8**, Standard **3**.

Table 1.2 Overview of the College and Career Readiness Anchor Standards for Reading

Cluster	Standards
Key Ideas and Details	1. Read closely to determine what the text says explicitly and to make logical inferences from it; cite specific textual evidence when writing or speaking to support conclusions drawn from the text. 2. Determine central ideas or themes of a text and analyze their development; summarize the key supporting details and ideas. 3. Analyze how and why individuals, events, and ideas develop and interact over the course of a text.
Craft and Structure	4. Interpret words and phrases as they are used in a text, including determining technical, connotative, and figurative meanings, and analyze how specific word choices shape meaning or tone. 5. Analyze the structure of texts, including how specific sentences, paragraphs, and larger portions of the text (e.g., a section, chapter, scene, or stanza) relate to each other and the whole. 6. Assess how point of view or purpose shapes the content and style of a text.
Integration of Knowledge and Ideas	7. Integrate and evaluate content presented in diverse media and formats, including visually and quantitatively, as well as in words. 8. Delineate and evaluate the argument and specific claims in a text, including the validity of the reasoning as well as the relevance and sufficiency of the evidence. 9. Analyze how two or more texts address similar themes or topics in order to build knowledge or to compare the approaches the authors take.
Range of Reading and Level of Text Complexity	10. Read and comprehend complex literary and informational texts independently and proficiently.

Note. From *Common Core State Standards for English Language Arts and Literacy in History/Social Studies, Science, and Technical Subjects* (p. 10), by the National Governors Association Center for Best Practices and the Council of Chief State School Officers, 2010, Washington, DC: Authors.

Why Should We Read the Standards Vertically Within Each Grade Level?

Within the CCSS, we need to read vertically to gain a general understanding of how the Standards are structured and what the more specific expectations are for each grade level. For example, if we were teaching eighth grade, we would read the eighth-grade Reading Standards for Informational Text 1–10 as detailed in Table 1.3.

When we read all of the English Language Arts Standards for eighth grade vertically, it becomes clear from the structure that as reading teachers, we are responsible not only for the Reading Standards but also for the Writing, Speaking and Listening, and Language Standards. This is a critical point because essential topics, such as vocabulary, which we would traditionally expect to encounter only in the Reading Standards, are far more detailed in the Language Standards.

Another reason to read the Standards vertically is to get a big picture of what students need to know and be able to do in English language arts by the end of each grade level. This is true when we review the Standards for the grades we teach, as well as when we want to review the CCSS expectations for other grade levels. We can then use this in-depth knowledge of grade-level information when engaging in planning and instruction.

Why Should We Read the Standards Horizontally Across Grade Levels?

Within each standard, we read horizontally to fully understand what each grade-level standard actually encompasses. The Common Core State Standards are not structured in a way that allows an eighth-grade teacher to teach only the eighth-grade standards. To fully understand what each

Table 1.3 Overview of the Common Core State Standards for Reading Informational Text for Grade 8

Cluster	Standards
Key Ideas and Details	1. Cite the textual evidence that most strongly supports an analysis of what the text says explicitly as well as inferences drawn from the text.
	2. Determine a central idea of a text and analyze its development over the course of the text, including its relationship to supporting ideas; provide an objective summary of the text.
	3. Analyze how a text makes connections among and distinctions between individuals, ideas, or events (e.g., through comparisons, analogies, or categories).
Craft and Structure	4. Determine the meaning of words and phrases as they are used in a text, including figurative, connotative, and technical meanings; analyze the impact of specific word choices on meaning and tone, including analogies or allusions to other texts.
	5. Analyze in detail the structure of a specific paragraph in a text, including the role of particular sentences in developing and refining a key concept.
	6. Determine an author's point of view or purpose in a text and analyze how the author acknowledges and responds to conflicting evidence or viewpoints.
Integration of Knowledge and Ideas	7. Evaluate the advantages and disadvantages of using different mediums (e.g., print or digital text, video, multimedia) to present a particular topic or idea.
	8. Delineate and evaluate the argument and specific claims in a text, assessing whether the reasoning is sound and the evidence is relevant and sufficient; recognize when irrelevant evidence is introduced.
	9. Analyze a case in which two or more texts provide conflicting information on the same topic and identify where the texts disagree on matters of fact or interpretation.
Range of Reading and Level of Text Complexity	10. By the end of the year, read and comprehend literary nonfiction at the high end of the grades 6–8 text complexity band independently and proficiently.

Note. From *Common Core State Standards for English Language Arts and Literacy in History/Social Studies, Science, and Technical Subjects* (p. 39), by the National Governors Association Center for Best Practices and the Council of Chief State School Officers, 2010, Washington, DC: Authors.

standard requires of students, we need to ensure that all of the preceding standards within a given anchor are being met (see Table 1.4).

For example, the Reading Informational Text Standard 1 for sixth grade is "Cite textual evidence to support analysis of what the text says explicitly as well as inferences drawn from the text" (NGA Center & CCSSO, 2010, p. 39). However, the standards for grades K–5 for the same benchmark address the following (NGA Center & CCSSO, 2010, pp. 13–14):

Kindergarten: "With prompting and support, ask and answer questions about key details in a text."

Grade 1: "Ask and answer questions about key details in a text."

Grade 2: "Ask and answer such questions as *who, what, where, when, why,* and *how* to demonstrate understanding of key details in a text."

Grade 3: "Ask and answer questions to demonstrate understanding of a text, referring explicitly to the text as the basis for the answers."

Grade 4: "Refer to details and examples in a text when explaining what the text says explicitly and when drawing inferences from the text."

Grade 5: "Quote accurately from a text when explaining what the text says explicitly and when drawing inferences from the text."

Table 1.4 Common Core State Standards 1–3 (Key Ideas and Details) for Reading Informational Text for Grades 6–8

Grade	Standards
6	1. Cite textual evidence to support analysis of what the text says explicitly as well as inferences drawn from the text.
	2. Determine a central idea of a text and how it is conveyed through particular details; provide a summary of the text distinct from personal opinions or judgments.
	3. Analyze in detail how a key individual, event, or idea is introduced, illustrated, and elaborated in a text (e.g., through examples or anecdotes).
7	1. Cite several pieces of textual evidence to support analysis of what the text says explicitly as well as inferences drawn from the text.
	2. Determine two or more central ideas in a text and analyze their development over the course of the text; provide an objective summary of the text.
	3. Analyze the interactions between individuals, events, and ideas in a text (e.g., how ideas influence individuals or events, or how individuals influence ideas or events).
8	1. Cite the textual evidence that most strongly supports an analysis of what the text says explicitly as well as inferences drawn from the text.
	2. Determine a central idea of a text and analyze its development over the course of the text, including its relationship to supporting ideas; provide an objective summary of the text.
	3. Analyze how a text makes connections among and distinctions between individuals, ideas, or events (e.g., through comparisons, analogies, or categories).

Note. From *Common Core State Standards for English Language Arts and Literacy in History/Social Studies, Science, and Technical Subjects* (p. 39), by the National Governors Association Center for Best Practices and the Council of Chief State School Officers, 2010, Washington, DC: Authors.

As a result, a more accurate phrasing that details what teachers and students need to know for grade 6 Standard 1 is: Ask and answer questions about key details in a text. Demonstrate understanding of key details by asking and answering *who, what, where, when, why,* and *how* questions. Ask and answer questions to demonstrate understanding of a text, referring explicitly to the text. Refer to examples in the text when explaining the text and drawing inferences from it. Quote accurately from a text when explaining what the text says explicitly and when drawing inferences from the text. Cite textual evidence to support analysis of what the text says explicitly as well as inferences drawn from the text.

Understanding the English language arts expectations for a particular grade level is important (reading vertically), but we must also be aware of the expectations that build to that grade level (reading horizontally).

How Can We Align the Content of the Standards With Viable Teaching Strategies?

Knowing the content of the Standards is essential for teaching students how to meet them. This requires studying each of the Standards in depth and aligning the content with viable teaching strategies. For example, Language Standard 4 for grades 9–10 (L.9–10.4) is "Determine or clarify the meaning of unknown and multiple-meaning words and phrases based on *grades 9–10 reading and content,* choosing flexibly from a range of strategies" (NGA Center & CCSSO, 2010, p. 55).

We could begin by examining a small part of the Standard: "Determine or clarify the meaning of unknown...words." Next, we could brainstorm strategies that we might use to help students meet this section of the Standard. Ideas such as the Semantic Map (Johnson & Pearson, 1984; see

Chapter 11, this volume) and Semantic Feature Analysis (Johnson & Pearson, 1984; see Chapter 10, this volume) would be among those that could be employed.

How Should We Assess Students When Using the CCSS?

We need to assess students in relation to their ability to meet the Standards before we plan effective instruction. Formative assessments provide viable options to determine student knowledge. According to the International Reading Association (2013), formative assessments are ongoing measures that teachers use to obtain information about various aspects of students' literacy. Examples of formative assessments include teacher observations (of discussions, patterned partner reading, and whisper reading); strategy applications, such as the Semantic Question Map (McLaughlin, 2010b), the Bookmark Technique (McLaughlin & Allen, 2009), retellings, and summaries; and brief written responses, such as Tickets Out (McLaughlin, 2012).

We can begin by using formative assessments to determine the degree of students' background knowledge. The results of such assessments provide a beginning point for effective instruction and illuminate any gaps in knowledge that may exist. Within each standard and across all of the standards, we can also use formative assessments to measure student progress.

Formative assessments occur every day during teaching and learning and provide information that informs multiple processes. Using formative assessments is not only an effective way to monitor student progress but also a viable way to glean information for planning future instruction. (Chapter 2 goes into further detail about formative assessment.)

How Should We Plan to Teach the English Language Arts CCSS?

According to the Common Core State Standards document, the ELA Standards are based on an integrated model of literacy, with expectations for research and media skills embedded throughout. Intentionally, there are no specific teaching strategies recommended. Instead, the document advocates flexibility in teaching methods. This means that teachers will need to find resources and plan curricula so their students can meet the English Language Arts Standards. First, however, teachers will need to study the Standards and decide what they mean.

What Can We Do Differently to Help Our Students Achieve?

The Common Core Standards are different from many state standards in terms of structure and content. For example, when considering structure, the CCSS are directly linked to the College and Career Readiness Standards, whereas state standards have traditionally stood on their own. When thinking about content, the English Language Arts Standards focus on skills such as interpretation, argumentation, and literary analysis, whereas more traditional standards focus on reader response and comprehension.

Secondary teachers who have been implementing the ELA Standards find that their thought processes about curricula, instruction, and assessment are being continually challenged. Even though standards for each grade level are provided, they are broad, and there is little direction about how to teach students to meet them. In fact, that is left for the teachers to determine. As stated in the introduction to the Common Core Standards (NGA Center & CCSSO, 2010), "By emphasizing required achievements, the Standards leave room for teachers, curriculum developers, and states to determine how those goals should be reached and what additional topics should be addressed" (p. 4). Yet, the expectations have clearly been set for students to be able to read texts on grade level with appropriate text complexity and write, speak, listen, and use language effectively. This has left educators wondering how to teach the aspects of literacy emphasized in the Standards.

Many teachers have been finding that they need to adapt their instruction to help students meet the expectations of the Standards. An example of how instruction may need to be different can be found in the challenges of Reading Standard 8 for Informational Text. It focuses on how an author uses reasoning and evidence to support points in informational text. It is associated with College and Career Readiness Reading Anchor Standard 8, which states that by the end of high school, students will be able to "delineate and evaluate the argument and specific claims in a text, including the validity of the reasoning as well as the relevance and sufficiency of the evidence" (NGA Center & CCSSO, 2010, p. 10). In Reading Standard 8 for Informational Text for grades 6–12, teachers are responsible for helping students learn a progression of skills that lay the foundation for instruction about evaluating arguments and evidence. The skill progressions for this standard in grades 6–12 are delineated in Table 1.5.

Of course, before students can analyze a text to determine the validity of the author's reasoning and the sufficiency of evidence, the students must first be able to comprehend the text.

Thus, reading comprehension strategies still need to be taught. A number of volumes about explicitly teaching reading comprehension strategies have been published (e.g., Harvey & Goudvis, 2007; McLaughlin, 2010a; McLaughlin & Allen, 2009). The research purports that comprehension is a multifaceted process that typically involves strategies such as activating relevant background knowledge, monitoring, visualizing, self-questioning, inferring, summarizing, and evaluating. Teaching these strategies helps enable students in each grade level to meet the expectations of all the CCR Anchor Standards, but especially Substrand 10: Range of Reading and Level of Text Complexity.

Ramon, an eighth-grade English language arts teacher, is an example of an educator who has experienced the challenge of teaching his students what they need to know to be efficient readers of more complex text, while simultaneously focusing on the instructional methods and materials necessary for students to meet the Common Core Standards. He has also observed that planning for literacy instruction has changed. Ramon notes,

Table 1.5 Common Core State Standard 8 for Reading Informational Text for Grades 6–12

Grade	Standard
6	Trace and evaluate the argument and specific claims in a text, distinguishing claims that are supported by reasons and evidence from claims that are not.
7	Trace and evaluate the argument and specific claims in a text, assessing whether the reasoning is sound and the evidence is relevant and sufficient to support the claims.
8	Delineate and evaluate the argument and specific claims in a text, assessing whether the reasoning is sound and the evidence is relevant and sufficient; recognize when irrelevant evidence is introduced.
9–10	Delineate and evaluate the argument and specific claims in a text, assessing whether the reasoning is valid and the evidence is relevant and sufficient; identify false statements and fallacious reasoning.
11–12	Delineate and evaluate the reasoning in seminal U.S. texts, including the application of constitutional principles and use of legal reasoning (e.g., in U.S. Supreme Court majority opinions and dissents) and the premises, purposes, and arguments in works of public advocacy (e.g., *The Federalist,* presidential addresses).

Note. From *Common Core State Standards for English Language Arts and Literacy in History/Social Studies, Science, and Technical Subjects* (pp. 39 and 40), by the National Governors Association Center for Best Practices and the Council of Chief State School Officers, 2010, Washington, DC: Authors.

I spend time with the other teachers on my interdisciplinary team planning how to meet the literacy needs of the kids on the team. We have to make sure all our students can all be engaged in standards-based instruction. My team teachers and I talk about the types of literacy instruction we have to include across the curriculum so kids can comprehend the text, and we monitor our students' progress. But I also spend time with other English language arts teachers on a vertical team interpreting ELA Standards and planning units and lessons based on the Standards. I talk a lot with other teachers about what instruction should be like that helps kids both read well and meet the Standards.

Previously, with state standards, Ramon planned literacy instruction with a focus on comprehension. He spent time introducing the text, teaching essential vocabulary, and encouraging students to make predictions and ask questions about the text. He taught comprehension strategies such as making connections, monitoring, visualizing, and summarizing. He also invited students to respond to the text in a variety of ways. Ramon taught those skills and strategies that were clearly delineated in the state standards, using whatever text he felt was appropriate for his students. He documented what he had taught and noted students' progress in meeting the state standards through formative assessments and required district measures.

Ramon knows that his students still need to be able to comprehend text. In fact, he feels it is even more important that students know how to apply comprehension strategies as they grapple with the more complex text required by the Standards. Consequently, in his teaching, Ramon knows that he needs to continue teaching his students not only to use a repertoire of reading comprehension strategies, which are not emphasized in the CCSS, but also to learn text analysis skills that are stressed in the Standards.

Since they began teaching students the expectations of the Common Core, Ramon and his colleagues have realized that teaching the concepts embedded in the English Language Arts Standards cannot be accomplished in a series of isolated lessons. Comprehension instruction remains a critical curricular component in all lessons focused on the Standards. In Standards-based lessons, teaching methods need to be carefully planned, and the content needs to be well coordinated. The teachers understand they must integrate what they know about best practices in the teaching of reading, writing, speaking and listening, and language and the CCSS every day. Teaching the Common Core State Standards is a complex task. The CCSS cannot simply be checked off a list.

Ramon and his colleagues integrate standards when they plan instruction. For example, Reading Informational Text Standard 8 for eighth grade is "Delineate and evaluate the argument and specific claims in a text, assessing whether the reasoning is sound and the evidence is relevant and sufficient; recognize when irrelevant evidence is introduced" (NGA Center & CCSSO, 2010, p. 39). When planning a focus on CCR Reading Anchor Standard 8, Ramon selects appropriate literary nonfiction (Reading Informational Text Standard 10), in which students can focus on identifying an author's claims and the reasoning supporting the claims (Reading Informational Text Standard 8). Then he plans how he will integrate numerous other ELA Standards to help students learn concepts at a deeper level, such as Reading Informational Text Standards 1, 4, and 6; Speaking and Listening Standards 1 and 4; Language Standard 6; and Writing Standards 1 and 9. Besides claims, reasons, and evidence, Ramon makes sure to address the author's point of view or purpose (Reading Informational Text Standard 6). Understanding the author's point of view or purpose for writing will help students identify the claims in the text, and whether those claims are supported by sound reasons and valid evidence. Ramon wants his students to be able to draw evidence from text to support analysis, reflection, and research (Writing Standard 9) and learn appropriate vocabulary associated with comprehension of the text (Reading Informational Text Standard 4). He plans for students to engage in collaborative conversations focused on the text (Speaking and Listening Standard 1), as discussion of text helps support comprehension. He expects students to use specific vocabulary associated with the topic in speaking or writing (Language Standard 6). He rarely teaches a reading lesson that does not involve identifying text-based evidence to support conclusions, so he needs to encourage students to cite textual evidence that will support their conclusions and explanations (Reading Informational Text Standard 1). He then guides his students to write their own well-constructed opinions, and teaches them to support their claims with sound reasoning and relevant and sufficient evidence (Writing Standard 1).

Further, because Ramon and his interdisciplinary team colleagues have planned together to help students develop disciplinary literacy, other teachers also focus on helping students understand the concepts of claims, reasons, and evidence in their content areas. Leroy, the team social studies teacher, teaches the eighth graders to meet Reading Standard 8 for Literacy in History/Social Studies, which is "Distinguish among fact, opinion, and reasoned judgment in a text" (NGA Center & CCSSO, 2010, p. 61) as they read social studies materials and websites while conducting short research projects during a social studies unit (CCR Anchor Standard 7 for Writing). Sara, the science teacher, reinforces and supports the students' learning as well. She teaches students how to meet Reading Standard 8 for Literacy in Science and Technical Subjects, which is "Distinguish among facts, reasoned judgment based on research findings, and speculation in a text" (NGA Center & CCSSO, 2010, p. 62), when they read a science article that aligns with her science lesson and draw evidence from the text to support analysis, reflection, and research (CCR Anchor Standard 9 for Writing).

Ramon and his colleagues know that for students to transfer their learning from one class to another, the teachers must explicitly talk with their students about how each teacher is teaching the ways in which fact and opinion, claims, reasons, and evidence pertain to text in their content areas (Perkins & Salomon, 1988). As Ramon states,

> My colleagues and I have to work together to think about how to develop literacy skills and strategies across the curriculum.

In Chapter 2, we discuss formative assessment: We define it, focus on the role that it plays in the successful implementation of the Common Core State Standards, and detail practical classroom applications.

ESSENTIAL RESOURCES

- Harvey, S., & Goudvis, A. (2007). *Strategies that work: Teaching comprehension for understanding and engagement* (2nd ed.). Portland, ME: Stenhouse.
- McLaughlin, M. (2010). *Content area reading: Teaching and learning in an age of multiple literacies.* Boston: Allyn & Bacon.
- McLaughlin, M., & Allen, M.B. (2009). *Guided Comprehension in grades 3–8* (Combined 2nd ed.). Newark, DE: International Reading Association.

References

Harvey, S., & Goudvis, A. (2007). *Strategies that work: Teaching comprehension for understanding and engagement* (2nd ed.). Portland, ME: Stenhouse.

International Reading Association. (2013). *Formative assessment* (Position statement). Newark, DE: Author. Retrieved February 7, 2013, from www.reading.org/Libraries/position-statements-and-resolutions/ps1080 _formative_assessment_web.pdf

Johnson, D.D., & Pearson, P.D. (1984). *Teaching reading vocabulary* (2nd ed.). New York: Holt, Rinehart and Winston.

McLaughlin, M. (2010a). *Content area reading: Teaching and learning in an age of multiple literacies.* Boston: Allyn & Bacon.

McLaughlin, M. (2010b). *Guided Comprehension in the primary grades* (2nd ed.). Newark, DE: International Reading Association.

McLaughlin, M. (2012). Tickets out. *The Reading Teacher, 65*(7), 477–479. doi:10.1002/TRTR.01071

McLaughlin, M., & Allen, M.B. (2009). *Guided Comprehension in grades 3–8* (Combined 2nd ed.). Newark, DE: International Reading Association.

National Governors Association Center for Best Practices & Council of Chief State School Officers. (2010). *Common Core State Standards for English language arts and literacy in history/social studies, science, and technical subjects.* Washington, DC: Authors. Retrieved August 3, 2012, from www.corestandards.org/assets/CCSSI_ELA%20 Standards.pdf

Perkins, D.N., & Salomon, G. (1988). Teaching for transfer. *Educational Leadership, 46*(1), 22–32.

CHAPTER 2

Assessment and the Common Core

ssessment and the Common Core State Standards (CCSS) are inextricably linked. We use formative assessment while we teach, and we use summative assessments to determine what our students have learned. We also use Partnership for Assessment of Readiness for College and Careers (PARCC; 2010), Smarter Balanced (2010), and other assessment consortia–developed resources to assess how well students have met the Standards.

According to the International Reading Association (IRA; 2013), formative assessment is an ongoing, goal-based process that occurs during teaching and learning. The results of formative assessment are used to check student understanding and inform instruction, whereas summative assessment documents student learning and school accountability. Summative assessment occurs after learning. It includes high-stakes tests and typically receives more public attention. McTighe and O'Connor (2005) distinguish between formative and summative assessments by viewing formative assessment as a means of improving learning, and summative assessment as a way to provide reliable information about what has been achieved.

In this chapter, we focus on these two aspects of assessment as they relate to the CCSS: formative assessment, which we use every day in our classrooms to help us understand students' progress, and summative assessments, such as those that have been developed by the Common Core assessment consortia. The latter are administered annually to measure students' progress in meeting the Common Core Standards. We also explore how we can prepare students to be successful when engaging in both types of assessment.

Particular questions that we address in this chapter are the following:

- What is formative assessment?
- How does formative assessment relate to the CCSS?
- What are examples of formative assessment strategies that we can use in our teaching?
- What is summative assessment?
- What CCSS assessments are being developed by the federally funded consortia?

What Is Formative Assessment?

Formative assessment is a goal-based process that provides descriptive feedback to teachers and students for use in adjusting both teaching and learning. In formative assessment, teachers and students share responsibility for learning. Then, they use the results to improve student learning.

Peer and self-assessment can also be viewed as elements of formative assessment. As Heritage (2010) notes, both processes evince the depth of students' thinking and how well they understand the learning goals.

It is important to note that formative assessment is not quizzes or tests. It is not graded. It is not associated with rubrics. It also has a research history that goes back more than 20 years and a teaching history that more than likely extends to the first teacher–student encounter.

Black and Wiliam (1998), often credited with writing about this topic first, note that formative assessment is everything in which teachers and students engage that provides information to be used as feedback to modify teaching and learning experiences. Shepard (2005) notes that formative assessment is a collaborative process in which how to improve learning is negotiated between the teacher and the student. Weber (1999, p. 26) proposes that formative assessment suggests future steps for teaching and learning. Such steps might result from observations that allow us to determine how well a student contributed to a class discussion, or informal writing that documents whether a student is able to apply a particular skill or strategy. Formative assessment not only helps reinforce how students learn and what students know but also helps identify what remains unclear.

Menken (2000) reminds us that effective assessments should be deeply entwined with teaching and learning driven by standards. Timely feedback on the part of both the teacher and the students is an essential ingredient of formative assessment. Figure 2.1 illustrates how teachers can base their instruction on the Common Core State Standards and use formative assessment to engage in continuous improvement.

Formative assessment is a natural part of teaching and learning (McLaughlin, 2010a). Formative assessment strategies include informal writing, strategy applications, short written responses, and teacher observation, which occurs during everyday learning experiences.

Researchers agree that formative assessment is characterized by the following:

- *Specified learning goals*—Formative assessment has a purpose. It is goal based. Results of the assessment strategies provide information that can be actively used to show how well the students are meeting the goals and to improve teaching and learning.

Figure 2.1 Common Core State Standards Continuous Improvement Teaching Loop

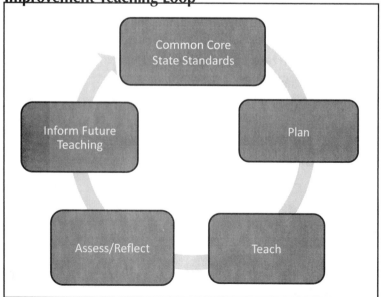

- *Collaboration*—Both teachers and students have active roles in formative assessment. Teachers plan lessons that integrate formative assessment strategies. They also observe, review, and make changes in their teaching based on descriptive feedback provided through student responses. Students actively engage with multiple formative assessment strategies every day. They use descriptive feedback from teachers to improve their learning.

- *Dynamic nature*—Formative assessment is active. It occurs during teaching and learning, is interwoven into lessons, and changes based on the nature of the activity. Formative assessment is ongoing and provides multiple measures of student learning.

- *Descriptive feedback to teachers and students*—As students actively engage in learning, they create feedback about their performances that is provided to teachers. Teachers typically use observation to record descriptive feedback about students' engagement in formative assessment. Then, teachers provide specific suggestions to students about how to improve.

- *Continuous improvement*—Teachers and students use the descriptive feedback to make meaningful adjustments in teaching and learning. It is important to note that we, as teachers, should be as specific as possible in our feedback to students. Complimenting them on their work does not provide direction for their work. Specific comments, such as those that follow, provide focus and purpose for students' revisions:

  > "In your literature response journal, you said you preferred the Hunger Games series by Suzanne Collins to the Harry Potter books by J.K. Rowling, but you didn't explain why. Will you please share at least three reasons? You might want to think about citing evidence from the texts, authors' points of view, and character development to support your thinking."

  > "You need to develop your description of the main character in the story you wrote. Questions to consider could be, How old is she? What does she look like? What can you tell us about her background?"

Formative assessment helps teachers differentiate instruction and helps students increase their achievement. Both help close the gap between what students understand at a given point and their achievement of the desired learning goals. Teachers use the information they glean from formative assessment to continually inform their understanding of students' strengths and needs, and then they use what they have learned to provide the most appropriate instruction for each student (IRA, 2013). Formative assessment supports learning as it occurs. It is a multifaceted information source that helps us use assessment results to provide appropriate reading instruction for all students. It also provides students with multiple opportunities for success.

How Does Formative Assessment Relate to the CCSS?

Formative assessment is not new. As teachers, we have been using it for decades—if not for centuries. We teach, observe student responses, and plan our next steps based on the descriptive feedback provided by formative assessment. The good news about its relation to the Common Core State Standards is that its value has finally been acknowledged, and although summative measures such as PARCC (2010) and Smarter Balanced (2010) are also being employed, in everyday teaching and learning, formative assessment is the focus.

When considering formative assessment's relation to the CCSS, IRA (2013) notes that teachers can use formative assessment to gain insights into student progress in all areas, including interaction with increasingly complex text. Formative assessment measures student growth and informs teachers' ongoing efforts to help students reach the Common Core State Standards. Assessing students' needs and strengths is an integral facet of meeting the Standards. Formative assessment is unique in its ability to meet this need.

It is important to remember that formative assessment strategies often address more than one Standard. As the ELA Common Core Standards (NGA Center & CCSSO, 2010) document states, "While the Standards delineate specific expectations in reading, writing, speaking, listening, and language, each standard need not be a separate focus for instruction and assessment. Often, several standards can be addressed by a single rich task" (p. 5).

What Are Examples of Formative Assessment Strategies That We Can Use in Our Teaching?

We use numerous formative assessment strategies in our teaching every day. We use the results to gauge student understanding and to inform our practice. Examples that we focus on in this section are the Concept of Definition Map (Schwartz & Raphael, 1985), Bookmark Technique (McLaughlin & Allen, 2009), the Lyric Summary (McLaughlin, 2010b, 2012a), discussion, Tickets Out (McLaughlin, 2012b), and teacher observation. Other formative assessment strategies are featured in Chapters 7–16.

Concept of Definition Map

We use the Concept of Definition Map (Schwartz & Raphael, 1985) to teach students to make connections to a focus term by responding to questions such as "What is it?" "What is it like?" and "What are some examples?" Students build personal understandings by connecting the new information to prior knowledge. Then, they can create a Concept of Definition Map Summary based on their completed maps.

When we observe students completing these maps or review the completed graphic organizers, we can discern what students understand about the focus term and its various characteristics, as well as how well they can summarize.

This formative assessment strategy can be used to support CCSS, such as Language Standard 4, in which students are required to determine words' meanings.

Bookmark Technique

We encourage students to engage in the Bookmark Technique (McLaughlin & Allen, 2009) to monitor their comprehension while reading. Students make four decisions related to the text: (1) the most interesting part; (2) a vocabulary word that the whole class needs to discuss; (3) something that was confusing; and (4) a chart, map, graph, or illustration that helped them understand what they read.

As we observe students completing the bookmarks or review their final efforts, we can discover multiple types of information about student performance. These include students' understanding of the text, knowledge of vocabulary words, and ability to use supports such as

Use these

maps, graphs, and illustrations. This formative assessment strategy can be used to support the multiple CCSS that require students to read narrative or informational text, such as Reading Standard 2 and Reading Standard 10 for both literature and informational text.

Lyric Summary

The Lyric Summary (McLaughlin, 2010b) offers an alternative format for students to create text summaries. This small-group approach to summarizing provides opportunities for students to use an alternative representation of thinking to share summaries. To begin, students gather in small groups and brainstorm lists of facts that they know about a topic of informational text or about the elements in narrative text. Next, they choose a song that they all know. Then, using their brainstormed lists, they write new lyrics to the song. Finally, each small group sings its Lyric Summary for the class.

When we observe students creating and performing their Lyric Summaries, we gain insights into their ability to work collaboratively, brainstorm ideas, summarize what they know, and transform the information into song lyrics.

This formative assessment strategy can be used to support CCSS, such as Reading Literature Standard 2, Reading Informational Text Standard 2, Writing Standard 8, and Speaking and Listening Standard 2, in which students are required to summarize narrative or informational text.

Discussion

Discussions are "forums for collaboratively constructing meaning and for sharing responses" (Almasi, 1996, p. 2). Gambrell (1996) notes that these collaborations integrate listening, speaking, and thinking skills. Because of the dynamic nature of these discussions, the meanings that readers construct are continually transformed by their experiences, interactions with others, and information from the text (Almasi, 1996). This social interaction is another aspect of literacy that is underpinned by Vygotsky's (1978) research. Discussion is a process that has cognitive, social, and affective dimensions. It affords students opportunities to engage in higher order thinking, interact with others, and take ownership of their learning (Almasi, 1996). Assessment feedback can be recorded through teacher observation or peer review.

This formative assessment strategy can be used to support many Common Core State Standards, particularly Speaking and Listening Standard 1, in which students are asked to participate in collaborative conversations.

Tickets Out

When using Tickets Out (McLaughlin, 2012b), students reflect on what they have learned and share two types of information: (1) What is the most important thing that you learned during class today? and (2) What questions do you have about what you learned today? Each student's response to what he or she learned that day is recorded on the front of an index card or blackline, and one question that the students may have is written on the back of the card or on the blackline. Students need less than five minutes to complete their tickets.

This type of writing is called Tickets Out because we collect the tickets as we stand at the door at the end of class. When the students hand us their tickets, they are able to leave the classroom.

After the students leave, it takes just a few minutes to read their tickets. We collect the tickets with the front side facing up so we can quickly read all the responses about the most important thing the students learned. As we read, we should be careful to set aside any responses that may need clarification. Then, we turn over the class tickets and read the questions that students have about their learning. As we read these, we should set aside questions that we think we need to respond to in a whole-group setting. This is often only four or five questions because several of them may be similar. The next day, we can begin class by clarifying any necessary information and responding to the students' questions.

This formative assessment strategy can be used to support CCSS, such as Reading Informational Text Standards 2 and 10.

Using Observation to Glean Student Feedback From Formative Assessment

When we integrate formative assessment in our teaching, we need to have a way to record and maintain information about each student. Observation provides opportunities for us to gather such details about students' engagement in all aspects of literacy. For example, we can observe if we want to assess students' fluency, record ideas about their engagement, or comment on students' roles in collaborative activities. Observation allows us to capture the essence of a live performance by watching students as they engage in a task. Observations are purposeful and offer evidence of student motivation, communication, interaction, risk taking, collaboration, and critical and creative thinking.

Before we begin observing, we need to establish a purpose and determine how we will use the information we glean. For example, if we are observing a student who is doing a retelling, we can use a checklist that includes information such as the characters, setting, problem, attempts to resolve, resolution, and a section for recording additional comments. In contrast, if we are observing a student's contribution to a cooperative activity, our checklist might include items such as the student's preparation for the group's work, engagement with peers, and contributions.

One way to organize and manage observations is to use a clipboard (McLaughlin, 2010a). We attach a sheet of mailing labels to a clipboard, with a label for each student in the class; student names are preprinted on each label. After we observe a student, we record our notes on a mailing label and date it. Then, we remove the label from the clipboard and place it on a piece of paper either in the student's portfolio or in his or her observation folder. The names of students who have not yet been observed remain on the clipboard. When all students have been observed, the mailing labels are replenished. As students are observed multiple times, the completed labels are placed chronologically on the designated sheet in either the portfolio or observation folder. This ongoing record of observations offers a running history of the student's engagement with formative assessments throughout a marking period and, eventually, throughout the year. LessonNote, a free app from iTunes, provides a way to record observations digitally.

Observation annotations can help us remember specific attributes of student performance, while simultaneously providing informal assessment information for each student. Keeping a dated record of student observations accommodates Tomlinson and McTighe's (2006) suggestion that we gather a "photo album" rather than a "snapshot" of evidence of student performance (p. 60). Using the results of multiple measures helps us differentiate instruction based on more accurate assessments of our students' learning needs.

It is important to note that there is no magic number of observations that should be completed each day. Starting slowly is a good way to begin. After all the students have been observed a few times, we typically find a comfort level with the timing of this process.

What Is Summative Assessment?

As teachers, we use both formative and summative assessment. Each of these types of assessment has particular characteristics, ranging from how often students engage in them to their informal and formal natures. For example, formative assessment is ongoing, classroom based, and informal. Summative assessment usually occurs at definitive times, such as the end of a chapter, a theme, or grading period and is a more formal type of assessment. Accountability is measured on a single day with a single summative test, but accountability is established across the school year when formative assessment is used on a regular basis in the classroom.

Summative assessments are usually more complex than formative assessments and take a longer period of time to complete. Examples of summative assessments include exhibitions, inquiry-based projects, and teacher-designed or textbook-related tests. These assessments are typically evaluated through the use of rubrics, or scoring guides, which we share with students before the assignment begins.

What CCSS Assessments Are Being Developed by the Federally Funded Consortia?

Five federally funded state assessment consortia have been approved: two comprehensive consortia, two alternate assessment consortia, and an English-language proficiency assessment consortium. The work of each is detailed in the Center for K–12 Assessment & Performance Management at ETS (K–12 Center at ETS; 2012) guide *Coming Together to Raise Achievement: New Assessments for the Common Core State Standards*. The publication provides a general overview of both standards and assessments, describes what it means for states involved in the consortia, and updates the progress of the five state assessment consortia. It also includes the future opportunities for each. The five assessment consortia are PARCC (2010), the Smarter Balanced Assessment Consortium (2010), the Dynamic Learning Maps (DLM) Consortium, the National Center and State Collaborative (NCSC) Consortium, and the Assessment Services Supporting ELs through Technology Systems (ASSETS) of the Wisconsin Department of Public Instruction and the World-Class Instructional Design and Assessment (WIDA) Consortium.

As we discuss the new assessments, we should consider the following seven elements viewed as common to successful assessment systems:

1. The student assessment process is guided by common standards and grounded in a thoughtful, standards-based curriculum. It is managed as part of a tightly integrated system of standards, curriculum, assessment, instruction, and teacher development.

2. A balance of assessment measures that includes evidence of actual student performance on challenging tasks that evaluate applications of knowledge and skills.

3. Teachers are integrally involved in the development of curriculum and the development and scoring of assessment measures for both the on-demand portion of state or national examinations and local tasks that feed into examination scores and course grades.

4. Assessment measures are structured to continuously improve teaching and learning.

5. Assessment and accountability systems are designed to improve the quality of learning and schooling.

6. Assessment and accountability systems use multiple measures to evaluate students and schools.

7. New technologies enable greater assessment quality and information systems that support accountability. (Darling-Hammond, 2010, pp. 3–5)

PARCC and Smarter Balanced

The publication *Coming Together to Raise Achievement: New Assessments for the Common Core State Standards* (K–12 Center at ETS, 2012) recounts the developments in PARCC (2010) and Smarter Balanced (2010), both of which received competitive grants from the U.S. Department of Education to develop new assessment systems by consortia of 15 or more states.

Both PARCC and Smarter Balanced committed to building assessment systems for grades 3–8 and high school that meet the following criteria:

- Builds upon **shared standards** in mathematics and English language arts (ELA) for college- and career-readiness;
- Measures **individual growth** as well as proficiency;
- Measures the extent to which each student is on track, at each grade level tested, toward **college or career readiness** by the time of high school completion; and
- Provides **information that is useful** in informing:
  - Teaching, learning, and program improvement;
  - Determinations of school effectiveness;
  - Determinations of principal and teacher effectiveness for use in evaluations and the provision of support to teachers and principals; and
  - Determinations of individual student college- and career-readiness, such as determinations made for high school exit decisions, college course placement to credit-bearing classes, or college entrance. (K–12 Center at ETS, 2012, p. 15)

Both consortia expect to be prepared with field-tested, technology-based assessments by the 2014–2015 school year. Examples of assessment prototypes can be found on the respective websites.

PARCC has designed model content frameworks to help educators understand how to align curricula with the CCSS for the new assessments.

> The purpose of the PARCC system is to increase the rates at which students graduate from high school prepared for success in college and the workplace. To reach this goal, PARCC intends the assessments to help educators increase student learning by providing data throughout the school year to inform instruction, interventions, and professional development as well as to improve teacher, school, and system effectiveness. The assessments will be designed to provide valid, reliable, and timely data; provide feedback on student performance; help determine whether students are college- and career-ready or on track; support the needs of educators in the classroom; and provide data for accountability, including measures of growth. (K–12 Center at ETS, 2012, p. 16)

(To keep pace with PARCC's continuing developments, visit parcconline.org.)

The design of the Smarter Balanced Assessment Consortium (Smarter Balanced) is intended to strategically "balance" summative, interim, and formative assessment through an integrated system of standards, curriculum, assessment, instruction, and teacher development, while providing accurate year-to-year indicators of students' progress toward college- and career-readiness. (K–12 Center at ETS, 2012, p. 24)

[handwritten: Smarter balance]

Smarter Balanced contracted with a national panel of experts in fall 2012 to develop exemplar modules of formative assessment tasks and tools in ELA and mathematics for Grades 3–8 and 11. Six exemplar instructional modules will be developed for each grade level, three in mathematics and three in ELA. Each module will address one or two learning progressions and will include formative tasks, scoring rubrics and samples of student work at multiple performance levels. (K–12 Center at ETS, 2012, p. 31)

*[handwritten: * Share this]*

(To stay informed about updates concerning Smarter Balanced, visit www.smarterbalanced.org.)

Dynamic Learning Maps and the National Center and State Collaborative

[handwritten: Dynamic Learning Maps is the alternate assessment]

Two alternate assessment consortia were also federally funded: the DLM and the NCSC (K–12 Center at ETS, 2012). These consortia were charged to create assessments "for those students with the most significant cognitive disabilities, who are unable to participate in general state assessments even with appropriate accommodations" (K–12 Center at ETS, 2012, p. 33). These measures were also planned to be ready for use by the 2014–2015 school year. The Wisconsin Department of Public Instruction, in collaboration with the Consortium, created ASSETS, the English-language proficiency assessment project. This was planned to be implemented for the 2015–2016 school year.

These new alternate assessments will be aligned to the Common Core State Standards (CCSS) and are expected to fit cohesively within the comprehensive assessment systems under development by the federal grant recipients: the Partnership for Assessment Readiness for College and Careers (PARCC) and the Smarter Balanced Assessment Consortium (Smarter Balanced). Both DLM and NCSC are to be ready for use by the 2014–15 school year, the same year in which the comprehensive assessment systems will be operational. (K–12 Center at ETS, 2012, p. 33)

[handwritten: Alternate Assessments are to be aligned w/ common core]

The purpose of the DLM assessment system is to significantly improve the academic outcomes of students with the most significant cognitive disabilities, thereby improving their preparedness for postsecondary options and the world of work. The assessment system will be designed to provide useful, timely diagnostic information and strong instructional support to teachers through a highly customizable system of instructionally embedded and end-of-year assessments.

In addition, professional development resources will be developed by DLM to provide Individualized Education Program (IEP)[1] teams with clear, consistent guidelines for the identification of students for the alternate assessment and to train teachers in the use of the assessment system. (K–12 Center at ETS, 2012, p. 34)

(To stay informed about updates concerning DLM, visit dynamiclearningmaps.org.)

[handwritten: use this site]

The NCSC is developing a comprehensive system that addresses the curriculum, instruction, and assessment needs of students with the most significant cognitive disabilities by:

1) producing technically defensible summative assessments;

2) incorporating evidence-based instruction and curriculum models; and

3) developing comprehensive approaches to professional development delivered through state-level Communities of Practice.

These resources will support educators and Individualized Education Program (IEP) teams as they design and implement appropriate instruction that addresses content and skill expectations aligned to the Common Core State Standards (CCSS), as well as help prepare students with the most significant cognitive disabilities for postsecondary life. When complete, the assessment system and accompanying resources will be made available to all states, regardless of their participation in the original grant. (K–12 Center at ETS, 2012, p. 38)

✳ To help teachers translate the CCSS into effective instruction, NCSC is developing curriculum resource guides for the concepts in math and ELA that are considered to be "big ideas" within the academic content. These guides will provide information on instruction within the general education setting (e.g., how the area can be taught to typically developing students); teaching and applying skills in meaningful contexts; linking skills to other content areas; differentiation of instruction through Universal Design for Learning; considerations for providing instruction of more basic skills to some students as embedded within instruction of grade level content; and tools for tiered interventions. (K–12 Center at ETS, 2012, p. 40)

(To remain informed of developments with the NCSC's comprehensive system, visit www.ncscpartners.org.)

Figure 2.2 details the similarities and differences among the assessments being developed by the two comprehensive consortia and the two alternate assessment consortia. The assessments featured are PARCC, Smarter Balanced, DLM, and NCSC.

ASSETS

English learners are the focus of ASSETS, a Common Core assessment that was developed by WIDA. WIDA's (2012) mission is to advance "academic language development and academic achievement for linguistically diverse students through high quality standards, assessments, research, and professional development for educators" (n.p.). Detailed information about ASSETS, as excerpted from *Coming Together to Raise Student Achievement: New Assessments for the Common Core State Standards*, follows. (More detailed information about English learners and the Common Core appears in Chapter 4, this volume.)

To support the development of next generation assessments of English proficiency, the U.S. Department of Education's 2011 competitive Enhanced Assessment Grant provided funding for the development of new assessments by consortia of 15 or more states. In addition to producing results that are valid, reliable and fair for the intended purpose, the new assessment system had to meet additional criteria, including:

- Be based on a common definition of English learner adopted by all Consortium states;
- Include diagnostic (e.g. screener or placement) and summative assessments;
- Assess English language proficiency across the four language domains of reading, writing, speaking and listening for each grade level from kindergarten through Grade 12;
- Produce results that indicate whether individual students have attained a level and complexity of English proficiency that is necessary to participate fully in academic instruction in English;
- Be accessible to all English learners with the one exception of those who are eligible for alternate assessments based on alternate academic standards; and

Figure 2.2 Side-by-Side Comparison of Four Common Core State Standards Assessment Systems

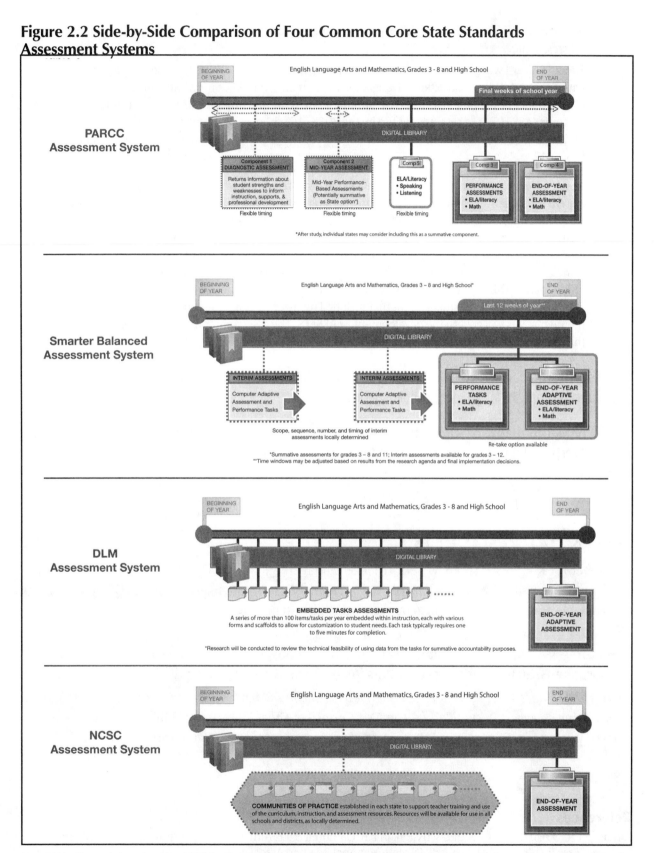

Note. DLM = Dynamic Learning Maps. NCSC = National Center and State Collaborative. PARCC = Partnership for Assessment of Readiness for College and Careers. Reprinted from *Coming Together to Raise Achievement: New Assessments for the Common Core State Standards* (p. 42), by Center for K–12 Assessment & Performance Management at ETS. (2012, April), Austin, TX: Author.

- Use technology to the maximum extent appropriate to develop, administer, and score assessments.

The sole award was given to the Wisconsin Department of Public Instruction, in collaboration with the World-Class Instructional Design and Assessment (WIDA) Consortium. The assessment system under development, called **Assessment Services Supporting ELs through Technology Systems** (ASSETS) is to be ready for use by the 2015–16 school year. A summary and illustration of the design of ASSETS can be found...at www.k12center.org/publications.html. (K–12 Center at ETS, 2012, p. 43)

The ASSETS Consortium will develop a next generation, technology-based language assessment system for students in grades K–12 who are learning English. The system will include a summative language assessment, an on-demand diagnostic screener, classroom interim assessments, and formative assessment tools for use in instruction, as well as accompanying professional development materials. All of these components will be grounded in English development standards linked to the Common Core State Standards (CCSS) in English language arts and mathematics. This Consortium will leverage the work of a Consortium formed in 2002 under another Enhanced Assessment Grant that included many of the same member states. ASSETS member states will govern the development of ASSETS. The assessments and tools developed by this Consortium will be available to all states. (K–12 Center at ETS, 2012, p. 44)

(To keep informed about new developments concerning ASSETS, visit www.k12center.org/publications/english_language_proficiency.html.)

Whether formative or summative, assessment permeates teaching and learning. Assessment is a shared responsibility. Motivating our students to join us in taking an active role in such measures is essential.

ESSENTIAL RESOURCES

- Center for K–12 Assessment & Performance Management at ETS. (2012, April). *Coming together to raise achievement: New assessments for the Common Core State Standards.* Austin, TX: Author. Available at www.k12center.org/publications/raise_achievement.html
- Darling-Hammond, L. (2010). *Performance counts: Assessment systems that support high-quality learning.* Washington, DC: Council of Chief State School Officers. Available at www.ccsso.org/Documents/2010/Performance_Counts_Assessment_Systems_2010.pdf
- Heritage, M. (2010, September). *Formative assessment and next-generation assessment systems: Are we losing an opportunity?* Washington, DC: Council of Chief State School Officers. Available at www.ccsso.org/Documents/2010/Formative_Assessment_Next_Generation_2010.pdf

References

Almasi, J.F. (1996). A new view of discussion. In L.B. Gambrell & J.F. Almasi (Eds.), *Lively discussions! Fostering engaged reading* (pp. 2–24). Newark, DE: International Reading Association.

Black, P., & Wiliam, D. (1998). Assessment and classroom learning. *Assessment in Education: Principles, Policy & Practice, 5*(1), 7–74.

Center for K–12 Assessment & Performance Management at ETS. (2012, April). *Coming together to raise achievement: New assessments for the Common Core State Standards*. Austin, TX: Author. Retrieved August 3, 2012, from www.k12center.org/rsc/pdf/Coming_Together_April_2012_Final.PDF

Darling-Hammond, L. (2010). *Performance counts: Assessment systems that support high-quality learning*. Washington, DC: Council of Chief State School Officers. Retrieved August 3, 2012, from www.ccsso.org/Documents/2010/Performance_Counts_Assessment_Systems_2010.pdf

Gambrell, L.B. (1996). What research reveals about discussion. In L.B. Gambrell & J.F. Almasi (Eds.), *Lively discussions! Fostering engaged reading* (pp. 25–38). Newark, DE: International Reading Association.

Heritage, M. (2010, September). *Formative assessment and next-generation assessment systems: Are we losing an opportunity?* Washington, DC: Council of Chief State School Officers. Retrieved August 3, 2012, from www.ccsso.org/Documents/2010/Formative_Assessment_Next_Generation_2010.pdf

International Reading Association. (2013). *Formative assessment* (Position statement). Newark, DE: Author. Retrieved February 7, 2013, from www.reading.org/Libraries/position-statements-and-resolutions/ps1080_formative_assessment_web.pdf

McLaughlin, M. (2010a). *Content area reading: Teaching and learning in an age of multiple literacies*. Boston: Allyn & Bacon.

McLaughlin, M. (2010b). *Guided Comprehension in the primary grades* (2nd ed.). Newark, DE: International Reading Association.

McLaughlin, M. (2012a). *Guided Comprehension for English learners*. Newark, DE: International Reading Association.

McLaughlin, M. (2012b). Tickets out. *The Reading Teacher, 65*(7), 477–479. doi:10.1002/TRTR.01071

McLaughlin, M., & Allen, M.B. (2009). *Guided Comprehension in grades 3–8* (Combined 2nd ed.). Newark, DE: International Reading Association.

McTighe, J., & O'Connor, J. (2005). Seven practices for effective learning. *Educational Leadership, 63*(3), 10–17.

Menken, K. (2000, September). *What are the critical issues in wide-scale assessment of English language learners?* (Issue Brief No. 6). Washington, DC: Center for the Study of Language & Education, National Clearinghouse for Bilingual Education. Retrieved August 3, 2012, from www.ncela.gwu.edu/files/rcd/BE020919/What_Are_The_Critical_Issues.pdf

National Governors Association Center for Best Practices & Council of Chief State School Officers. (2010). *Common Core State Standards for English language arts and literacy in history/social studies, science, and technical subjects*. Washington, DC: Authors. Retrieved August 3, 2012, from www.corestandards.org/assets/CCSSI_ELA%20Standards.pdf

Partnership for Assessment of Readiness for College and Careers. (2010). *The Partnership for Assessment of Readiness for College and Careers (PARCC) application for the Race to the Top comprehensive assessment systems competition*. Retrieved October 2, 2010, from www.fldoe.org/parcc/pdf/apprtcasc.pdf

Schwartz, R.M., & Raphael, T.E. (1985). Concept of definition: A key to improving students' vocabulary. *The Reading Teacher, 39*(2), 198–205.

Shepard, L.A. (2005). Linking formative assessment to scaffolding. *Educational Leadership, 63*(3), 66–70.

Smarter Balanced Assessment Consortium. (2010). *Race to the Top assessment program application for new grants: Comprehensive assessment systems*. Retrieved August 3, 2012, from www2.ed.gov/programs/racetothetop-assessment/applicant.html

Tomlinson, C.A., & McTighe, J. (2006). *Integrating differentiated instruction and understanding by design: Connecting content and kids*. Alexandria, VA: Association for Supervision and Curriculum Development.

Vygotsky, L.S. (1978). *Mind in society: The development of higher psychological processes* (M. Cole, V. John-Steiner, S. Scribner, & E. Souberman, Eds. & Trans.). Cambridge, MA: Harvard University Press.

Weber, E. (1999). *Student assessment that works: A practical approach*. Boston: Allyn & Bacon.

World-Class Instructional Design and Assessment. (2012). Who we are & the WIDA story. Retrieved from www.wida.us/aboutus/mission.aspx

CHAPTER 3

Implementation of the Common Core Standards

The Common Core State Standards Initiative is progressing at lightning speed. Every day, new policy statements, documents to support implementation, and resources related to the Common Core State Standards (CCSS) are emerging. States are either actively engaged in implementation or in the planning stages. Future implementations will build on current efforts.

As we contemplate teaching the Standards, we can think about implementation efforts as the responsibility of every educator. Even though the Common Core State Standards Initiative began as a policy decision, professional organizations, publishers, states, universities, districts, and schools are pulling together to create tools, resources, and materials to help with implementation.

In this chapter, we respond to the following questions:

- What is the role of professional development in the implementation of the Common Core State Standards?
- How can national organizations, professional associations, and publishers support implementation of the Standards?
- How can multistate regions support implementation of the CCSS?
- How can states support professional development and Standards implementation?
- How can institutions of higher education support teacher preparation and professional development in CCSS implementation?
- How can school districts support schools and administrators in professional development and CCSS implementation?
- How can schools support teachers in professional development and Standards implementation?

In this chapter, we respond to these questions with a variety of suggestions for implementing the Common Core State Standards. Examples of implementation plans at various levels are also presented.

What Is the Role of Professional Development in the Implementation of the Common Core State Standards?

At first glance, it may seem to some educators that the Common Core Standards represent little change from the standards that they have been using. However, educators who have been involved in the in-depth implementation of the CCSS are finding the Standards quite different from any previous state standards. There is an intentional focus on informational text, and classrooms are abuzz with terms that may be unfamiliar, such as *close reading, text complexity, argumentation*, and *text-based evidence*. Researchers at the Center on Policy Education (Kober & Rentner, 2012) noted that most educators in their survey believed that the Common Core Standards are more rigorous than previous state standards. In the same survey, Kober and Rentner found that providing professional development in sufficient quality and quantity to ensure that teachers and administrators are prepared for the new demands will be quite a challenge.

Share w/ staff

Yet, it stands to reason that intensive, ongoing professional development will be the key to quality Standards implementation. Teachers and administrators working together to interpret the CCSS, ensure a common understanding, align curricula at the state and local levels, and plan for lessons, units, and related assessments is paramount. To meet this challenge, teachers need time for extensive group planning, as well as access to a variety of instructional resources and necessary funding. To successfully implement the Standards, educators at every level need to begin with a Common Core Implementation Model (see Figure 3.1).

When using the Model, states, districts, and schools should clearly delineate participants and their responsibilities, as well as create a timeline of professional development and strategic tasks. The resulting Common Core Implementation Plan should be thoughtful, extensive, and connected to all relevant Common Core initiatives. For example, if a state has a grant to implement components of the CCSS that extends to districts, this effort should be reflected in both the state and district Common Core Implementation Plans. If districts have Common Core–based expectations for teachers, the ideas should be supported by professional development opportunities. This should appear in the Common Core Implementation Plans for both the district and the school. It should be clear how the Standards initiative is connected and will be implemented.

Are there grants for this?

Figure 3.1 The Common Core Implementation Model

State → Collaborative groups → Districts → Schools → Teachers →

Resources to assist in implementation of such plans are beginning to emerge in a variety of Web-based and traditional publications. The Essential Resources section at the end of this chapter includes specific links to many of these resources. *Resources*

How Can National Organizations, Professional Associations, and Publishers Support Implementation of the Standards?

National organizations, professional associations, and educational publishers are rallying around the Common Core State Standards. Each is making efforts to provide information and resources that are being connected across the United States in a rapid and unprecedented manner. National organizations, such as the Council of Chief State School Officers (CCSSO) and the National Governors Association Center for Best Practices (NGA Center), have been leading the Common Core implementation at the national level by providing tools and resources for state and district leadership. Many other national organizations are also involved in developing resources to support professional development and implementation at the state, district, and classroom level. Examples of these include the following:

- The CCSSO (www.ccsso.org) is a co-leader of the Common Core State Standards Initiative and has developed a list of resources that is continually being updated for parents, teachers, principals, and higher education to help with implementation.

- The NGA Center (www.nga.org) is the other co-leader of the charge and has created a Common Core implementation guide aimed at assisting state governors with transition to the Standards.

- Achieve (www.achieve.org), an organization focused on college and career readiness, has developed a wealth of materials to assist in Common Core planning and implementation for policymakers and state and district leaders.

- The Hunt Institute (www.hunt-institute.org) has sponsored a series of videos on YouTube about the Standards and what they mean.

- Student Achievement Partners (www.achievethecore.org) has been instrumental in the Common Core initiative and is building a bank of resources and lesson plans with video examples of classroom practice and examples of student work that demonstrate the instructional shifts required by the Common Core Standards.

- The National PTA (www.pta.org) has developed the *Parents' Guide to Student Success* (www.pta.org/4446.htm), a set of grade-level guides explaining to parents what students should know and be able to do to meet the expectations of the CCSS.

- Learning Forward (www.learningforward.org) has published a collection of studies and materials to support professional development and implementation of the Standards.

- PARCC and Smarter Balanced, the national assessment consortia discussed in Chapter 2, are developing resources aligned with the Standards and the related assessments.

These are a few examples of the type of support being developed to assist educators and policymakers as they grapple with the implications of implementation across the United States.

Professional associations have also responded to lend support to educators in their implementation of the Common Core. For example, the International Reading Association Common Core State Standards (CCSS) Committee (2012) has developed the white paper *Literacy Implementation Guidance for the ELA Common Core State Standards* to guide teachers, administrators, curriculum developers, and publishers to make sound instructional decisions as they align literacy and content area curriculum, plan lessons and assessment, and create resources to meet individual student needs. These principles address the following topics:

1. Use of challenging texts
2. Foundational skills

3. Comprehension

4. Vocabulary

5. Writing

6. Disciplinary literacy

7. Diverse learners

IRA has also created webinars, resources, and professional development institutes. Further, it sponsors a Q and A about the Common Core on the Association's website. The IRA Annual Convention also has featured sessions, institutes, and strands based on Common Core Standards issues, literacy components, and approaches to implementation.

Other professional organizations have supported professional development and implementation of the Common Core. Examples of these include, but are not limited to, the National Council of Teachers of English (www.ncte.org), ASCD (www.ascd.org), and the National Association of Elementary School Principals (www.naesp.org). Professional associations are continually updating information for their members and the general public on their websites.

Publishers are aligning their materials to the Common Core State Standards and developing new curricular materials and supplemental resources to support teachers in the implementation of the CCSS. Publishers are also supporting professional development for teachers transitioning to the Common Core. A quick look at most educational publisher websites will yield a variety of resources or opportunities for professional development. For example, Pearson Education (www.pearsoned.com) has developed a series of webinars explaining different aspects of the Common Core Standards. McGraw-Hill Education has published materials to be used in lesson planning and professional development, which can be found on their Common Core Solutions website (www.commoncoresolutions.com). Creative Commons (www.creativecommons.org) and the Association of Educational Publishers (www.aepweb.org) have begun a collaborative project involving the major Internet search engines (Google, Yahoo, and Bing). Together, they are partnering in a project called the Learning Resource Metadata Initiative (www.lrmi.net) that will develop a tagging system to help educators find specific Internet resources about the Common Core. Further, a number of publishers and nonprofit organizations are assisting with the Learning Resource Metadata Initiative tagging system so the Common Core tags are accurate and useful for teachers.

Links to these organizations and other helpful resources from national organizations, professional associations, and publishers can be found in the Essential Resources section at the end of this chapter. The resulting responsibilities for professional development and implementation of the Standards rest with educators in states, institutions of higher education, school districts, and schools.

How Can Multistate Regions Support Implementation of the CCSS?

In some instances, groups of states are uniting to pool expertise and resources to create implementation tools. For example, leaders from Massachusetts, New York, and Rhode Island, facilitated by Achieve, collaborated to develop the Tri-State Quality Review Rubric for Lessons and Units: ELA/Literacy (Grades 3–5) and ELA (Grades 6–12). The rubric is intended to be used when evaluating Common Core–aligned curricular resources in developing lessons and units that represent the rigor of the Common Core's English language arts expectations. This is an excellent resource for any classroom teacher or school administrator. (To see the latest version of the Tri-State Rubric, visit www.achieve.org.)

How Can States Support Professional Development and Standards Implementation?

The Common Core State Standards are a state-led initiative. Consequently, states have the responsibility to ensure that districts and schools have the support they need to implement the CCSS in ways that connect seamlessly with other state initiatives and requirements. States have the following responsibilities:

- Add content to the CCSS, including information concerning pre-K students, struggling readers, English learners, and students with disabilities.
- Provide funding to facilitate the changes necessitated by the CCSS.
- Require quality, meaningful assessment of the CCSS.
- Provide opportunities and resources for quality professional development that focuses on the content of the Standards, curricular alignment, and the development of related assessments for educators at multiple levels, including state departments of education, school administrators, curriculum planners, supervisors, specialists, classroom teachers, and teacher educators.

When contemplating implementation, states may choose to use a regional approach to ensure that knowledge and implementation of the Standards is comprehensive. Kentucky, which was the first state to adopt the Standards, is a model of a state that has ensured a statewide, systemic approach to professional development on the Standards (Overturf, 2011). In 2009, the legislature of the state of Kentucky voted to overhaul the state's education system. Senate Bill 1 required the Kentucky Department of Education to create a new system of standards and assessments by the spring of 2012. Because the Common Core Standards were being developed at the same time, Kentucky decided to join the effort. Educators in Kentucky provided feedback on the CCR Anchor Standards as well as the K–12 Common Core Standards. Kentucky used an interim assessment to measure students' achievement of the CCSS in spring 2012.

To prepare educators for this massive undertaking, the Kentucky Department of Education led regional, monthly CCSS implementation sessions as part of the Kentucky Content Leadership Network. The sessions were comprised of teams of teachers and school administrators from every school district in the state, as well as university professors from all institutions of higher learning within the state, who were required to participate in ongoing professional development to ensure the successful implementation of the Common Core. The purposes of the regional sessions were to analyze the Standards, develop assessments, plan for instruction, and learn from one another. Educators then returned to their classrooms to implement their new learning and share with others in their schools. It was—and continues to be—a truly collaborative effort.

The Kentucky Department of Education website (www.education.ky.gov) features a variety of instructional resources for school districts and teachers that were developed by regional representatives. These resources, many of which emerged from the monthly regional meetings, include the state's Model Curriculum Framework, English Language Arts Deconstructed Standards with learning targets, and webcasts about the Standards. Kentucky also distributes an electronic newsletter every month that includes updates and resources for teaching the Standards, and hosts periodic Twitter days when educators share resources that they are using to teach the Standards. Kentucky is developing the state-of-the-art Continuous Instructional Improvement Technology System, which will connect the Standards, electronically stored instructional resources, curriculum, formative assessment strategies, and lessons. Many of these resources were developed by Kentucky educators working together across the state in the Content Leadership Network and other state-led professional development, but the plan is to also include outside resources. Kentucky is also involved in a partnership with Learning Forward to develop a statewide, comprehensive professional learning system to support educators in Kentucky's implementation of the Common Core.

There are many other examples of leadership from state departments of education. For example, the New Mexico Department of Education has developed a clear, coherent website that provides information and resources. The Kansas Department of Education has created a website with numerous resources for implementation of the Common Core, including excellent materials for understanding text complexity. The New York Department of Education has created a website called EngageNY, with resources and videos focused on implementation. Additionally, the Ohio Department of Education has created a model curriculum that includes teaching ideas and strategies. The links to these and other selected state resources can be found in Table 3.1.

Table 3.1 Selected State Resources

- *Kansas Department of Education: Common Core Resources*—Includes a collection of tools for use in understanding and measuring text complexity: www.ksde.org/Default.aspx?tabid=4778
- *Kentucky Department of Education: Content Leadership Networks deliverables*—Contains resources to use in implementation of the ELA Standards, including standards "placemats" and gap alignment tools: www.education.ky.gov/kde/administrative+resources/school+improvement/instructional+support+network/leadership+networks+-+deliverables.htm
- *Kentucky Department of Education: English Language Arts Deconstructed Standards*—Created through a collaboration of Kentucky educators, including teachers, district administrators, higher education faculty, regional consultants, and department of education consultants: www.education.ky.gov/KDE/Instructional+Resources/Curriculum+Documents+and+Resources/English+Language+Arts+Deconstructed+Standards.htm
- *New Mexico Public Education Department: Common Core State Standards*—Contains a wealth of information for students, parents, teachers, and administrators: newmexicocommoncore.org
- *New York State Education Department: EngageNY: Common Core*—Includes videos explaining the instructional shifts in the Common Core Standards: engageny.org/common-core
- *Ohio Department of Education: English Language Arts Model Curriculum*—Includes strategies for students with disabilities, gifted students, and English learners: www.education.ohio.gov/GD/Templates/Pages/ODE/ODEDetail.aspx?page=3&TopicRelationID=1696&ContentID=83819
- *Utah Education Network: Utah Core Standards for Mathematics & English Language Arts*—Includes resources and videos to support the ELA Common Core Standards: www.uen.org/commoncore/#eresources

How Can Institutions of Higher Education Support Teacher Preparation and Professional Development in CCSS Implementation?

Institutions of higher education have the responsibility to prepare preservice and inservice teachers for the increased demands of teaching in a Common Core world. Participants in this effort should include faculty and administrators in teacher preparation programs, graduate literacy programs, and the arts and sciences.

College and university faculties who are involved in preservice teacher preparation should study the Standards and engage in collaborative discussions and projects to help develop their knowledge of the Standards and the challenges of implementation. Faculty members should take every opportunity to engage with schools that are transitioning to the Common Core State Standards and participate fully in professional learning communities at the university level. Preservice coursework, assignments, assessments, and field-based experiences should be aligned with the CCSS to ensure that preservice candidates are prepared for the Common Core expectations in public schools.

At the inservice level, teachers and administrators need research-based support from institutions of higher education to make appropriate instructional decisions and design suitable assessments. Higher education faculty members should be in a position to help provide that support, which means that universities need to be fully engaged in and knowledgeable about the Standards and the expectations for public school educators. Graduate faculty need to address the Standards and provide research-based theoretical underpinnings as well as practical, classroom-based assignments and strategies for their students.

National projects are underway to involve institutions of higher education fully in the Common Core Standards initiative. The American Association of State Colleges and Universities, the Council of Chief State School Officers, and the State Higher Education Executive Officers are collaborating to lead an initiative called the College Readiness Partnership. This partnership currently involves teams from seven states who are working to create resources outlining how institutions of higher education and states can work together to ensure Standards implementation and college and career readiness.

How Can School Districts Support Schools and Administrators in Professional Development and CCSS Implementation?

School district offices have a responsibility to ensure that educators in their districts are equipped to implement the Common Core. That includes a plan to do so. Local school districts and schools have the following responsibilities:

- Address the needs of struggling readers, English learners, students with disabilities, and pre-K students in relation to the Standards.

- Provide opportunities and resources for quality professional development that focuses on the content of the Standards, curricular alignment, instructional methods, and the development of related assessments for teachers and building-level administrators.

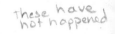
These have not happened

- Provide resources, including time and materials, for teachers attempting to learn best teaching practices for the CCSS.
- Design and implement instruction and formative assessments that will help all students achieve.

To lead CCSS initiatives at the school district levels, administrative personnel need to be proactive in supporting building-level administrators and teachers, providing material and financial resources, ensuring curricular alignment support, and leading professional development opportunities. For example, in the first year of implementation of the Common Core, Kentucky's Jefferson County Public Schools developed a summer institute to introduce the CCSS to secondary teachers. Representatives from each secondary school participated in the professional development institute and prepared to lead CCSS professional development in their schools. The district then placed all professional development materials online. These include links to the Standards, materials from the training sessions, directions for developing a Standards-based writing workshop, and a document containing Standards-related terminology. Ongoing district support included posting tools for implementing the ELA Standards that featured curriculum standards maps, curriculum unit maps, K–12 Standards progression documents, and sets of reading tools such as posters, rubrics (scoring guides), and resource lists. Jefferson County also created Standards-based guided practice documents that feature student passages, related questions, and additional queries that require students to compare and contrast passages. Teacher support materials, including detailed lesson plans on how to teach to help students reach the Standards, were incorporated in these documents. The district also sent sets of texts representing required text complexity at each grade level to be made available for teachers in schools' library/media centers.

idea for curriculum director

look up this example

The New York City Department of Education is another example of a school district that has supported teachers with excellent CCSS resources. The NYC Department of Education website features a Common Core Library section with resources for teacher teams, including professional development materials and lesson plans with rubrics and examples of annotated student work. Many other school districts will engage in these types of efforts as the Standards implementation progresses.

＊ NY

How Can Schools Support Teachers in Professional Development and Standards Implementation?

Schools have the ultimate responsibility for ensuring that faculty members are knowledgeable, skillful, and thoughtful about implementation of the Common Core. At the school level, administrators in Kentucky have found that their efforts to help teachers understand and teach the CCSS is a massive task that requires time, funding, and instructional resources. For example, Melinda is a principal in a middle school that is implementing the CCSS. She found that most of her school's professional development time and resources for the first year of implementation needed to be focused on supporting teachers in learning the Standards. To facilitate group learning and planning, a strategic professional plan, consisting of multiple levels of professional development, was put into place to support implementation of the Standards. This included district-based days in the summer with representatives of the English language arts department, professional

tell this part to staff

＊ start here

Establishing
PLC

Start here

development days with the entire faculty before the beginning of school, and establishing professional learning communities (PLCs) focused on the expectations of the Common Core. As a principal, Melinda also engaged teachers in team-based expectations, extended faculty meetings, and after-school professional development opportunities. She notes,

> The Common Core Standards have a few things in common with our former state standards, but there are many more differences. My teachers had to really dig in to the Standards, talk with each other and other teachers in the district to interpret the CCSS, and think about how instruction and assessment needed to be different. Also, there is an expectation that content teachers will focus on literacy, as well. Both interdisciplinary teams and content area departments had to have time to think about how to plan to help students meet the expectations of the Standards.

Part of the district Standards rollout plan included developing teacher leaders within each building. Melinda, like other middle school principals in her district, identified an English language arts teacher at each grade level to serve as a cohort teacher leader responsible for attending district summer training. The cohort teacher leaders worked together as a district cadre to understand the Standards and to prepare to lead professional development at the school level. The cohort teacher leaders received 12 hours of intense training on the Standards during a district summer conference. The training included an introduction to the Standards, how to read the Standards, understanding the CCSS appendixes, understanding the organization of the Standards by strands and clusters, the progression of the Standards from grade to grade, how to deconstruct the Standards, using the Standards to plan Standards-based instructional units, formative assessment practices, and Characteristics of Highly Effective Teaching and Learning (a state initiative).

Part of the cohort teacher leader training included spending time planning the first instructional unit using curriculum documents created by the district Literacy Team. The expectation was for cohort teacher leaders to implement the plan and bring in work samples to analyze by grade-level groups during five teacher cohort meeting sessions scheduled after school throughout the year. The meetings focused on the ELA instructional shifts, sharing lessons and student work samples, analysis of student formative assessments, understanding text complexity, and so on.

At the school level, Melinda made sure the cohort teacher leaders replicated much of the training they received at the district level with the school faculty. This included content area teachers as well as the rest of the English language arts teachers. As Melinda notes,

> We had to think about the school as a whole. At first, my content teachers didn't understand that the literacy standards affected them. We all had to realize that this is not only an English language arts responsibility. And my English language arts teachers had a lot to learn, as well.

To further support the implementation of the Standards, Melinda made sure there was protected time in the master schedule so the cohort teacher leaders could lead ongoing professional development. The schedule was designed to ensure that interdisciplinary teachers had common planning time and could continue to work together during the school year. Teams created plans in which each teacher on the team addressed the literacy standards in their disciplines. The schedule also allowed the English language arts department to work together in a PLC once a month. PLCs are characterized by shared leadership, collective creativity, shared values and vision, supportive conditions, and shared personal practice. The schedule provided time for each PLC to work together and afforded teachers much needed time to discuss interpretations of the Standards, share ideas from classrooms at the same grade level, and analyze assessments and set learning goals.

The PLCs worked collaboratively to understand each standard at each grade level. For example, Reading Standard 4 for Literature for grade 7 is as follows:

> Determine the meaning of words and phrases as they are used in a text, including figurative and connotative meanings; analyze the impact of rhymes and other repetitions of sounds (e.g., alliteration) on a specific verse or stanza of a poem or section of a story or drama. (NGA Center & CCSSO, 2010, p. 36)

At first, some of the teachers thought they were teaching students to meet the standard by asking students to write poetry that included similes, metaphors, and other figurative language. As teachers worked together in the PLC, they realized this particular standard is not about the knowledge of poetry styles. Instead, this particular standard is about analyzing how an author uses language in a poem, story, or drama. This knowledge redirected the teachers' instruction to focus on student understanding of how a poet uses figurative language and other diction devices. Although teachers still ask students to write poetry, now they also ask students to explain their language choices as part of the lesson.

Because of gaps in student knowledge about the concepts represented in the Standards, the teachers in Melinda's school realized that they would need to become intentional about meeting individual students' needs. To begin to accommodate their students, one PLC task was to develop assessments to gauge students' misconceptions and knowledge of the standards from earlier grades, including questions to informally gauge their ability to contend with each standard. For example, in an informal survey of students' knowledge of determining an author's point of view (Reading Informational Text Standard 6), teachers asked, "What was the author's purpose for writing this text? How do you know?" The PLCs also worked on curriculum maps and developed plans for assessing student progress in meeting the Standards by creating formative assessments and analyzing data from district assessments to identify instructional gaps.

In extended faculty meetings, the entire faculty engaged in professional development activities to ensure continuity from grade level to grade level and across the curriculum. After-school professional development opportunities gave teachers the chance to conduct backward planning: reviewing important vocabulary that students should know, writing assessments, and developing lesson plans together. Some teachers also began study groups based on increasing their knowledge of the concepts in the Standards. For example, they knew developing vocabulary was important, but many teachers did not know engaging instructional methods to use in their classrooms. By participating in study groups, these teachers were able to learn better methods for teaching vocabulary.

Implementing the ELA Standards is a complex task, but teachers across the country are working diligently to meet the challenge. Melinda believes that the students in her school have directly benefited from the time the school personnel spent engaging in professional development. She notes,

> Everyone is much more on the same page. We have worked out meanings of a lot of the standards and shared ways to teach students to meet the standards. Even though it has taken a lot of time and effort, we have a more distinct mission and vision about literacy across the whole

school. We want our students to be literate citizens and be ready for college. Implementation of the Common Core Standards is a colossal endeavor, one that requires a great deal of time, effort, and collaboration among all who have responsibility for student achievement. Implementing the CCSS must, most assuredly, be a united effort.

In Chapter 4, we focus on the Common Core and how it affects special populations such as English learners, students with disabilities, and gifted and talented learners.

ESSENTIAL RESOURCES

- ASCD has created a number of Common Core resources: www.ascd.org/common-core-state-standards/common-core.aspx.
- The Council of Chief State School Officers has created a list of resources for implementing the Standards: www.ccsso.org/Resources/Programs/The_Common_Core_State_Standards_Initiative.html.
- The Hunt Institute has published a series of YouTube videos with information and explanations of the Standards: www.youtube.com/user/TheHuntInstitute.
- The International Reading Association has a webpage dedicated to the ELA Standards, as well as publications and other resources for professional development: www.reading.org/CommonCore.
- Literacy Design Collaborative has developed templates for content area teachers to design literacy tasks: www.literacydesigncollaborative.org.
- The National Council of Teachers of English has a webpage focused on the Common Core Standards and resources for professional development: www.ncte.org/standards/commoncore.
- The National PTA has created a parents' guide to explain the Common Core at each grade level entitled the *Parents' Guide to Student Success*: www.pta.org/4446.htm.
- Open Educational Resources has developed a collection of online, copyright-free teaching and learning materials available in the public domain with a section specifically focused on resources for the Common Core: www.oercommons.org.
- Pearson Education provides resources for teachers, as well as a series of webinars about the Standards: commoncore.pearsoned.com/index.cfm?locator=PS11T9.
- *Publishers' criteria*—David Coleman and Susan Pimentel, two of the major writers of the Common Core State Standards, have published two publishers' criteria guides for publishers and curriculum developers. The guidelines are helpful for districts, schools, and teachers as they work to plan lessons and units focused on the ELA/Literacy Standards.
  - Revised Publishers' Criteria for the Common Core State Standards in English Language Arts and Literacy, Grades K–2: www.corestandards.org/assets/Publishers_Criteria_for_K-2.pdf
  - Revised Publishers' Criteria for the Common Core State Standards in English Language Arts and Literacy, Grades 3–12: www.corestandards.org/assets/Publishers_Criteria_for_3-12.pdf

- Student Achievement Partners has created examples of lesson plans for demonstrating the instructional shifts in the ELA Standards, which includes video and examples of student work: www.achievethecore.org.
- The Teaching Channel's website includes a section with videos of teaching practices related to the Common Core: www.teachingchannel.org/videos?categories=topics_common-core.
- Tri-State Quality Review Rubric for Lessons and Units: ELA/Literacy (Grades 3–5) and ELA (Grades 6–12) was developed by Massachusetts, New York, and Rhode Island: www.achieve.org.

References

International Reading Association Common Core State Standards (CCSS) Committee. (2012). *Literacy implementation guidance for the ELA Common Core State Standards* [White paper]. Newark, DE: Author. Retrieved February 2, 2013, from www.reading.org/ccssguidelines

Kober, N., & Rentner, D.S. (2012, January). *Year two of implementing the Common Core State Standards: States' progress and challenges.* Washington, DC: Center on Education Policy. Retrieved August 3, 2012, from www.cep-dc.org/displayDocument.cfm?DocumentID=391

National Governors Association Center for Best Practices & Council of Chief State School Officers. (2010). *Common Core State Standards for English language arts and literacy in history/social studies, science, and technical subjects.* Washington, DC: Authors. Retrieved August 3, 2012, from www.corestandards.org/assets/CCSSI_ELA%20 Standards.pdf

Overturf, B.J. (2011). Kentucky leads the US in implementing Common Core Standards. *Reading Today, 29*(2), 24–25.

CHAPTER 4

English Learners, Students With Disabilities, Gifted and Talented Learners, and the Common Core

As we plan to implement the Common Core State standards, it is important to remember that all students are responsible for achieving the Standards. This means that populations such as English learners, students with disabilities, and gifted and talented learners are also accountable for them. Unfortunately, the Common Core initiative has barely addressed these students' needs.

The Common Core State Standards for English Language Arts were written for regular education students, and at this point, there are no plans to modify them in any way. Consequently, English learners, students with disabilities, and gifted and talented learners have neither Standards nor related materials that accommodate their needs.

In this chapter, we focus on these learners. We respond to a variety of queries about each, including what research has to say and how we can differentiate instruction. The questions that guide our exploration of these topics include

- What do we know about these learners?
- What connections can we make to the CCSS?
- What types of instructional considerations need to occur?

English Learners

What Do We Know About English Learners?

According to Young and Hadaway (2006), English learners (ELs) are the fastest growing educational population. Goldenberg (2010) further notes, "ELL students in the United States come from over 400 different language backgrounds; however, by far the largest proportion—80%—is Spanish speakers" (p. 17).

When teaching ELs, we need to view their previous experiences as strengths and maintain high expectations for their performance. As Helman (2009) has observed, "When students' knowledge and background experiences, as well as their abilities, languages, and family heritage, are seen as strengths, students are empowered to be successful at school" (p. 9).

August and Shanahan (2008) have found that ELs learning to read in English benefit from the explicit teaching of the components of literacy (e.g., phonemic awareness, phonics, vocabulary, comprehension, writing), just as English speakers learning to read in English do. Goldenberg (2010) notes, "ELLs appear to be capable of learning at levels comparable to those of English speakers, if they are provided with good, structured, explicit teaching" (p. 27).

A wide range of accessible text at a variety of levels should be available to English learners. Further, an array of supports, including pictures, wait time, and collaboration, should be included in our teaching.

When assessing ELs, we need to be particularly aware of their language development. Our goal is to ensure that language issues do not interfere with the content of the assessments. We can monitor English learners' progress through formative assessment. Observing their progress through formative assessments provides us with ongoing insights into their thinking and abilities. This information helps us understand whether the supports we provided were effective or need to be changed.

[handwritten margin note: We need to develop formative assessment]

What Connections Can We Make to the CCSS?

The National Governors Association Center for Best Practices and the Council of Chief State School Officers (2010a) have created a document entitled "Application of Common Core State Standards for English Language Learners." The authors suggest that English learners should be held to the high expectations of the Common Core State Standards. They further note that "these students may require additional time, appropriate instructional support, and aligned assessments as they acquire both English language proficiency and content area knowledge" (p. 1).

The document also notes that to meet the Standards, it is essential that ELs have access to the following:

- Teachers and personnel at the school and district levels who are well prepared and qualified to support ELLs while taking advantage of the many strengths and skills they bring to the classroom;
- Literacy-rich school environments where students are immersed in a variety of language experiences;
- Instruction that develops foundational skills in English and enables ELLs to participate fully in grade-level coursework;
- Coursework that prepares ELLs for postsecondary education or the workplace, yet is made comprehensible for students learning content in a second language (through specific pedagogical techniques and additional resources);
- Opportunities for classroom discourse and interaction that are well-designed to enable ELLs to develop communicative strengths in language arts;
- Ongoing assessment and feedback to guide learning; and
- Speakers of English who know the language well enough to provide ELLs with models and support. (NGA Center & CCSSO, 2010a, pp. 1–2)

What Types of Instructional Considerations Need to Occur?

Bao is a 10th-grade student who immigrated to the United States with her family from Vietnam last year. Bao is working with Mrs. Sherman, an ESL teacher, who has taught Bao's other teachers how to use a variety of supports when teaching English learners. The supports include access to motivational text, extended wait time, short written responses, and pictures. Mrs. Sherman has suggested that paired and small-group instructional settings work best for Bao. She also has encouraged the teachers to create culturally responsive classrooms and integrate multiple representations of thinking in their instruction.

Mrs. Sherman focuses on encouraging Bao to take an active role in reading. She often uses culturally relevant text, discussion, graphic organizers, and technology to engage her. She pays particular attention to Bao's background knowledge and often enhances it by reading aloud informational articles, accessing pertinent websites, and encouraging Bao to partner with other students—either native English speakers or same language speakers, depending on the task.

Our goal is to teach the English learners in our classes to become active, engaged readers. To help our students do this, we need to understand all that we can about how to teach them (Young & Hadaway, 2006). According to McLaughlin (2012), there are numerous ways in which we can modify our teaching to accommodate these students, including the following:

- Emphasize student motivation and engagement
- Employ a structured literacy lesson format with appropriate supports
- Teach students to generate and respond to questions
- Teach patterns for narrative and informational texts
- Read aloud texts that present content, useful language patterns, or vocabulary in context to help foster oral language development
- Interact with text to make content more comprehensible
- Encourage students to engage in written responses to provide time for thought and reflection
- Provide numerous daily opportunities for students to engage in discussion
- Integrate visual aids to support and extend understanding, including picture books as supports for English learners of all ages
- Teach integrated, engaging, and enriching lessons that deepen understandings (p. 6)

✳ An additional strategy is to encourage students to represent their thinking in multiple ways (e.g., dramatization, music, photography).

Helman (2009) notes, "Educational factors that influence the literacy learning of ELLs involve in-class instruction, the types and quality of lessons, involvement of the students and their communities, teacher knowledge, and students' opportunities to use language in cognitively challenging activities" (p. 13). As English learners strive to meet the Common Core Standards, high-quality instruction will support their efforts.

Students With Disabilities

What Do We Know About Students With Disabilities?

Since 1975, federal laws have been in place to provide accommodations for learning and other types of disabilities. Currently, four federal regulations govern special education in the United

States: the Individuals with Disabilities Education Act, Section 504 of the Rehabilitation Act, the Americans with Disabilities Act, and the No Child Left Behind Act. One of the qualifications for special-education services is that a student must be in need of specially designed instruction to receive a free, appropriate public education in the least restrictive environment that conforms to an individualized education plan (IEP). Once the student is eligible to receive special-education services, there are a multitude of policies that govern those services, the process for receiving them, and the student's privacy (Osborne & Russo, 2007).

Response to Intervention (RTI) is often associated with special education but is actually a general education system. The National Center on Response to Intervention (2010) defines RTI as such:

> Response to Intervention integrates assessment and intervention within a multi-level prevention system to maximize student achievement and to reduce behavioral problems. With RTI, schools use data to identify students at risk for poor learning outcomes, monitor student progress, provide evidence-based interventions and adjust the intensity and nature of those interventions depending on a student's responsiveness, and identify students with learning disabilities or other disabilities. (p. 2)

Each state has its own particular guidelines for RTI; however, the bottom line is that districts are required to have an RTI process in place before referring a student for special education. The RTI system is designed to provide information about students' achievement, provide learning supports to students who need them, and put in place a monitoring system that allows students to acquire the supports as needed. Students can be referred for special education services after receiving interventions in the regular classroom. Only after a student has demonstrated that he or she still needs specialized instruction after interventions in the regular education setting can the student be referred for special education services. For many students, RTI interventions are focused on reading achievement.

According to researchers in the field of reading disabilities, students with learning disabilities may display poor phonological awareness, which affects their reading ability in other areas (Shankweiler et al., 1995). Students may have problems with auditory, visual, phonological, or language processing or may have difficulties with memory or attention. Some students have physical disabilities such as visual or hearing impairment that affect reading achievement. Each student who qualifies for special education has an IEP that is specifically designed to meet his or her particular needs. A student's IEP in reading, based on assessment, is likely to be focused on gaps in basic skills knowledge in phonemic awareness or phonics, fluency issues, lack of vocabulary development, comprehension strategies, written language processing, or a combination of these areas. The IEP includes specially designed instruction (SDI) to specify evidence-based practice, and may note modification and/or accommodations for the student on reading assessments should the reading disability negatively impact expected reading behaviors. Reading instruction for students with disabilities is always required; accommodations are not a replacement for effective instruction and student practice.

What Connections Can We Make to the CCSS?

The Common Core Standards document includes a caveat for students with disabilities. A brief document attached to the Standards is entitled "Application to Students With Disabilities" (NGA Center & CCSSO, 2010b). The writers of this document state that students who are eligible under the Individuals with Disabilities Education Act "must be challenged to excel within the general curriculum" (p. 1). In other words, students with disabilities are expected to participate fully in instruction based on the CCSS. The Standards should not be made easier; instead, students should be provided supports and accommodations to achieve within the expectations of the Common Core (Council for Exceptional Children, 2011).

To promote a culture of high expectations, the CCSS document goes on to recommend three types of supports and services for students with disabilities:

- Instructional supports for learning—based on the principles of Universal Design for Learning (UDL)...

- Instructional accommodations (Thompson, Morse, Sharpe & Hall, 2005)—changes in materials or procedures—which do not change the standards...

- Assistive technology devices and services to ensure access to the general education curriculum and the Common Core State Standards. (NGA Center & CCSSO, 2010b, pp. 1–2)

What Types of Instructional Considerations Need to Occur?

Calvin, a ninth grader, is eligible for special education services in reading. When other students read and analyze the author's purpose in a science article or read literature closely for deep comprehension, Calvin struggles with basic comprehension. He has an IEP with accommodations for reading. In the Common Core classroom, students with disabilities that affect their reading progress still need specialized instructional attention provided by a literacy expert. These students should receive comprehension instruction geared to meet their particular literacy needs. However, Calvin also needs to be part of the whole-class instruction in lessons relating to the ELA Standards. To help meet the needs of students like Calvin and other diverse learners, his teachers plan instruction for their classes with supports for learning based on the principles of the Universal Design for Learning (UDL; CAST, 2011).

The UDL Model is a framework to address curricular planning that meets the needs of all learners. This framework was created to anticipate the needs of diverse learners when designing a curriculum, but its principles can be used when planning classroom units and lessons as well. The three principles are as follows (CAST, 2011, p. 5):

- Provide multiple means of representation.

- Provide multiple means of action and expression.

- Provide multiple means of engagement.

These can essentially be summarized as using multiple modes of teaching, learning, and engagement.

Multiple Means of Representation

Multiple means of representation relates to the "what" of learning—the ways that learners perceive and comprehend information. To provide multiple means of representation means students have a variety of ways to acquire information. We must understand student needs based on assessment and plan to use different modes (e.g., visual, auditory, language) when planning instructional activities and assessing reading performance. This can be accomplished through the use of technology as well as research-based teaching methods and strategies that take into account the different ways that students learn. For special-education students, indeed for all students, assessment is used to help them build on knowledge that they already possess to build new knowledge.

For students with reading disabilities, instruction in the Common Core Standards needs to be explicit. For struggling readers like Calvin to be able to participate in the instruction and meet the expectations, his teachers engage in explicit instruction: modeling for their students, scaffolding students' learning, giving multiple opportunities for their students to practice, and planning frequent check-ins using formative assessment. The teachers intentionally model the thinking processes they want Calvin and his classmates to use when approaching a literacy task focused on the CCSS in English, science, social studies, or technical subjects. The teachers are transparent in their teaching, talking in detail about what they are doing and why. They know what to emphasize and ensure that they are clear when talking to their students about what they need to learn. Calvin's teachers provide learning supports for his reading of more complex text in the disciplines. These include using highlighting to focus on vocabulary words, using technology to provide background on the reading, and preparing a digital recording of the text if Calvin needs to listen to the passage. Calvin's teachers provide numerous learning supports so Calvin can achieve the expectations of the Standards.

Multiple Means of Action and Expression

Multiple means of action and expression in UDL addresses the "how" of learning—the ways in which students demonstrate their learning. To provide multiple means of expression means to ensure that students have varied options to demonstrate what they have learned. For Calvin, this means his teachers provide increased opportunities to respond in lessons focused on the Common Core Standards, and they accept different ways for him to communicate. Calvin and his classmates can dramatize passages or create illustrations to demonstrate interpretations of the text, as well as participate in explicit writing instruction of the types of texts required to meet the Standards. He can also participate in academic discussions of the ideas found in the text.

Multiple Means of Engagement

Multiple means of engagement in UDL has to do with the "why" of learning—the reasons students learn. Multiple means of engagement means teachers know their students well enough to know their interests and abilities, and the teachers know what it takes to motivate the students to learn at high levels. Calvin's teachers offer options for individual choice and autonomy, provide instruction that is culturally responsive and relevant to his interests, and help him develop skills and procedures for tasks so he can gain a sense of academic confidence. Calvin and several other students in the class may need more or extended time, so his teachers plan for that. They help their students learn to set goals for success that will be valuable in helping them meet the appropriate Common Core Standards.

When we design classroom instruction following the principles of UDL, we increase the likelihood that the needs of students with disabilities will be met. A student who meets the eligibility criteria under the Individuals with Disabilities Education Act will have an IEP. It may designate that teachers will provide instructional modifications within mainstream classroom instruction. Any instructional modifications should support instruction in the Common Core Standards. The expectation is that to meet the CCSS, students with disabilities must be engaged in appropriate instruction. More information about the UDL principles can be found at www.udlcenter.org/aboutudl/udlguidelines.

Gifted and Talented Students

What Do We Know About Gifted and Talented Students?

Although there are no federal mandates to serve gifted and talented students at this time, the federal definition of gifted and talented, included in the Elementary and Secondary Education Act (2004), states that gifted and talented learners are

> students, children, or youth who give evidence of high achievement capability in areas such as intellectual, creative, artistic, or leadership capacity, or in specific academic fields, and who need services and activities not ordinarily provided by the school in order to fully develop those capabilities. (National Association for Gifted Children, 2008, para. 1)

Catron and Wingenbach (1986) define gifted readers as "students who have been identified both as gifted and as reading on a level two or more years beyond their chronological grade placement" (p. 134). They make a distinction between a gifted reader and a good reader, saying that

> the gifted reader is quick to integrate prior knowledge and experience with text information, is comfortable and productive in the application of higher level thinking skills (analysis, synthesis, evaluation) to the written text, and is capable of communicating the outcome of this individualized processing of print. (p. 134)

Gifted readers appear to effortlessly employ comprehension skills such as anticipation of meaning based on visual cues, organization of text, and syntax; reader and text interaction through use of prior knowledge and experience; and metacognitive awareness. Gifted readers, according to these researchers, process "text for immediate comprehension, going directly from visual features to meaning" (p. 135). Catron and Wingenbach add that gifted readers generally add so much of their own knowledge and experience as they comprehend text that sometimes it interferes with literal levels of comprehension.

There have been few studies examining effective instructional programs for gifted and talented readers, but experts and advocates of gifted education consistently agree about the nature of instruction for these readers. Wood (2008) discusses what gifted and talented readers need from an instructional reading program, including

- Opportunities to read challenging materials
- Deeper reading comprehension instruction
- Critical reading of text, including interpretation and analysis
- Development of an appreciation of diverse, multicultural literature
- Opportunities for group discussion of selected texts
- Development of creative reading behaviors, including writing and dramatic interpretation
- Choice and self-selection of texts to promote motivation and reading enjoyment

Experts in gifted and talented education have recommended that an instructional program for these readers should include flexible grouping based on reading level and interest, acceleration, enrichment, discussion opportunities, challenging literature, and reading that is critical, creative, and inquiry-based (Wood, 2008).

At the high school level, opportunities often exist for gifted students to enroll in Advanced Placement English courses. Such classes usually concentrate on literary analysis and require students to read texts such as *How to Read Literature Like a Professor: A Lively and Entertaining Guide to Reading Between the Lines* (Foster, 2003), so they can learn how to analyze complex literature. Students in AP English courses read and analyze a variety of college-level works of literature and literary nonfiction.

What Connections Can We Make to the CCSS?

The ability to read complex text is an expectation of the Common Core, and grade-level text exemplars are included in Appendix B of the CCSS (NGA Center & CCSSO, 2010e). Gifted readers can most likely comprehend these types of texts with little difficulty; however, many will still need teacher guidance in contemplating deeper meanings of the text and analyzing the author's craft. It would be surprising if many gifted readers in grades 6–12 had already read a great number of texts such as these independently, which include classic and complex short stories, poems, novels, and literary nonfiction such as memoirs, biographies, and speeches. As such, they need experiences with a wide variety of literature and literary nonfiction to meet the expectations of the Standards. At the same time, teachers should recognize that gifted readers will rarely need to spend extended instructional time learning how to read such texts, but will need opportunities to dig deeper into the meaning.

The introduction to the English Language Arts Standards includes a statement that the CCSS "do not define the nature of advanced work for students who meet the Standards prior to the end of high school" (NGA Center & CCSSO, 2010c, p. 6). In Appendix A of the Standards, the issue of text complexity for advanced readers is addressed with this statement:

> *Students reading well above and well below grade-band level need additional support.* Students for whom texts within their text complexity grade band (or even from the next higher band) present insufficient challenge must be given the attention and resources necessary to develop their reading ability at an appropriately advanced pace. (NGA Center & CCSSO, 2010d, p. 9)

Beyond these statements there is little direction for teachers regarding gifted and talented readers in the Common Core Standards. However, as teachers, we know that there will be students who are advanced beyond the CCSS at that particular grade level. Although details are lacking, the expectation of the Standards is that gifted and talented readers will have the opportunity to learn at the levels of which they are capable. These students must have special consideration in the planning of curriculum, instruction, and assessment in order for their needs to be met. Gifted readers have the right to carefully planned instruction that allows them to achieve at their greatest potential in the comprehension of more challenging materials and to more sophisticated methods of response within the Common Core classroom. While most students need teacher guidance to learn to comprehend complex text, gifted readers may need teacher guidance in selecting and analyzing even more complex texts that will help them achieve at higher levels.

What Types of Instructional Considerations Need to Occur?

Sylvia is an 11th-grade student who is considered a gifted reader. She began reading before she started kindergarten and has been an avid reader throughout all her years of school. She loves fiction, especially science fiction and fantasy, and enjoys discussing short stories and novels with other students who read these genres for pleasure. Her favorite books include *The Hitchhiker's Guide to the Galaxy* (Adams, 2009) and *A Wizard of Earthsea* (Le Guin, 2012), as well as more modern works of fantasy. Sylvia is considered an "underground reader" (Miller, 2009), a student who reads voraciously and often covertly outside of school. She not only comprehends the texts she reads but more often than not also understands the larger ideas included in them.

Although Sylvia has been reading advanced-level texts for most of her life, Ms. Zhang, her 11th-grade English teacher, finds Sylvia still has gaps in her knowledge. The Standards require 11th graders to be able to analyze different types of text, including plays by Shakespeare; 18th-, 19th-, and early-20th-century foundational works of American literature; and seminal U.S. texts such as presidential speeches (NGA Center & CCSSO, 2010c, p. 38). Because Sylvia has concentrated her personal reading on science fiction, a genre she loves, Ms. Zhang sees that Sylvia needs experience with other types of text, including literary nonfiction and more traditional literature. At the same time, Ms. Zhang notes that Sylvia quickly and easily learns the concepts of text analysis with text she is reading in class and therefore does not have to spend as much time with comprehension of the text as other students. Ms. Zhang arranges for Sylvia to engage in discussions of texts with equally capable peers both in the classroom and elsewhere in order to think critically and creatively about the text; furthermore, she conducts whole-class lessons in close reading focused on literary analysis. Ms. Zhang also provides opportunities for Sylvia and her peers who are gifted readers to engage in inquiry-based literacy—that is, reading, writing, speaking, and listening in order to find answers to broad questions and solve authentic problems, often using technology.

The National Association for Gifted Children (2008) notes that for advanced students, "fidelity to grade-level standards will limit learning" (para. 23). These readers need instructional considerations that stretch beyond the grade-level boundaries of the CCSS. Students who demonstrate the characteristics of gifted and talented readers need opportunities to analyze, discuss, and explore the possibilities of text to the extent of their abilities, rather than focusing only on the expectations of the Standards.

In the Common Core classroom, we need to ensure that gifted and talented readers have opportunities to engage in Standards instruction that allows them to use their abilities for text comprehension and analysis with materials that are appropriately challenging for their needs. The possibilities for text analysis, writing, research, speech and debate, and multimedia presentations are endless for gifted and talented readers in grades 6–12.

English learners, students with disabilities, and gifted and talented learners are three types of students whose needs must be considered as we implement the Common Core State Standards. Because there are relatively few CCSS resources available for these students, we need to be especially diligent in ensuring that they can reach their maximum potential in our classrooms.

ESSENTIAL RESOURCES

- Chi, Y., Garcia, R.B., Surber, C., & Trautman, L. (2012). *Alignment study between the Common Core State Standards in English language arts and mathematics and the WIDA English language proficiency standards, 2007 Edition, prekindergarten through grade 12.* Retrieved July 29, 2012, from www.wida.us/Research/agenda/Alignment

- McLaughlin, M. (2012). *Guided Comprehension for English learners.* Newark, DE: International Reading Association.

- National Governors Association Center for Best Practices & Council of Chief State School Officers. (2010). *Application of Common Core State Standards for English language learners.* Retrieved July 29, 2012, from www.corestandards.org/assets/application-for-english-learners.pdf

- National Governors Association Center for Best Practices & Council of Chief State School Officers. (2010). *Application to students with disabilities.* Retrieved July 29, 2012, from www.corestandards.org/assets/application-to-students-with-disabilities.pdf

References

August, D., & Shanahan, T. (Eds.). (2008). *Developing reading and writing in second-language learners: Lessons from the report of the National Literacy Panel on language-minority children and youth.* New York: Routledge; Washington, DC: Center for Applied Linguistics; Newark, DE: International Reading Association.

CAST. (2011). *Universal Design for Learning (UDL) guidelines version 2.0.* Wakefield, MA: Author. Retrieved August 4, 2012, from www.udlcenter.org/aboutudl/udlguidelines

Catron, R.M., & Wingenbach, N. (1986). Developing the potential of the gifted reader. *Theory Into Practice, 25*(2), 134–140. doi:10.1080/00405848609543213

Council for Exceptional Children. (2011). Common Core Standards: What special educators need to know. *CEC Today.* Retrieved July 10, 2012, from www.cec.sped.org/AM/Template.cfm?Section=CEC_Today1&TEMPLATE=/CM/ContentDisplay.cfm&CONTENTID=15269

Goldenberg, C. (2010). Improving achievement for English learners: Conclusions from recent reviews and emerging research. In G. Li & P.A. Edwards (Eds.), *Best practices in ELL instruction* (pp. 15–43). New York: Guilford.

Helman, L. (2009). Factors influencing second-language literacy development: A road map for teachers. In L. Helman (Ed.), *Literacy development with English learners: Research-based instruction in grades K–6* (pp. 1–17). New York: Guilford.

McLaughlin, M. (2012). *Guided Comprehension for English learners.* Newark, DE: International Reading Association.

Miller, D. (2009). Mind the gap: Engaging gifted readers. *Education Week Teacher: The Book Whisperer.* Retrieved October 5, 2012, from blogs.edweek.org/teachers/book-whisperer/2009/03/mind_the_gap_engaging_gifted_r.html

National Association for Gifted Children. (2008). *Frequently asked questions.* Retrieved July 11, 2012, from www.nagc.org/index2.aspx?id=548

National Center on Response to Intervention. (2010, April). *Essential components of RTI—a closer look at Response to Intervention.* Washington, DC: U.S. Department of Education, Office of Special Education Programs, National Center on Response to Intervention. Retrieved August 22, 2012, from www.rti4success.org/pdf/rtiessentialcomponents_042710.pdf

National Governors Association Center for Best Practices & Council of Chief State School Officers. (2010a). *Application of Common Core State Standards for English language learners.* Retrieved July 29, 2012, from www.corestandards.org/assets/application-for-english-learners.pdf

National Governors Association Center for Best Practices & Council of Chief State School Officers. (2010b). *Application to students with disabilities.* Retrieved August 7, 2012, from www.corestandards.org/assets/application-to-students-with-disabilities.pdf

National Governors Association Center for Best Practices & Council of Chief State School Officers. (2010c). *Common Core State Standards for English language arts and literacy in history/social studies, science, and technical subjects.* Washington, DC: Authors. Retrieved August 4, 2012, from www.corestandards.org/assets/CCSSI_ELA%20Standards.pdf

National Governors Association Center for Best Practices & Council of Chief State School Officers. (2010d). *Common Core State Standards for English language arts and literacy in history/social studies, science, and technical subjects: Appendix A: Research supporting key elements of the Standards and glossary of key terms.* Washington, DC: Authors. Retrieved August 7, 2012, from www.corestandards.org/assets/Appendix_A.pdf

National Governors Association Center for Best Practices & Council of Chief State School Officers. (2010e). *Common Core State Standards for English language arts and literacy in history/social studies, science, and technical subjects: Appendix B: Text exemplars and sample performance tasks.* Washington, DC: Authors. Retrieved August 3, 2012, from www.corestandards.org/assets/Appendix_B.pdf

Osborne, A.G., Jr., & Russo, C.J. (2007). *Special education and the law: A guide for practitioners* (2nd ed.). Thousand Oaks, CA: Corwin.

Shankweiler, D., Crain, S., Katz, L., Fowler, A., Liberman, A., Brady, S., et al. (1995). Cognitive profiles of reading-disabled children: Comparison of language skills in phonology, morphology, and syntax. *Psychological Science, 6*(3), 149–156. doi:10.1111/j.1467-9280.1995.tb00324.x

Wood, P.F. (2008). Reading instruction with gifted and talented readers: A series of unfortunate events or a sequence of auspicious results? *Gifted Child Today, 31*(3), 16–25.

Young, T.A., & Hadaway, N.L. (Eds.). (2006). *Supporting the literacy development of English learners: Increasing success in all classrooms.* Newark, DE: International Reading Association.

Literature Cited

Adams, D. (2009). *The hitchhiker's guide to the galaxy* (25th anniversary ed.). New York: Crown.

Foster, T.C. (2003). *How to read literature like a professor: A lively and entertaining guide to reading between the lines.* New York: Harper Perennial.

Le Guin, U.K. (2012). *A wizard of Earthsea.* Boston: Graphia/Houghton Mifflin.

CHAPTER 5

Reshaping Curriculum to Accommodate the Common Core and the Teaching of Reading

When we review the Common Core State Standards, several dichotomies emerge between what the Standards are suggesting and what we, as reading teachers, know to be research-based best practices. Examples of such issues include the following:

1. Current best practices purport that reading is a social-constructivist process, but close reading advocates that our students should read complex text with little or no activation of background knowledge.

2. The Standards address *reading closely*, which many perceive to be deep comprehension, but ACT (formerly American College Testing; 2006) advocates for *close reading*, a literary analysis technique.

3. Metacognitive reading comprehension strategies are not included in the CCSS, but students still need to use them.

4. There are content gaps in the Standards. For example, students are expected to ask and answer questions in the primary grades, but there is little emphasis on questioning in grades 4–12. A similar gap is found in student expectations for using text structures.

5. The Reading Standards note that students will read complex text at their grade levels, but the CCSS do not address the teaching of reading beyond the inclusion of literacy skills.

Each of these points has an impact on curriculum, instruction, and assessment. Consequently, it is crucial that we, as literacy professionals, develop curricula that integrate what research and best practices support as essential for the high-quality teaching of reading—as well as what the Common Core requires. As we engage in this discussion, it is important to remember that each state has the opportunity to add 15% to the content of the Common Core State Standards. These topics are among those that states might consider including in their versions of the CCSS.

In this chapter, we address these issues by responding to the following questions:

- What do we know about reading as a social-constructivist process?
- What do we know about reading closely?
- What is close reading?
- What can we do to ensure that our students continue to learn reading comprehension strategies?
- How can we address the Standards' requirement for students to read complex text?
- How can we make certain that our students learn higher levels of thinking and questioning?
- How can we ensure that all students receive appropriate reading instruction?

What Do We Know About Reading as a Social-Constructivist Process?

To understand reading comprehension as a social-constructivist process, we must first understand constructivism as a theory about knowledge and learning. From a constructivist perspective, learning "is understood as a self-regulated process of resolving inner cognitive conflicts that often become apparent through concrete experience, collaborative discourse, and reflection" (Brooks & Brooks, 1993, p. vii). Constructivists believe that students construct knowledge by linking what is new to what is already known. They construct meaning through these connections when educators pose relevant problems, structure learning around primary concepts, seek and value students' ideas, and assess student learning in context (Brooks & Brooks, 1993).

Cambourne (2002) suggests that instructional principles emerge from constructivist theory. These include:

- Creating a classroom culture that encourages deep engagement with effective reading.
- Using strategies that are a blend of explicitness, systematicity, mindfulness, and contextualization.
- Creating continuous opportunities to develop intellectual unrest.
- Encouraging students to develop their conscious awareness of how text functions and how we create meaning.
- Designing and using tasks that will support the authentic use of the processes and understandings that are implicit in reading behavior.

Constructivism is manifested in classrooms that are characterized by engagement, accessible text, student-generated ideas, discussion, interaction, higher levels of thinking, and personal construction of meaning (McLaughlin, 2010). In such contexts, authentic literacy tasks assimilate real-world experiences, provide a purpose for learning, and encourage students to take ownership of learning (Hiebert, 1994).

In reading, constructivism is reflected in schema-based learning development, which purports that learning takes place when new information is integrated with what is already known. Prior knowledge is the key factor in this process. The more students know about a particular topic, the easier it is for them to make connections between what they know and what they are learning (Anderson, 1994; Anderson & Pearson, 1984). Constructivists view comprehension as the construction of the meaning of a written or spoken communication through a reciprocal, holistic interchange of ideas between the interpreter and the message in a particular communicative context. *Note:* The presumption here is that meaning resides in the intentional problem-solving, thinking processes of the interpreter during such an interchange, that the content of meaning is influenced by that person's prior knowledge and experience, and that the message so constructed by the receiver may or may not be congruent with the message sent. (Harris & Hodges, 1995, p. 39)

Vygotsky's principles enhance the constructivist perspective by addressing the social context of learning (Dixon-Krauss, 1996). According to Vygotsky, a student should be taught within his or her zone of proximal development (Forman & Cazden, 1994; Vygotsky, 1978), which is the level at which the student can learn with the support of a more knowledgeable other. As the student's understanding increases, the support from the more knowledgeable other decreases, and the student takes on more responsibility. This gradual release of responsibility is also known as scaffolding instruction.

Instruction within the zone should incorporate both scaffolding and social mediation. When discussing this Vygotskian principle, Dixon-Krauss (1996) notes that language concepts are learned through discussion—social dialogue—with more capable others. Such social interaction encourages students to think and share their ideas. Current beliefs about the teaching of reading also include students' use of reading comprehension strategies when constructing meaning.

What Do We Know About Reading Closely?

When students read closely, they examine evidence and draw logical conclusions to support their thinking and interpret the author's message. Reading closely is also known as deep comprehension. As current best practice suggests, reading closely begins with activation of students' background knowledge. Next, students read the text multiple times for different purposes, generate and answer text-dependent questions, and discuss ideas that arise from the text based on textual evidence. Then we guide students to think critically about the text, striving to explore ideas stated explicitly and implicitly by the author. Common Core Reading Standard 1 for grades K–12 builds to CCR Standard 1. The expectation of CCR Reading Standard 1 in all disciplines is that students will be able to engage in the fundamental tasks required to "read closely to determine what the text says explicitly" (NGA Center & CCSSO, 2010, p. 10). For information about reading closely in various disciplines, see Chapter 7, this volume.

What Is Close Reading?

Close reading, the term ACT (2006) has suggested to describe "reading closely," is a literary analysis technique.

In close reading, a great deal of attention is paid to how the author presents ideas, intentional word choice, and the message being conveyed based on minute clues in the text. In informational and argumentative text, readers also need to examine the author's claims and the evidence provided to support those claims. Close reading examples beginning as early as third grade are posted as models on websites such as that of Student Achievement Partners (2012; www.achievethecore.org).

In such examples, students are expected to read complex text independently and then participate in a whole-group discussion based on text-dependent questions asked by the teacher.

College and Career Readiness (CCR) Reading Anchor Standard 1 states, "Read closely to determine what the text says explicitly and to make logical inferences from it; cite specific textual evidence when writing or speaking to support conclusions drawn from the text" (NGA Center & CCSSO, 2010, p. 10). Common Core Reading Standard 1 builds to CCR Reading Anchor Standard 1 by expecting early primary children to be able to ask and answer questions about key details in a text. By grade 5, and with increasing sophistication up through grade 12, students are expected to read closely and cite textual evidence to support logical conclusions per the ELA Reading Literature and Reading Informational Standards. The same is expected in grades 6–12 for literacy in history/social studies, science, and technical subjects.

Proponents of close reading advocate that teachers should not provide background information about complex text, should not engage students in prereading activities, and should not teach lessons in reading strategies. Instead, students should approach a text with little prior discussion to glean what they can about the author's message and ideas, and to engage in a "productive struggle," a term used in the *Publishers' Criteria for the Common Core State Standards in ELA and Literacy, Grades 3–12* (Coleman & Pimentel, 2012b). In a productive struggle, students first read the text with no help and then participate in discussion to figure out the meaning of words and the author's message. In a video explaining the concept of close reading, Coleman (2011), one of the chief contributing writers of the ELA Standards and an author of the publishers' criteria for the CCSS, puts forth statements about prereading, such as "predicting what's in a text before you read it is not an essential college- and career-ready skill" (2:14). Coleman also dismisses the idea of teaching a "generic reading strategy" (2:34) before a close reading of a complex text. These and similar statements have sparked a debate over the use of close reading (Gewetz, 2012). Such statements have the potential to negate decades of research on how students learn to read. As reading teachers, we know that students who cannot read well enough to comprehend today's classroom materials are not going to magically develop the skills and strategies they need to read and analyze complex text independently.

When commenting on close reading, literacy experts have shared thinking that provides insights into its nature. For example, Fisher and Frey (personal communication, July 7, 2012) see close reading as an important aspect of reader response. As they observe,

> Rosenblatt (1995) cautioned, "The reader must remain faithful to the author's text and must be alert to the potential clues concerning character and motive" (p. 11). This requires a careful reading and often re-reading of the same text, which has not been common practice.

Pearson (personal communication, July 7, 2012) notes,

> Empson (1930) in no way meant to divorce close reading from the deployment of existing knowledge and insight in the interpretive process. Knowledge has to be tamed, sometimes even held at bay, but it is intimately involved at every step.

Pearson also suggests a series of probes to support the use of close reading. They begin with "What do you think?" and "What makes you think so?" Next, he suggests that readers follow up with one of the following prompts, which he notes range from literal to interpretive to critical and even evaluative:

- What's the point of this piece?
- What's the flow of the author's fundamental argument? What's the nature of the author's evidence base?
- What other piece from this year's syllabus does it most remind you of?
- Does this author know anything about _____ (subject of the text)?
- How would this author have responded to _____ (another piece of fiction or nonfiction)?

Pearson further elaborates,

> Another way of thinking about close reading is that it puts the reader into a frame of conducting what some would call a textual reading (in contrast to a writerly reading—focusing on authorial moves and history, or a readerly reading—focusing on examining the text in light of reader's knowledge, response preferences, and dispositions). Still another way of thinking about close reading is that it gives due respect to the text—not, by the way, to the author, but to the text.

Finally, Pearson notes, "The real truth is that close reading is as grounded in knowledge and context as it is in text. It just ensures that text has a role—and a voice—at the table."

Calfee (personal communication, July 8, 2012) concludes that the Introduction to the Common Core State Standards

> lays out a full and rich portrayal of the concept of literacy—in all its forms—as a tool that serves individuals for thinking and communicating. "Close reading" and "reading closely" are mentioned, once in the Introduction, and as part of Anchor Standard 1. In reasonable proportion and with appropriate developmental attention, this idea certainly has a place in what we would expect of a high school graduate, but it does not warrant placement as the keystone in the arch of literacy that is portrayed by the Standards.

When we read the Standards and the supporting documents closely ourselves, we see more into the nature of reading closely. We see that the term *close reading* can be used in two ways: as a literary analysis technique and as a way to describe reading deeply for enhanced comprehension. The Standards state that students should be able to "readily undertake the close, attentive reading that is at the heart of understanding and enjoying complex works of literature" (NGA Center & CCSSO, 2010, p. 3). It is important that adolescents learn to comprehend and learn to read closely for deeper comprehension.

What Can We Do to Ensure That Our Students Continue to Learn Reading Comprehension Strategies?

The primary difficulty with the Common Core's decision not to include reading comprehension strategies is that most school curricula will be built on the Standards—and will not include the additional content that teachers know students need. The fact is that a good number of states have adopted the CCSS without making any changes to content—much less the 15% that they have been invited to add. Individual states need to include the teaching of reading comprehension strategies in their versions of the Standards.

Studies have demonstrated that explicit instruction of comprehension strategies improves students' comprehension of new texts and topics (Dole, Duffy, Roehler, & Pearson, 1991; Duffy et al., 1987; Hiebert, Pearson, Taylor, Richardson, & Paris, 1998). Research supports the teaching of reading comprehension strategies beginning in the primary grades (Duffy, 2001; Duke & Pearson, 2002; Hilden & Pressley, 2002; McLaughlin, 2002). In fact, Duke and Pearson (2002) suggest incorporating "both explicit instruction in specific comprehension strategies and a great deal of time and opportunity for actual reading, writing, and discussion of text" (p. 207).

Fielding and Pearson (1994) recommend a framework for comprehension instruction that encourages the gradual release of responsibility from teacher to student. This four-step approach includes teacher modeling, guided practice, independent practice, and application of the strategy in authentic reading situations. This framework is underpinned by Vygotsky's (1978) work on instruction within the zone of proximal development and also supported by scaffolding, the gradual relinquishing of support as students become more competent in using the strategy.

Linking skills and strategies can facilitate comprehension. Comprehension strategies are generally more complex than comprehension skills and often require the orchestration of several skills. Effective instruction links comprehension skills and strategies to promote strategic reading. For example, the comprehension skills of sequencing, making judgments, noting details, making generalizations, and using text structure can be linked to summarizing, which is a comprehension strategy (Lipson, 2001). These and other skills, including generating questions, making inferences, distinguishing between important and less important details, and drawing conclusions, facilitate students' use of one or more comprehension strategies. Generating questions is an example of a skill that permeates all reading comprehension skills. Several such skills, including asking and answering questions, are addressed in the Reading Standards (see Reading Standard 1.1).

After explaining and modeling skills and strategies, we can scaffold instruction to provide the support necessary as students attempt new tasks. As we observe students gaining competence in using the strategies, we can gradually release responsibility for learning to the students, who apply the strategies independently after practicing them in a variety of settings.

In the Key Design Considerations section in the Introduction to the Common Core State Standards, reading comprehension strategies are addressed in a subsection labeled "A focus on results rather than means." It details the Standards' results-oriented approach:

> By emphasizing required achievements, the Standards leave room for teachers, curriculum developers, and states to determine how those goals should be reached and what additional topics should be addressed. Thus, the Standards do not mandate such things as a particular writing process or the full range of metacognitive strategies that students may need to monitor and direct their thinking and learning. Teachers are thus free to provide students with whatever tools and knowledge their professional judgment and experience identify as most helpful for meeting the goals set out in the Standards. (NGA Center & CCSSO, 2010, p. 4)

How Can We Address the Standards' Requirement for Students to Read Complex Text?

CCR Reading Anchor Standard 10 states that students will "Read and comprehend complex literary and informational texts independently and proficiently" (NGA Center & CCSSO, 2010, p. 10). As reading teachers, we can support the need for students to read increasingly complex texts, but we also know that not all students are capable of reading such texts, particularly at grade level. As the authors of the publishers' criteria for the CCSS note, "Many students will need careful instruction—including effective scaffolding—to enable them to read at the level required by the Common Core State Standards" (Coleman & Pimentel, 2012a, p. 8; Coleman & Pimental, 2012b). The complex nature of text is not new to those of us who teach reading. We fully understand its multifaceted features and its relation to readers. As Hiebert (2012) has observed,

- The complexity of a text is a function of the reader's proficiency. There are complex beginning reading texts, there are complex middle-grade texts, etc.
- Numerous features can make a text complex.
- Typically: Complex texts have complex ideas and, usually, complex ideas are conveyed with rare and infrequent vocabulary. (slide 8)

In 2006, ACT based its definition of text complexity on three levels of increasingly complex text: uncomplicated, more challenging, and complex. ACT (2006) further delineated the characteristics of text on its continuum as

- Relationships (interactions among ideas or characters)
- Richness (amount and sophistication of information conveyed through data or literary devices)
- Structure (how the text is organized and how it progresses)
- Style (author's tone and use of language)
- Vocabulary (author's word choice)
- Purpose (author's intent in writing the text) (p. 15)

Table 5.1 shows further details of ACT's definition.

Table 5.1 Characteristics of Uncomplicated, More Challenging, and Complex Texts on the ACT Reading Test

Aspect of Text	Degree of Text Complexity		
	Uncomplicated	More Challenging	Complex
Relationships	Basic, straightforward	Sometimes implicit	Subtle, involved, deeply embedded
Richness	Minimal/limited	Moderate/more detailed	Sizable/highly sophisticated
Structure	Simple, conventional	More involved	Elaborate, sometimes unconventional
Style	Plain, accessible	Richer, less plain	Often intricate
Vocabulary	Familiar	Some difficult, context-dependent words	Demanding, highly context dependent
Purpose	Clear	Conveyed with some subtlety	Implicit, sometimes ambiguous

Note. From *Reading Between the Lines: What the ACT Reveals About College Readiness in Reading* (p. 14), by ACT, 2006, Iowa City, IA: Author. Copyright 2006 by ACT. Reprinted with permission.

Although several of the characteristics developed by ACT are rooted more in literary analysis than in reading, ACT's three categories of text complexity—uncomplicated, more challenging, and complex—strongly parallel the terms used by literacy professionals when discussing text levels: independent, instructional, and frustration. Students can read at the independent level with no assistance, and they can read at the instructional level with some assistance from the teacher. Frustration-level text is often shared in different ways. For example, we can provide detailed supports and share such text in small groups, as well as through disciplinary read-alouds, and books on CD.

As reading teachers, we know that students have diverse reading abilities; not all students are capable of reading text at their grade level. There are general guidelines for determining students' reading levels related to word accuracy, comprehension, and fluency. For word accuracy, the text is considered easy if students can read it with 95–100% accuracy, provided their fluency and comprehension are appropriate. The instructional level is reached when students can read most of the text but have some challenges with words or content. This is usually between 90% and 94% accuracy. Students who read a text with accuracy below 90% often struggle with fluency and comprehension because they must use so much of their cognitive focus to figure out unknown words. This is considered the frustration level. At this level, keywords are often misunderstood, and comprehension is compromised.

In addition to word accuracy, comprehension must also be assessed. This often involves determining students' background knowledge as well as their ability to retell or summarize what was read, effectively discuss the text, or predict what will happen next. If a student is unable to successfully complete such tasks, the text may be too difficult.

Fluency, the third factor, is directly related to comprehension. In fact, Rasinski (2010) notes that fluency is the ability to read accurately and expressively at a natural rate with good phrasing and good comprehension. Research suggests that lack of fluency may be an issue that still affects comprehension for many students at the high school level (Rasinski et al., 2005).

When we assess students' word accuracy, comprehension, and fluency, we gain insights into their reading abilities. Although the results of these informal measures are approximations, they provide a starting point for planning appropriate instruction for adolescents who still need to learn to read grade-level materials.

How Can We Make Certain That Our Students Learn Higher Levels of Thinking and Questioning?

The Common Core State Standards are built on the CCR Anchor Standards, which purport to ensure that our students are prepared for their future endeavors. However, when reviewing the CCSS, it becomes clear that there is little, if any, emphasis on students' ability to engage in divergent and evaluative thinking, a necessity for their future success. The emphases within the 6–12 Standards appear to be on finding answers to text-dependent questions. Consequently, we, as teachers, must continue to teach students how to think at higher levels.

Importantly, although the writers of the Common Core created the Standards, they also noted that teaching is in the hands of the educators. For example, Reading Standard 1 for all types of text is focused on citing specific textual evidence to support analysis of text, but the essential skill of

Table 5.2 Ciardiello's Levels of Questioning

Question Level	Signal Words and Phrases	Cognitive Operations
Memory	*Who?, What?, Where?, When?*	Naming, defining, identifying, designating
Convergent thinking	*Why?, How?, In what ways?*	Explaining, stating relationships, comparing/contrasting
Divergent thinking	*imagine, suppose, predict, if/then*	Predicting, hypothesizing, inferring, reconstructing
Evaluative thinking	*defend, judge, justify, What do you think?*	Valuing, judging, defending, justifying

asking and answering questions is only addressed in the primary grades. Grade 6–12 students need to be able to generate and respond to questions at multiple levels of thinking, including convergent, divergent, and evaluative. This skill supports students' learning and, in turn, directly effects their attainment of the Standards. Because asking and answering questions is not included in the grade 6–12 Standards, it is our task to teach this information.

To continue to engage our students in higher level thinking, we can follow Ciardiello's (1998, 2007) suggestions for teaching students how to generate and respond to questions at four levels: memory, convergent, divergent, and evaluative. Ciardiello also provides question prompts for each level. Ciardiello's questioning levels, including signal words and cognitive operations for each category, are featured in Table 5.2.

How Can We Ensure That All Students Receive Appropriate Reading Instruction?

In 2000, the International Reading Association published a set of children's literacy rights in response to the growing concern about narrowed reading instruction. The document states, "We must ensure that all children receive the excellent instruction and support they need to learn to read and write" (p. 1). We think this statement is as true today as it was then. All students have the right to engage in the social-constructivist nature of reading, use reading comprehension strategies, read increasingly challenging text, and understand how to successfully engage in higher order thinking. As teachers, we can honor these rights by providing our students with a full range of research-based, best literacy practices when implementing the ELA Common Core Standards.

The IRA (2012) position statement on adolescent literacy provides direction on the teaching of grade 6–12 students. The statement discusses eight considerations that adolescents deserve to support their literacy development. IRA believes that adolescents need access to engaging and motivating content and instruction to support their continued development. Specifically, adolescents deserve

1. Content area teachers who provide instruction in the multiple literacy strategies needed to meet the demands of the specific discipline

2. A culture of literacy in their schools with a systematic and comprehensive programmatic approach to increasing literacy achievement for all

3. Access to and instruction with multimodal, multiple texts

4. Differentiated literacy instruction specific to their individual needs

5. Opportunities to participate in oral communication when they engage in literacy activities

6. Opportunities to use literacy in the pursuit of civic engagement

7. Assessments that highlight their strengths and challenges

8. Access to a wide variety of print and nonprint materials

As we plan for literacy development and Standards-based instruction in grades 6–12, we need to thoughtfully consider the diverse needs of adolescents.

References

ACT. (2006). *Reading between the lines: What the ACT reveals about college readiness in reading.* Iowa City, IA: Author. Retrieved August 22, 2012, from www.act.org/research/policymakers/pdf/reading_report.pdf

Anderson, R.C. (1994). Role of the reader's schema in comprehension, learning, and memory. In R.B. Ruddell, M.R. Ruddell, & H. Singer (Eds.), *Theoretical models and processes of reading* (4th ed., pp. 469–482). Newark, DE: International Reading Association.

Anderson, R.C., & Pearson, P.D. (1984). A schema-theoretic view of basic processes in reading comprehension. In P.D. Pearson, R. Barr, M.L. Kamil, & P. Mosenthal (Eds.), *Handbook of reading research* (pp. 255–291). New York: Longman.

Brooks, J.G., & Brooks, M.G. (1993). *In search of understanding: The case for constructivist classrooms.* Alexandria, VA: Association for Supervision and Curriculum Development.

Cambourne, B. (2002). Holistic, integrated approaches to reading and language arts instruction: The constructivist framework of an instructional theory. In A.E. Farstrup & S.J. Samuels (Eds.), *What research has to say about reading instruction* (3rd ed., pp. 25–47). Newark, DE: International Reading Association. doi:10.1598/0872071774.2

Ciardiello, A.V. (1998). Did you ask a good question today? Alternative cognitive and metacognitive strategies. *Journal of Adolescent & Adult Literacy*, 42(3), 210–219.

Ciardiello, A.V. (2007). *Puzzle them first! Motivating adolescent readers with question-finding.* Newark, DE: International Reading Association.

Coleman, D. (2011, July 31). *Close reading of text: Letter from Birmingham jail, Martin Luther King, Jr.* [Video]. Albany, NY: EngageNY. Retrieved June 24, 2012, from engageny.org/resource/close-reading-of-text-mlk-letter-from-birmingham-jail/

Coleman, D., & Pimentel, S. (2012a, May). *Revised publishers' criteria for the Common Core State Standards in English language arts and literacy, grades K–2.* Washington, DC: National Governors Association, Council of Chief State School Officers, Achieve, Council of the Great City Schools, & National Association of State Boards of Education. Retrieved July 12, 2012, from corestandards.org/assets/Publishers_Criteria_for_K-2.pdf

Coleman, D., & Pimentel, S. (2012b, April). *Revised publishers' criteria for the Common Core State Standards in English language arts and literacy, grades 3–12.* Washington, DC: National Governors Association, Council of Chief State School Officers, Achieve, Council of the Great City Schools, & National Association of State Boards of Education. Retrieved August 4, 2012, from corestandards.org/assets/Publishers_Criteria_for_3-12.pdf

Dixon-Krauss, L. (1996). *Vygotsky in the classroom: Mediated literacy instruction and assessment.* White Plains, NY: Longman.

Dole, J.A., Duffy, G.G., Roehler, L.R., & Pearson, P.D. (1991). Moving from the old to the new: Research on reading comprehension instruction. *Review of Educational Research*, 61(2), 239–264.

Duffy, G.G. (2001, December). *The case for direct explanation of strategies.* Paper presented at the 51st annual meeting of the National Reading Conference, San Antonio, TX.

Duffy, G.G., Roehler, L.R., Sivan, E., Rackliffe, G., Book, C., Meloth, M.S., et al. (1987). Effects of explaining the reasoning associated with using reading strategies. *Reading Research Quarterly*, 22(3), 347–368. doi:10.2307/747973

Duke, N.K., & Pearson, P.D. (2002). Effective practices for developing reading comprehension. In A.E. Farstrup & S.J. Samuels (Eds.), *What research has to say about reading instruction* (3rd ed., pp. 205–242). Newark, DE: International Reading Association.

Empson, W. (1930). *Seven types of ambiguity.* London: Chatto & Windus.

Fielding, L.G., & Pearson, P.D. (1994). Reading comprehension: What works. *Educational Leadership, 51*(5), 62–68.

Forman, E.A., & Cazden, C.B. (1994). Exploring Vygotskian perspectives in education: The cognitive value of peer interaction. In R.B. Ruddell, M.R. Ruddell, & H. Singer (Eds.), *Theoretical models and processes of reading* (4th ed., pp. 155–178). Newark, DE: International Reading Association.

Gewetz, C. (2012). Common standards ignite debate over prereading. *Education Week, 31*(29), 1, 22–23.

Harris, T.L., & Hodges, R.E. (Eds.). (1995). *The literacy dictionary: The vocabulary of reading and writing.* Newark, DE: International Reading Association.

Hiebert, E.H. (1994). Becoming literate through authentic tasks: Evidence and adaptations. In R.B. Ruddell, M.R. Ruddell, & H. Singer (Eds.), *Theoretical models and processes of reading* (4th ed., pp. 391–413). Newark, DE: International Reading Association.

Hiebert, E.H. (2012, February). *Seven actions that teachers can take right now: Text complexity.* Retrieved June 22, 2012 from textproject.org/assets/Uploads/Hiebert_2012-03-10_CRLP-slides.pdf

Hiebert, E.H., Pearson, P.D., Taylor, B.M., Richardson, V., & Paris, S.G. (1998). *Every child a reader.* Ann Arbor, MI: Center for the Improvement of Early Reading Achievement.

Hilden, K., & Pressley, M. (2002, December). *Can teachers become comprehension strategies teachers given a small amount of training?* Paper presented at the 52nd annual meeting of the National Reading Conference, Miami, FL.

International Reading Association. (2000). *Making a difference means making it different: Honoring children's rights to excellent reading instruction.* Newark, DE: International Reading Association.

International Reading Association. (2012). *Adolescent literacy* (Position statement). Newark, DE: Author. Retrieved December 18, 1012, from www.reading.org/Libraries/resources/ps1079_adolescentliteracy_rev2012.pdf

Lipson, M.Y. (2001). *A fresh look at comprehension.* Paper presented at the Reading/Language Arts Symposium, Chicago, IL.

McLaughlin, M. (2002). *Guided Comprehension in the primary grades: Curricularizing strategy instruction.* Paper presented at the 52nd annual meeting of the National Reading Conference, Miami, FL.

McLaughlin, M. (2010). *Content area reading: Teaching and learning in an age of multiple literacies.* Boston: Allyn & Bacon.

National Governors Association Center for Best Practices & Council of Chief State School Officers. (2010). *Common Core State Standards for English language arts and literacy in history/social studies, science, and technical subjects.* Washington, DC: Authors.

Rasinski, T.V. (2010). *The fluent reader: Oral and silent reading strategies for building fluency, word recognition, and comprehension* (2nd ed.). New York: Scholastic.

Rasinski, T.V., Padak, N.D., McKean, C.A., Wilfong, L.G., Friedauer, J.A., & Heim, P. (2005) Is reading fluency a key for successful high school reading? *Journal of Adolescent & Adult Literacy, 49*(1), 22–27. doi:10.1598/JAAL.49.1.3

Rosenblatt, L.M. (1995). *Literature as exploration* (5th ed.). New York: Modern Language Association of America.

Student Achievement Partners. (2012). *Close reading exemplars.* Retrieved June 27, 2012, from www.achievethe core.org/steal-these-tools/close-reading-exemplars

Vygotsky, L.S. (1978). *Mind in society: The development of higher psychological processes* (M. Cole, V. John-Steiner, S. Scribner, & E. Souberman, Eds. & Trans.). Cambridge, MA: Harvard University Press.

CHAPTER 6

Disciplinary Literacy

One of the ways in which the Common Core differs from previous standards is in its expectation that middle school and high school students read, write, think about, and discuss ideas in a variety of disciplines. To be college and career ready, students need to be able to read various types of disciplinary text with deep understanding. Literacy permeates this expectation, and, subsequently, literacy pervades all middle school and high school teaching and learning. In fact, the Common Core has created Reading and Writing Standards in History/Social Studies, Science, and Technical Subjects, in addition to those delineated in the grades 6–12 English Language Arts Standards. It has also designated exemplar texts, which can be used to parallel more contemporary texts, in CCSS Appendix B (NGA Center & CCSSO, 2010b).

Our task is to teach our grades 6–12 students to use various aspects of literacy to think through the disciplines and meet the CCSS. To that end, we address these related queries:

- Why should we teach our students to think through the disciplines?
- Who is responsible for teaching students to think through the disciplines?
- How can we teach students to use disciplinary strategies to engage, guide, and extend their thinking?

Why Should We Teach Our Students to Think Through the Disciplines?

Disciplinary experts know how to think to advance knowledge in their content areas. Thinking through a discipline involves the ability to comprehend text and communicate ideas. For example, scientists routinely read technical journal articles and trade magazines, historians read archived primary and secondary sources, and mathematicians read problems and explanations of mathematical concepts to learn about and contribute to their fields (Moje, 2008; Shanahan & Shanahan, 2008). Disciplinary experts think, write, and discuss ideas. They engage in debate and argue their positions. As Moje (2008) explained, "Knowledge production in the disciplines operates according to particular norms for everyday practice, conventions for communicating and representing knowledge and ideas, and ways of interacting, defending ideas, and challenging the deeply held ideas of others in the discipline" (p. 100). Literacy skills are undisputedly essential for disciplinary experts to be able to function well in their professional roles.

There is emerging research that suggests competent readers do approach the reading task differently according to concepts that may be important in the specific discipline. In their study, Shanahan and Shanahan (2008) found that content experts and secondary content teachers read text in quite different ways according to the discipline. For example, mathematicians emphasized rereading and reading with a focus on how even function words such as *a* and *the* can be important for comprehending mathematical concepts. Scientists focused on the transformation of information into different forms. The scientists in the study discussed the importance of charts, graphs, pictures, text, and diagrams for comprehending science concepts. Social studies experts, however, were most interested in the credibility of the source and were aware of interpretations of different sources, believing the author of texts to be fallible. Shanahan and Shanahan concluded that advanced literacy instruction embedded in the content areas should focus on disciplinary literacy, or the literate practices particular to the discipline. Disciplinary literacy must become an emphasis for students to be college and career ready (ACT, 2006; Biancarosa & Snow, 2006; Buehl, 2011; IRA, 2006; McLaughlin, 2010; Moje, 2008; Shanahan & Shanahan, 2008).

Who Is Responsible for Teaching Students to Think Through the Disciplines?

If we are teaching the disciplines, we are responsible for integrating literacy into our instruction. This does not mean that we, as content area teachers, are expected to teach reading and writing— quite the contrary. We are expected to engage students in discipline-related learning experiences that encourage learners to think, read, and write like historians, scientists, or mathematicians. Students should be able to do this in whichever discipline they are engaging (McLaughlin, 2010; Moje, 2008; Shanahan & Shanahan, 2008).

Engaging in such discipline-related instruction from a collaborative perspective is particularly vital, because the resulting thinking skills typically benefit all disciplines. The Common Core supports that this is a shared responsibility. In particular, the CCSS (NGA Center & CCSSO, 2010a) note the following:

> The Standards insist that instruction...be a shared responsibility within the school.... The grades 6–12 standards are divided into two sections, one for ELA and the other for history/social studies, science, and technical subjects. This division reflects the unique, time-honored place of ELA teachers in developing students' literacy skills while at the same time recognizing that teachers in other areas must have a role in this development as well.
>
> Part of the motivation behind the interdisciplinary approach to literacy promulgated by the Standards is extensive research establishing the need for college and career ready students to be proficient in reading complex informational text independently in a variety of content areas. Most of the required reading in college and workforce training programs is informational in structure and challenging in content; postsecondary education programs typically provide students with both a higher volume of such reading than is generally required in K–12 schools and comparatively little scaffolding. (p. 4)

Taking a closer look at how the grades 6–12 standards are structured reinforces our thinking about the literacy standards being a shared responsibility. Explorations of the CCSS for reading, writing, speaking and listening, and language throughout the disciplines follow. All of these standards are based on the overarching College and Career Readiness Standards.

Standards for Reading Throughout the Disciplines

The English Language Arts Standards are stated at the beginning of the grades 6–12 standards section of the CCSS (p. 35), but similar standards also appear in the Literacy in History/Social Studies, Science, and Technical Subject Standards later in the document. Within the disciplines, each standard changes slightly to reflect particular challenges. For example, in Table 6.1 we show how Reading Standard 2 changes slightly for disciplines in grades 9–10.

As we collaborate, we need to integrate literacy in our content area teaching. For example, the ability to determine central ideas is part of Reading Standard 2 for English Language Arts, Literacy in History/Social Studies, and Literacy in Science and Technical Subjects. Students are expected to be able to determine the central idea in a text in all disciplines. This is a shared responsibility that needs to be included in the teaching of every content area. If we are teaching about DNA in biology, we are responsible for teaching our students how to determine the central idea of that concept. Similarly, if we are teaching the history of World War II, we are responsible for teaching our students to determine the central idea of that. The good news is that we are all responsible for our own disciplines. The additional good news is that our students will be taught many skills, including how to determine the central idea, in multiple subject areas. Their knowledge will be reinforced across the curriculum.

Another factor in our collaborative efforts is the percentage of narrative and informational text that students are expected to read during grades 6–12. This is one of the major differences between the Common Core and previous state standards. The ELA Reading Standards for grades 6–12 are

Table 6.1 Common Core State Standard 2 for Reading Across the Disciplines in Grades 9–10

Discipline	Standard
College and Career Readiness Anchor Standard 2 for Reading (Overarching standard)	Determine central ideas or themes of a text and analyze their development; summarize the key supporting details and ideas. (p. 35)
English Language Arts Reading Standard 2 for Literature	Determine a theme or central idea of a text and analyze in detail its development over the course of the text, including how it emerges and is shaped and refined by specific details; provide an objective summary of the text. (p. 38)
English Language Arts Reading Standard 2 for Informational Text	Determine a central idea of a text and analyze its development over the course of the text, including how it emerges and is shaped and refined by specific details; provide an objective summary of the text. (p. 40)
Literacy in History/Social Studies Reading Standard 2	Determine the central ideas or information of a primary or secondary source; provide an accurate summary of how key events or ideas develop over the course of the text. (p. 61)
Literacy in Science and Technical Subjects Reading Standard 2	Determine the central ideas or conclusions of a text; trace the text's explanation or depiction of a complex process, phenomenon, or concept; provide an accurate summary of the text. (p. 62)

Note. From *Common Core State Standards for English Language Arts and Literacy in History/Social Studies, Science, and Technical Subjects,* by the National Governors Association Center for Best Practices and the Council of Chief State School Officers, 2010, Washington, DC: Authors.

based on the 2009 Reading Framework of the National Assessment for Educational Progress (NAEP; National Assessment Governing Board, 2008). According to the NAEP framework, by grade 8 students should be engaged in instruction based on 45% literary text and 55% informational text. By grade 12, students should be engaged in 30% literary text and 70% informational text. The NAEP distribution for reading is delineated in Table 6.2.

Table 6.2 Distribution of Literary and Informational Passages in the 2009 NAEP Reading Framework

Grade	Literary	Informational
4	50%	50%
8	45%	55%
12	30%	70%

Note. From Reading Framework for the 2009 National Assessment of Educational Progress (p. 11), by the National Assessment Governing Board, 2008, Washington, DC: U.S. Government Printing Office.

The writers of the Standards were careful to point out that integrating literacy development and adhering to percentages of narrative and informational text is a team effort:

> In accord with NAEP's growing emphasis on informational texts in the higher grades, the Standards demand that a significant amount of reading of informational texts take place in and outside the ELA classroom. Fulfilling the Standards for 6–12 ELA requires much greater attention to a specific category of informational text—literary nonfiction—than has been traditional. Because the ELA classroom must focus on literature (stories, drama, and poetry) as well as literary nonfiction, a great deal of informational reading in grades 6–12 must take place in other classes if the NAEP assessment framework is to be matched instructionally. To measure students' growth toward college and career readiness, assessments aligned with the Standards should adhere to the distribution of texts across grades cited in the NAEP framework. (NGA Center & CCSSO, 2010a, p. 5)

This postscript was added to the statement:

> The percentages on the table reflect the sum of student reading, not just reading in ELA settings. Teachers of senior English classes, for example, are not required to devote 70 percent of reading to informational texts. Rather, 70 percent of student reading across the grade should be informational. (NGA Center & CCSSO, 2010a, p. 5)

In English courses, teachers need to plan for students to engage in reading literature (stories, dramas, and poetry) and informational text (literary nonfiction): "personal essays, speeches, opinion pieces, essays about art or literature, biographies, memoirs, journalism, and historical, scientific, technical, or economic accounts (including digital sources) written for a broad audience" (NGA Center & CCSSO, 2010a, p. 57). Some may expect that English teachers possess the skills to teach reading at the secondary level and, therefore, these teachers would be the obvious choice to teach all of the Reading Standards. However, there are serious flaws in this thinking. First, ACT (2006) has reported that secondary ELA teachers, who usually have a background in English grammar and literature, often have no more preparation to teach reading than teachers of other content areas. The assumed preparation of English teachers to teach reading at the secondary level was also a lesson learned in the Kentucky Striving Readers project, a federal grant focused on developing adolescent literacy (Pallangyo et al., 2012). When the Kentucky Striving Readers project began in 2006, the partners in the grant assumed that English teachers would be more prepared to become literacy coaches in middle and high schools than teachers who had degrees in other subject areas. However, further study found that English teachers had taken no more coursework in reading than teachers of science, social studies, or mathematics (Overturf & Bronger, 2011). In addition, classroom English teachers involved in the Kentucky project were not perceived to demonstrate higher levels of literacy strategy implementation than other content area teachers (Cantrell, Almasi, Carter, & Rintamaa, 2011). A second issue is that the ELA Standards for grades 6–12 seem to suggest that English teachers are responsible for teaching students to read both literature and informational text, often with very specific requirements in the Standards. As an example, we can consider Reading Informational Text Standard 9 for grades 9–10: "Analyze seminal U.S. documents of historical and literary significance (e.g., Washington's Farewell Address, the Gettysburg Address, Roosevelt's Four Freedoms speech, King's 'Letter from Birmingham Jail'), including how they address related themes and concepts" (NGA Center & CCSSO, 2010a, p. 40). This falls under the Informational Text substandard in the ELA Reading Standards, but it is obvious that both English teachers and social studies teachers need to collaborate to teach students to meet this standard.

As teachers in various disciplines, we need to plan instruction to ensure students meet the Reading Standards for Literacy in History/Social Studies, Science, and Technical Subjects. Teaching students to think through text will help them learn concepts within the disciplines. Buehl (2012) suggests that we consider the idea of reading as inquiry, in which students learn to self-question when reading disciplinary texts.

Standards for Writing Throughout the Disciplines

The ability to write about content area concepts is another facet of disciplinary literacy. Within each discipline, students write to explore concepts, respond to reading, communicate thoughts, and better understand theories. Writing helps students learn to think about topics and has traditionally been considered an effective way to learn content. Recent research suggests that writing also increases reading comprehension. Graham and Hebert (2010) found that students' comprehension of science, social studies, and language arts texts in grades 2–12 increased when they wrote about what they read. The strongest evidence suggested that students improved comprehension when they responded to a text in writing, wrote summaries of the text, wrote notes about a text, answered questions about a text in writing, or created and answered written questions about a text. There was also evidence to suggest that students' reading skills and comprehension were enhanced when students learned the writing skills and processes that go into creating text, and comprehension seemed to improve by asking students to increase how often they produced their own texts.

The Common Core emphasizes writing in its grade-specific ELA Standards. The emphasis extends to Writing Standards for Literacy in History/Social Studies, Science, and Technical Subjects. The Writing Standards include a strong emphasis on the ability to write arguments in different disciplines. The Writing Standards also involve standards for conducting research. An example is Writing Standard 7 for grades 6–8, as seen in Table 6.3.

As with the expectations for reading, the Common Core views the integration of writing as a shared responsibility across disciplines. The expectations for writing are aligned with the 2011 NAEP Writing Framework (National Assessment Governing Board, 2007), as shown in Table 6.4. Again, a postscript in the CCSS states, "As with reading, the percentages in the table reflect the sum of student writing, not just writing in ELA settings" (NGA Center & CCSSO, 2010a, p. 5). Although ELA teachers may teach the specifics of writing development, writing in all disciplines is important and necessary for students to be college and career ready.

Speaking and Listening Throughout the Disciplines

The Common Core Standards for Speaking and Listening are a strand of the ELA Standards. They address issues such as the ability to engage in peer collaboration, participate in lively discussions, follow and understand the ideas of a speaker, create effective presentations, and use digital media, all of which most certainly enhance comprehension and content learning. Table 6.5 presents an overview of the CCR Anchor Standards for Speaking and Listening. Specific grade-level standards for speaking and listening are delineated in CCSS.

Proponents of disciplinary literacy engage in speaking and listening experiences to comprehend, collaborate, share ideas, and present information. Students need to meet the speaking and listening expectations in all disciplines to be college and career ready.

Language Standards (Vocabulary Acquisition and Use) Throughout the Disciplines

Reading Standard 4 in Literature, Informational Text, History/Social Studies, and Science and Technical Subjects focuses on determining the meanings of unfamiliar words and phrases in all content areas. The ELA Writing Standards for grades 6–12 and the Writing Standards for Literacy in History/Social Studies, Science, and Technical Subjects also concentrate on the use of precise language and domain-specific vocabulary when writing in all disciplines.

More specific expectations for vocabulary development can be found in the ELA Language Standards. They are grouped within a cluster of standards entitled "Vocabulary Acquisition and

Table 6.3 Common Core State Standard 7 for Writing Across the Disciplines in Grades 6–8

Discipline	Standard
College and Career Readiness Anchor Standard 7 for Writing (Overarching standard)	Conduct short as well as more sustained research projects based on focused questions, demonstrating understanding of the subject under investigation. (p. 41)
English Language Arts Writing Standard 7 (Grade 6)	Conduct short research projects to answer a question, drawing on several sources and refocusing the inquiry when appropriate. (p. 44)
English Language Arts Writing Standard 7 (Grade 7)	Conduct short research projects to answer a question, drawing on several sources and generating additional related, focused questions for further research and investigation. (p. 44)
English Language Arts Writing Standard 7 (Grade 8)	Conduct short research projects to answer a question (including a self-generated question), drawing on several sources and generating additional related, focused questions that allow for multiple avenues of exploration. (p. 44)
Writing Standard 7 for Literacy in History/Social Studies, Science, and Technical Subjects (Grades 6–8)	Conduct short research projects to answer a question (including a self-generated question), drawing on several sources and generating additional related, focused questions that allow for multiple avenues of exploration. (p. 66)

Note. From *Common Core State Standards for English Language Arts and Literacy in History/Social Studies, Science, and Technical Subjects*, by the National Governors Association Center for Best Practices and the Council of Chief State School Officers, 2010, Washington, DC: Authors.

Table 6.4 Distribution of Communicative Purposes in the 2011 NAEP Writing Framework

Grade	To Persuade	To Explain	To Convey Experience
4	30%	35%	35%
8	35%	35%	30%
12	40%	40%	20%

Note. From *Writing Framework for the 2011 National Assessment of Educational Progress* (Prepublication ed., p. 17), by the National Assessment Governing Board, 2008, Iowa City, IA: ACT.

Table 6.5 Overview of the College and Career Readiness Anchor Standards for Speaking and Listening

Cluster	Standard
Comprehension and Collaboration	1. Prepare for and participate effectively in a range of conversations and collaborations with diverse partners, building on others' ideas and expressing their own clearly and persuasively.
	2. Integrate and evaluate information presented in diverse media and formats, including visually, quantitatively, and orally.
	3. Evaluate a speaker's point of view, reasoning, and use of evidence and rhetoric.
Presentation of Knowledge and Ideas	4. Present information, findings, and supporting evidence such that listeners can follow the line of reasoning and the organization, development, and style are appropriate to task, purpose, and audience.
	5. Make strategic use of digital media and visual displays of data to express information and enhance understanding of presentations.
	6. Adapt speech to a variety of contexts and communicative tasks, demonstrating command of formal English when indicated or appropriate.

Note. From *Common Core State Standards for English Language Arts and Literacy in History/Social Studies, Science, and Technical Subjects* (p. 48), by the National Governors Association Center for Best Practices and the Council of Chief State School Officers, 2010, Washington, DC: Authors.

Use." For more information about vocabulary development in the disciplines, including teaching examples, see Chapter 10, this volume.

How Can We Teach Students to Use Strategies to Engage, Guide, and Extend Their Thinking?

When reading disciplinary text (textbook, informational article, or other format), it is vital that students be engaged. To meet this goal, we can teach students a variety of strategies that will help them to think through texts and fully understand the authors' message. These strategies emerge in three categories: engaging, guiding, and extending students' thinking. They focus on helping students to make connections, monitor understanding, summarize, and evaluate. It is important to note that discussion and writing, which directly support the Common Core Standards for grades 6–12, permeate all of these strategies.

Engaging Students' Thinking

As they approach texts in various disciplines, students need to be motivated to learn. There are a number of strategies we can teach students to use before reading that will help engage them in reading text. These include previewing and making connections.

When previewing text, students activate background knowledge. They examine what they already know about the topic or related ideas. If students don't have background knowledge, we can provide a knowledge base by engaging in brief teacher read-alouds, discussion, use of supportive visuals, selected vocabulary, and strategy applications such as Purpose Questions (McLaughlin, 2010), Concept of Definition Maps (Schwartz & Raphael, 1985; see Chapter 10, this volume), and Semantic Question Maps (McLaughlin, 2010; see Chapter 10, this volume). Other examples of applications to engage students' thinking can be found in Chapters 7–15.

Guiding Students' Thinking

As students read text, we encourage them to make connections to ideas discussed during previewing and to focus on understanding what they are reading. To accomplish this, we can teach students to use strategy applications such as Bookmark Technique (McLaughlin, 2010; McLaughlin & Allen, 2009), K-W-L (Ogle, 1986), K-W-D-L (Shaw, 1997), K-W-H-L (adapted from Ogle, 1986), and INSERT Method (Vaughn & Estes, 1986). Examples of other applications to guide students' thinking can be found in Chapters 7–15.

Extending Students' Thinking

After students have read text, we invite them to extend their thinking beyond the text to other aspects of the discipline and other subject areas. Students can begin by summarizing in a variety of ways. Alternate summarizing applications include the Bio-Pyramid (Macon, 1991; see Chapter 8, this volume) and Sketch Summary (McLaughlin & Overturf, 2013). When evaluating the text, the perspectives, and consistency of message, students can use Discussion Webs (Alvermann, 1991), Text-Based Viewpoint Organizer (McLaughlin & Overturf, 2013; see Chapter 12, this volume), and Mind and Alternative Mind Portraits (McLaughlin, 2010). Other examples of applications to extend students' thinking can be found in Chapters 7–15. Students can also extend their understanding by engaging in a variety of more long-term performance-based projects, such as Electronic Informational Books (McLaughlin, 2010), Press Conferences (McLaughlin, 2010), The Rest of the Story (McLaughlin, 2010), and First Person Experiences (McLaughlin, 2010).

Teaching students to think through text is a goal in every discipline. As we engage in this process, we can make connections to a variety of disciplinary Standards to help ensure that our students are college and career ready.

References

ACT. (2006). *Reading between the lines: What the ACT reveals about college readiness in reading.* Iowa City, IA: Author.

Alvermann, D.E. (1991). The discussion web: A graphic aid for learning across the curriculum. *The Reading Teacher, 45*(2), 92–99.

Biancarosa, C., & Snow, C.E. (2006). *Reading next—A vision for action and research in middle and high school literacy: A report to Carnegie Corporation of New York* (2nd ed.). Washington, DC: Alliance for Excellent Education.

Buehl, D. (2011). *Developing readers in the academic disciplines.* Newark, DE: International Reading Association.

Buehl, D. (2012, October). *Disciplinary literacy: The intersection with the Common Core Standards.* Presented at Kentucky Reading Association annual conference, Lexington, KY.

Cantrell, S.C., Almasi, J.F., Carter, J.C., & Rintamaa, M. (2011). *Striving Readers final evaluation report: Danville, Kentucky.* Washington, DC: United States Department of Education. Retrieved November 23, 2012 from www2.ed.gov/programs/strivingreaders/danvilleeval32011.pdf

Graham, S., & Hebert, M.A. (2010). *Writing to read: Evidence for how writing can improve reading. A Carnegie Corporation Time to Act Report.* Washington, DC: Alliance for Excellent Education.

International Reading Association. (2006). *Standards for middle and high school literacy coaches.* Newark, DE: Author.

Macon, J.M. (1991). *Literature response.* Paper presented at the Annual Literacy Workshop, Anaheim, CA.

McLaughlin, M. (2010). *Content area reading: Teaching and learning in an age of multiple literacies.* Boston: Pearson.

McLaughlin, M., & Allen, M.B. (2009). *Guided Comprehension in grades 3–8* (Combined 2nd ed.). Newark, DE: International Reading Association.

McLaughlin, M., & Overturf, B.J. (2013). *The Common Core: Graphic organizers for teaching K–12 students to meet the Reading Standards.* Newark, DE: International Reading Association. Retrieved from www.reading.org/general/Publications/Books/bk021.aspx

Moje, E.B. (2008). Foregrounding the disciplines in secondary literacy teaching and learning: A call for change. *Journal of Adolescent & Adult Literacy, 52*(2), 96–107. doi:10.1598/JAAL.52.2.1

National Assessment Governing Board. (2007). *Writing framework for the 2011 National Assessment of Educational Progress* (Prepublication ed.). Iowa City, IA: ACT. Retrieved December 19, 2012, from www.state.nj.us/education/assessment/naep/results/writing/2011naep_writing_framework.pdf

National Assessment Governing Board. (2008). *Reading framework for the 2009 National Assessment of Educational Progress*. Washington, DC: U.S. Government Printing Office. Retrieved December 19, 2012, from www.nagb.org/content/nagb/assets/documents/publications/frameworks/reading09.pdf

National Governors Association Center for Best Practices & Council of Chief State School Officers. (2010a). *Common Core State Standards for English language arts and literacy in history/social studies, science, and technical subjects.* Washington, DC: Authors. Retrieved August 3, 2012, from www.corestandards.org/assets/CCSSI_ELA%20Standards.pdf

National Governors Association Center for Best Practices & Council of Chief State School Officers. (2010b). *Common Core State Standards for English language arts and literacy in history/social studies, science, and technical subjects: Appendix B: Text exemplars and sample performance tasks.* Washington, DC: Authors. Retrieved August 3, 2012, from www.corestandards.org/assets/Appendix_B.pdf

Ogle, D.M. (1986). K-W-L: A teaching model that develops active reading of expository text. *The Reading Teacher, 39*(6), 564–570.

Overturf, B.J., & Bronger, L.P. (2011). *Meeting the gold standard: Preparation of middle and high school literacy coaches in the field* (Issue paper). Washington DC: U.S. Department of Education. Retrieved November 23, 2012 from www2.ed.gov/programs/slcp/finalmeeting.pdf

Pallangyo, A.A., Walker, D., Belcher, K., Overturf, B., Bronger, L., & Parker, C. (2012). *Lessons learned. The Kentucky Content Literacy Consortium: A Striving Readers Project.* Frankfurt: Kentucky Department of Education. Retrieved November 9, 2012, from education.ky.gov/curriculum/lit/Documents/KCLCStrivingReadersLessonsLessonedPaperFinal32712.pdf

Schwartz, R.M., & Raphael, T.E. (1985). Concept of definition: A key to improving students' vocabulary. *The Reading Teacher, 39*(2), 198–205.

Shanahan, T., & Shanahan, C. (2008). Teaching disciplinary literacy to adolescents: Rethinking content-area literacy. *Harvard Educational Review, 78*(1), 40–59.

Shaw, J.M. (1997). Cooperative problem solving: Using KWDL as an organizational technique. *Teaching Children Mathematics, 3*(9), 482–486.

Vaughn, J.L., & Estes, T.H. (1986). *Reading and reasoning beyond the primary grades.* Boston: Pearson.

PART II

Teaching the Common Core State Standards for Reading

The Common Core State Standards (CCSS) are based on the set of 10 College and Career Readiness (CCR) Anchor Standards. The CCR Anchor Standards describe what college students should know and be able to do in the areas of reading (for both literature and informational text), writing, speaking and listening, and language (which includes conventions of standard English, knowledge of language, and vocabulary acquisition and use). The Anchor Standards for Reading are the basis for the English Language Arts (ELA) Common Core State Standards. Students are expected to read and comprehend, and perform more sophisticated tasks with text than ever before to prepare for college and careers in the future. Each expectation in the CCSS begins with a text of some sort—a book, story, magazine article, poem, play, brochure, webpage, digital resource, piece of student writing, and so forth. Meeting the CCR Anchor Standards for Reading is key to achieving the Standards across the curriculum.

In Part II, we describe each CCR Anchor Standard for Reading and its corresponding Common Core State Standards for grades 6–12. As we contemplated the Standards, we assigned each an icon as a helpful way to remember the focus of each standard. The College and Career Readiness Anchor Standards for Reading chart provides a quick reference to the concepts and expectations that each icon and related Standards represent.

Each of the CCR Anchor Standards for Reading is discussed in a chapter that follows. Our exploration of the Standards is guided by these five queries:

1. What does this CCR Anchor Standard mean for college success?

2. How do the grade 6–12 CCSS build to this CCR Anchor Standard?

3. What literacy skills and strategies support this reading standard at each grade level?

4. How can we teach this reading standard so our students achieve?

5. What other ELA Standards can be integrated with this reading standard?

Details concerning each question follow.

College and Career Readiness Anchor Standards for Reading

CCR Reading Anchor Standard 1		
Reading closely		Thinking like a detective

CCR Reading Anchor Standard 2		
Central idea/theme		Getting to the point

CCR Reading Anchor Standard 3		
Development of characters, events, and ideas		Following the thread

CCR Reading Anchor Standard 4		
Word meanings		Knowing the word

CCR Reading Anchor Standard 5		
Text structures		Examining how the text is built

CCR Reading Anchor Standard 6		
Point of view		Seeing in different ways

CCR Reading Anchor Standard 7		
Content in diverse media		Putting it together

CCR Reading Anchor Standard 8		
Reasons and evidence		Hearing the argument

CCR Reading Anchor Standard 9		
Comparing and contrasting		Weighing the works

CCR Reading Anchor Standard 10		
Text complexity		Stepping higher

What Does This CCR Anchor Standard Mean for College Success?

The Common Core State Standards were created by taking each College and Career Readiness Anchor Standard and backward mapping to what the earliest primary-grade students would need to know and be able to do to build a foundation for the expectations of the CCR Anchor Standard. The first section of each chapter focuses on an examination of the rationale for the CCR Standard.

How Do the Grade 6–12 CCSS Build to This CCR Anchor Standard?

In the second section of each chapter, we include the vertical alignment from grades 6–12 for each standard. We describe special considerations that we may need to think through when planning to teach the standard at each grade level.

What Literacy Skills and Strategies Support This Reading Standard at Each Grade Level?

In the next section of each chapter, we list and discuss the skills and concepts that students need to achieve the Common Core Standard at each grade level. We keep in mind that some students may not have mastered the skills and concepts from the previous grades, so it is important to plan instruction that meets the additional needs of students in the class.

How Can We Teach This Reading Standard So Our Students Achieve?

In the fourth section of each chapter, we include a collection of teaching ideas that we can use in our classrooms to teach the literacy skills and strategies that support each standard. At the close of each chapter, a rich instructional task, which integrates several standards, is discussed.

What Other ELA Standards Can Be Integrated With This Reading Standard?

The CCSS were not designed to be used as a checklist and should not be taught in isolation. They must be part of a carefully designed curriculum and include comprehensive instruction that integrates related standards. We believe that the effective teaching of the Reading Standards means integrating the ELA Standards into a series of rich, connected instructional tasks. The Writing, Speaking and Listening, and Language Standards are naturally integrated into any authentic reading task. We should consider the following when planning to incorporate ELA Standards.

Reading

For each reading standard, there are a number of other reading standards that can be taught together. The Reading Standards were designed so reading can be used as a tool for learning. Most of the Reading Standards support the ability to read complex text closely and deliberately. Few of them can be deeply taught in isolation.

Writing

Reading and writing are inextricably linked, so writing is a natural part of reading instruction. Writing from sources, writing text-based answers, and engaging in brief research tasks can lead to writing to explore ideas and demonstrate learning in social studies, science, and other content areas. Writing longer pieces and deriving ideas from a variety of texts, including digital sources, are also student focuses. Writing Standards 1–3 describe expectations for three types of writing: (1) writing argumentation, (2) writing informative/explanatory texts, and (3) writing narratives. Writing Standards 4–6 support the standards for the writing process, which should be addressed in every formal writing experience. Writing Standards 7–9 are the standards for conducting research, including the use of technology. Writing Standard 10 establishes the expectation for students to write for varied time frames.

Speaking and Listening

The Speaking and Listening Standards establish an expectation that students collaborate with one another, discuss ideas and content, listen carefully to others, and present their learning in different ways, including multimedia presentations. The Common Core Standards cannot be taught in a classroom in which students consistently sit quietly with no interaction. Teaching the CCSS for Reading requires active learning that addresses multiple modalities, including lots of opportunities for academic conversation.

Language

There are two main parts to the Language Standards. Language Standards 1–3 support writing conventions and language use and should be considered in every lesson that includes writing. Language Standards 4–6 target vocabulary acquisition and use. Direct instruction and learning from context should be balanced in grades 6–12. The vocabulary standards should always be addressed when teaching the Reading Standards.

In the Common Core in Action section at the end of each chapter, multiple ELA Standards are integrated with practical classroom applications. This shows that teachers study the Common Core Standards carefully and decide how particular ELA Standards can be combined and taught within the content expectations of the grade 6–12 Standards.

Part II is an important resource when planning for the ELA Standards at the state, district, school, team, and classroom levels. Each of the chapters that follows is focused on one of the CCR Anchor Standards. Chapters 7–16 are especially valuable resources as we develop curriculum, units, and lessons to help our students achieve the Standards.

CHAPTER 7

CCR Reading Anchor Standard 1: Reading Closely and Citing Textual Evidence

 **Thinking Like a Detective**	**College and Career Readiness Reading Anchor Standard 1** Read closely to determine what the text says explicitly and to make logical inferences from it; cite specific textual evidence when writing or speaking to support conclusions drawn from the text. (NGA Center & CCSSO, 2010a, p. 10)

What Does CCR Reading Anchor Standard 1 Mean?

The aim of College and Career Readiness (CCR) Reading Anchor Standard 1 is to ensure that students can read and comprehend the text at deep and thoughtful levels. Readers need to be able to draw conclusions about what they read and make inferences that make sense, even when the text is challenging. Being able to cite specific evidence from the text in discussion or writing is an indication that the student can support a thoughtful and logical conclusion when reading literary or informational text. CCR Reading Standard 1 complements CCR Reading Standard 10, which focuses on text complexity and the need for students to be able to read more challenging texts independently.

Reading Anchor Standard 1 focuses on three college and career readiness reading skills:

1. The ability to read closely to determine what the text says explicitly

2. The ability to support logical inferences from the text when writing or speaking

3. The ability to cite specific textual evidence to support conclusions

Reading Closely

The term "reading closely" can be likened to reading like a detective. Just like Sherlock Holmes, when students read closely, they examine evidence and draw logical conclusions to support their ideas and interpret those of the author.

There are varying interpretations of "close reading" and "reading closely." These include descriptions suggested by the Aspen Institute (Brown & Kappes, 2012), as well as an interpretation of "reading closely," the wording used in the Common Core State Standards. For example, the Aspen Institute notes that

Close Reading of text involves an investigation of a short piece of text, with multiple readings done over multiple instructional lessons. Through text-based questions and discussion, students are guided to deeply analyze and appreciate various aspects of the text, such as key vocabulary and how its meaning is shaped by context; attention to form, tone, imagery and/or rhetorical devices; the significance of word choice and syntax; and the discovery of different levels of meaning as passages are read multiple times. The teacher's goal in the use of Close Reading is to gradually release responsibility to students—moving from an environment where the teacher models for students the strategies to one where students employ the strategies on their own when they read independently. (Brown & Kappes, 2012, p. 2)

The Aspen Institute further notes,

In the context of a comprehensive literacy framework, Close Reading is an instructional strategy that provides modeling and guided practice of the skills and strategies needed to independently read increasingly complex text and apply newly acquired knowledge in text-based demonstrations of deep understanding. (Brown & Kappes, 2012, p. 4)

This differs from the ACT (2006) definition that describes close reading as a literary analysis technique used in many college-level English classes. In ACT's view of close reading, students are expected to observe carefully as they read, searching for facts and details to help them interpret the text. In a close reading of literature, readers discover and interpret aspects of a narrative or poetic text, such as theme, interactions among characters, and events. Students take note of literary devices such as irony, tone, and the author's specific word choice. In informational text, readers analyze an author's use of evidence to make his or her point, looking for claims the author makes and reasons used to support these claims. In both literature and informational text, students are asked to interpret their observations to make inferences or to support an opinion about the text, most often in a written analysis.

Finally, "reading closely," the term that actually appears in the Common Core State Standards, has been interpreted as referring to reading for deep comprehension. Common Core Reading Standard 1 for grades K–12 builds to CCR Standard 1 with the expectation that students do the fundamental tasks required to "read closely to determine what the text says explicitly" (NGA Center & CCSSO, 2010a, p. 10). When students read closely, they activate background knowledge, read the text multiple times for different purposes, construct meaning, generate and respond to questions, engage in discussion, and contemplate ideas that arise from both the text and the negotiation of meaning. As teachers, we demonstrate how to use research-based strategies that will help students understand the text. We guide students to think critically about the text, striving to explore ideas stated explicitly and implicitly by the author.

It is important to note that engaging students in close reading is not the only type of reading that occurs in grade 6–12 classes. For example, teachers can occasionally use read-alouds to introduce topics or enhance background knowledge. Students can also read with partners, read silently, engage in discussion circles, and listen to text on CD.

Making Logical Inferences

An author does not include every literal idea in a text. When readers comprehend, they are continually making inferences. Students must look for clues in the text to help them understand the passage. The clues in the text, along with the reader's background knowledge of the topic, the author, or the context, help the reader make logical leaps in understanding to something that makes sense. Readers are typically required to make inferences to understand the author's intent.

Citing Textual Evidence

Students are expected to be able to draw inferences from challenging text and be credible when talking or writing about the text. Citing text as the source of evidence involves being able to extract words verbatim to prove a point. Students must be able to read a text, determine the main idea or key details, and explain their reasoning using the explicit examples in a text that helped them make decisions about what the text means. Citing textual evidence means being able to quote the author accurately to support conclusions.

Reading Closely Across the Curriculum

The instructional shift from a focus on literature in English language arts to a balance between literature and informational text is one of the major differences between the Common Core Standards and previous state standards. In English courses, teachers need to plan for students to engage in reading literature such as stories, dramas, and poetry, as well as literary nonfiction such as personal essays, speeches, opinion pieces, essays about art or literature, biographies, memoirs, journalism, and historical, scientific, technical, or economic accounts (including digital sources) written for a broad audience (NGA Center & CCSSO, 2010a, p. 57). In all disciplines, students are expected to read a variety of materials, determine what the text says explicitly, make logical inferences, and cite textual evidence to support conclusions. Our responsibility is to ensure that students can read text closely—that is, they can read with deep comprehension and respond to the ideas found in literature, literary nonfiction, and informational texts in history/social studies, science, and technical subjects.

In Common Core lessons focused on reading text closely, teachers select texts that align to the level of the text exemplars found in Appendix B of the Common Core Standards for the grades 6–8, 9–10, and 11–12 text complexity bands (NGA Center & CCSSO, 2010b). The text exemplars in Appendix B show the types of texts appropriate for English Language Arts (both literature and literary nonfiction), and discipline-based texts in history/social studies, science, and technical subjects (such as mathematics, technology, engineering, etc.). Although these texts are not mandated, they can be used as examples of the level of difficulty required in Common Core lessons for reading closely. The text exemplars can also be used to parallel more contemporary texts across the curriculum. For more information about paralleling contemporary texts with the Common Core text exemplars, see the Text Complexity Final Recommendation Forms (i.e., "placemats") in the ELA and Literacy Resources for the Kansas Common Core State Standards section of the Kansas Department of Education website (2012; see www.ksde.org/Default.aspx?tabid=4778). See Chapter 16, this volume, for a complete placemat for *The Hunger Games*.

How Do the Common Core Standards Build to CCR Reading Anchor Standard 1?

Common Core Reading Standard 1 in grades 6–12 builds toward College and Career Readiness Reading Anchor Standard 1 by addressing reading skills in four substrands. The Reading substrands addressed in grades 6–12 are as follows:

Table 7.1 Common Core State Standard 1 for Reading Literature in Grades 6–12

Grade	Standard
6	Cite textual evidence to support analysis of what the text says explicitly as well as inferences drawn from the text.
7	Cite several pieces of textual evidence to support analysis of what the text says explicitly as well as inferences drawn from the text.
8	Cite the textual evidence that most strongly supports an analysis of what the text says explicitly as well as inferences drawn from the text.
9–10	Cite strong and thorough textual evidence to support analysis of what the text says explicitly as well as inferences drawn from the text.
11–12	Cite strong and thorough textual evidence to support analysis of what the text says explicitly as well as inferences drawn from the text, including determining where the text leaves matters uncertain.

Note. The standards are from *Common Core State Standards for English Language Arts and Literacy in History/Social Studies, Science, and Technical Subjects* (pp. 36 and 38), by National Governors Association Center for Best Practices and Council of Chief State School Officers, 2010, Washington, DC: Authors.

Table 7.2 Common Core State Standard 1 for Reading Informational Text in Grades 6–12

Grade	Standard
6	Cite textual evidence to support analysis of what the text says explicitly as well as inferences drawn from the text.
7	Cite several pieces of textual evidence to support analysis of what the text says explicitly as well as inferences drawn from the text.
8	Cite the textual evidence that most strongly supports an analysis of what the text says explicitly as well as inferences drawn from the text.
9–10	Cite strong and thorough textual evidence to support analysis of what the text says explicitly as well as inferences drawn from the text.
11–12	Cite strong and thorough textual evidence to support analysis of what the text says explicitly as well as inferences drawn from the text, including determining where the text leaves matters uncertain.

Note. The standards are from *Common Core State Standards for English Language Arts and Literacy in History/Social Studies, Science, and Technical Subjects* (pp. 39 and 40), by National Governors Association Center for Best Practices and Council of Chief State School Officers, 2010, Washington, DC: Authors.

- Reading Standards for Literature (English Language Arts)
- Reading Standards for Informational Text (English Language Arts)
- Reading Standards for Literacy in History/Social Studies
- Reading Standards for Literacy in Science and Technical Subjects

Common Core Reading Standard 1 is worded in exactly the same way in both the Reading Literature and Reading Informational Text Standards for English Language Arts at every grade level. Students in grade 6 are expected to cite textual evidence to support analysis of what the text says explicitly as well as inferences drawn from the text. Seventh graders are expected to cite several pieces of textual evidence to support analysis and eighth graders to cite the textual evidence that most strongly supports analysis. Students in grades 9 and 10 cite strong and thorough evidence to support analysis. Eleventh- and 12th-grade students also cite textual evidence to support analysis and inferences when the text leaves matters uncertain. The expectations of ELA Reading Standard 1 are listed in Table 7.1 for Literature and Table 7.2 for Informational Text.

Reading Standard 1 for Literacy in History/Social Studies focuses on the ability to cite textual evidence when reading social studies materials. In grades 6–8, students cite textual evidence to support analysis of primary and secondary sources. In grades 9–10, students also attend to features such as date and origin of the information. In grades 11–12, students build on this knowledge and connect insights gained from specific details to an understanding of the text as a whole. The expectations of Reading Standard 1 for Literacy in History/Social Studies are outlined in Table 7.3.

Reading Standard 1 for Literacy in Science and Technical Subjects requires students in grades 6–8 to cite specific textual evidence to support analysis of science and technical texts. In grades

9–10, students are expected to attend to the precise details of explanations or descriptions. Students in grades 11–12 should also be able to attend to important distinctions the author makes and to any gaps or inconsistencies in the account. Table 7.4 shows the expectations of Reading Standard 1 for Literacy in Science and Technical Subjects.

What Literacy Skills and Strategies Support Reading Anchor Standard 1?

When we review the literacy skills and strategies in the Common Core State Standards, we can readily determine that gaps exist. As educators, we may find ourselves asking whether we should be teaching a particular concept because it does not appear in the CCSS. However, it is important to note that the Standards are not the determining factor. If the skill or strategy is included in our curriculums, we should teach it. For example, students in grades K–3 are expected to be able to ask and answer questions. Similarly, students in grades 4 and 5 are expected to know and use text structures such as comparison/contrast and problem/ solution. The grade 6–12 CCSS do not address either of these topics, but the students still need to know what they are and how to use them to successfully meet the Standards. That is why we noted in Chapter 1 the importance of our reading the CCSS both vertically (our grade levels) and horizontally (what students are expected to know before they reach our grade levels).

Many of the essential skills that grade 6–12 students need to know, including asking and answering questions and using text structure, are delineated in the grade K–5 Standards. For example, Common Core Reading Standard 1 (for both literature and informational text) is associated with Reading Standard 10, which focuses on the expectation that students will read complex text. For students to be able to read, discuss, and write about complex text and fulfill the expectations of Reading Standard 1, they must be able to use the supporting skills and strategies that were introduced in earlier grades. Details are featured in Table 7.5 for Literature (English Language Arts) and Table 7.6 for Informational Text (ELA, Reading in History/Social Studies, and Reading in Science and Technical Subjects).

Table 7.3 Common Core Reading Standard 1 for Literacy in History/Social Studies in Grades 6–12

Grade	Standard
6–8	Cite specific textual evidence to support analysis of primary and secondary sources.
9–10	Cite specific textual evidence to support analysis of primary and secondary sources, attending to such features as the date and origin of the information.
11–12	Cite specific textual evidence to support analysis of primary and secondary sources, connecting insights gained from specific details to an understanding of the text as a whole.

Note. The standards are from *Common Core State Standards for English Language Arts and Literacy in History/Social Studies, Science, and Technical Subjects* (p. 61), by National Governors Association Center for Best Practices and Council of Chief State School Officers, 2010, Washington, DC: Authors.

Table 7.4 Common Core Reading Standard 1 for Literacy in Science and Technical Subjects in Grades 6–12

Grade	Standard
6–8	Cite specific textual evidence to support analysis of science and technical texts.
9–10	Cite specific textual evidence to support analysis of science and technical texts, attending to the precise details of explanations or descriptions.
11–12	Cite specific textual evidence to support analysis of science and technical texts, attending to important distinctions the author makes and to any gaps or inconsistencies in the account.

Note. The standards are from *Common Core State Standards for English Language Arts and Literacy in History/Social Studies, Science, and Technical Subjects* (p. 62), by National Governors Association Center for Best Practices and Council of Chief State School Officers, 2010, Washington, DC: Authors.

Table 7.5 K–5 Reading Standard 1: Supporting Skills and Strategies for Literature in Grades 6–12

Grade	Standards
K	With prompting and support, ask and answer questions about key details in a text.
1	Ask and answer questions about key details in a text.
2	Ask and answer such questions as *who, what, where, when, why,* and *how* to demonstrate understanding of key details in a text.
3	Ask and answer questions to demonstrate understanding of a text, referring explicitly to the text as the basis for the answers.
4	Refer to details and examples in a text when explaining what the text says explicitly and when drawing inferences from the text.
5	Quote accurately from a text when explaining what the text says explicitly and when drawing inferences from the text.

Note. The standards are from *Common Core State Standards for English Language Arts and Literacy in History/Social Studies, Science, and Technical Subjects* (pp. 11 and 12), by National Governors Association Center for Best Practices and Council of Chief State School Officers, 2010, Washington, DC: Authors.

Table 7.6 K–5 Reading Standard 1: Supporting Skills and Strategies for Informational Text in Grades 6–12

Grade	Standards
K	With prompting and support, ask and answer questions about key details in a text.
1	Ask and answer questions about key details in a text.
2	Ask and answer such questions as *who, what, where, when, why,* and *how* to demonstrate understanding of key details in a text.
3	Ask and answer questions to demonstrate understanding of a text, referring explicitly to the text as the basis for the answers.
4	Refer to details and examples in a text when explaining what the text says explicitly and when drawing inferences from the text.
5	Quote accurately from a text when explaining what the text says explicitly and when drawing inferences from the text.

Note. The standards are from *Common Core State Standards for English Language Arts and Literacy in History/Social Studies, Science, and Technical Subjects* (pp. 13 and 14), by National Governors Association Center for Best Practices and Council of Chief State School Officers, 2010, Washington, DC: Authors.

How Can We Teach Reading Anchor Standard 1 So Our Students Achieve?

In this section, we discuss the CCSS expectations for students. For example, the first Common Core Standard for Reading requires that students be able to analyze what the text says explicitly, analyze inferences drawn from the text, and cite textual evidence to support conclusions. We also describe teaching ideas and how they support the Standard. Because technology should be integrated into the curriculum along with the Standards, we embed examples of how to use 21st-century skills in meaningful ways.

Analyzing What the Text Says Explicitly

Although the CCSS expect students to identify key details in earlier grades, this is still an important skill for students in grades 6–12. The key details in a narrative text are the characters, setting, problem, attempts to resolve the problem, and resolution. The key ideas in informational text typically reflect text structures such as description, cause/effect, comparison/contrast, problem/solution, and chronology/sequence.

The Narrative Text Map (McLaughlin & Overturf, 2013) is a widely used graphic organizer designed to promote student understanding of the key details of narrative texts. This organizer provides an alternative format for summarizing stories. When it is completed, students can use the information to create an oral summary of the text. Figure 7.1 shows an example of a Narrative Text Map based on *To Kill a Mockingbird* (Lee, 1958/2008).

Figure 7.1 Narrative Map Based on *To Kill a Mockingbird*

Title/Chapter: *To Kill a Mockingbird,* Chapter 9

Characters
Scout Finch, Jem Finch, Atticus Finch, Boo Radley, Uncle Jack, Aunt Alexandra, Francis, Dill Harris, and Tom Robinson

Setting
Maycomb County, Alabama, in the 1930s

Problem
Scout was getting into fights at school because her father, Atticus, was defending a black man, who was on trial for raping a white girl.

Event 1
Scout walked away from a fight at school because she did not want to disappoint her father.

Event 2
Atticus had to defend Tom Robinson, the black man accused of raping a white girl, even though he knew he wouldn't win.

Event 3
Uncle Jack, Atticus's younger brother, came to spend Christmas with the Finch family.

Event 4
On Christmas Day, Uncle Jack disciplined Scout for getting into a fight with her cousin Francis.

Event 5
Atticus knew that his daughter lashed out to defend him, but he wanted her to know that fighting wasn't the way to resolve the issue.

Resolution
While Scout was listening, Atticus and Uncle Jack had a conversation about the difficult times ahead because of the trial. Atticus said he hoped his children would not listen to the townspeople or engage in hatred.

Theme
Race is a major theme in the story. The characters' remarks frequently refer to race, and people in the story are treated unfairly because of race. Gender is also a recurring element of the theme because Scout, who is a tomboy, is always getting into fights.

The Informational Text Map (McLaughlin & Overturf, 2013), which is also directly linked to text structure, is a flexible graphic organizer. For example, when reading material that has a problem/solution text structure, the graphic organizer focuses on those elements. Other versions of this graphic organizer focus on informational text structures such as comparison/contrast and cause/effect. The Informational Text Map for Problem and Solution based on climate change appears in Figure 7.2.

Analyzing What the Text Says Implicitly

Asking and answering questions helps students to analyze what the Standards say implicitly. Although this is not a focus of the grade 6–12 CCSS, it is an essential skill for students in those grades. Thick and Thin Questions (Lewin & Shoemaker, 1998) is a teaching idea designed to help students to create questions pertaining to a text. It also helps students discern the depth of the questions they ask. Students use the questions they generate and to which they respond to facilitate their understanding of a text. Thin Questions are created at the literal level, and answers may easily be found in the text. Thick Questions are queries raised at the convergent, divergent, or evaluative levels. The answer to these questions may not be as noticeable in the text or may need to be inferred. Figure 7.3 features examples of Thick and Thin Questions based on the textbook *America: History of Our Nation, Beginnings through 1877* (Davidson, 2009).

Figure 7.2 The Informational Text Map for Problem and Solution Based on Climate Change

Informational Text Map: Problem and Solution
Topic: Climate Change
Source: epa.gov/climatechange/kids/index.html

Problem:
Human activity is causing the Earth to warm up at astounding rates. This global increase in temperature is due to human activities, which are the major cause of climate change. Examples of human activities that contribute to climate change are the deforestation of large areas and the burning of fossil fuels for making electricity and driving cars.

Factors in the Text That Contribute to the Solution:
1. Use less fossil fuel by using public transportation, walking, or riding a bike.
2. Turn off electronic devices such as televisions or computers when they are not in use.
3. Create less waste. Don't take receipts at gas stations and recycle cans, bottles, and paper.

Solution:
Human activity is the major cause of climate change, which could be reduced if people made a few changes in their daily activities. For example, people could use less fossil fuel by using public transportation, walking, or riding their bikes. People could also use less energy by turning off electronic devices when they are not in use. In addition, people could create less waste by recycling cans, bottles, and paper. All of these factors could decrease the rate of climate change.

Figure 7.3 Thick and Thin Questions Based on the Textbook *America: History of Our Nation, Beginnings through 1877*

Text: Davidson, J.W. (2009). *America: History of our nation: Beginnings through 1877*. Boston: Pearson Prentice Hall.

Page	Thin Questions	Thick Questions
Page 67	Where did England build its first permanent settlement in North America? *Response:* Jamestown, Virginia	How could the colonists have prevented so many settlers from dying at Jamestown? *Response:* The colonists who settled at Jamestown were tradespeople, not farmers. They spent most of their time searching for gold and relied on the Native Americans for their food. They should have been learning how to grow their own food for survival.
Page 68	Who was the Native American chief who feared that the English settlers were going to invade his people and country? *Response:* Chief Powhatan	How did the tobacco crop provide support to the colonists? *Response:* People in European countries, including England, liked smoking tobacco. The colonists grew and sold tobacco, so exporting it provided colonists with a way to make money.
Page 69	What was the main job of the House of Burgesses? *Response:* The House of Burgesses passed laws and set taxes.	How did the Pilgrims and Jamestown settlers' reasons for coming to America differ? *Response:* The Pilgrims were persecuted and left England to gain religious freedom, but the Jamestown settlers wanted to search for gold and gain wealth.
Page 70	What was the first document that the American colonists created to govern themselves? *Response:* The Mayflower Compact	Why was it important for the colonists to develop The Mayflower Compact? *Response:* The settlers needed a form of self-government. This document provided them with laws. If they did not have laws, there would have been chaos. The Mayflower Compact was a way to keep order.

Making Inferences

To achieve Reading Standard 1, students must refer to the text to make logical inferences. In this standard, grade 6–12 students are expected to refer to details and examples in a text when explaining what the text says explicitly and when drawing inferences from the text. We have selected the Inferring Equation (Harvey & Goudvis, 2007) for teaching this.

The Inferring Equation, "Background Knowledge + Text Clues = Inference" (Harvey & Goudvis, 2007, p. 141), can be used with any text. Harvey and Goudvis explain that when readers infer, they merge "background knowledge with clues in the text to come up with an idea that is not explicitly stated by the author. Reasonable inferences need to be tied to the text" (p. 132). Students can use the words on the page and any illustrations, charts, graphs, or photographs as text clues. As they see the clues, the students think about what they already know about the topic (background knowledge). Using background knowledge plus the text clues, the students arrive at a conclusion, or inference, about what is happening in the narrative or informational text. Harvey and Goudvis suggest creating an anchor chart with the Inferring Equation written at the top and completing the chart as students read and discuss the text. An Inferring Equation based on the *ScienceNews* article "Brain Learns While You Snooze" appears in Figure 7.4.

Figure 7.4 Inferring Equation

Text: Sanders, L. (2012). Brain learns while you snooze. *ScienceNews, 182*(7), p. 9. Retrieved from www.sciencenews.org/view/generic/id/343362/title/Brain_learns_while_you_snooze

BK (background knowledge)	TC (text clues)	I (inference)
Evidence shows that people can learn in their sleep.	"The results don't mean that Spanish vocabulary tapes have a place on the nightstand."	Only certain things can be learned while a person is asleep.

Citing Textual Evidence

In Reading Standard 1, students are responsible for making logical inferences and citing textual evidence. A useful idea to teach this is the What I Read…What Is in My Head…What the Text Said graphic organizer (McLaughlin & Overturf, 2013). Figure 7.5 shows an example based on *Dragonwings* by Laurence Yep (1975; see NGA Center & CCSSO, 2010b). As students read, they can

Figure 7.5 Example of Citing Textual Evidence

Text: Yep, L. (1975). *Dragonwings*. New York: Harper & Row.

What I Read (summary of passage)	What Is In My Head (inference)	What the Text Said (evidence from the text)
White Shadow did not go to school during the day. Instead, he attended the Tang school at night.	He did not go to regular school because of American prejudice.	p. 50 "…the demons would not allow me to go to any of their schools just a few blocks away. I could only go to a special school the demons had set up in the Tang people's town, which was so poorly equipped and so poorly staffed that I was better off in the Company."

use the graphic organizer to keep track of their inferences and the textual evidence that supports them. In the "What I Read" column, students summarize in a sentence or phrase what the text passage says. In the "What Is in My Head" column, students record their inference. In the "What the Text Said" column, students write the word or phrase included in the text that explicitly caused them to develop the inference. In this last column, words or phrases from the text are direct quotes and should be enclosed in quotation marks.

Understanding Text

The goal of Reading Standard 1 is for students to use textual analysis skills to come to a deep understanding of text. One way to facilitate the integration of skills and help students better understand text is for students to engage in peer discussion. Literature Circles (narrative text) and Discussion Circles (informational text) are teaching methods that provide students opportunities to discuss the ideas in the text.

Engaging students in Literature Circles when reading literary text or in Discussion Circles when reading informational text provides a means for students to engage in small-group, text-based conversations in which they share meaningful ideas about texts as they read them (McLaughlin, 2010). As Ketch (2005) notes, "Conversation helps individuals make sense of their world. It helps to build empathy, understanding, respect for different opinions, and ownership of the learning process" (p. 8). Researchers also report that small-group conversations motivate students, foster higher order thinking, and promote reading comprehension (Berne & Clark, 2008; Gambrell, 2004; Ketch, 2005; Kucan & Beck, 2003). Blanton, Pilonieta, and Wood (2007) further note that students of diverse linguistic and cultural backgrounds benefit from participating in small-group discussions.

It is important to remember that both the text and students' personal interpretations drive these discussions. There is not a list of questions to be answered, but rather a focus on students' inquiries, connections, and interpretations concerning the text they are reading. The time spent in Literature or Discussion Circles varies by length of text but is usually about 20 minutes per class for a certain number of days. We can, on occasion, use a minilesson to demonstrate strategies (e.g., making connections, visualizing, summarizing) or a particular literary element (e.g., plot, theme, characterization) on which the students may focus their discussion, but it is critical that each group's conversation evolves on its own. Teaching students how to assume the roles of discussion director, vocabulary finder, text connector, illustrator, and summarizer often facilitates the implementation of these types of independent discussion groups (Daniels, 1994). Circle roles are rotated in each meeting.

Literary or informational texts can be the source of these discussions. Students typically self-select what they read from choices we provide. For example, students may choose to read a CCSS exemplar text such as *The Old Man and the Sea* (Hemingway, 1952) in literature class or a variety of informational articles about meiosis and mitosis in biology class.

To learn more about Literature Circles, visit the Literature Circle Resource Center online (www.litcircles.org) and "Literature Circles: Getting Started" on ReadWriteThink's website (www .readwritethink.org/classroom-resources/lesson-plans/literature-circles-getting-started-19.html).

21st-Century Skill Applications for Reading Anchor Standard 1

In this section, we share ideas to help students meet the Reading Standards through the use of 21st-century tools and skills. Although online tools can be used for a variety of purposes, we have chosen to highlight specific tools for use with each particular standard. As teachers, we should select tools we think will work best for our students, using the same tools in multiple ways when possible.

CCR Reading Standard 1 focuses on reading closely to determine what the text says explicitly and to make logical inferences from it, citing specific textual evidence when writing or speaking to support conclusions drawn from the text. To meet Reading Standard 1, students learn to read carefully and closely, often marking up or annotating the text for deeper comprehension.

Many appropriate texts relevant to content area study can be found on related websites. If students are planning to read a PDF of an article, poem, or story, they can use an electronic tool to annotate or mark up the text. Free programs such as Adobe Reader have highlight and sticky note features to help students do this, but these tools are not as versatile as those in other programs. Figure 7.6 illustrates how Adobe Reader's sticky note feature can be used to annotate a PDF.

Mobile apps such as Notability (www.gingerlabs.com/cont/notability.php), GoodReader (itunes.apple.com/us/app/goodreader-for-ipad/id363448914?mt=8), or iAnnotate PDF

Figure 7.6 Annotated PDF, "A Sound of Thunder"

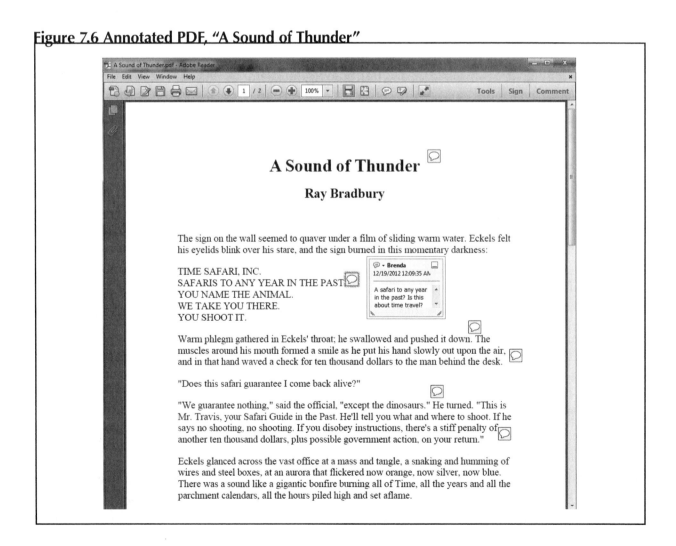

(www.branchfire.com/iannotate) must be purchased, but they have many more options for students to annotate, highlight, draw, place sticky notes, etc. These apps can be used to highlight text or add comments with the convenience of a touch screen. Students can use a finger to highlight words or phrases, draw circles around words or ideas, or connect ideas with lines, arrows, or boxes. Students can also zoom in to write notes in the margins and capture thoughts about the text, note reactions to an idea or to the author's style, or focus on key vocabulary.

Adolescents often need to engage in a motivating experience to begin to think about a text, especially when it is an unfamiliar complex text. Spillane (2012) used a free Web-based program called Tag Galaxy as a brief motivational activity for her high school students. In Tag Galaxy, the teacher or student enters a word or phrase as a tag. A "solar system" appears, with a word related to the target word attached to each "planet." The planets revolve around the "sun" (target word). By clicking on the planets, more related planets (words) appear. When the user clicks on the sun, images from Flickr (a photo sharing site) related to the target word cover the planet. For example, by entering *Hamlet* as the first tag, planets appeared with the words *England, Ophelia, Shakespeare, castles, Denmark, village, skull,* and *Kronborg.* Clicking on the planet with the tag *Ophelia* brought up related planets labeled *love, self, water, portrait,* and *self-portrait.* From there, clicking on *water* brought up images of girls dressed as a drowning Ophelia in dramatic plays from around the world. Students can view images related to the text in order to get a brief idea of the story or topic. This is also a way to motivate students to read the text without giving away too much of what is to come. Spillane does caution that because photos are posted on Flickr by the public, some may be unsuitable for students. She advises teachers to use professional judgment and view images before using them with the class.

For students to learn to read closely, they must have many experiences with complex text. Kajder (2012), an expert in instructional technology in English Language Arts, used a program called Subtext (www.subtext.com) in her eighth-grade classroom as a tool for her students to read, think about, and discuss complex text. Subtext is a free iPad app that allows students to read and discuss a book together online. In a classroom in which each student has an iPad, students can interact with the text and collaborate with each other to exchange ideas in the pages of digital texts even when they are not in class together. Teachers can layer in enrichment materials, assignments, opinion polls, and strategy instruction to help increase students' thinking at higher levels. The CCSS exemplar texts are included in a special section in Subtext.

Social bookmarking is a way for students to work collaboratively to highlight and annotate webpages. Diigo (www.diigo.com) is a versatile tool that can be used for social bookmarking. Diigo is a tool that allows students to interact with Web-based text by highlighting and commenting back and forth. This allows for student analysis of text, citing textual evidence and engaging in conversation about online text. Students can tag the webpage they are working on, and when they return, their highlights and comments will have been preserved. An archive can thus be created and teachers can engage in analysis of student work.

It is easy for these types of online tools to become merely a series of activities. Instead, teachers often use a classroom Web space for organizing online tools as well as student work and information. A social learning network site such as Edmodo (www.edmodo.com) allows for flexible use and developmental approaches to skills, and it easily incorporates other online tools. Establishing a classroom blog on a service like Edublogs (www.edublogs.org), Kidblog (www.kidblog.org), or

Wordpress (www.wordpress.org) is another way to consolidate online tools. Creating an online space for students is a good way to form a bigger picture of literacy development rather than simply instituting an activity-based approach to technology integration.

How Can We Integrate Other ELA Standards With Reading Anchor Standard 1?

When planning to teach CCR Reading Anchor Standard 1, we can integrate several other ELA standards to design rich instructional tasks. Examples of ideas to include when creating these tasks follow.

Integrating Other ELA Standards With Reading Literature Standard 1

- Reading Literature Standard 2 focuses on the ability to determine the author's theme or central idea. *Example:* When reading text closely, engage students in inferring the theme of a literary text by exploring particular details in the text and supporting their conclusions by citing specific textual evidence.

- Reading Literature Standard 3 focuses on being able to analyze characters, settings, and events in a story or drama, drawing on specific details in the text. *Example:* When reading literature closely, encourage students to carefully describe and discuss the traits of the characters, the significance of the setting, and the manner in which the events in a literary text take place.

- Reading Literature Standard 4 refers to the author's choice and use of words in a literary text. *Example:* When reading literature closely, discuss the author's use of particular words and phrases when writing about or discussing text, including examples of figurative and connotative language. Explicitly teach students how to create examples of figurative language to include in their writing.

- Reading Literature Standard 5 refers to analyzing the structure of literary texts. *Example:* As they read literary text closely, ask students to discuss the structure of stories, dramas, and poems and how that structure helps develop ideas.

- Reading Literature Standard 6 refers to point of view. *Example:* Encourage students to analyze an author's or character's point of view when reading closely.

- Reading Literature Standard 7 focuses on comparing a written version of a text with multimedia or artistic versions of the text. *Example:* Explicitly teach students how to carefully study and analyze the authors' choices in different versions of text.

- Writing Standard 9 states that students will be able to draw evidence from literary texts to support analysis, reflection, and research. *Example:* After students read a literary text closely, teach students to write or discuss opinions about the text and justify their thinking by providing supporting information.

- Speaking and Listening Standard 1 describes the expectation that students engage in a range of collaborative discussions, with specific indicators to demonstrate how to participate in an effective academic conversation. *Example:* Engage students in whole-group and small-group collaborative conversations when reading stories, dramas, and poems closely.

- Language Standard 5 is the vocabulary standard that refers to demonstrating understanding of use of figurative language, word relationships, and nuances in word meaning. *Example:* When students engage in close reading of a literary text, teach them to identify or analyze the way authors use shades of word meaning and figurative language.

Integrating Other ELA Standards With Reading Informational Text Standard 1

- Reading Informational Text Standard 2 focuses on the ability to determine central ideas of an informational text and provide an objective summary of the text. *Example:* When students read an informational text closely, encourage them to summarize the central ideas of the text.

- Reading Informational Text Standard 3 focuses on analyzing the connections and relationships among people, events, ideas, or pieces of information in a text. *Example:* When students read closely, teach them to use the clues in the text (connections and relationships among people, events, ideas, or pieces of information) to better understand events or ideas.

- Reading Informational Text Standard 4 focuses on determining the meanings of words and phrases, including figurative, connotative, or technical meanings, in an informational text. *Example:* When students read an informational text closely, teach them to identify and use the domain-specific words and phrases included in the author's discussion of the topic.

- Reading Informational Text Standard 5 refers to analysis of text structure and organization of the text. *Example:* When students are reading closely, teach students to analyze the structure the author uses to organize the text, whether in print or digital form.

- Reading Informational Text Standard 6 is point of view or purpose. *Example:* When students are reading an informational text closely, encourage them to analyze the author's point of view or purpose for writing the text.

- Reading Informational Text Standard 7 focuses on different mediums and versions of text. *Example:* After reading a text closely, ask students to compare and contrast a film version of the text with the written version.

- Reading Informational Text Standard 8 addresses reading arguments, including claims, reasons, and evidence to support various points in the text. *Example:* Teach students to evaluate the author's arguments and specific claims in the text when students are reading closely.

- Reading Informational Text Standard 10 refers to the expectation that students be able to read more challenging text. *Example:* Teach students to read increasingly complex texts over time.

- Writing Standard 9 addresses the expectation that students will be able to draw evidence from informational texts to support analysis, reflection, and research. *Example:* Teach students to write an opinion about a topic or text and support their points of view.

- Speaking and Listening Standard 1 describes the expectation that students engage effectively in a range of collaborative discussions, with specific indicators to demonstrate how to participate in an effective academic conversation. *Example:* To help students read closely, ensure that they regularly engage in collaborative academic conversations about texts.

THE COMMON CORE IN ACTION

In this section of Chapters 7–16, we examine one of the foundational ideas that underpin each of the College and Career Readiness Anchor Standards for Reading. For the first Standard, "Read closely to determine what the text says explicitly and to make logical inferences from it; cite specific textual evidence when writing or speaking to support conclusions drawn from the text" (NGA Center & CCSSO, 2010a, p. 10), we have elected to share more detailed information about the process of reading text closely.

Common Core Literacy Task

In the following example, we describe how Jamal, a tenth-grade English teacher, prepares to engage his students in close reading based on the Aspen Institute's definition (Brown & Kappes, 2012). To address Reading Standard 1, Jamal plans to teach a small group of his students to engage in close reading of a complex text that is new to them. Researchers have found that using a small-group setting helps students to read complex text with greater understanding.

He will begin by briefly activating students' background knowledge through discussion of a related issue and by making connections to recent topics they have studied. Next, he will explain to the students that they will be reading the short selection of text three times. Then he will invite the students to engage in the first reading. After the initial reading, he will encourage the students to think about what they have read and then engage them in a brief discussion about the central themes of the passage and any ideas the students may find confusing. During the second reading, the students will annotate the text, noting context clues used to determine vocabulary meaning, connections they make, questions they generate based on their reading, and other information. This reading will also be followed by a brief discussion based primarily on students' annotations. During the third reading, students will focus on the author's message and the perspective from which the text was written. After the final reading, students will pause to reflect and then write a brief reflection on the meaning of the text.

Jamal, who has noted students' deepening understanding of text as the three readings progress, believes that reading a short selection of text several times provides students with more opportunities to analyze text and comprehend at deeper levels. He notes that the quality of discussion increases and that students' written reflections have greater depth.

When Jamal teaches this lesson, he will teach it in a small-group setting, which will enable him to support all students as they engage in close reading. He has found that reading closely in small groups appears to encourage students to be more confident and more eager to respond. Jamal will follow these steps:

1. Introduce the text by sharing the genre, cover and title, and author of the book. He will introduce the text with minimal activation of background knowledge to help students make connections to the topic and set purposes for reading. He will be careful not to reveal the outcome of the text. The students will need to read to determine the author's message.

2. *First reading*—Students will read the entire text independently. (When students are reading poetry, Jamal will read the poem aloud for the first reading, providing students with a good fluency model.)

3. *Second reading*—During the second reading, students will annotate the text as they read. (When reading hard copy articles or short stories, students will annotate directly on the text. When reading texts from the Internet, students will use an electronic form of annotating.)

4. *Third reading*—Jamal and the students will generate and respond to text-dependent questions, as well as questions requiring higher levels of thinking, as they think through the text. They may choose to use graphic organizers, short written reflections, music, or sketching to clarify and express their understanding.

5. To extend student learning, encourage them to self-select an aspect of the topic about which they have been reading and engage in Internet Inquiry (Leu & Leu, 1999) to deepen their understanding.

Although Jamal's lesson is primarily focused on Reading Standard 1 (reading closely), he is careful to integrate several other standards in his lesson to create a rich instructional task. In this lesson, the additional standards include Reading Standard 4 (meanings of words and phrases), Reading Standard 5 (text structure), Reading Standard 10 (complex text), Writing Standard 9 (response to text), Speaking and Listening Standard 1 (academic discussion), and Language Standard 6 (meanings of general academic and domain-specific vocabulary). Prior to teaching this lesson, Jamal engaged in teaching his students a number of Common Core–related skills, including how to generate and respond to questions, use text structures, engage in meaningful academic discussion, and create short written responses.

Reading Standard 1 focuses on ensuring that students can read and analyze text. It requires students to analyze what the text says explicitly and implicitly and cite specific textual evidence to support their conclusions. When students read like a detective, they read closely.

References

ACT. (2006). *Reading between the lines: What the ACT reveals about college readiness in reading.* Iowa City, IA: Author. Retrieved August 22, 2012, from www.act.org/research/policymakers/pdf/reading_report.pdf

Berne, J.I., & Clark, K.F. (2008). Focusing literature discussion groups on comprehension strategies. *The Reading Teacher, 62*(1), 74–79.

Blanton, W.E., Pilonieta, P., & Wood, K.D. (2007). Promoting meaningful adolescent reading instruction through integrated literacy circles. In J. Lewis & G. Moorman (Eds.), *Adolescent literacy instruction: Policies and promising practices* (pp. 212–237). Newark, DE: International Reading Association.

Brown, S. & Kappes, L. (2012). *Implementing the Common Core State Standards: A primer on "close reading of text."* Washington, DC: The Aspen Institute. Retrieved January 14, 2013, from www.aspeninstitute.org/sites/default/files/content/docs/pubs/CR.Primer.print_.pdf

Environmental Protection Agency. (2012). *A student's guide to global climate change.* Retrieved January 14, 2013, from epa.gov/climatechange/kids/index.html

Daniels, H. (1994). *Literature circles: Voice and choice in a student-centered classroom.* York, ME: Stenhouse.

Gambrell, L.B. (2004). Shifts in the conversation: Teacher-led, peer-led, and computer-mediated discussions. *The Reading Teacher, 58*(2), 212–215.

Harvey, S., & Goudvis, A. (2007). *Strategies that work: Teaching comprehension for understanding and engagement* (2nd ed.). Portland, ME: Stenhouse.

Kajder, S. (2012, November). *Reports from cyberspace.* Presentation at the annual National Council of Teachers of English/Language Arts conference, Las Vegas.

Kansas Department of Education. (2012). Text complexity final recommendation forms (i.e., "placemats"). *ELA and literacy resources for the Kansas Common Core Standards.* Retrieved from www.ksde.org/Default.aspx?tabid=4778

Ketch, A. (2005). Conversation: The comprehension connection. *The Reading Teacher, 59*(1), 8–13.

Kucan, L., & Beck, I.L. (2003). Inviting students to talk about expository texts: A comparison of two discourse environments and their effects on comprehension. *Reading Research and Instruction, 42*(3), 1–31.

Lewin, L., & Shoemaker, B.J. (1998). *Great performances: Creating classroom-based assessment tasks.* Alexandria, VA: ASCD.

Leu, D.J., Jr., & Leu, D.D. (1999). *Teaching with the Internet: Lessons from the classroom* (Rev. ed.). Norwood, MA: Christopher-Gordon.

McLaughlin, M. (2010). *Content area reading: Teaching and learning in an age of multiple literacies.* Boston: Allyn & Bacon.

McLaughlin, M., & Overturf, B.J. (2013). *The Common Core: Graphic organizers for teaching K–12 students to meet the Reading Standards.* Newark, DE: International Reading Association. Retrieved from www.reading.org/general/Publications/Books/bk021.aspx

National Governors Association Center for Best Practices & Council of Chief State School Officers. (2010a). *Common Core State Standards for English language arts and literacy in history/social studies, science, and technical subjects.* Washington, DC: Authors. Retrieved August 3, 2012, from www.corestandards.org/assets/CCSSI _ELA%20Standards.pdf

National Governors Association Center for Best Practices & Council of Chief State School Officers. (2010b). *Common Core State Standards for English language arts and literacy in history/social studies, science, and technical subjects: Appendix B: Text exemplars and sample performance tasks.* Washington, DC: Authors. Retrieved August 3, 2012, from www.corestandards.org/assets/Appendix_B.pdf

Spillane, L.A. (2012). *Reading amplified: Digital tools that engage students in words, books, and ideas.* Portland, ME: Stenhouse.

Literature and Informational Text Cited

Davidson, J.W. (2009). *America: History of our nation, beginnings through 1877.* Boston: Pearson Prentice Hall.

Hemingway, E. (1952). *The old man and the sea.* New York: Scribners.

Lee, H. (2008). *To kill a mockingbird.* New York: HarperCollins. (Original work published 1958)

Sanders, L. (2012). Brain learns while you snooze. *ScienceNews, 182*(7), p. 9. Retrieved from www.sciencenews.org/view/generic/id/343362/title/Brain_learns_while_you_snooze.

Yep, L. (1975). *Dragonwings.* New York: Harper & Row.

CHAPTER 8

CCR Reading Anchor Standard 2: Determining Central Ideas and Themes

Getting to the Point

College and Career Readiness Reading Anchor Standard 2
Determine central ideas or themes of a text and analyze their development; summarize the key supporting details and ideas. (NGA Center & CCSSO, 2010, p. 10)

What Does CCR Reading Anchor Standard 2 Mean?

For readers to understand the author's message, they must be able to determine the point of the text—the central idea. Being able to "identify clear main ideas or purposes of complex passages or their paragraphs" (ACT, 2006, p. 36) has been identified as a college and career readiness requirement for academic success. In College and Career Readiness (CCR) Reading Anchor Standard 2, students are expected to know how to get to the point by determining the central idea of a text and summarizing the key details that support it.

Students encounter the expectations of CCR Reading Anchor Standard 2 in every text. They need to be able to determine the central idea of texts in order to learn the content of the course. Being able to determine the theme or central idea and summarize a text is a key comprehension skill used across all disciplines.

Reading Anchor Standard 2 focuses on three college and career readiness reading skills:

1. The ability to determine the central idea or theme of a text

2. The ability to analyze the development of ideas or themes in a text

3. The ability to summarize key supporting details and ideas in a text

Central Ideas in Informational Text

Determining the central idea of an informational text means understanding the message the author is trying to convey. Because students are asked to read a variety of types of materials, they should prepare to determine the central idea in an array of informational texts: magazine and journal articles, speeches, newspapers, textbooks, webpages, biographies, primary and secondary sources, scientific writing, and technical materials. Being able to analyze the development of ideas in a text is a component of logical thinking. If students can explain how supporting ideas relate to central ideas, they are more likely to be able to write a logical, coherent essay or a thoughtful, organized answer to a question.

Themes in Literature

In English language arts classes, students read and analyze texts, including books, short stories, plays, and poetry. Theme is one of the concepts addressed in literary analysis. The theme of a literary text is the author's message to the reader—what the author wants the reader to remember after reading the text. The theme is often a value judgment by the author about aspects of life and can typically be expressed in a proverb such as "money can't buy happiness." Short stories usually have one theme, but a novel can have several.

Authors express themes in several different ways: through the title of the text, how the characters feel, what the characters think or say, what the characters learn, and the conflict, events, or actions in the story. Students must infer to draw logical conclusions about the author's intent. The theme can often be determined by the conflict in which the main character is involved—man vs. nature, good vs. evil, and so on. A more sophisticated way that authors help establish a theme is by making allusions to history, mythology, culture, art, music, or other literary works. Of course, for allusions to be effective, the reader must be familiar with the person or event that is referred to in the allusion. The following are examples of allusions to mythology and literature in everyday conversation:

- "Chocolate is my sister's Achilles' heel." (Her weakness. Achilles, a character in Greek mythology, was invincible everywhere except for his heel.)
- "When we were buying holiday gifts for our families, my friend reminded me of Scrooge because she spent so little money." (Scrooge, a character from Charles Dickens' *A Christmas Carol*, was known for being a penny-pinching miser.)

Authors also give clues to the themes in literary texts through archetypes and motifs. An archetype is a character, action, or situation with fairly stereotypical traits. Familiarity with an archetype helps the reader understand how he or she is supposed to feel about a character or plot element, adding to the establishment of the theme. Nathaniel Hawthorne's *The Scarlet Letter* is an example of an archetypal novel; the battle between good and evil is an archetypal plot, and Hester Prynne and her daughter are the archetypal mother and illegitimate daughter. A motif is any element that is repeated throughout the literary work and can be an image, sound, phrase, or idea. A motif is symbolic of the theme and helps establish the theme by repetition throughout the text.

Summarizing Key Supporting Details and Ideas

Summarizing is extracting the most important ideas from a text. In content area classes, students are often expected to extract the most important information from the text and write a brief synopsis of the ideas presented.

How Do the Common Core Standards Build to CCR Reading Anchor Standard 2?

The Common Core Standards in grades 6–12 build toward College and Career Readiness Anchor Standard 2 by addressing reading skills in four substrands. The Reading Standard 2 substrands addressed in grades 6–12 are as follows:

- Reading Standards for Literature (English Language Arts)
- Reading Standards for Informational Text (English Language Arts)

- Reading Standards for Literacy in History/Social Studies
- Reading Standards for Literacy in Science and Technical Subjects

In Reading Literature Standard 2, sixth graders learn to use details to determine the theme or central idea of a literary text. Seventh-grade students also learn to analyze the development of the theme or central idea over the course of a text. Eighth-grade students build on this skill by taking into account the relationship of the theme or central idea to the characters, setting, and plot. Students in grades 9 and 10 add to this knowledge by including how the theme or central idea emerges and is shaped by specific details. Students in grades 11 and 12 determine two or more themes or central ideas in a literary text. These students analyze the development of each theme or central idea and how they interact and build upon one another. In Reading Standard 2 for Literature, students also focus on learning to provide an objective summary of a literary text. Reading Standard 2 for Literature is given in Table 8.1.

For Reading Standard 2 for Informational Text, sixth graders use particular details to determine a central idea of literary nonfiction. Seventh graders determine two or more central ideas and analyze their development over the course of the text. Eighth-grade students add to this knowledge by learning to determine the relationship of the central idea to supporting ideas in literary nonfiction. Students in grades 9 and 10 add to this knowledge by including how the theme or central idea emerges and is shaped by specific details. Students in grades 11 and 12 determine two or more themes or central ideas. They analyze the development of each theme or central idea and analyze how these themes and central ideas interact and build upon one another. Reading Standard 2 for Informational Text is detailed in Table 8.2.

Table 8.1 Common Core State Standard 2 for Reading Literature in Grades 6–12

Grade	Standard
6	Determine a theme or central idea of the text and how it is conveyed through particular details; provide a summary of the text distinct from personal opinions or judgments.
7	Determine a theme or central idea of a text and analyze its development over the course of the text; provide an objective summary of the text.
8	Determine a theme or central idea of the text and analyze its development over the course of the text, including its relationship to the characters, setting, and plot; provide an objective summary of the text.
9–10	Determine a theme or central idea of a text and analyze in detail its development over the course of the text, including how it emerges and is shaped and refined by specific details; provide an objective summary of the text.
11–12	Determine two or more themes or central ideas of a text and analyze their development over the course of the text, including how they interact and build on one another to produce a complex account; provide an objective summary of the text.

Note. The standards are from *Common Core State Standards for English Language Arts and Literacy in History/Social Studies, Science, and Technical Subjects* (pp. 36 and 38), by National Governors Association Center for Best Practices and Council of Chief State School Officers, 2010, Washington, DC: Authors.

Table 8.2 Common Core State Standard 2 for Reading Informational Text in Grades 6–12

Grade	Standard
6	Determine a central idea of a text and how it is conveyed through particular details; provide a summary of the text distinct from personal opinions or judgments.
7	Determine two or more central ideas in a text and analyze their development over the course of the text; provide an objective summary of the text.
8	Determine a central idea of the text and analyze its development over the course of the text, including its relationship to supporting ideas; provide an objective summary of the text.
9–10	Determine a central idea of a text and analyze its development over the course of the text, including how it emerges and is shaped and refined by specific details; provide an objective summary of the text.
11–12	Determine two or more central ideas of a text and analyze their development over the course of the text, including how they interact and build on one another to provide a complex analysis; provide an objective summary of the text.

Note. The standards are from *Common Core State Standards for English Language Arts and Literacy in History/Social Studies, Science, and Technical Subjects* (pp. 39 and 40), by National Governors Association Center for Best Practices and Council of Chief State School Officers, 2010, Washington, DC: Authors.

Table 8.3 Common Core Reading Standard 2 for Literacy in History/Social Studies in Grades 6–12

Grade	Standard
6–8	Determine the central ideas or information of a primary or secondary source; provide an accurate summary of the source distinct from prior knowledge or opinions.
9–10	Determine the central ideas or information of a primary or secondary source; provide an accurate summary of how key events or ideas develop over the course of the text.
11–12	Determine the central ideas or information of a primary or secondary source; provide an accurate summary that makes clear the relationships among the key details and ideas.

Note. The standards are from *Common Core State Standards for English Language Arts and Literacy in History/Social Studies, Science, and Technical Subjects* (p. 61), by National Governors Association Center for Best Practices and Council of Chief State School Officers, 2010, Washington, DC: Authors.

Table 8.4 Common Core Reading Standard 2 for Literacy in Science and Technical Subjects in Grades 6–12

Grade	Standard
6–8	Determine the central ideas or conclusions of the text; provide an accurate summary of the text distinct from prior knowledge or opinions.
9–10	Determine the central ideas or conclusions of a text; trace the text's explanation or depiction of a complex process, phenomenon, or concept; provide an accurate summary of the text.
11–12	Determine the central ideas or conclusions of a text; summarize complex concepts, processes, or information presented in a text by paraphrasing them in simpler but still accurate terms.

Note. The standards are from *Common Core State Standards for English Language Arts and Literacy in History/Social Studies, Science, and Technical Subjects* (p. 62), by National Governors Association Center for Best Practices and Council of Chief State School Officers, 2010, Washington, DC: Authors.

In Reading Standard 2 for Literacy in History/Social Studies, students at all levels learn to determine the central idea or information of a primary or secondary source. Students in grades 6–8 learn to provide an accurate summary of the source that is not dependent on prior knowledge or opinions. Students in grades 9–10 accurately summarize how key events or ideas develop over the course of the text, and students in grades 11–12 also make clear the relationships among key detail and ideas when summarizing primary and secondary sources. Reading Standard 2 for Literacy in History/Social Studies is outlined in Table 8.3.

Reading Standard 2 for Literacy in Science and Technical Subjects focuses on students' ability to determine the central ideas or conclusions of a scientific or technical text. Students in grades 6–8 are expected to determine the central ideas or conclusions of the text. By grades 9–10, students should also be able to trace the text's explanation or depiction of a complex process, phenomenon, or concept. Students in grades 6–8 learn to provide an accurate summary of the text distinct from prior knowledge or opinions. By grades 11–12, students should be able to summarize complex concepts, processes, or information presented in the text by paraphrasing in accurate but simpler language. Reading Standard 2 for Literacy in Science and Technical Subjects is shown in Table 8.4.

What Literacy Skills and Strategies Support Reading Anchor Standard 2?

When we review the literacy skills and strategies in the Common Core State Standards, we can readily determine that gaps exist. As teachers, we may find ourselves asking whether we should be teaching a particular concept because it does not appear in the CCSS. However, it is important to note that the Standards are not the determining factor. If the skill or strategy is included in our curriculums, we should teach it. For example, students in grades K–3 are expected to be able to ask and answer questions. Similarly, students in grades 4 and 5 are expected to know and use text structures, such as comparison/contrast and problem/solution. The grade 6–12 CCSS do not address either of these topics, but the students still need to know what they are and how to use them to successfully meet the Standards. That is why we noted in Chapter 1 the importance of our reading the CCSS both vertically (our grade levels) and horizontally (what students are expected to know before they reach our grade levels).

Many of the essential skills that grade 6–12 students need to know, including asking and answering questions and using text structures, are delineated in the grade K–5 Standards. For example, Common Core Reading Standard 1 (for both literature and informational text) is associated with Reading Standard 10, which focuses on the expectation that students will read complex text. For students to be able to read, discuss, and write about complex text, they must be able to use the supporting skills and strategies that were introduced in earlier grades. Details for Reading Standard 2, the focus of this chapter, are featured in Table 8.5 for Literature (English Language Arts) and Table 8.6 for Informational Text (ELA, Reading in History/Social Studies, and Reading in Science and Technical Subjects).

Table 8.5 K–5 Reading Standard 2: Supporting Skills and Strategies in Literature in Grades 6–12

Grade	Standards
K	With prompting and support, retell familiar stories, including key details.
1	Retell stories, including key details, and demonstrate understanding of their central message or lesson.
2	Recount stories, including fables and folktales from diverse cultures, and determine their central message, lesson, or moral.
3	Recount stories, including fables, folktales, and myths from diverse cultures; determine the central message, lesson, or moral and explain how it is conveyed through key details in the text.
4	Determine a theme of a story, drama, or poem from details in the text; summarize the text.
5	Determine a theme of a story, drama, or poem from details in the text, including how characters in a story or drama respond to challenges or how the speaker in a poem reflects upon a topic; summarize the text.

Note. The standards are from *Common Core State Standards for English Language Arts and Literacy in History/Social Studies, Science, and Technical Subjects* (pp. 11 and 12), by National Governors Association Center for Best Practices and Council of Chief State School Officers, 2010, Washington, DC: Authors.

Table 8.6 K–5 Reading Standard 2: Supporting Skills and Strategies for Informational Text in Grades 6–12

Grade	Standards
K	With prompting and support, identify the main topic and retell key details of a text.
1	Identify the main topic and retell key details of a text.
2	Identify the main topic of a multiparagraph text as well as the focus of specific paragraphs within the text.
3	Determine the main idea of a text; recount the key details and explain how they support the main idea.
4	Determine the main idea of a text and explain how it is supported by key details; summarize the text.
5	Determine two or more main ideas of a text and explain how they are supported by key details; summarize the text.

Note. The standards are from *Common Core State Standards for English Language Arts and Literacy in History/Social Studies, Science, and Technical Subjects* (pp. 13 and 14), by National Governors Association Center for Best Practices and Council of Chief State School Officers, 2010, Washington, DC: Authors.

How Can We Teach Reading Anchor Standard 2 So Our Students Achieve?

In this section, we discuss the CCSS expectations for students. For example, the second Common Core Standard for Reading requires that students be able to determine central ideas or themes of a text and analyze their development and to summarize the key supporting details and ideas. We also describe teaching ideas and how they support the Standard. Because technology should be integrated into the curriculum along with the Standards, we embed examples of how to use 21st-century skills in meaningful ways.

Retelling: Sketch and Label Retelling, "The Gift of the Magi"

Retelling (Morrow, 1985), which involves summarizing narrative elements, is a very flexible teaching idea. It can be completed orally, in writing, by sketching, or through dramatization. The Sketch and Label Retelling (McLaughlin, 2010), which appears in Figure 8.1, focuses on four points: Who? Where? What happened? and How did it end? These parallel the narrative elements characters, setting, problem, and resolution, and they also support students' determination of theme.

Figure 8.1 Sketch and Label Retelling for O. Henry's "The Gift of the Magi"

Analyzing Development of Literary Theme

The Evolution of Calpurnia Tate (Kelly, 2011) offers a prime example of theme development. This young adult novel delineates Calpurnia Tate's journey of self-discovery. Callie is interested in science and wants to learn about nature, so she spends as much time as possible with her grandfather, who is a naturalist. Science and the complexities of family life are both themes in the novel. Callie is the only daughter in a family of seven children. She emerges as an inquisitive young woman who is torn between what she wants to do and what is socially expected of young ladies in Texas in 1899. Novels often have more than one theme, representing models of everyday life.

The main character in a short story or novel is always involved in some type of conflict—internal, external, or both. Theme is often determined by the ways in which the main character meets the challenges of the conflict and then changes over the course of a text. Once students determine a main character, a conflict, and how the character changes, they are on the path to determining possible themes. As another example, Figure 8.2 features Theme Search (McLaughlin & Overturf, 2013), a graphic organizer, based on "The Monkey's Paw" by W.W. Jacobs.

Figure 8.2 Theme Search for "The Monkey's Paw"

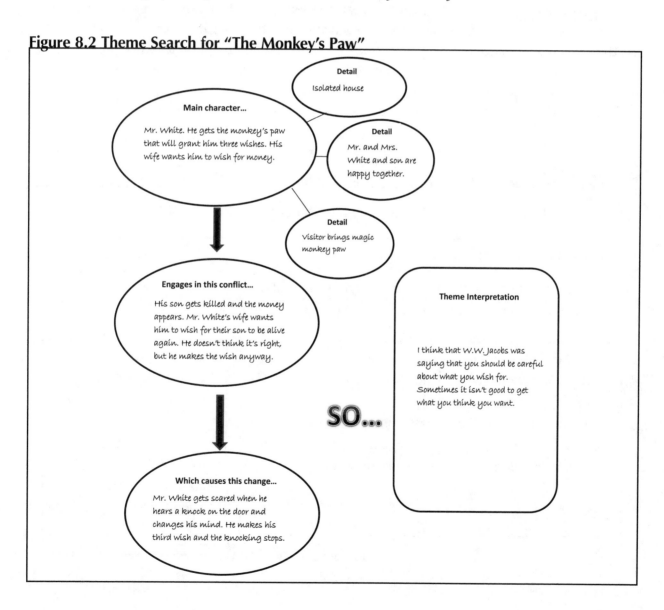

Determining Central Idea and Supporting Ideas in Informational Text

The Main Idea Table (McLaughlin & Allen, 2009) is designed to provide students with opportunities to record the main idea and three supporting details from a text. In the example included in Figure 8.3, the main idea is about science. A variety of details are also included.

Providing an Accurate and Objective Summary

The Bio-Pyramid is an alternative way to summarize facts about a person's life (Macon, 1991). It involves students' inserting information to complete eight lines about a person's life. The pyramid begins with one word and expands to eight. Figure 8.4 shows a Bio-Pyramid about President Abraham Lincoln.

21st-Century Skill Applications for Reading Anchor Standard 2

In this section, we share ideas to help students meet the Reading Standards through the use of 21st-century tools and skills. Although online tools can be used for a variety of purposes, we have chosen to highlight specific tools for use with each particular standard. As teachers, we should select tools we think will work best for our students, using the same tools in multiple ways when possible.

CCR Reading Standard 2 focuses on determining central ideas or themes of a text and analyzing their development. Students are also expected to summarize key supporting details and ideas. One way to explore the central idea in a text is through using a tool to visualize words.

Figure 8.3 Main Idea and Supporting Details for *Biology*

Text: Miller, K.R., & Levine, J.S. (2008). *Biology*. Boston: Pearson Prentice Hall.

Main Idea:

Science is a way to examine and understand the natural world around us; it is the information resulting from observation, study, and experimentation.

• Science deals only with the natural world. • Information is collected and organized in a systematic order.	• Explanations can be tested and explained. • It involves using evidence to discover the natural world.	• Investigations are created to understand nature. • Science is a way of questioning, observing, concluding, and testing hypotheses.

←   **Supporting Details**   →

Figure 8.4 Bio-Pyramid About Abraham Lincoln

Text: Biography. (2012). "Abraham Lincoln." Retrieved November 26, 2012, from www.biography.com/people/abraham-lincoln-9382540

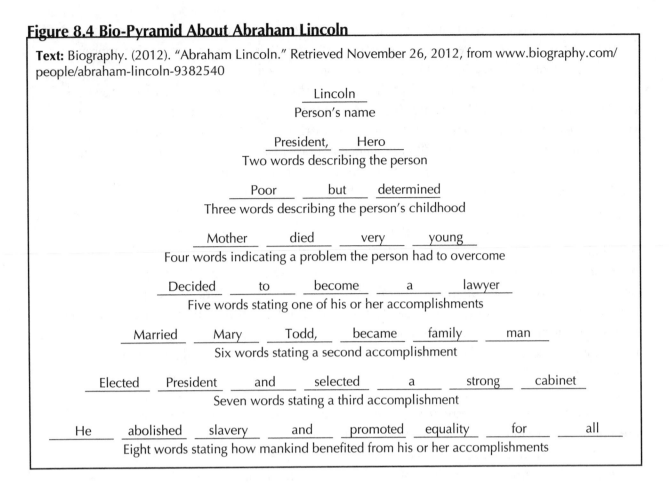

Lincoln
Person's name

President,   Hero
Two words describing the person

Poor   but   determined
Three words describing the person's childhood

Mother   died   very   young
Four words indicating a problem the person had to overcome

Decided   to   become   a   lawyer
Five words stating one of his or her accomplishments

Married   Mary   Todd,   became   family   man
Six words stating a second accomplishment

Elected   President   and   selected   a   strong   cabinet
Seven words stating a third accomplishment

He   abolished   slavery   and   promoted   equality   for   all
Eight words stating how mankind benefited from his or her accomplishments

WordSift (www.wordsift.com) is especially suited for this purpose. When students paste text into a text box, WordSift displays a word cloud that shows the words representing the most prominent concepts. These words can be arranged from most rare to most common and vice versa. WordSift also displays a word map of the most-used word, images that relate to the word, and sentences in the student's pasted text where the word is used. For example, in Martin Luther King Jr.'s "I Have a Dream" speech, the word *freedom* appears as the major word used in the text. In WordSift, a selection of images of posters with the word *freedom* is displayed, the word *freedom* is mapped, and sentences in which King used the word *freedom* in the speech are listed. If a student clicks on another word in the word cloud, related information will appear. Students can discuss the most prominent words in any informational text as a clue to the central idea. If student blogging is part of the classroom routine, teachers can help students develop their skills to analyze text and share what they are finding in WordSift.

Social bookmarking and tagging can be used together to develop students' ability to identify key/main ideas. Social bookmarking is a collaborative activity in which students highlight, annotate, and comment on websites and share with others. When students tag a webpage in order to search for it again, they determine keywords and terms to assign to a piece of information. Not only does this help the student with research, it requires the student to consider which words would best indicate the main idea of the Web-based information.

Literary Graffiti, on the ReadWriteThink website (www.readwritethink.org/classroom-resources/student-interactives/literary-graffiti-30023.html), is a student interactive appropriate for older students. Literary Graffiti helps students visualize and contemplate symbols to represent text. Using the computer, students create literary graffiti that represents the theme or central idea of a literary text. Students then write a summary of the text, a description of the graffiti, and the significance of the graffiti to the text. Completed graffitis can be printed and shared.

Dredger, Kajder, and Beach (2012) explained a more advanced way for students to explore the theme or central idea of a text while also developing writing, speaking, and listening skills. Students create a PechaKucha (www.pechakucha.org) presentation about the text. The PechaKucha (Japanese for "chitchat") presentation began as a way for architects and designers to showcase their work. PechaKucha is built on the idea that a presentation does not need to be long and complicated. A PechaKucha is 20 PowerPoint slides with 20 seconds allotted for each slide (programmed to automatically advance) for a presentation that is just over 6.5 minutes long. PechaKucha presentations are focused on images (photographs, clip art, artwork, etc.) that represent ideas and concepts with very little or no text added to the slides. Students choose their topic, write notes on their information, create their slides, and practice their presentation until they know it well enough that they can discuss each slide in the allotted time. Sometimes, teachers allow students to use the "record slide show" feature to record their written text as a scaffold for spoken presentations. The audience is welcome to ask questions or discuss the ideas that have been presented.

Ignite talks (www.igniteshow.com) work on the same principle as PechaKucha, but the presentations are shorter and not limited to images. An Ignite presentation is 20 slides that are programmed to advance every 15 seconds. Presentations take 5 minutes. In both formats, students can explain the theme or central idea of a text by discussing the images they have chosen and the slides they have created to represent their ideas. In a successful Ignite talk, the presenter condenses the content into the main ideas and includes only the most important details. Presentations should include how the student believes the author developed the central themes or ideas of the text. Students can embed their recorded PechaKucha or Ignite presentations in a class blog with an explanation of how they developed their ideas.

Songify and AutoRap are examples of free mobile apps that students can use in creative ways to explore the theme or central idea of a text. After students write a description of the theme or central ideas, they can read their text into Songify, which will automatically turn their recorded text into an electronic song. Likewise, AutoRap turns recorded text into rap. These tools may be an option for students to express their understanding of the text through creative expression. Musical representation of themes is often motivational for students in grades 6–12.

In Reading Standard 2, students are also expected to summarize text. Cube Creator is another student interactive on the ReadWriteThink website (www.readwritethink.org/classroom-resources/student-interactives/cube-creator-30850.html) that can be a tool for summarizing different text types. For example, students can use the Cube Creator to summarize a variety of genres. Students can create a Bio Cube (McLaughlin & Allen, 2009) to describe a person's significance, background, and personality. The Mystery Cube (McLaughlin & Allen, 2009) can help students identify elements of mysteries, practice vocabulary, and sort and summarize information. The Mystery Cube requires students to describe the setting, clues, crime or mystery, victim, detective, and solution. With the Story Cube, students summarize the key elements of a story, including character, setting, conflict, resolution, and theme. In the Create-Your-Own Cube option, students or teachers can construct their own questions or topics.

Summaries can also be audio-recorded. Greenstone (2012) discussed summarizing text by creating voice memos in NoteShare (www.aquaminds.com). Programs such as NoteShare and Evernote (a popular free program available at www.evernote.com) allow students to take notes, organize projects and notes in virtual notebooks, and share notebooks with others to collaborate on a project. Text can be downloaded into the program. Students can read sections of the text, then attach a voice-recorded summary to each section of the text.

How Can We Integrate Other ELA Standards With Reading Anchor Standard 2?

When planning to teach College and Career Readiness Reading Anchor Standard 2, we can integrate several other ELA standards to design rich instructional tasks. Examples of ideas to include when creating rich instructional tasks follow.

Integrating Other ELA Standards With Reading Literature Standard 2

- Reading Literature Standard 1 focuses on reading a narrative text closely. *Example:* During a close reading, ask text-dependent questions that will encourage students to determine the theme or central idea of a text and analyze its development. Encourage students to summarize the text.

- Reading Literature Standard 3 focuses on being able to analyze characters, settings, and events in a story or drama, drawing on specific details in the text. *Example:* Encourage students to analyze characters, settings, and events as a clue to determine the theme or central idea of a literary text.

- Reading Literature Standard 5 refers to analyzing the structure of literary texts. *Example:* Teach students to analyze the way the author structured the text as a clue to theme or central idea.

- Reading Literature Standard 6 refers to point of view. *Example:* Teach students to consider an author's or character's point of view to help determine the theme.

- Reading Literature Standard 7 focuses on comparing a written version of a text with multimedia or artistic versions of the text. *Example:* Teach students to compare and contrast how the theme is expressed in multimedia or artistic versions of the text.

- Reading Literature Standard 9 focuses on comparing and contrasting aspects of literary text. *Example:* Encourage students to compare and contrast the themes of two literary texts.

- Writing Standard 3 describes expectations for students to write narratives to develop real or imagined experiences or events using effective technique, relevant descriptive details, and well-structured event sequences. *Example:* Teach students to write narratives in which they establish and develop their own theme.

- Speaking and Listening Standard 1 describes the expectation that students engage effectively in a range of collaborative discussions, with specific indicators to demonstrate how to participate in an effective academic conversation. *Example:* Engage students in a number of collaborative discussions, such as Literature Circles and whole-class discussions, when exploring theme or central ideas in literature.

- Speaking and Listening Standard 5 refers to creating multimedia presentations to develop and support ideas. *Example:* Encourage students to create multimedia presentations that focus on the theme or central idea of a text they have read or as a way to summarize the text.

- Language Standard 5 is the vocabulary standard that refers to demonstrating understanding of figurative language, word relationships, and nuances in word meanings. *Example:* Ask students to discuss connotations and denotations in word meanings as a clue to the theme or central idea of a text.

Integrating Other ELA Standards With Reading Informational Text Standard 2

- Reading Informational Text Standard 1 refers to closely reading an informational text. *Example:* When engaging in close reading of an informational text, ask students to cite textual evidence to support analysis of central and supporting ideas.

- Reading Informational Text Standard 3 focuses on analyzing the connections and relationships among people, events, ideas, or pieces of information in a text. *Example:* Encourage students to make connections between and among ideas to determine the central idea and supporting details of an informational text.

- Reading Informational Text Standard 4 focuses on determining the meanings of words and phrases, including figurative, connotative, or technical meanings, in an informational text. *Example:* Teach students to identify and use domain-specific words and phrases included in the author's discussion of the topic to help determine the central idea and supporting details.

- Reading Informational Text Standard 5 refers to analysis of text structure and organization of the text. *Example:* Teach students to analyze the structure the author uses to organize the text as a clue to the central idea and supporting ideas and key details.

- Reading Informational Text Standard 6 is point of view or purpose. *Example:* Encourage students to consider the author's point of view or purpose for writing the text as a clue to the text's central ideas.

- Reading Informational Text Standard 8 addresses reading arguments, including claims, reasons, and evidence, to support various points in the text. *Example:* Teach students to trace an author's reasons and evidence in the argument and specific claims in a text.

- Writing Standard 1 describes expectations for students to write arguments to support claims with reasons and evidence. *Example:* Teach students to develop and write well-reasoned arguments that consist of a claim (central idea) and supporting evidence.

- Speaking and Listening Standard 1 describes the expectation that students will engage effectively in a range of collaborative discussions, with specific indicators to demonstrate how to participate in an effective academic conversation. *Example:* Engage students in a number of collaborative academic conversations about text in a variety of settings (paired, small group, whole group) in which they discuss the central and supporting ideas in a text.

- Speaking and Listening Standard 5 refers to creating multimedia presentations to develop and support ideas. *Example:* Invite students to create multimedia presentations to enhance understanding of central ideas and key details in informational text in various disciplines.

- Language Standard 6 is the vocabulary standard that refers to general academic and domain-specific words and phrases. *Example:* Teach students to become word conscious by learning and using meaningful new vocabulary related to the central idea in texts in various disciplines.

THE COMMON CORE IN ACTION

In this section, we examine one of the foundational ideas that underpins each of the Common Core Standards for Reading. For the second standard, "Determine central ideas or themes of a text and analyze their development; summarize the key supporting details and ideas" (NGA Center & CCSSO, 2010, p. 10), we have elected to share more detailed information about determining the central idea of an informational text, which is an explicit part of the Reading Standards for Informational Text in English Language Arts.

Common Core Literacy Task: Analyzing the Development of Central Ideas in an Informational Text

Julia, a high school biology teacher, plans to include Reading Standard 2 for Science and Technical Subjects in grades 9–10, which is "Determine the central ideas or conclusions of a text; trace the text's explanation or depiction of a complex process, phenomenon, or concept; provide an accurate summary of the text" (NGA Center & CCSSO, 2010, p. 62) in her unit on genetics. As she reviews the Reading standards, she sees that Reading Standard 2 for Informational Text is "Determine a central idea of a text and analyze its development over the course of the text, including how it emerges and is shaped and refined by specific details; provide an objective summary of the text" (p. 40). She decides that looking at the wording in the complementary standards is helpful for her own understanding.

Although Julia could choose any number of informational articles, for this lesson, she decides to motivate her students' interest in genetics by connecting to the popular novel *The Hunger Games* (Collins, 2008). Through conversations with her students, Julia knows that many of them have read the book, seen the movie, or both. The *New York Times* article "D.I.Y. Biology, on the Wings of the Mockingjay" by James Gorman (2012) seems to be a perfect text for this task.

1. Julia introduces the article by asking her students to read the title and think about what they know about the fictional mockingjay in *The Hunger Games*. After a brief and lively whole-class discussion about the significance of the mockingjay, Julia invites her students to work in pairs. (SL.9-10.1)

2. Julia distributes the "D.I.Y. Biology" article to her students and asks them to read to find the "big ideas" in the article. Students also mark up and annotate the text to indicate central ideas and key details. (RI.9-10.1)

3. Julia distributes the graphic organizer Analyzing the Development of Central Ideas (see Figure 8.5) to each student pair. Then she explicitly teaches how to use it. Students determine the first central idea and write it in the top rectangular box. (RI.9-10.2; RST.9-10.2)

4. Student pairs continue to discuss and add specific supporting details in the smaller boxes. (SL.9-10.1; RI.9-10.2)

5. Students complete each of the boxes for the rest of the article.

Figure 8.5 Analyzing the Development of Central Ideas Using "D.I.Y. Biology, on the Wings of the Mockingjay"

Text: Gorman, J. (2012). D.I.Y. biology, on the wings of the mockingjay. *New York Times.* Retrieved January 14, 2013, from www.nytimes.com/2012/05/15/science/the-hunger-games-mockingjay-fiction-for-now.html

In *The Hunger Games*, a mockingjay is a cross between a mockingbird and a genetically engineered bird called a jabberjay.

The mockingjay first appears as a symbol.	The jabberjay was not expected to survive in the wild, but it bred with mockingbirds.	In the story, there were unexpected consequences.

Tools to modify organisms are already available in real life.

Dr. Slonczewski, a microbiologist and science fiction writer, wrote about modified organisms.	Tools to modify organisms are already in industry and beyond.	Anyone can do it.

Do-it-yourself biology is growing.

Tools of biotechnology can be bought on eBay.	Pet breeders and children may have access.	There could be "an explosion of diversity in new living creatures."

6. After students finish the graphic organizer, Julia facilitates a whole-class discussion about the central ideas in the text. (SL.9-10.1)

7. Each student then follows his or her graphic organizer as a guide to write a summary of the article. (W.9-10.9b)

Reading Anchor Standard 2 focuses on determining the central idea or theme, analyzing its development, and summarizing literary text. It requires students to determine central ideas, analyze their development, and provide objective summaries of informational text. When students get to the point, they think about the big idea of the text—an important college and career readiness skill.

References

ACT. (2006). *Reading between the lines: What the ACT reveals about college readiness in reading.* Iowa City, IA: Author. Retrieved August 22, 2012, from www.act.org/research/policymakers/pdf/reading_report.pdf

Dredger, K., Kajder, S., & Beach, C. (2012, November). *Ignite spotlight: The PechaKucha as creative connection.* Paper presented at the annual conference of the National Council of Teachers of English, Las Vegas, NV.

Greenstone, B. (2012). *Strategies for reading digital text.* Maine Learning Technology Initiative webinar. Retrieved October 23, 2012, from stateofmaine.adobeconnect.com/_a827390218/p5u8jb2u9ke/?launcher=false&fcs Content=true&pbMode=normal

Macon, J.M. (1991). *Literature response.* Paper presented at the Annual Literacy Workshop, Anaheim, CA.

McLaughlin, M. (2010). *Guided Comprehension in the primary grades* (2nd ed.). Newark, DE: International Reading Association.

McLaughlin, M., & Allen, M.B. (2009). *Guided Comprehension in grades 3–8* (Combined 2nd ed.). Newark, DE: International Reading Association.

McLaughlin, M., & Overturf, B.J. (2013). *The Common Core: Graphic organizers for teaching K–12 students to meet the Reading Standards.* Newark, DE: International Reading Association. Retrieved from www.reading.org/general/Publications/Books/bk021.aspx

Morrow, L.M. (1985). Retelling stories: A strategy for improving young children's comprehension, concept of story structure, and oral language complexity. *The Elementary School Journal, 85*(5), 647–661.

National Governors Association Center for Best Practices & Council of Chief State School Officers. (2010). *Common Core State Standards for English language arts and literacy in history/social studies, science, and technical subjects.* Washington, DC: Authors. Retrieved August 3, 2012, from www.corestandards.org/assets/CCSSI_ELA%20 Standards.pdf

Literature and Informational Text Cited

Biography. (2012). "Abraham Lincoln." Retrieved November 26, 2012, from www.biography.com/people/abraham-lincoln-9382540

Collins, S. (2008). *The Hunger Games.* New York: Scholastic.

Gorman, J. (2012). D.I.Y. biology, on the wings of the mockingjay. *New York Times.* Retrieved January 14, 2013, from www.nytimes.com/2012/05/15/science/the-hunger-games-mockingjay-fiction-for-now.html

Henry, O. The gift of the Magi. Retrieved December 12, 2012, from www.online-literature.com/donne/1014

Kelly, J. (2011). *The evolution of Calpurnia Tate.* New York: Square Fish.

Miller, K.R., & Levine, J.S. (2008). *Biology.* Boston: Pearson Prentice Hall.

CHAPTER 9

CCR Reading Anchor Standard 3: Individual, Event, and Idea Development

Following the Thread

| **College and Career Readiness Reading Anchor Standard 3** |
| Analyze how and why individuals, events, and ideas develop and interact over the course of a text. (NGA Center & CCSSO, 2010, p. 10) |

What Does CCR Reading Anchor Standard 3 Mean?

Students need to read and comprehend text that is not always explicit. According to ACT (2006), one of the characteristics of complex text is that of relationships in the text. Relationships in a complex text have been defined as "interactions among ideas or characters in the text [that] are subtle, involved, or deeply embedded" (ACT, 2006, p. 17). College and Career Readiness (CCR) Reading Anchor Standard 3 is related to the author's development of relationships in a text and is highly connected with Reading Standard 1 (read closely) and Reading Standard 10 (text complexity). Students must be able to follow the thread that the author establishes for character and idea development.

Reading Anchor Standard 3 focuses on four college and career readiness reading skills:

1. The ability to analyze how individuals develop and interact

2. The ability to analyze how events develop and interact

3. The ability to analyze how ideas develop and interact

4. The ability to recognize how individuals, events, and ideas interact

Authors of literature often show the relationships between and among characters, events, and ideas in an understated way, using literary devices to help build the relationships. The way the author describes characters, the dialogue among them, and their actions toward one another help the reader get a deeper sense of the story or poem. The structure of a literary text (characters, setting, problem, attempts to resolve the problem, resolution) helps build relationships over the course of events in the text.

In informational text, readers understand how ideas are related and build to the main idea. If students can explain the relationships or interactions among individuals and ideas in a text, they better understand the concepts in the text and are better prepared to write coherently.

How Do the Common Core Standards Build to CCR Reading Anchor Standard 3?

The Common Core Standards in grades 6–12 build toward College and Career Readiness Anchor Standard 3 by addressing reading skills in four substrands. The Reading Standard 3 substrands addressed in grades 6–12 are as follows:

- Reading Standards for Literature (English Language Arts)
- Reading Standards for Informational Text (English Language Arts)
- Reading Standards for Literacy in History/Social Studies
- Reading Standards for Literacy in Science and Technical Subjects

In Reading Standard 3 for Literature, sixth-grade students learn to describe how a plot unfolds as well as how characters respond or change as a result. Seventh graders learn to analyze how particular elements of a story or drama interact, and eighth graders analyze how dialogue or incidents in literary text propel the action, reveal aspects of a character, or provoke a decision in the story or drama. In grades 9–10, Reading Standard 3 for Literature is focused on analyzing complex characters, while in grades 11–12, students learn to analyze the impact of author's choices regarding how to develop the story or drama. The expectations for Standard 3 for Reading Literature are delineated in Table 9.1.

For informational text, the expectations for Reading Standard 3 focus on the interactions among individuals, events, and ideas. In grade 6, students learn to analyze how key individuals, events, or ideas are introduced, illustrated, and elaborated. Seventh graders analyze how individuals, events, and ideas are influenced by interactions among them, and eighth graders analyze how a text uses comparisons, analogies, or categories to make connections and distinctions between individuals, ideas, or events. Students in grades 9–10 analyze how an author unfolds an analysis or series of ideas or events, and in grades 11–12, students learn to analyze a complex set of ideas or sequence of events as well as explain how they develop over the course of a text. The expectations of Reading Standard 3 for Informational Text appear in Table 9.2.

Table 9.1 Common Core State Standard 3 for Reading Literature in Grades 6–12

Grade	Standard
6	Describe how a particular story's or drama's plot unfolds in a series of episodes as well as how the characters respond or change as the plot moves toward a resolution.
7	Analyze how particular elements of a story or drama interact (e.g., how setting shapes the characters or plot).
8	Analyze how particular lines of dialogue or incidents in a story or drama propel the action, reveal aspects of a character, or provoke a decision.
9–10	Analyze how complex characters (e.g., those with multiple or conflicting motivations) develop over the course of a text, interact with other characters, and advance the plot or develop the theme.
11–12	Analyze the impact of the author's choices regarding how to develop and relate elements of a story or drama (e.g., where a story is set, how the action is ordered, how the characters are introduced and developed).

Note. The standards are from *Common Core State Standards for English Language Arts and Literacy in History/Social Studies, Science, and Technical Subjects* (pp. 36 and 38), by National Governors Association Center for Best Practices and Council of Chief State School Officers, 2010, Washington, DC: Authors.

Table 9.2 Common Core State Standard 3 for Reading Informational Text in Grades 6–12

Grade	Standard
6	Analyze in detail how a key individual, event, or idea is introduced, illustrated, and elaborated in a text (e.g., through examples or anecdotes).
7	Analyze the interactions between individuals, events, and ideas in a text (e.g., how ideas influence individuals or events, or how individuals influence ideas or events).
8	Analyze how a text makes connections among and distinctions between individuals, ideas, or events (e.g., through comparisons, analogies, or categories).
9–10	Analyze how the author unfolds an analysis or series of ideas or events, including the order in which the points are made, how they are introduced and developed, and the connections that are drawn between them.
11–12	Analyze a complex set of ideas or sequence of events and explain how specific individuals, ideas, or events interact and develop over the course of the text.

Note. The standards are from *Common Core State Standards for English Language Arts and Literacy in History/Social Studies, Science, and Technical Subjects* (pp. 39 and 40), by National Governors Association Center for Best Practices and Council of Chief State School Officers, 2010, Washington, DC: Authors.

Table 9.3 Common Core Reading Standard 3 for Literacy in History/Social Studies in Grades 6–12

Grade	Standard
6–8	Identify key steps in a text's description of a process related to history/social studies (e.g., how a bill becomes a law, how interest rates are raised or lowered).
9–10	Analyze in detail a series of events described in a text; determine whether earlier events caused later ones or simply preceded them.
11–12	Evaluate various explanations for actions or events and determine which explanation best accords with textual evidence, acknowledging where the text leaves matters uncertain.

Note. The standards are from *Common Core State Standards for English Language Arts and Literacy in History/Social Studies, Science, and Technical Subjects* (p. 61), by National Governors Association Center for Best Practices and Council of Chief State School Officers, 2010, Washington, DC: Authors.

Table 9.4 Common Core Reading Standard 3 for Literacy in Science and Technical Subjects in Grades 6–12

Grade	Standard
6–8	Follow precisely a multistep procedure when carrying out experiments, taking measurements, or performing technical tasks.
9–10	Follow precisely a complex multistep procedure when carrying out experiments, taking measurements, or performing technical tasks, attending to special cases or exceptions defined in the text.
11–12	Follow precisely a complex multistep procedure when carrying out experiments, taking measurements, or performing technical tasks; analyze the specific results based on explanations in the text.

Note. The standards are from *Common Core State Standards for English Language Arts and Literacy in History/Social Studies, Science, and Technical Subjects* (p. 62), by National Governors Association Center for Best Practices and Council of Chief State School Officers, 2010, Washington, DC: Authors.

In Reading Standard 3 for Literacy in History/Social Studies, students in grades 6–8 identify key steps in a text's description of a process related to social studies. In grades 9–10, students learn to analyze in detail events described in a text and to decide cause and effect. Students in grades 11–12 evaluate explanations and determine which explanation fits best with textual evidence, acknowledging where the text leaves matters uncertain. Table 9.3 delineates the expectations of Reading Standard 3 for Literacy in History/Social Studies.

In Science and Technical Subjects, Reading Standard 3 focuses on the ability to read the steps of a process. Students in grades 6–8 are expected to precisely follow a multistep procedure to carry out experiments, take measurements, or perform technical tasks. In grades 9–10, students are expected to follow a complex multistep procedure but also expected to attend to special cases or exceptions defined in the text. Students in grade 11–12 build on this knowledge to analyze the specific results based on explanations in the text as well. The expectations of Reading Standard 3 for Literacy in Science and Technical subjects are outlined in Table 9.4.

What Literacy Skills and Strategies Support Reading Standard 3?

When we review the literacy skills and strategies in the Common Core State Standards, we can readily determine that gaps exist. As educators, we may find ourselves asking whether we should be teaching a particular concept because it does not appear in the CCSS. However, it is important to note that the Standards are not the determining factor. If the skill or strategy is included in our curriculums, we should teach it. For example, students in grades K–3 are expected to be able to ask and answer questions. Similarly, students in grades 4 and 5 are expected to know and use text structures such as comparison/contrast and problem/solution. The grade 6–12 CCSS do not address either of these topics, but the students still need to know what they are and how to use them to successfully meet the Standards. That is why we noted in Chapter 1 the importance of our reading the CCSS both vertically (our grade levels) and horizontally (what students are expected to know before they reach our grade levels).

Many of the essential skills that grade 6–12 students need to know, including asking and answering questions and using text structure, are delineated in the grade K–5 Standards. For example, Common Core Reading Standard 1 (for both literature and informational text) is associated with Reading Standard 10, which focuses on the expectation that students will read complex text. For students to be able to read, discuss, and write about complex text, they must be able to use the supporting skills and strategies that were introduced in earlier grades. Details for Reading Standard 3, the focus of this chapter, are featured in Table 9.5 for Literature (English Language Arts) and Table 9.6 for Informational Text (ELA, Reading in History/Social Studies, and Reading in Science and Technical Subjects).

How Can We Teach Reading Anchor Standard 3 So Our Students Achieve?

In this section, we discuss the CCSS expectations for students. For example, the third College and Career Readiness Standard requires that students be able to analyze how and why individuals,

Table 9.5 K–5 Reading Standard 3: Supporting Skills and Strategies for Literature in Grades 6–12

Grade	Skills and Strategies
K	With prompting and support, identify characters, settings, and major events in a story.
1	Describe characters, settings, and major events in a story, using key details.
2	Describe how characters in a story respond to major events and challenges.
3	Describe characters in a story (e.g., their traits, motivations, or feelings) and explain how their actions contribute to the sequence of events.
4	Describe in depth a character, setting, or event in a story or drama, drawing on specific details in the text (e.g., a character's thoughts, words, or actions).
5	Compare and contrast two or more characters, settings, or events in a story or drama, drawing on specific details in the text (e.g., how characters interact).

Note. The skills and strategies are from *Common Core State Standards for English Language Arts and Literacy in History/Social Studies, Science, and Technical Subjects* (pp. 11 and 12), by National Governors Association Center for Best Practices and Council of Chief State School Officers, 2010, Washington, DC: Authors.

Table 9.6 K–5 Reading Standard 3: Supporting Skills and Strategies for Informational Text in Grades 6–12

Grade	Skills and Strategies
K	With prompting and support, describe the connection between two individuals, events, ideas, or pieces of information in a text.
1	Describe the connection between two individuals, events, ideas, or pieces of information in a text.
2	Describe the connection between a series of historical events, scientific ideas or concepts, or steps in technical procedures in text.
3	Describe the relationship between a series of historical events, scientific ideas or concepts, or steps in technical procedures in a text, using language that pertains to time, sequence, and cause/effect.
4	Explain events, procedures, ideas, or concepts in a historical, scientific, or technical text, including what happened and why, based on specific information in the text.
5	Explain the relationships or interactions between two or more individuals, events, ideas, or concepts in a historical, scientific, or technical text based on specific information in the text.

Note. The skills and strategies are from *Common Core State Standards for English Language Arts and Literacy in History/Social Studies, Science, and Technical Subjects* (pp. 13 and 14), by National Governors Association Center for Best Practices and Council of Chief State School Officers, 2010, Washington, DC: Authors.

events, and ideas develop and interact over the course of a text. We also describe teaching ideas and how they support the Standard. Because technology should be integrated into the curriculum along with the Standards, we embed examples of how to use 21st-century skills in meaningful ways.

Development of Characters, Settings, and Events: Story Impression

Story Impressions were developed by McGinley and Denner (1987) to encourage students to make predictions about stories, acquaint students with story vocabulary, and provide a framework for narrative writing. We begin by selecting a published story on which we will base the Story Impression. Next, we provide students with a list of words that relate to the literary elements: characters, setting, problem, attempts to resolve the problem, and resolution. These are the clues for the Story Impression. When we give the list to the students, the words are connected by downward arrows to show the sequence in which they appear in the story. Next, the students work in small groups to create a story based on the clues provided. Then, each group reads its story aloud. After each group has shared its story, we read the published story. Finally, we discuss by comparing and contrasting the stories that the students have written and the original. Example clues and a Story Impression based on Jack London's short story "To Build a Fire" appear in Figure 9.1.

Figure 9.1 Example of a Story Impression

Example Text: "To Build a Fire," Jack London

Sequential Clues:

- Mysterious, far-reaching trail
- Man and dog
- Freezing cold
- Fire
- Falling snow douses it
- 75 degrees below zero
- Lack of feeling
- Sleep off to death

Prediction

On a mysterious, far-reaching trail, a man and dog walked for a long time. It was freezing cold, but the man pushed on. He was trying to reach his friends. They had become separated in a blizzard. He built a fire, but falling snow extinguished it. He walked until he could not take another step. It was 75 degrees below zero and the man could no longer feel his feet. He could not move. He felt powerless. He knew he would fall asleep and die in the wilderness. Then the director called, "Cut!" and everyone took a break while they staged the next scene in the movie.

Note. Story Impressions from McGinley, W.J., & Denner, P.R. (1987). Story impressions: A prereading/writing activity. *Journal of Reading, 31*(3), 248–253.

Characterization: Character, Trait, and Quote Map

To teach characterization, we created the Character, Trait, and Quote Map. The character's name is written in an oval in the center. Students can then list characteristics related to the focus character in circles around the oval. Under each trait, students also include a quote from the text that supports the characteristic. For example, Figure 9.2 is based on the short story "The Tell-Tale Heart" by Edgar Allan Poe (1835). The young man is the focus character. Traits include *determined, guilty, consistent, irritated,* and *mad.* Each is supported by a quote that students took directly from the text.

Figure 9.2 Example of a Character, Trait, and Quote Map

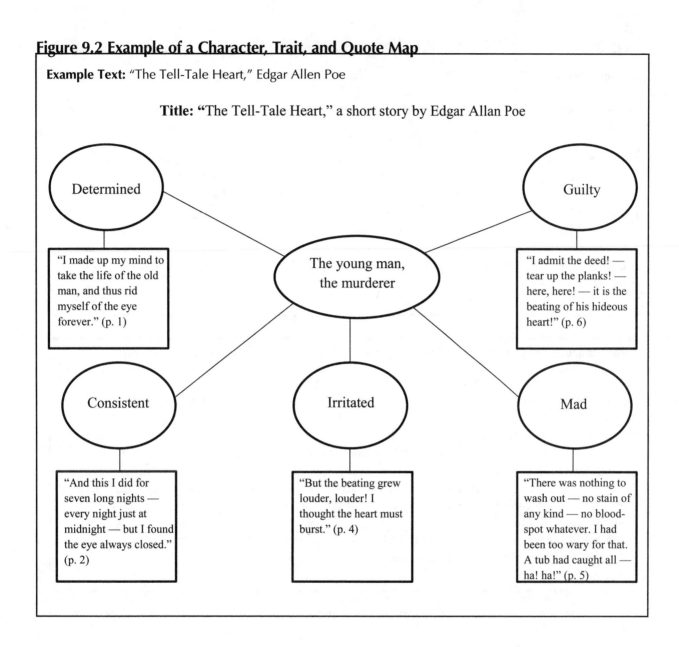

Example Text: "The Tell-Tale Heart," Edgar Allen Poe

Title: "The Tell-Tale Heart," a short story by Edgar Allan Poe

Determined

"I made up my mind to take the life of the old man, and thus rid myself of the eye forever." (p. 1)

The young man, the murderer

Guilty

"I admit the deed! — tear up the planks! — here, here! — it is the beating of his hideous heart!" (p. 6)

Consistent

"And this I did for seven long nights — every night just at midnight — but I found the eye always closed." (p. 2)

Irritated

"But the beating grew louder, louder! I thought the heart must burst." (p. 4)

Mad

"There was nothing to wash out — no stain of any kind — no blood-spot whatever. I had been too wary for that. A tub had caught all — ha! ha!" (p. 5)

Comparing and Contrasting Story Elements

To help students compare and contrast story elements, we created the Comparison/Contrast Story Map (McLaughlin & Overturf, 2013). The information presented in the graphic organizer includes the five narrative elements (characters, setting, problem, attempts to resolve the problem, and resolution) and two short story titles, all for students to complete. The short stories that are compared and contrasted in Figure 9.3 are "The Lottery" and "The Most Dangerous Game."

Connections Among Individuals, Events, and Ideas

We provide three examples in this section to accommodate the expectations of Reading Standard 3 for Informational Text.

Figure 9.3 Example of a Comparison/Contrast Story Map

Example Texts: "The Lottery" by Shirley Jackson and "The Most Dangerous Game" by Richard Connell

Text #1: "The Lottery"

The citizens of a small village have been participating in a lottery where a chosen person is stoned by the townspeople once a year. Mr. Summers holds the lottery and uses the same black tattered box every year. The oldest town member, Old Man Warner, declared that the lottery has been going on for as long as he has been alive, 77 years, and should continue even though some people question the ritual. Because they are set in their beliefs, the townspeople continue to hold the lottery and Tessie Hutchinson is the one chosen to be stoned. The people of the town do not seem to think anything of taking a human life, and they continue this barbaric practice because of their fixed view.

Text Analysis: Style, Characters, Settings, Themes, Connections to Another Literary Work

Both short stories are written in a very direct style that reflects the themes. The characters have fixed beliefs. They do not appear to value human life because they kill for pleasure. In "The Lottery," the characters kill because it is their yearly ritual, and in "The Most Dangerous Game," the General kills for his own excitement. Both story settings are also private; in "The Lottery," the stoning takes place in a small town with only the townspeople present, and in "The Most Dangerous Game," the killings take place on a secluded island with only Rainsford, the General, and Ivan present. The recurring themes in both stories are that the characters do not value human life and that the characters go along with the majority's beliefs. These stories reminded me of *The Hunger Games*. Katniss lived in a time when the games were viewed as an annual sporting event. The people did not value the lives of the tributes. The style of writing is different in the novel, though. There are many more details and, unlike the short stories, the novel moves at a much slower pace.

Text #2: "The Most Dangerous Game"

Whitney and Rainsford are sailing on their yacht in the dark Caribbean night when Rainsford finds himself overboard, having tried to catch his fallen pipe. Rainsford, who is a world-class hunter, swims to the nearest island and stumbles upon a magnificent mansion. He is welcomed and treated with the finest food and clothing by the owner of the mansion, General Zaroff. What Rainsford doesn't know is that the General is fascinated with hunting and has given up on hunting animals. Due to the lack of excitement, his new prey is human beings. General Zaroff informs Rainsford that he will be his next challenge to hunt. Rainsford is horrified at the General's mindset but has no choice but to participate. While being hunted, Rainsford kills Ivan, the General's servant, but the killing was meant for the General. In the end, for the sake of his survival, Rainsford does kill the General. It was a barbaric game that the General played, and it was evident that the General had no feelings when taking human life.

For an example of steps in a procedure, using language that pertains to time, sequence, and cause/effect, see the Sequence Chain in Chapter 11 (Figure 11.1). The scientific method is the topic of this sample graphic organizer.

An example of events in history, including what happened and why based on specific information in the text, can be found in Chapter 11 (Figure 11.3). The Cherokee Trail of Tears and the political move that caused it are the focus of this sample Cause and Effect Text Organizer.

For an example of the relationships between two concepts in a scientific text, see the Venn Diagram in Chapter 11 (Figure 11.2). Planets and stars are compared and contrasted in this sample graphic organizer. Similarities appear in the overlapping part of the circles and differences appear in the outer parts of each circle.

Explaining Relationships Between Two or More Individuals, Events, Ideas, or Concepts in Informational Texts

To show the relations between two concepts in informational text, we use a Contrast Chart (McLaughlin & Allen, 2009) to focus on the differences between World War I and World War II. The Contrast Chart is featured in Figure 9.4.

21st-Century Skill Applications for Reading Anchor Standard 3

In this section, we share ideas to help students meet the Reading Standards through the use of 21st-century tools and skills. Although online tools can be used for a variety of purposes, we have chosen

Figure 9.4 Example of a Contrast Chart

World War I	World War II
1. The assassination of Archduke Franz Ferdinand, heir to the Austro-Hungarian Empire, set off a chain of events that started World War I.	1. Adolf Hitler and his Nazi Party rose to power and invaded Poland; as a result, Great Britain and France declared war on Germany.
2. WWI lasted for four years (1914–1918).	2. WWII lasted for six years (1939–1945).
3. Modern weaponry such as machine guns, tanks, and chemical weapons were used.	3. Modern weaponry and the atomic bomb were used.
4. 9 million soldiers were killed and 22 million were wounded.	4. It is estimated that 45–60 million people were killed and 6 million Jews were murdered in concentration camps.
5. The war ended with a cease-fire agreement followed by a treaty.	5. The war ended when Germany and Japan were defeated and surrendered.
Source: http://www.history.com/topics/world-war-i	Source: http://www.history.com/topics/world-war-ii

to highlight specific tools for use with each particular standard. As teachers, we should select tools we think will work best for our students, using the same tools in multiple ways when possible.

CCR Reading Standard 3 focuses on analyzing how and why individuals, events, and ideas develop and interact over the course of a text. The ReadWriteThink Trading Cards mobile app (www.readwritethink.org/classroom-resources/mobile-apps/trading-cards-30922.html) can be used to analyze fictional or real persons, fictional or real places, objects (or ideas), events, or vocabulary. The Trading Card Creator can also be accessed as an online student interactive on the ReadWriteThink website (www.readwritethink.org/classroom-resources/student-interactives/ trading-card-creator-30056.html). The Trading Card Creator guides students to create trading cards that help them think about specific details and inferences about different aspects of literary and nonfiction texts. They can then describe how the individuals, events, and ideas on their trading cards develop and interact over the course of a text.

The use of QR ("quick response") codes on mobile devices is another engaging way to motivate students (Kajder, 2012; Schrock, 2012). Black and white QR bar codes are ubiquitous in our daily lives, found on posters, ads, food products, restaurants, and real estate signs. Figure 9.5 shows an example QR code. Students can create their own QR codes that connect peers to a written text, recorded audio, website, YouTube video, and more. QR codes can often store up to 4296 characters, making them perfect for written text, explanations of content, or linking a project to additional information. Libraries and classroom teachers are finding creative ways to use these codes every day, such as having students record book reviews to attach to a book that others will read (Kajder, 2012) or creating information scavenger hunts for other students (for a QR Treasure Hunt Generator, see www.classtools.net/QR).

Figure 9.5 Example of a QR Code

Students can create their own QR codes as a way to retell a narrative text, summarize content text, or present an analysis of how and why individuals, events, and ideas develop and interact over the course of a text. First, students write their retelling, summary, or analysis. Then, students use a website such as QRStuff (www.qrstuff.com) to create QR codes for their writing. On QRStuff, students choose the "plain text" option and enter their written text in the text box (it can be cut and pasted from a word-processed document). The QR code is automatically created as the text is entered into the box. After all the text is entered, students can download the QR code to a computer, print it, or e-mail it to share with others. To access a QR code, students must have a QR code reader (such as the Scan or Qrafter apps) installed on a mobile device.

Students can share their analysis of a book through carefully placed QR codes within a text. QR codes can be linked to a VoiceThread (www.voicethread.com) or online discussion board where students share their insights into how a character is developing at a certain point in a story or predict where they think the story is going. QR codes can also be linked to website URLs, YouTube videos, Google maps, and Dropbox files, making them perfect for placing within an informational text to help students develop background information about the topic. Students can create QR codes at "stop and analyze" intervals to contemplate how and why individuals, events, and ideas are developing and interacting over the course of a text.

As another way for students to explore how individuals, ideas, and events interact over the course of the text, students can use online tools to express those interactions. Map tools such as Google Lit Trips (www.googlelittrips.com) allow students to create maps of what is happening during a story or novel. Students can then draw conclusions based on the interaction of characters and setting. There are also great timeline tools available for exploring the timeline of a story or event. With tools such as Tiki-Toki (www.tiki-toki.com), Timeglider (timeglider.com), and Preceden (www.preceden.com), students can create timelines to describe the major events in a story or historical episode.

How Can We Integrate Other ELA Standards With Reading Anchor Standard 3?

When planning to teach Common Core Reading Standard 3, we can integrate several other ELA standards to design rich instructional tasks. Examples of ideas to include when creating rich instructional tasks follow.

Integrating Other ELA Standards With Reading Literature Standard 3

- Reading Literature Standard 1 focuses on reading a literary text closely. *Example:* When reading a literary text, invite students to analyze characters, dialogue, or the impact of the author's choices regarding elements of literature.

- Reading Literature Standard 5 refers to analyzing the structure of literary texts. *Example:* When discussing the development of characters, settings, or ideas in a story or drama, encourage students to analyze the way the author structured the text to develop these narrative elements.

- Reading Literature Standard 6 refers to point of view. *Example:* Encourage students to refer to a character's or author's point of view when writing or speaking about a text.

- Reading Literature Standard 9 focuses on comparing and contrasting aspects of literary text. *Example:* Teach students to compare and contrast characters, events, and ideas in texts.

- Writing Standard 3 describes expectations for students to write narratives to develop real or imagined experiences or events using effective technique, relevant descriptive details, and well-structured event sequences. *Example:* Teach students to write a story with descriptive characters, settings, and event sequences following the criteria in Writing Standard 3.

- Speaking and Listening Standard 1 describes the expectation that students will engage effectively in a range of collaborative discussions, with specific indicators to demonstrate how to participate in an effective academic conversation. *Example:* When reading stories, dramas, and poetry, engage students in whole-group discussions and small-group Literature Circles.

- Language Standard 5 is the vocabulary standard that refers to demonstrating understanding of figurative language, word relationships, and nuances in word meanings. *Example:* Ask students to describe the nuances in language an author uses to describe characters, settings, or events in a story or drama.

Integrating Other ELA Standards With Reading Informational Text Standard 3

When planning to teach Common Core Reading Standard 3 for literary nonfiction and other informational texts, we can integrate several other ELA standards to design rich instructional tasks. Examples of ideas to include when creating rich instructional tasks follow.

- Reading Informational Text Standard 1 refers to closely reading an informational text. *Example:* Ask students to read closely to find connections and interactions between individuals, events, ideas, or concepts in historical, scientific, or technical texts.

- Reading Informational Text Standard 2 focuses on the ability to summarize the central idea and supporting details of an informational text. *Example:* Teach students to summarize the central idea and supporting details when discussing interactions between individuals, events, ideas, or concepts in a historical, scientific, or technical text.

- Reading Informational Text Standard 5 refers to analysis of text structure and organization of the text. *Example:* Encourage students to discuss how the structure and organization of the text helps the author develop ideas in the text.

- Reading Informational Text Standard 6 is point of view. *Example:* When reading an informational text, teach students to analyze the author's point of view.

- Reading Informational Text Standard 8 addresses analyzing arguments, including claims, reasons, and evidence, to support various points in the text. *Example:* Teach students to evaluate the reasoning and analyze the interaction of ideas as they discuss an author's arguments in a text.

- Writing Standard 2 lays out the expectations for informative/explanatory writing. *Example:* Teach students to write an informative/explanatory paragraph or essay to analyze individuals, events, ideas, or concepts in an informational text, following the criteria found in Writing Standard 2.

- Writing Standard 7 refers to participating in short research projects that build knowledge about a topic. *Example:* Create situations in which students engage in short research projects to build knowledge about individuals, events, ideas, or concepts.

- Writing Standard 8 focuses on recalling information from experiences or gathering information from sources to answer questions about a topic. *Example:* While engaged in research, encourage students to explore two or more informational texts to generate and respond to questions on a given topic and/or to make connections between individuals, events, ideas, or concepts.

- Writing Standard 9 addresses the expectation that students will be able to draw evidence from informational texts to support analysis, reflection, and research. *Example:* Invite students to write responses that emphasize the interaction and development of an individual's ideas and events in the text.

- Speaking and Listening Standard 1 describes the expectation that students will engage effectively in a range of collaborative discussions, with specific indicators to demonstrate how to participate in an effective academic conversation. *Example:* Engage students in collaborative academic conversations about the individuals, events, ideas, or concepts in informational text.

- Language Standard 6 is the vocabulary standard that refers to general academic and domain-specific words and phrases. *Example:* Ask students to use vocabulary specific to informational text when writing or speaking about disciplinary concepts.

THE COMMON CORE IN ACTION

In this section, we examine one of the foundational ideas that underpins each of the Common Core's Anchor Standards for Reading. For the third standard, "Analyze how and why individuals, events, and ideas develop and interact over the course of the text" (NGA Center & CCSSO, 2010, p. 10), we have elected to share more detailed information about characterization, which is an explicit part of the standard for grades 6–12.

Common Core Literacy Task: Characterization

Jim is an eighth-grade English teacher whose students have been reading *The Hunger Games*. He and his colleagues have been planning together to use the Suzanne Collins novel to teach their students to meet the eighth-grade Reading Standard 3 for Literature: "Analyze how particular lines of dialogue or incidents in a story or drama propel the action, reveal aspects of a character, or provoke a decision" (NGA Center & CCSSO, 2010, p. 36). He plans to particularly focus on teaching students to analyze how dialogue or incidents in literary text propel the action, reveal a character, or provoke a decision in the story or drama.

Jim has been involved in professional development in which the teachers in his middle school have studied the 6–12 Standards and focused on developing rich instructional tasks. He wants to ensure that his students are prepared to address Reading Literature Standard 3, so he plans to begin by teaching lessons about how incidents in a novel reveal characters.

Jim has decided to use the Text-Based Characterization Organizer (McLaughlin & Overturf, 2013). His students have already read *The Hunger Games*, so he will teach his students how to use specific evidence in the novel to reveal a character. He explains and models using the Text-Based Characterization Organizer with a different text. Then he gradually releases responsibility to the students, who will work with partners to choose a character and show how he or she is revealed by the text. After the students select their characters, partners will select incidents from the novel that support their thinking.

Jim plans to use the following lesson sequence:

1. Briefly review the content of *The Hunger Games* and invite students to generate inferences based on textual evidence. (RL.8.1)

2. Invite students to discuss text-based inferences about various characters. (RL.8.1; SL.8.1; SL.8.2)

3. Encourage students to choose partners, select a character, and write a brainstormed list of traits they believe the character possesses. (SL.8.1; SL.8.2, W.8.9)

4. Guide the students to search the text for evidence of the various characteristics, and record the text-based evidence on the graphic organizer. (RL.8.1; RL.8.3)

5. Encourage students to discuss their selections with another pair. (SL.8.1)

6. Invite students to use the completed graphic organizer to write a summary about the character and the text-based evidence that reveals his or her traits. (RL.8.3, W.8.2; W.8.9)

Figure 9.6 shows a completed Text-Based Characterization Organizer about Katniss, the protagonist in *The Hunger Games*.

Figure 9.6 Example of a Text-Based Characterization Organizer

Prim

Loving: Katniss treated her sister, Prim, in loving ways. She made sure her family had food, even though hunting was against the law.

Gael

Adventurous: Katniss was adventurous every time she got her bow and went hunting with Gael.

Katniss

The Hunger Games

Peeta

Grateful, caring, and frightened: Depending on the point in the story, Katniss was grateful to Peeta, took care of him, and was sometimes frightened when with him.

Rue

Protective and compassionate: Rue was Katniss' partner for a brief time, but then Rue was killed. Katniss protected Rue and covered her in flowers when she died.

Summary: Katniss exhibited many characteristics in *The Hunger Games*. She was loving, protective, and compassionate toward Prim and Rue. She shared a sense of adventure with Gael and she displayed several qualities toward Peeta. When he gave her bread to feed her family, she was grateful. When he was injured, she was caring, and after the games, when he was confused, she feared him at times.

Reading Standard 3 focuses on ensuring that students can analyze the development of characters, events, and ideas in texts. It requires students to analyze how incidents and/or dialogue propel action, reveal character traits, or provoke a decision. When students can follow the thread, they better understand how to comprehend the text.

References

ACT. (2006). *Reading between the lines: What the ACT reveals about college readiness in reading.* Iowa City, IA: Author. Retrieved August 22, 2012, from www.act.org/research/policymakers/pdf/reading_report.pdf

Kajder, S. (2012, November). *Reports from cyberspace.* Paper presented at the annual conference of the National Council of Teachers of English, Las Vegas, NV.

McGinley, W.J., & Denner, P.R. (1987). Story impressions: A prereading/writing activity. *Journal of Reading, 31*(3), 248–253.

McLaughlin, M., & Allen, M.B. (2009). *Guided Comprehension in grades 3–8* (Combined 2nd ed.). Newark, DE: International Reading Association.

McLaughlin, M., & Overturf, B.J. (2013). *The Common Core: Graphic organizers for teaching K–12 students to meet the Reading Standards.* Newark, DE: International Reading Association. Retrieved from www.reading.org/general/Publications/Books/bk021.aspx

National Governors Association Center for Best Practices & Council of Chief State School Officers. (2010). *Common Core State Standards for English language arts and literacy in history/social studies, science, and technical subjects.* Washington, DC: Authors. Retrieved August 3, 2012, from www.corestandards.org/assets/CCSSI_ELA%20 Standards.pdf

Schrock, K. (2012). QR codes in the classroom. *Kathy Schrock's guide to everything.* Retrieved November 25, 2012, from www.schrockguide.net/qr-codes-in-the-classroom.html

Literature Cited

Collins, S. (2010). *The Hunger Games.* New York: Scholastic.

Connell, R. (1924). The most dangerous game. Retrieved December 12, 2012, from fiction.eserver.org/short/the_most_dangerous_game.html

Jackson, S. (1948). The lottery. Retrieved December 12, 2012, from www.americanliterature.com/author/shirley-jackson/short-story/the-lottery

London, J. (1908). To build a fire. Retrieved December 12, 2012, from www.jacklondons.net/Media/to_build_a_fire_print_ver.html

Poe, E.A. (1843). The tell-tale heart. Retrieved December 12, 2012, from xroads.virginia.edu/~hyper/poe/telltale.html

CCR Reading Anchor Standard 4: Meanings of Words and Phrases

Knowing the Word

| **College and Career Readiness Reading Anchor Standard 4** |
| Interpret words and phrases as they are used in a text, including determining technical, connotative, and figurative meanings, and analyze how specific word choices shape meaning or tone. (NGA Center & CCSSO, 2010, p. 10) |

What Does CCR Reading Anchor Standard 4 Mean?

College and Career Readiness (CCR) Reading Anchor Standard 4 focuses on the words and phrases that authors choose to use in their writing. In a report on college and career readiness, ACT (2006) notes that a characteristic of complex text is the author's use of language, which is often intricate. In Reading Standard 4, students are expected to be able to interpret and analyze the words an author uses in a text and the way the author uses words and phrases to bring meaning to the text. This standard helps fulfill expectations that students be able to "determine, even when the language is richly figurative and the vocabulary is difficult, the appropriate meaning of context-dependent words, phrases, or statements in virtually any passage" (ACT, 2006, p. 37).

CCR Reading Anchor Standard 4 is focused on understanding words in context. It is also focused on the concept of diction. Diction means not only the exact way a person pronounces words but also an author's word choice and style of expression. An author's diction helps determine the message of the text. When students analyze a text for diction, they identify the diction devices the author used and try to interpret why the author chose those words for the text. Examples of diction devices are denotation (technical meaning of a word), connotation (interpretive meaning of a word or phrase), and figurative language, such as similes and metaphors.

When studying literature, teachers may ask students to write a diction analysis of a text. This type of analysis is an essay in which students analyze a piece of text for the author's vocabulary choices, style of expression, type of language (formal, informal, colloquial, or poetic), and tone. The essay focuses on how the text was written to create a certain effect, which then ties back to the purpose of the text.

When reading an informational text, students are expected to determine the meanings of symbols, key terms, and domain-specific words and phrases as they are used in the text in order to comprehend and learn from it. Determining the meanings of domain-specific words and phrases will help students learn the content of a disciplinary text.

Reading Anchor Standard 4 focuses on five College and Career Readiness reading skills:

1. The ability to interpret words and phrases as they are used in a text

2. The ability to determine technical meanings

3. The ability to determine connotative meanings

4. The ability to determine figurative meanings

5. The ability to analyze how word choices determine meaning or tone

Interpreting Words and Phrases

Authors choose words and phrases very carefully to create a mood or tone and to help the reader visualize the characters, setting, and events. In poetry especially, just a few words can sketch a host of images. The reader is expected to interpret the text using the words and phrases that the author chose as clues to the meaning. For example, in Carl Sandburg's (1970) poem "Fog," the first two lines are "The fog comes / on little cat feet" (p. 33). The poet creates a metaphor comparing fog to a cat, but through his word choice, he also creates a mood of quiet and mystery that helps the reader visualize the fog.

Technical Meanings

When students read disciplinary texts such as textbooks, newspapers, magazines, informational articles, and websites, they will encounter a large number of words with technical meanings that are specialized for particular fields of study. For example, scientists study matter and DNA, literature experts interpret monologues and soliloquies, and mathematicians examine rhombuses and parallelograms. Each field has its own specialized vocabulary.

Connotative Meanings

Connotation is the way we interpret the author's words to help paint a picture in our minds. For example, an author may describe a thin woman as "slender as a willow tree" or "skinny as a fence post." The connotation of the word *slender* coupled with the simile "as a willow tree" may give us an image of a young, beautiful girl, whereas the connotation of *skinny* along with the simile "as a fence post" may give us quite a different image of a woman who has known a hard life. Authors deliberately use words to attempt to influence the reader's connotation—the way the reader might interpret the word or phrase. The opposite of connotation is denotation, which means the literal dictionary definition of a word.

Figurative Language

Authors use figurative language to help the reader visualize the text and to add interest to their writing. Readers interpret figurative language to visualize the text and determine the author's message and intent. The following are common examples of figurative language:

- *Alliteration*—Words that repeat the same letters or sounds. *Example:* Gabby's gainer was as good as gold.

- *Euphemism*—The substitution of an inoffensive or more agreeable word for a word that may offend or suggest something unpleasant. *Example*: The doctor said, "You may feel some pressure." (She meant, "This is going to hurt!")

- *Hyperbole*—A figure of speech that uses exaggeration and is not meant to be taken literally. *Example:* I'm so hungry, I could eat an elephant.

- *Idiom*—A phrase whose meaning is not predictable from the words in the phrase. *Example:* "That test was a piece of cake." (It was easy.)

- *Metaphor*—A figure of speech that compares two things that are basically unalike, but says the first thing actually is the second thing. *Example:* Coffee was my life preserver that morning.

- *Onomatopoeia*—Words or phrases that sound like the object they are describing. *Example:* The firecrackers popped and crackled in the night sky.

- *Oxymoron*—The combination of seemingly contradictory words. *Example:* "hopelessly optimistic"

- *Paradox*—A sentence that is a contradiction. *Example:* This statement is false. (The statement cannot be both false and true at the same time.)

- *Personification*—A figure of speech in which the author gives an object the qualities of a person. *Example:* The raindrops tiptoed across the window.

- *Simile*—A figure of speech that compares two things that are basically different, often using the words *like* or *as*. *Example:* The race car was like lightning.

Analyzing How Word Choices Shape Meaning or Tone

The ability to analyze the author's word choice in poetry or prose is a college readiness skill. To analyze how the author's word choice shapes meaning or tone, The College Board (College Entrance Examination Board, 2002) suggests using the acronym DIDLS, which stands for diction, imagery, details, language, and sentence structure (or syntax). Diction was discussed previously as the connotation or denotation of a word the author chose to use. Imagery consists of words the author chose to appeal to the senses, and that can sway meaning from positive to negative. When an author uses details for effect in writing, he or she adds (or omits) facts that emphasize certain aspects of the characters, settings, or events. This focuses the reader's attention on that aspect. Language refers to the overall type of language the author uses: Is the tone formal, clinical, or informal, or does the passage use jargon? Sentence structure (syntax) refers to the author's use of sentence structure for effect, such as the use of short, choppy sentences to be emphatic or longer, more complex sentences to be thoughtful.

How Do the Common Core Standards Build to CCR Reading Anchor Standard 4?

The Common Core Standards in grades 6–12 build toward College and Career Readiness Anchor Standard 4 by addressing skills in four substrands of reading. The Reading Standard 4 substrands included in grades 6–12 are as follows:

- Reading Standards for Literature (English Language Arts)
- Reading Standards for Informational Text (English Language Arts)
- Reading Standards for Literacy in History/Social Studies
- Reading Standards for Literacy in Science and Technical Subjects

In Literature, the expectations of Reading Standard 4 are that every student in grades 6–12 will determine the meaning of words and phrases as they are used in a text, including figurative and connotative meanings. Sixth graders learn to analyze the impact of the author's specific word choice on the meaning and tone of the text. Seventh graders analyze the impact of rhymes and other repetitions of sounds on a specific verse or stanza of the poem or section of a story or drama. Eighth graders build on that knowledge to analyze the impact of word choices on meaning and tone, including analogies or allusions to other texts. Students in ninth and tenth grade analyze the cumulative impact of specific word choices on meaning and tone, and students in eleventh and twelfth grade add to that knowledge by analyzing words with multiple meanings or language that is particularly fresh, engaging, or beautiful. There is a pointed caveat that analysis of the language of Shakespeare as well as other authors should be included at this level. Reading Standard 4 for Literature for grades 6–12 is delineated in Table 10.1.

Reading Standard 4 for Informational Text is very similar to Reading Standard 4 for Literature. The major difference is that students in grades 11–12 will analyze how an author uses and refines the meaning of a key term or terms over the course of a text. A specific example is included regarding the way in which Madison defined the term *faction* in *Federalist* No. 10. Reading Standard 4 for Informational Text for grades 6–12 appears in Table 10.2.

Reading Standard 4 for Literacy in History/ Social Studies focuses on vocabulary germane to understanding concepts in history/social studies. In grades 6–8, students learn to determine the meanings of words and phrases as they are used in a history/social studies text. In grades 9–10, there is a focus on determining the meanings of vocabulary describing political, social, or economic aspects of history/social studies. In grades 11–12, Reading Standard 4 for Literacy in History/Social Studies is exactly the same as Reading Standard 4 for Informational Text in English Language Arts, which is to analyze how an author uses and refines the meaning of a key term or terms over the course of a text. The same specific example is included regarding the way in which Madison defined *faction* in *Federalist* No. 10. The expectations of Reading Standard 4 for Literacy in History/Social Studies are shown in Table 10.3.

Table 10.1 Common Core State Standard 4 for Reading Literature in Grades 6–12

Grade	Standard
6	Determine the meaning of words and phrases as they are used in a text, including figurative and connotative meanings; analyze the impact of the specific word choice on meaning and tone.
7	Determine the meaning of words and phrases as they are used in a text, including figurative and connotative meanings; analyze the impact of rhymes and other repetitions of sounds (e.g., alliteration) on a specific verse or stanza of a poem or section of a story or drama.
8	Determine the meaning of words and phrases as they are used in a text, including figurative and connotative meanings; analyze the impact of specific word choices on meaning and tone, including analogies or allusions to other texts.
9–10	Determine the meaning of words and phrases as they are used in the text, including figurative and connotative meanings; analyze the cumulative impact of specific word choices on meaning and tone (e.g., how the language evokes a sense of time and place; how it sets a formal or informal tone).
11–12	Determine the meaning of words and phrases as they are used in the text, including figurative and connotative meanings; analyze the impact of specific word choices on meaning and tone, including words with multiple meanings or language that is particularly fresh, engaging, or beautiful. (Include Shakespeare as well as other authors.)

Note. The standards are from *Common Core State Standards for English Language Arts and Literacy in History/Social Studies, Science, and Technical Subjects* (pp. 36 and 38), by National Governors Association Center for Best Practices and Council of Chief State School Officers, 2010, Washington, DC: Authors.

Table 10.2 Common Core State Standard 4 for Reading Informational Text in Grades 6–12

Grade	Standard
6	Determine the meaning of words and phrases as they are used in a text, including figurative, connotative, and technical meanings.
7	Determine the meaning of words and phrases as they are used in a text, including figurative, connotative, and technical meanings; analyze the impact of the specific word choice on meaning and tone.
8	Determine the meaning of words and phrases as they are used in a text, including figurative, connotative, and technical meanings; analyze the impact of specific word choices on meaning and tone, including analogies or allusions to other texts.
9–10	Determine the meaning of words and phrases as they are used in a text, including figurative, connotative, and technical meanings; analyze the cumulative impact of specific word choices on meaning and tone (e.g., how the language of the court opinion differs from that of a newspaper).
11–12	Determine the meaning of words and phrases as they are used in a text, including figurative, connotative, and technical meanings; analyze how an author uses and refines the meaning of a key term or terms over the course of a text (e.g., how Madison defines *faction* in *Federalist* No. 10).

Note. The standards are from *Common Core State Standards for English Language Arts and Literacy in History/Social Studies, Science, and Technical Subjects* (pp. 39 and 40), by National Governors Association Center for Best Practices and Council of Chief State School Officers, 2010, Washington, DC: Authors.

Table 10.3 Common Core Reading Standard 4 for Literacy in History/Social Studies in Grades 6–12

Grade	Standard
6–8	Determine the meaning of words and phrases as they are used in a text, including vocabulary specific to domains related to history/social studies.
9–10	Determine the meaning of words and phrases as they are used in a text, including vocabulary describing political, social, or economic aspects of history/social studies.
11–12	Determine the meaning of words and phrases as they are used in a text, including analyzing how an author uses and refines the meaning of the key term over the course of a text (e.g., how Madison defines *faction* in *Federalist* No. 10).

Note. The standards are from *Common Core State Standards for English Language Arts and Literacy in History/Social Studies, Science, and Technical Subjects* (p. 61), by National Governors Association Center for Best Practices and Council of Chief State School Officers, 2010, Washington, DC: Authors.

Reading Standard 4 for Literacy in Science and Technical Subjects states that students in grades 6–12 will determine the meaning of symbols, key terms, and other domain-specific words and phrases as they are used in a specific scientific or technical context relevant to each particular grade level. Reading Standard 4 for Literacy in Science and Technical Subjects appears in Table 10.4.

Reading Standard 4 is also the standard that connects to vocabulary expectations outlined in the Language Standards. We address the standards for vocabulary acquisition and use across the curriculum in conjunction with the expectations for Reading Standard 4. These are located in Language Standards 4–6.

All students need to develop a broad vocabulary base. Research shows that vocabulary development and knowledge are key for reading comprehension (Anderson & Nagy, 1991; Blachowicz, Fisher, Ogle, & Watts-Taffe, 2010; Graves & Watts-Taffe, 2002; Stahl & Fairbanks, 1986). To develop a robust vocabulary, students in grades 6–12 need to engage in intentional and varied learning experiences with words. To meet Reading Standard 4, students need to be engaged in regular vocabulary instruction designed to help them learn a host of skills and strategies. Teaching the vocabulary concepts found in the Language Standards for vocabulary acquisition and use supports Reading Standard 4.

There are three major areas of focus for vocabulary instruction to meet the Language (Vocabulary Acquisition and Use) Standards:

1. Meanings of unknown and multiple-meaning words and phrases (Language Standard 4)

2. Figurative language, word relationships, and nuances in word meanings (Language Standard 5)

3. General academic and domain-specific words and phrases (Language Standard 6)

Language Standard 4 relates to determining or clarifying the meanings of unknown and multiple-meaning words and phrases. Students at all grades are expected to identify the meanings of words and use context as a clue to determine the meanings of unfamiliar words. Students in grades 6–8 learn to use grade-appropriate Greek or Latin affixes and roots as clues to the meaning of a word. All students in grades 6–12 should be able to use appropriate reference materials to help them determine precise word meanings and pronunciations and be able to verify the preliminary determination of a word or phrase by checking the inferred meaning in context or in a dictionary. Students in grades 9–12 should also be able to identify and correctly use patterns of word changes that indicate different meanings or parts of speech. Table 10.5 delineates the skills and strategies needed to meet Language Standard 4 in grades 6–12.

Table 10.4 Common Core Reading Standard 4 for Literacy in Science and Technical Subjects in Grades 6–12

Grade	Standard
6–8	Determine the meaning of symbols, key terms, and other domain-specific words and phrases as they are used in a specific scientific or technical context relevant to *grades 6–8 texts and topics*.
9–10	Determine the meaning of symbols, key terms, and other domain-specific words and phrases as they are used in a specific scientific or technical context relevant to *grades 9–10 texts and topics*.
11–12	Determine the meaning of symbols, key terms, and other domain-specific words and phrases as they are used in a specific scientific or technical context relevant to *grades 11–12 texts and topics*.

Note. The standards are from *Common Core State Standards for English Language Arts and Literacy in History/Social Studies, Science, and Technical Subjects* (p. 62), by National Governors Association Center for Best Practices and Council of Chief State School Officers, 2010, Washington, DC: Authors.

Language Standard 5 focuses on word relationships and nuances in word meanings. In the elementary grades, students concentrated on understanding categories of words and their uses. Students also began to distinguish shades of meaning among verbs describing the same general action and among adjectives describing degrees of intensity. Students began to examine literal and nonliteral meanings of words and phrases. They were also expected to explore word relationships and nuances more deeply as they studied figurative language. This included similes and metaphors; idioms, adages, and proverbs; and related words to their synonyms, antonyms, and homographs. In grades 6–8, students are expected to interpret figures of speech in context, use the relationship between particular words to better understand each of the words, and distinguish among the connotations of words with similar denotations. In grades 9–12, students are expected to demonstrate understanding of figurative language, word relationships, and nuances in word meanings. They should be able to interpret figures of speech in context and analyze their role in the text and to analyze nuances in the meaning of words with similar denotations. Table 10.6 delineates the skills and strategies needed to meet Language Standard 5 in grades 6–12.

Language Standard 6 requires students to acquire and use grade-appropriate words and phrases. This standard focuses on what Beck, McKeown, and Kucan (2002) call Tier Two words (general academic) and Tier Three words (domain-specific). Tier One words are those that students already know. Tier Two words are more unfamiliar words that students will encounter across various texts, such as descriptive adjectives (e.g., *instinctual*), nouns (e.g., *resonance*), and active verbs (e.g., *extol*). Tier Three words are domain-specific words and phrases that are more often found in disciplinary texts, such as *isotope* and *quadratic function*. The skills and strategies needed to meet Language Standard 6 in grades 6–12 appear in Table 10.7.

Table 10.5 CCR Anchor Standard 4 for Language: Supporting Skills and Strategies for Vocabulary Acquisition and Use

Grade	Skills and Strategies
6	Determine or clarify the meaning of unknown and multiple-meaning words and phrases based on *grade 6 reading and content*, choosing flexibly from a range of strategies. a. Use context (e.g., the overall meaning of a sentence or paragraph; a word's position or function in a sentence) as a clue to the meaning of a word or phrase. b. Use common, grade-appropriate Greek or Latin affixes and roots as clues to the meaning of a word (e.g., *audience, auditory, audible*). c. Consult reference materials (e.g., dictionaries, glossaries, thesauruses), both print and digital, to find the pronunciation of a word or determine or clarify its precise meaning or its part of speech. d. Verify the preliminary determination of the meaning of a word or phrase (e.g., by checking the inferred meaning in context or in a dictionary).
7	Determine or clarify the meaning of unknown and multiple-meaning words and phrases based on *grade 7 reading and content*, choosing flexibly from a range of strategies. a. Use context (e.g., the overall meaning of the sentence or paragraph; a word's position or function in a sentence) as a clue to the meaning of a word or phrase. b. Use common, grade-appropriate Greek or Latin affixes and roots as clues to the meaning of a word (e.g., *belligerent, bellicose, rebel*). c. Consult general and specialized reference materials (e.g., dictionaries, glossaries, thesauruses), both print and digital, to find the pronunciation of a word or determine or clarify its precise meaning or its part of speech. d. Verify the preliminary determination of the meaning of a word or phrase (e.g., by checking the inferred meaning in context or in a dictionary).
8	Determine or clarify the meaning of unknown and multiple-meaning words or phrases based on *grade 8 reading and content*, choosing flexibly from a range of strategies. a. Use context (e.g., the overall meaning of the sentence or paragraph; a word's position or function in a sentence) as a clue to the meaning of a word or phrase. b. Use common, grade-appropriate Greek and Latin affixes and roots as clues to the meaning of the word (e.g., *precede, recede, secede*). c. Consult general and specialized reference materials (e.g., dictionaries, glossaries, thesauruses), both print and digital, to find the pronunciation of a word or determine or clarify its precise meaning or its part of speech. d. Verify the preliminary determination of the meaning of a word or phrase (e.g., by checking the inferred meaning in context or in a dictionary).
9–10	Determine or clarify the meaning of unknown and multiple-meaning words and phrases based on *grades 9–10 reading and content*, choosing flexibly from a range of strategies. a. Use context (e.g., the overall meaning of a sentence, paragraph, or text; a word's position or function in a sentence) as a clue to the meaning of a word or phrase. b. Identify and correctly use patterns of word changes that indicate different meanings or parts of speech (e.g., *analyze, analysis, analytical; advocate, advocacy*). c. Consult general and specialized reference materials (e.g., dictionaries, glossaries, thesauruses), both print and digital, to find the pronunciation of a word or determine or clarify its precise meaning, its part of speech, or its etymology. d. Verify the preliminary determination of the meaning of a word or phrase (e.g., by checking the inferred meaning in context or in a dictionary).

(continued)

Table 10.5 CCR Anchor Standard 4 for Language: Supporting Skills and Strategies for Vocabulary Acquisition and Use (continued)

Grade	Skills and Strategies
11–12	Determine or clarify the meaning of unknown and multiple-meaning words and phrases based on *grades 11–12 reading and content*, choosing flexibly from a range of strategies. a. Use context (e.g., the overall meaning of a sentence, paragraph, or text; a word's position or function in a sentence) as a clue to the meaning of a word or phrase. b. Identify and correctly use patterns of word changes that indicate different meanings or parts of speech (e.g., *conceive, conception, conceivable*). c. Consult general and specialized reference materials (e.g., dictionaries, glossaries, thesauruses), both print and digital, to find the pronunciation of a word or determine or clarify its precise meaning, its part of speech, its etymology, or its standard usage. d. Verify the preliminary determination of the meaning of a word or phrase (e.g., by checking the inferred meaning in context or in a dictionary).

Note. The skills and strategies are from *Common Core State Standards for English Language Arts and Literacy in History/Social Studies, Science, and Technical Subjects* (pp. 53 and 55), by National Governors Association Center for Best Practices and Council of Chief State School Officers, 2010, Washington, DC: Authors.

Table 10.6 CCR Anchor Standard 5 for Language: Supporting Skills and Strategies for Vocabulary Acquisition and Use

Grade	Skills and Strategies
6	Demonstrate understanding of figurative language, word relationships, and nuances in word meanings. a. Interpret figures of speech (e.g., personification) in context. b. Use the relationship between particular words (e.g., cause/effect, part/whole, item/category) to better understand each of the words. c. Distinguish among the connotations (associations) of words with similar denotations (definitions) (e.g., *stingy, scrimping, economical, unwasteful, thrifty*).
7	Demonstrate understanding of figurative language, word relationships, and nuances in word meanings. a. Interpret figures of speech (e.g., literary, biblical, and mythological allusions) in context. b. Use the relationship between particular words (e.g., synonym/antonym, analogy) to better understand each of the words. c. Distinguish among the connotations (associations) of words with similar denotations (definitions) (e.g., *refined, respectful, polite, diplomatic, condescending*).
8	Demonstrate understanding of figurative language, word relationships, and nuances in word meanings. a. Interpret figures of speech (e.g., verbal irony, puns) in context. b. Use the relationship between particular words to better understand each of the words. c. Distinguish among the connotations (associations) of words with similar denotations (definitions) (e.g., *bullheaded, willful, firm, persistent, resolute*).
9–10	Demonstrate understanding of figurative language, word relationships, and nuances in word meanings. a. Interpret figures of speech (e.g., euphemism, oxymoron) in context and analyze their role in the text. b. Analyze nuances in the meaning of words with similar denotations.
11–12	Demonstrate understanding of figurative language, word relationships, and nuances in word meanings. a. Interpret figures of speech (e.g., hyperbole, paradox) in context and analyze their role in the text. b. Analyze nuances in the meaning of words with similar denotations.

Note. The skills and strategies are from *Common Core State Standards for English Language Arts and Literacy in History/Social Studies, Science, and Technical Subjects* (pp. 53 and 55), by National Governors Association Center for Best Practices and Council of Chief State School Officers, 2010, Washington, DC: Authors.

Table 10.7 CCR Anchor Standard 6 for Language: Supporting Skills and Strategies for Vocabulary Acquisition and Use

Grade	Skills and Strategies
6	Acquire and use accurately grade-appropriate general academic and domain-specific words and phrases; gather vocabulary knowledge when considering a word or phrase important to comprehension or expression.
7	Acquire and use accurately grade-appropriate general academic and domain-specific words and phrases; gather vocabulary knowledge when considering a word or phrase important to comprehension or expression.
8	Acquire and use accurately grade-appropriate general academic and domain-specific words and phrases; gather vocabulary knowledge when considering a word or phrase important to comprehension or expression.
9–10	Acquire and use accurately general academic and domain-specific words and phrases, sufficient for reading, writing, speaking, and listening at the college and career readiness level; demonstrate independence in gathering vocabulary knowledge when considering a word or phrase important to comprehension or expression.
11–12	Acquire and use accurately general academic and domain-specific words and phrases, sufficient for reading, writing, speaking, and listening at the college and career readiness level; demonstrate independence in gathering vocabulary knowledge when considering a word or phrase important to comprehension or expression.

Note. The skills and strategies are from *Common Core State Standards for English Language Arts and Literacy in History/Social Studies, Science, and Technical Subjects* (pp. 53 and 55), by National Governors Association Center for Best Practices and Council of Chief State School Officers, 2010, Washington, DC: Authors.

What Literacy Skills and Strategies Support Reading Anchor Standard 4?

When we review the literacy skills and strategies in the Common Core State Standards, we can readily determine that gaps exist. As educators, we may find ourselves asking whether we should be teaching a particular concept because it does not appear in the CCSS. However, it is important to note that the Standards are not the determining factor. If the skill or strategy is included in our curriculums, we should teach it. For example, students in grades K–3 are expected to be able to ask and answer questions. Similarly, students in grades 4 and 5 are expected to know and use text structures such as comparison/contrast and problem/solution. The grade 6–12 CCSS do not address either of these topics, but the students still need to know what they are and how to use them to successfully meet the Standards. That is why we noted in Chapter 1 the importance of our reading the CCSS both vertically (our grade levels) and horizontally (what students are expected to know before they reach our grade levels).

Many of the essential skills that grade 6–12 students need to know, including asking and answering questions and using text structure, are delineated in the grade K–5 Standards. For example, Common Core Reading Standard 1, for both literature and informational text, is associated with Reading Standard 10, which focuses on the expectation that students will read complex text. For students to be able to read, discuss, and write about complex text, they must be able to use the supporting skills and strategies that were introduced in earlier grades. Details of Reading Standard 4, the focus of this chapter, are featured in Table 10.8 for Literature (English Language Arts) and Table 10.9 for Informational Text (ELA, Reading in History/Social Studies, and Reading in Science and Technical Subjects).

How Can We Teach Reading Anchor Standard 4 So Our Students Achieve?

In this section, we discuss the CCSS expectations for students. For example, the fourth College and Career Readiness Standard for Reading requires that students be able to interpret words and phrases as they are used in a text, including how specific sentences, paragraphs, and larger portions

Table 10.8 K–5 Reading Standard 4: Supporting Skills and Strategies for Literature in Grades 6–12

Grade	Skills and Strategies
K	Ask and answer questions about unknown words in a text.
1	Identify words and phrases in stories or poems that suggest feelings or appeal to the senses.
2	Describe how words and phrases (e.g., regular beats, alliteration, rhymes, repeated lines) supply rhythm and meaning in a story, poem, or song.
3	Determine the meaning of words and phrases as they are used in a text, distinguishing literal from nonliteral language.
4	Determine the meaning of words and phrases as they are used in a text, including those that allude to significant characters found in mythology (e.g., Herculean).
5	Determine the meaning of words and phrases as they are used in a text, including figurative language such as metaphors and similes.

Note. The standards are from *Common Core State Standards for English Language Arts and Literacy in History/Social Studies, Science, and Technical Subjects* (pp. 11 and 12), by National Governors Association Center for Best Practices and Council of Chief State School Officers, 2010, Washington, DC: Authors.

Table 10.9 K–5 Reading Standard 4: Supporting Skills and Strategies for Informational Text in Grades 6–12

Grade	Skills and Strategies
K	With prompting and support, ask and answer questions about unknown words in a text.
1	Ask and answer questions to help determine or clarify the meaning of words and phrases in a text.
2	Determine the meaning of words and phrases in a text relevant to a *grade 2 topic or subject area*.
3	Determine the meaning of general academic and domain-specific words and phrases in a text relevant to a *grade 3 topic or subject area*.
4	Determine the meaning of general academic and domain-specific words or phrases in a text relevant to a *grade 4 topic or subject area*.
5	Determine the meaning of general academic and domain-specific words and phrases in a text relevant to a *grade 5 topic or subject area*.

Note. The standards are from *Common Core State Standards for English Language Arts and Literacy in History/Social Studies, Science, and Technical Subjects* (pp. 13 and 14), by National Governors Association Center for Best Practices and Council of Chief State School Officers, 2010, Washington, DC: Authors.

of the text relate to each other and to the whole. We also describe teaching ideas and how they support the Standard. Because technology should be integrated into the curriculum along with the Standards, we embed examples of how to use 21st-century skills in meaningful ways.

Determining the Meanings of Unfamiliar Words and Phrases Through Context

The ability to infer word meaning in context is an important word-solving strategy that helps students become independent readers of more complex text. Research on use of context as a word learning strategy shows positive results and is recommended as part of vocabulary instruction (Blachowicz, Fisher, Ogle, & Watts-Taffe, 2010; Graves & Watts-Taffe, 2002).

There are eight different kinds of context clues (McLaughlin, 2010). Teaching our students how to use the various types of clues increases their ability to understand words in context. The context clues are definition, root words and affixes, example-illustration, grammar, comparison/contrast, logic, cause/effect, and mood and tone. The Context Clue Organizer (McLaughlin & Overturf, 2013) appears in Figure 10.1.

Figure 10.1 Example of a Context Clue Organizer

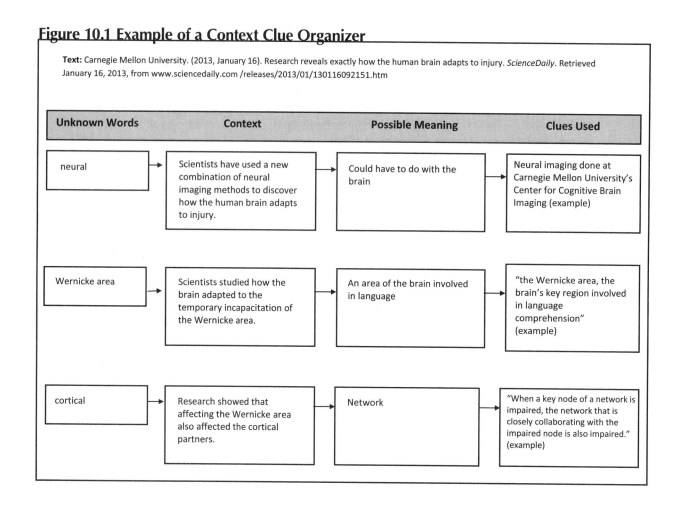

Text: Carnegie Mellon University. (2013, January 16). Research reveals exactly how the human brain adapts to injury. *ScienceDaily*. Retrieved January 16, 2013, from www.sciencedaily.com /releases/2013/01/130116092151.htm

Unknown Words	Context	Possible Meaning	Clues Used
neural	Scientists have used a new combination of neural imaging methods to discover how the human brain adapts to injury.	Could have to do with the brain	Neural imaging done at Carnegie Mellon University's Center for Cognitive Brain Imaging (example)
Wernicke area	Scientists studied how the brain adapted to the temporary incapacitation of the Wernicke area.	An area of the brain involved in language	"the Wernicke area, the brain's key region involved in language comprehension" (example)
cortical	Research showed that affecting the Wernicke area also affected the cortical partners.	Network	"When a key node of a network is impaired, the network that is closely collaborating with the impaired node is also impaired." (example)

Using Graphic Organizers to Teach Word Meanings

Thinking through the components of a graphic organizer helps students to learn disciplinary terminology. The Concept of Definition Map (Schwartz & Raphael, 1985) and the Semantic Question Map (McLaughlin, 2010) are examples of graphic organizers that students can use to increase their understanding of words.

When using the Concept of Definition Map (Schwartz & Raphael, 1985), students provide specific information about a term. Questions embedded in the organizer focus on the term, its meaning, its characteristics, examples, and a synonym. Figure 10.2 shows a Concept of Definition Map and summary about the branches of the United States government.

The Semantic Question Map (McLaughlin, 2010) includes three to six questions related to a given term. The questions, which are written specifically for each term, are used to spark student responses. As the students respond, we record their ideas under the related question. The completed Semantic Question Map can be used to summarize ideas about the term. A completed map about matter appears in Figure 10.3.

Using Greek and Latin Roots as Clues to Meaning

Many unfamiliar words can be determined through the use of context, but many cannot. In the latter case, readers often use morphemic analysis to decide the meanings of the parts of a word.

Figure 10.2 Example of a Concept of Definition Map

Source: Bens' Guide to U.S. Government for Kids: http://bensguide.gpo.gov/6-8/index.html

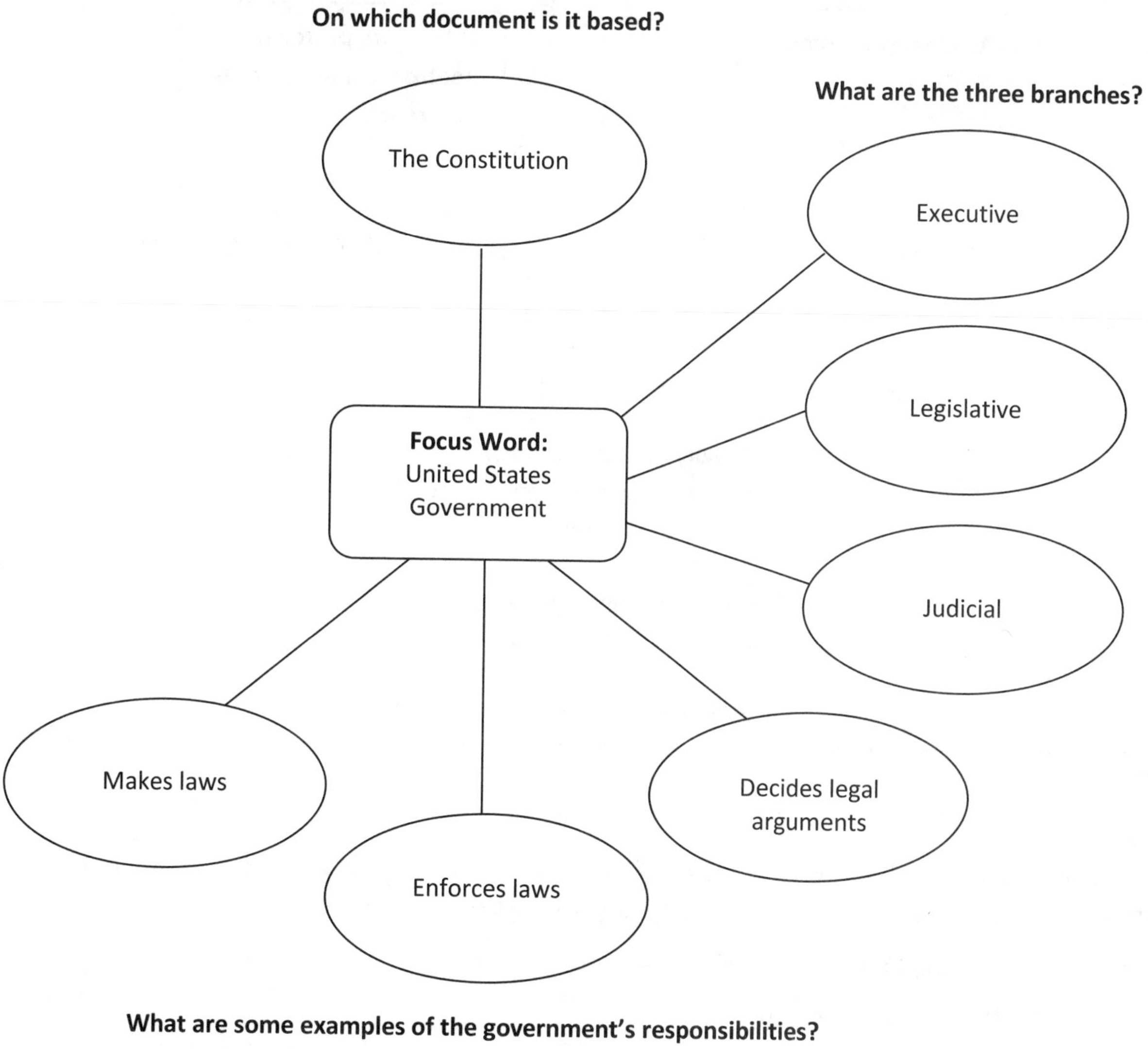

On which document is it based?

What are the three branches?

The Constitution

Executive

Legislative

Focus Word:
United States
Government

Judicial

Makes laws

Decides legal
arguments

Enforces laws

What are some examples of the government's responsibilities?

Summary: The United States government is based on The Constitution. It is comprised of three branches: executive, legislative, and judicial. Some of its responsibilities are to make laws, enforce laws, and decide legal arguments.

Learning the meanings of affixes and word roots helps students determine the meanings of unfamiliar words and better comprehend the text (Biemiller, 2004; Graves & Hammond, 1980; Nagy, 1988; Templeton et al., 2010). When older students engage in the study of morphology, they often more deeply understand concept words in the disciplines.

Goodwin, Lipsky, and Ahn (2012) conducted a meta-analysis of the results of 30 studies involving morphological instruction, which underscores the value of teaching morphemic analysis

Figure 10.3 Example of a Semantic Question Map

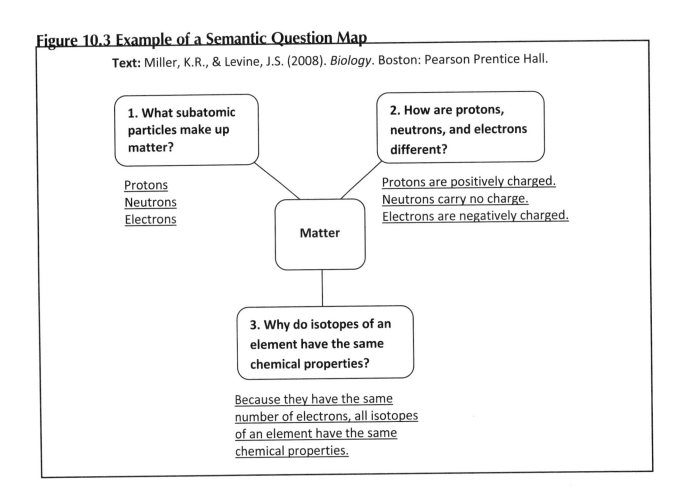

Text: Miller, K.R., & Levine, J.S. (2008). *Biology*. Boston: Pearson Prentice Hall.

1. What subatomic particles make up matter?

Protons
Neutrons
Electrons

2. How are protons, neutrons, and electrons different?

Protons are positively charged.
Neutrons carry no charge.
Electrons are negatively charged.

Matter

3. Why do isotopes of an element have the same chemical properties?

Because they have the same number of electrons, all isotopes of an element have the same chemical properties.

to students. Based on their results, these researchers suggest five morphological instructional strategies that should be included in vocabulary instruction for K–8 students:

1. Segment and build with morphemes

2. Use affix and root meanings

3. Use morphemes to improve spelling

4. Segment compound words and combine words to create common compound words

5. Identify cognates to support ELs

Templeton, Bear, Invernizzi, and Johnston (2010) describe a teaching idea entitled "Explore-a-Root" that can be employed in each discipline. Each student is assigned a Greek or Latin root that is associated with the subject area (e.g., *sal* meaning salt, *hydro* meaning water, *gon* meaning angle, *jud* meaning judge). Students can use online sources or comprehensive dictionaries to explore the meaning and origin of the root and to find as many words as possible that can be derived from it. Students can then create a display with sketches of different words derived from the root or develop an electronic resource of roots and their related information. An example of a root students may choose to explore is *sect*, which means to cut or separate. Related words include *dissect, bisect, trisect, transect, intersection, insect,* and *section.*

Using Reference Materials

To motivate students to explore terms in multiple references, invite them to engage in a Reference Scavenger Hunt (see Figure 10.4). Ask teams of students to create questions that pertain to the discipline and exchange them with another team. Each team finds the answers to questions it is researching and identifies the reference materials or websites they used to find the information.

Interpreting Figurative Language

Authors frequently use figurative language such as similes, metaphors, personification, hyperbole, onomatopoeia, alliteration, idioms, oxymorons, and euphemisms to make their writing more expressive. The ability to determine the meaning of both literal and nonliteral language is a key to comprehension and is an expectation of Language Standard 5 for vocabulary acquisition and use.

Figure 10.4 Reference Materials Scavenger Hunt

Question	Answer	Reference Information
1. Why did the Boston Massacre occur?	British soldiers and American patriots did not agree and clashed in the streets. The conflict led to the Boston Massacre.	www.bostonmassacre.net/academic/essay2.htm
2. Why is the Boston Massacre considered the first battle in the Revolutionary War?	American "patriots" threw sticks and snowballs at British soldiers in Boston. The British soldiers fired into the crowd and killed five Americans. The Royal Governor evacuated the British troops from Boston. This reinforced the American rebellion against the British.	www.ushistory.org/declaration/related/massacre.htm
3. What were the outcomes of the trial of the British soldiers?	The British soldiers were found guilty of manslaughter and had their thumbs branded with an "M" for "murder" as their punishment. The Boston Massacre was advertised as the reason for American revolution against the British.	www.history.com/this-day-in-history/the-boston-massacre
4.		

Students should have numerous experiences with analyzing the use of figurative language in text and writing their own examples of figurative language.

Before reading a text that includes several examples of figurative language, we can ask students to explore what they think a few of the examples might mean. Each student should have a sheet of paper folded in half lengthwise. The paper should be folded top to bottom and then top to bottom again so when it is opened, the paper has eight sections. After reviewing the text, students find several examples of figurative language from the text and write one of the examples at the top of each of the eight sections. Then, in each section, students sketch or add words that illustrate the example of figurative language. For example, Carl Sandburg's (1970) poem "Chicago" is filled with images such as "fierce as a dog with tongue lapping for action" and "City of the Big Shoulders." Students can share and discuss their interpretations with others in small groups.

Dalton and Grisham (2011) discuss using media as a form of creative expression as students learn about words and their relationships, and report that "recent research suggests that students may also benefit from creating multimedia representations of words" (p. 311). Students can use digital tools, such as Animoto (www.animoto.com) or GoAnimate for Schools (www.goanimate4schools.com) to create multimedia presentations to demonstrate their interpretations of figurative language in selected poems or short stories.

Connotation, Denotation, and Technical Meanings

Templeton et al. (2010) discussed a "Word Museum" project in which students researched a selected word and its origin to explore denotations and connotations. Students used reference websites such as the Online Etymology Dictionary (www.etymonline.com) or the Oxford English Dictionary (www.oed.com) to answer questions such as these: From which language did your word derive? What is the first recorded instance of its use in the English language? Write down some of the most interesting or surprising citations recorded over the years. Students were asked to find and copy an encyclopedia article that helped explain what their word means or meant in the past and why the information was important. Students also found a poem that helped explain what their word meant. They did an online search to find how many sites used the word and how it was used differently. Students collected evidence of their word in print, on TV, or in public sources to determine connotations and they interviewed people about their understanding of the meaning of the word. Students then created a multidimensional museum display of their word, their research, their sources, and a written narrative explaining their findings.

General Academic and Domain-Specific Words and Phrases

Nagy and Townsend (2012) discussed the importance of developing academic vocabulary as language acquisition in the disciplines. According to these researchers, "academic words are tools for communicating and thinking about disciplinary content" (p. 105). Learning the key vocabulary helps students learn content area concepts.

Semantic Feature Analysis (Johnson & Pearson, 1984) is a graphic organizer that allows students to show which of the categories being discussed possess which of the listed characteristics. Students can use this chart before reading to make predictions and after reading to revise their thinking as necessary, based on the information revealed in the text. Figure 10.5 is a Semantic Feature Analysis Chart that describes possible ways we can classify triangles by sides and angles.

Flocabulary (www.flocabulary .com) is a digital program that promotes key terms and vocabulary in different disciplines by using hip-hop as a learning tool. There is speculation (and emerging research) that hip-hop can help some students learn (Borgia & Owles, 2009; Morrell & Duncan-Andrade, 2002) and that the Flocabulary program can help students learn vocabulary (Farr et al., n.d.). Flocabulary (which has a small library of free materials but requires a small fee for the full library) includes songs, videos, and lyrics for various discipline-based concepts. Teacher materials come with the paid version. Teachers can use an electronic whiteboard to project the lyrics and video and to engage students in rapping about topics such as figurative language, the Industrial Revolution, atoms and elements, and linear equations.

Figure 10.5 Example of a Semantic Feature Analysis Chart

Topic: Triangles

	Angles		
Sides	Acute	Right	Obtuse
Scalene	+	+	+
Isosceles	+	+	+
Equilateral	+	−	−
Response Key:	+ = Yes	− = No	? = Don't know

21st-Century Skill Applications for Reading Anchor Standard 4

In this section, we share ideas to help students meet the Reading Standards through the use of 21st-century tools and skills. Although online tools can be used for a variety of purposes, we have chosen to highlight specific tools for use with each particular standard. As teachers, we should select tools we think will work best for our students, using the same tools in multiple ways when possible.

CCR Reading Standard 4 focuses on students interpreting words and phrases as they are used in a text, including determining technical, connotative, and figurative meanings. They also analyze how specific word choices shape meaning or tone. Using an online word mapping tool such as the Thinkmap Visual Thesaurus (www.visualthesaurus.com) or the Visuwords Online Graphical Dictionary (www.visuwords.com) can help students understand word relationships. These tools show the ways in which different uses of a word "map" to other words, showing visual representations of vocabulary networks. InstaGrok (www.instagrok.com) extends the word-mapping concept with related websites, video clips, and online quizzes about words and their connected concepts. InstaGrok is available as a stand-alone tool and is also an app on the Edmodo (www.edmodo.com) classroom social networking site used by many teachers.

To quickly retrieve the definition of a word or phrase, students can use cell phone technology and SMS Search feature on Google mobile (Spillane, 2012a). Students text "define" followed by a word to 466453. For example, a student enters the phrase "define connotation" as a text message. Google will return a text message with a definition of the word "connotation." Similarly, students can enter idioms such as "define wet blanket" and receive an immediate explanation of the idiom.

Wordle (www.wordle.net) is a popular word cloud tool that can be used to explore how word choices shape meaning or tone. Wordle creates colorful word clouds from text that is pasted into it. Words used the most in the text appear larger in size, and students can change the colors, shape, and appearance of the word cloud. Spillane (2012b) used Wordle as a tool to help students learn to analyze the author's word choice in a literary text. In Spillane's classroom, high school students analyzed the relationship among the most prominent words in the first chapter of F. Scott Fitzgerald's *The Great Gatsby* in order to begin a textual analysis of the novel. WordSift (www.wordsift.com) and Tagxedo (www.tagxedo.com) are also appropriate tools for making word clouds. Tagxedo will create shapes within a word cloud, and word clouds are easy to export for use in papers, blog posts, and other online venues.

Literary Graffiti at ReadWriteThink (described in Chapter 8, this volume) allows students the opportunity to "interpret words and phrases as they are used in a text" in a way that makes the student a generator of content rather than just a consumer. This tool pushes the idea beyond "I don't understand" to "here's what I think."

How Can We Integrate Other ELA Standards With Reading Anchor Standard 4?

Integrating Other ELA Standards With Reading Literature Standard 4

When planning to teach Common Core Reading Standard 4, we can integrate several other ELA standards to design rich instructional tasks. Examples of ideas to include when creating such tasks follow.

- Reading Literature Standard 1 focuses on reading a narrative text closely. *Example:* When students engage in close reading of a narrative text, ask questions about expressive words and phrases the author chose to use in the text.

- Writing Standard 3 describes expectations for narrative writing. *Example:* Encourage students to use expressive words, phrases, and sensory details and follow criteria found in Writing Standard 3 when writing narrative text.

- Speaking and Listening Standard 1 describes students engaging effectively in a range of collaborative discussions, with specific indicators to demonstrate how to participate in an effective academic conversation. *Example:* When reading stories, dramas, and poems, engage students in both whole-group and small-group collaborative conversations related to analyzing the expressive words and phrases that the author chose to include in the text.

Integrating Other ELA Standards With Reading Informational Text Standard 4

- Reading Informational Text Standard 1 refers to closely reading an informational text. *Example:* When students read an informational text closely, encourage them to discuss the general academic and domain-specific words that the author chose to use in the text.

- Writing Standard 1 focuses on the expectations for writing arguments with claims supported by reasons and evidence. *Example:* Teach students to use linking words such as *because* and *consequently* and to follow the criteria in Writing Standard 1 when writing arguments.

- Writing Standard 2 describes the expectations for informative/explanatory writing. *Example:* Ask students to use precise academic language and domain-specific vocabulary as well as the criteria found in Writing Standard 2 to inform about or explain a topic found in informational texts.

- Speaking and Listening Standard 5 describes the expectations for students to create multimedia presentations. *Example:* Encourage students to use domain-specific words and phrases when creating audio recordings or recounting experiences to clarify ideas, enhance facts or details, or develop main ideas.

THE COMMON CORE IN ACTION

In this section of Chapters 7–16, we examine one of the foundational ideas that underpin each of the College and Career Readiness Anchor Standards for Reading. For the fourth Standard, "Interpret words and phrases as they are used in a text, including determining technical, connotative, and figurative meanings, and analyze how specific word choices shape meaning or tone" (NGA Center & CCSSO, 2010, p. 10), we have elected to share more detailed information about determining the meaning of domain-specific words and phrases.

Common Core Literacy Task: Determining the Meanings of Domain-Specific Words and Phrases

Andre is a high school mathematics teacher. As part of a unit on chaos theory and fractals, Andre plans to have his geometry students read a *Discover Magazine* article he himself found quite fascinating. The article is entitled "Pollock's Fractals" (Ouellette, 2001) and can be found on *Discover Magazine's* website (discovermagazine.com/2001/nov/featpollock#.UL-g1IM80pk). In the article, Ouellette examines art historian Richard Taylor's finding that the drip paintings of abstract artist Jackson Pollock, which at first glance look entirely random, are actually founded in fractal geometry. In fact, using computer methods, Taylor has found that authentic Pollock paintings can be distinguished from imitators and forgers by analyzing their fractal dimension. Pollock paintings have fractal dimensions. The paintings of Pollock imitators do not.

Andre plans to use this article in a lesson to extend his students' understanding of fractal dimensions. Reading the article will also help his students apply vocabulary that is specific to mathematics and help them meet Standard 4 for grades 9–10 in the Reading Standards for Literacy in Science and Technical Subjects. Standard 4 is "Determine the meaning of symbols, key terms, and other domain-specific words and phrases as they are used in a specific scientific or technical context relevant to grades 9–10 texts and topics" (RST.9-10.4).

Andre has already introduced chaos theory and fractals and his students have experimented with fractal-generating software. To use the article in his class, Andre plans to do the following:

1. Distribute the article with specific mathematical words and phrases underlined or highlighted. For example, *chaos theory*, *fractal*, *magnifications*, *chaotic systems*, and *fractal dimensions* might be underlined.

2. Distribute and explicitly teach students how to use the Domain-Specific Word Connections graphic organizer (McLaughlin & Overturf, 2013), which appears in its preview form in Figure 10.6. Students think about the math vocabulary words and phrases, and they write them in the column that best describes what they know about the words at this point. If they know a definition, they should write it. If they can write a sentence using the word, they should do so. This serves as a preview of the concepts in the article.

3. Introduce Jackson Pollock's drip paintings by showing several examples online (especially *Number 14: Gray* at artsy.net/artwork/jackson-pollock-number-14-gray and *Blue Poles* at www.wikipaintings.org/en/jackson-pollock/blue-poles-number-11-1952-1). A number of

Figure 10.6 Example of a Domain-Specific Word Connections Organizer

Words From Text:

chaos theory   fractal   magnifications   chaotic systems   fractal dimensions

New to Me	Heard It Before	Know a Definition	Can Write a Sentence
	chaos theory		The "butterfly effect" illustrates the essential idea of chaos theory.
	fractal	a self-similar pattern that repeats	
	magnifications	enlargements	The magnifications of the cells were much easier to see.
chaotic systems			
fractal dimensions			

YouTube videos tell about Jackson Pollock's painting style (for example, see the four-minute video from the Museum of Modern Art at www.youtube.com/watch?v=EncR_T0faKM). Engage students in a brief discussion of Jackson Pollock's paintings and his style to help build their background knowledge about Pollock's paintings. (SL.9-10.1; SL.9-10.2)

4. Divide the students into pairs. Ask students to read the article together, stopping periodically to discuss the ideas presented. (SL.9-10.1)

5. As students work, ask them to complete the graphic organizer. (RST.9-10.4; L.9-10.6) Students list words in the boxes that most describe their competency with the word:

    a. New to me

    b. Heard it before

    c. Know a definition

    d. Can write a sentence

6. After students read the article and complete graphic organizers, teach a lesson on the concept of fractal dimensions found in Pollock's paintings. Refer to the article and the vocabulary in class discussion. (SL.9-10.1)

7. Ask students to revisit the graphic organizer, completing definition and sentence boxes to more clearly reflect their current understanding. (RST.9-10.4; L.9-10.6) The goal is for students to get to the point of being able to write an accurate sentence using each word.

8. Review graphic organizers as a quick formative assessment and reteach as needed.

9. Ask students to write a response to the article using the math terms correctly in their writing. (WHST.9-10.9)

Reading Standard 4 focuses on ensuring that students can determine unfamiliar words in a text and analyze the author's word choice. It requires students to ask and answer questions about unknown words in a text, identify and evaluate words and phrases that suggest feelings or appeal to the senses, determine the meanings of general academic and domain-specific words and phrases, and understand figurative language. When students know the word, they can more deeply comprehend a text.

References

ACT. (2006). *Reading between the lines: What the ACT reveals about college readiness in reading.* Iowa City, IA: Author. Retrieved August 22, 2012, from www.act.org/research/policymakers/pdf/reading_report.pdf

Anderson, R.C., & Nagy, W.E. (1991). Word meanings. In R. Barr, M.L. Kamil, P. Mosenthal, & P.D. Pearson (Eds.), *Handbook of reading research* (Vol. 2, pp. 690–724). New York: Longman.

Beck, I.L., McKeown, M.G., & Kucan, L. (2002). *Bringing words to life: Robust vocabulary instruction.* New York: Guilford.

Biemiller, A. (2004). Teaching vocabulary in the primary grades: Vocabulary instruction needed. In J.F. Baumann & E.J. Kame'enui (Eds.), *Vocabulary instruction: Research to practice* (pp. 28–40). New York: Guilford.

Blachowicz, C.L.Z., Fisher, P.J.L., Ogle, D., & Watts-Taffe, S. (2010). Vocabulary: Questions from the classroom. *Reading Research Quarterly, 41*(4), 524–539.

Borgia, L., & Owles, C. (2009). Using pop culture to aid literacy instruction. *Illinois Reading Council Journal, 38*(1), 47–51.

College Entrance Examination Board. (2002). *The AP vertical teams guide for English.* New York: Author.

Dalton, B., & Grisham, D.L. (2011). eVoc strategies: 10 ways to use technology to build vocabulary. *The Reading Teacher, 64*(5), 306–317.

Farr, R., Conner, J., Haydel, E., & Munroe, K. (n.d.). *The Word Up project: Multisensory instruction to build vocabulary proficiency and reading skills.* Retrieved October 8, 2012, from flocabulary.s3.amazonaws.com/pdfs/flat/the -word-up-project-research-base.pdf

Goodwin, A., Lipsky, M., & Ahn, S. (2012). Word detectives: Using units of meaning to support literacy. *The Reading Teacher, 65*(7), 461–470.

Graves, M.F., & Hammond, H.K. (1980). A validated procedure for teaching prefixes and its effect on students' ability to assign meanings to novel words. In M.L. Kamil & A.J. Moe (Eds.), *Perspectives on reading research and instruction* (pp. 184–188). Washington, DC: National Reading Conference.

Graves, M.F., & Watts-Taffe, S.M. (2002). The place of word consciousness in a research-based vocabulary program. In A.E. Farstrup & S.J. Samuels (Eds.), *What research has to say about reading instruction* (3rd ed., pp. 140–165). Newark, DE: International Reading Association.

Johnson, D.D., & Pearson, P.D. (1984). *Teaching reading vocabulary* (2nd ed.). New York: Holt, Rinehart and Winston.

McLaughlin, M. (2010). *Content area reading: Teaching and learning in an age of multiple literacies.* Boston: Allyn & Bacon.

McLaughlin, M., & Overturf, B.J. (2013). *The Common Core: Graphic organizers for teaching K–12 students to meet the Reading Standards.* Newark, DE: International Reading Association. Retrieved from www.reading.org/general/ Publications/Books/bk021.aspx

Morrell, E., & Duncan-Andrade, J.M.R. (2002). Promoting academic literacy with urban youth through engaging hip-hop culture. *English Journal, 91*(6), 88–92.

Nagy, W.E. (1988). *Teaching vocabulary to improve reading comprehension.* Washington, DC: ERIC Clearinghouse on Reading and Communication Skills; Urbana, IL: National Council of Teachers of English; Newark, DE: International Reading Association.

Nagy, W., & Townsend, D. (2012). Words as tools: Learning academic vocabulary as language acquisition. *Reading Research Quarterly, 47*(1), 91–108.

National Governors Association Center for Best Practices & Council of Chief State School Officers. (2010). *Common Core State Standards for English language arts and literacy in history/social studies, science, and technical subjects.* Washington, DC: Authors. Retrieved August 3, 2012, from www.corestandards.org/assets/CCSSI_ELA%20 Standards.pdf

Ouellette, J. (2001). Pollock's fractals. *Discover Magazine.* Retrieved December 5, 2012, from discovermagazine .com/2001/nov/featpollock#.UL-g1IM80pk

Schwartz, R.M., & Raphael, T.E. (1985). Concept of definition: A key to improving students' vocabulary. *The Reading Teacher, 39*(2), 198–205.

Spillane, L.A. (2012a). 13 ways of looking at the cell phone. Presented at the annual conference of the National Council of Teachers of English, Las Vegas, NV.

Spillane, L.A. (2012b). *Reading amplified: Digital tools that engage students in words, books, and ideas.* Portland, ME: Stenhouse.

Stahl, S.A., & Fairbanks, M.M. (1986). The effects of vocabulary instruction: A model-based meta-analysis. *Review of Educational Research, 56*(1), 72–110.

Templeton, S., Bear, D.R., Invernizzi, M., & Johnston, F. (2010). *Vocabulary their way: Word study with middle and secondary students.* Boston: Pearson.

Literature Cited

Fitzgerald, F.S. (2004). *The great Gatsby.* New York: Scribner.

Sandburg, C. (1970). Chicago. In *The complete poems of Carl Sandburg* (p. 3). Orlando, FL: Harcourt.

Sandburg, C. (1970). Fog. In *The complete poems of Carl Sandburg* (p. 33). Orlando, FL: Harcourt.

CHAPTER 11

CCR Reading Anchor Standard 5: Structure of Texts

Examining How It Is Built

| **College and Career Readiness Reading Anchor Standard 5** |
| Analyze the structure of texts, including how specific sentences, paragraphs, and larger portions of the text (e.g., a section, chapter, scene, or stanza) relate to each other and the whole. (NGA Center & CCSSO, 2010, p. 10) |

What Does CCR Reading Anchor Standard 5 Mean?

College and Career Readiness (CCR) Reading Anchor Standard 5 requires students to be able to read texts that are highly challenging in terms of their structure. According to ACT (2006), students should be able to "understand the function of a part of a passage when the function is subtle or complex" (p. 36). When reading, students need to be able to understand the structure of a particular complex text to comprehend it. Just as a building is constructed in a certain way, so is text. Students need to examine how it is built to understand a text, which is often written in intricate ways. Text structure is the organizational pattern that the author uses to arrange the content and the ideas.

When reading literature, students may be asked not only to read complex text but also to analyze how an author's choices about the structure of specific parts of a text contribute to its overall structure and meaning. Students need to be prepared not only to use text structure to comprehend but also to analyze the author's choices regarding structure. This includes how the author chose to order events within the text, connect ideas, and manipulate time to create effect.

For informational text, students are expected to analyze how an author's ideas are developed and refined by particular text structures. This is the focus for Reading Informational Text Standard 5.

Reading Anchor Standard 5 focuses on two reading skills:

1. The ability to analyze the structure of texts

2. The ability to relate sentences, paragraphs, and larger portions of text to one another and to the whole

Book Structures

Before we discuss text structures, we need to address the bigger picture: book structure. The structure of books typically includes their front and back covers, the title page, the table of contents, the way the text is organized, the glossary, and the index. Books are generally viewed as either literary or informational. These types of text have some characteristics in common and some that are unique.

Typically, literary books (stories) have information about the title and content on the front and back covers. Next a title page, featuring the title, the author's name, and often the publisher, is included at the beginning of the book. The copyright information usually appears on the back of the title page. Then, depending on the length of the work, there may or may not be a table of contents that chronicles chapter titles and the page numbers on which each chapter begins. Pictures and other visual supports may or may not be included in literary books. The structure seems to be tied to the nature of the text and, oftentimes, left to the publisher.

Textbooks and other factual works usually have information on the front and back covers. They also have a title page. The copyright information usually appears on the back of the title page. This type of book usually includes a table of contents, or some sort of content listing, that chronicles chapter titles and the page numbers on which the chapters begin. If we are examining textbooks, pictures and other visual supports are usually included. If we are exploring a different type of informational text, pictures and other visuals may or may not be included. These types of books are typically organized by chapter number. Headings and subheadings are used to arrange the information within the chapters. Glossaries, or minidictionaries, are often included toward the end of textbooks. Textbooks and other informational works also often have an index, which is arranged alphabetically to help readers quickly locate a topic and the page(s) on which it appears. For example, *The Ancient Romans* by Allison Lassieur (2004) has information on both covers, a table of contents, picture supports, chapter titles, subheadings, a glossary, and an index. In addition, this volume has a biographical dictionary, which provides information about 10 leaders of ancient Rome, and a section entitled "To Find Out More" (p. 100) that lists resources, including books, videos, and websites.

Text Structures

Although text structures are the focus of Common Core Standards in grades 3, 4, and 5, students in grades 6–12 need to be able to recognize and use them. Consequently, we begin this section with a focus on traditional text structures and then explore how to analyze not only the structures, but also their component parts.

When discussing particular text structures, we generally begin by focusing on literary (story-based) text and informational (fact-based) text. When we examine these types of structure, we focus on how the text is organized. As Armbruster (2004) notes, the organization of the text is the arrangement of ideas and the relationships among them. Understanding and using text organization supports comprehension (Akhondi, Malayeri, & Samad, 2011). Researchers note that students who know about text structure comprehend better (Duke & Pearson, 2002).

Goldman and Rakestraw (2000) further note that experience in reading multiple genres provides students with knowledge of numerous text structures and improves their text-driven processing. Gambrell (2001) also observes that transacting with a wide variety of genres, including biography, historical fiction, legends, poetry, mythology, folk tales, and brochures, increases students' reading performance.

In grades 6–8, the student expectations of Reading Standard 5 for Literature include analyzing how components such as sentences, chapters, scenes, or stanzas fit into the overall structure of text and contribute to the development of the theme, setting, or plot. Other expectations include determining how a drama's or poem's form or structure contributes to its meaning and comparing and contrasting the structure of two or more texts and analyzing how structure influences meaning and style.

For grade 9–10 students, expectations include analyzing authors' choices concerning how to structure a text, order events within it (e.g., parallel plots), and manipulate time (e.g., pacing, flashbacks) to create such effects as mystery, tension, or surprise. Students in grades 11–12 are also expected to analyze how an author's choices concerning how to structure specific parts of a text (e.g., the choice of where to begin or end a story, the choice to provide a comedic or tragic resolution) contribute to its overall structure and meaning as well as its aesthetic impact.

In Reading Standard 5 for Informational Text, sixth-grade students are expected to analyze how particular sentences, paragraphs, chapters, or sections fit into the overall structure of texts and contribute to the development of the ideas. Seventh graders analyze the structure authors use to organize text, including how the major sections contribute to the whole and to the development of the ideas. Eighth graders analyze in detail the structure of a specific paragraph in a text, including the role of particular sentences in developing and refining a key concept.

In grades 9–10, expectations include analyzing in detail how authors' ideas or claims are developed and refined by particular sentences, paragraphs, or larger portions of a text (e.g., a section or chapter), and students in grades 11–12 are expected to analyze and evaluate the effectiveness of the structure authors use in their exposition or argument, including whether the structure makes points clear, convincing, and engaging.

Narrative Text Structure. Narrative text structure is comprised of the five narrative elements: characters, setting, problem, attempts to resolve the problem, and resolution. Instruction in story structure has shown positive results in comprehension for a wide range of students (Duke & Pearson, 2002). Teaching ideas such as Retellings and Narrative Text Maps help students to learn this text structure. (For an example of the Sketch and Label Retelling, see Chapter 8, Figure 8.1. For an example of the Narrative Text Map, see Chapter 7, Figure 7.1.)

Informational Text Structure. Description, sequence (chronology), comparison/contrast, cause/ effect, and problem/solution are the five informational text structures (McLaughlin, 2010). A brief description of each and related signal words follow.

1. *Description*—This pattern focuses on characteristics, facts, and features related to a topic, person, event, or object. Signal words for the description text pattern include *above, below, behind, down, across,* and *under.* For an example of this structure, see the Concept of Definition Map and summary (Schwartz & Raphael, 1985) in Chapter 10.

2. *Sequence (chronology)*—This pattern relates steps in a process or the order in which things happened. Signal words for the sequence text pattern include *first, second, third, then, next, during,* and *finally.* An example of a completed Sequence Chain about the scientific method, which illustrates the sequence text structure, is featured in Figure 11.1.

3. *Comparison/contrast*—This pattern illuminates similarities (comparisons) and differences (contrasts). Signal words and phrases for comparison/contrast text include *although, but, compared with, however, on the one hand, on the other hand, similarly,* and *different from.* Figure 11.2 features a Venn Diagram about planets and stars. The similarities appear in the overlapping parts of the circle; the differences appear in the outer portions of each circle.

4. *Cause/effect*—This pattern shows how events or ideas (effects) come to be because of certain other ideas, acts, or events (causes). Signal words and phrases for cause/effect text

Figure 11.1 Example of a Sequence Chain

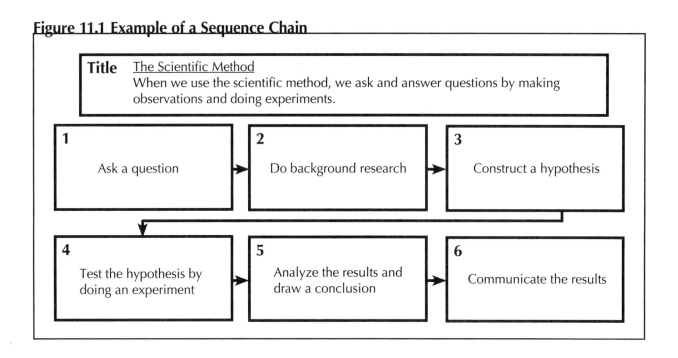

| **Title** | The Scientific Method |
| When we use the scientific method, we ask and answer questions by making observations and doing experiments. |

1 Ask a question → **2** Do background research → **3** Construct a hypothesis

4 Test the hypothesis by doing an experiment → **5** Analyze the results and draw a conclusion → **6** Communicate the results

Figure 11.2 Example of a Venn Diagram (Comparison/Contrast)

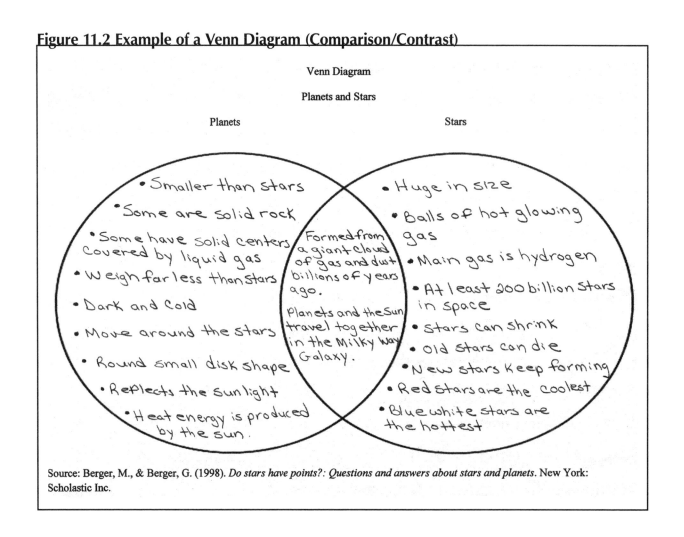

Venn Diagram

Planets and Stars

Planets

Stars

- Smaller than stars
- Some are solid rock
- Some have solid centers covered by liquid gas
- Weigh far less than stars
- Dark and cold
- Move around the stars
- Round small disk shape
- Reflects the sunlight
- Heat energy is produced by the sun.

Formed from a giant cloud of gas and dust billions of years ago.
Planets and the Sun travel together in the Milky Way Galaxy.

- Huge in size
- Balls of hot glowing gas
- Main gas is hydrogen
- At least 200 billion stars in space
- Stars can shrink
- Old stars can die
- New stars keep forming
- Red stars are the coolest
- Blue white stars are the hottest

Source: Berger, M., & Berger, G. (1998). *Do stars have points?: Questions and answers about stars and planets.* New York: Scholastic Inc.

include *because, as a result, since, for this reason, in order to, if...then,* and *therefore.* Figure 11.3 is an Informational Text Cause/Effect Organizer (McLaughlin & Overturf, 2013) about the Cherokee Trail of Tears.

5. *Problem/solution*—This pattern showcases a difficulty (problem) and provides an example of how it can be resolved (solution). Signal words and phrases for the problem/solution text pattern include *because, since, therefore, consequently, as a result, cause, solve,* and *resolve.* This structure is featured in Figure 11.4, an Informational Text Problem/Solution Organizer (McLaughlin & Overturf, 2013) about transportation in the United States in the 1860s.

Researchers suggest that we should explicitly teach text structures to our students (Pressley, 2002). Research reports that if students know the text patterns and understand how to generate questions, they

Figure 11.3 Example of an Informational Text Cause/Effect Organizer

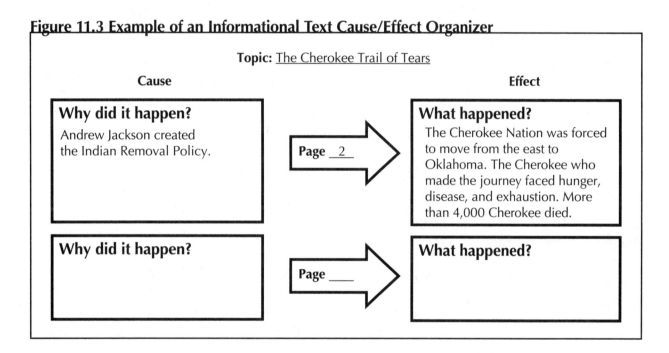

Figure 11.4 Example of an Informational Text Problem/Solution Organizer

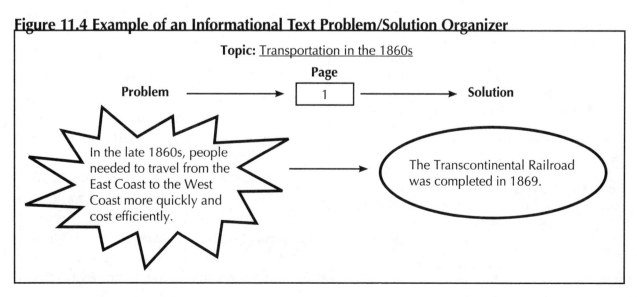

will improve their comprehension of text (Gambrell, 2001). Moss (2004) suggests that we should teach each text structure individually, encouraging students to master one structure before learning another.

Recognizing and using text structures will help students understand the type of information included in the text and predict the types of questions that may be raised about it. For example, if students are reading a biography and realize that the text pattern is sequential (chronological), their questions may focus on what happened when. When reading a section of text in which the pattern is comparison/contrast, students' questions may focus on similarities and differences.

How Do the Common Core Standards Build to CCR Reading Anchor Standard 5?

The Common Core Standards in grades 6–12 build toward College and Career Readiness Anchor Standard 5 by addressing skills in four substrands of reading. The Reading Standard 4 substrands included in grades 6–12 are as follows:

- Reading Standards for Literature (English Language Arts)

- Reading Standards for Informational Text (English Language Arts)

- Reading Standards for Literacy in History/Social Studies

- Reading Standards for Literacy in Science and Technical Subjects

For Reading Standard 5 in Literature, students in grade 6 are expected to analyze how a particular sentence, chapter, scene, or stanza fits into the overall structure of the text and contributes to the development of the theme, setting, or plot. Seventh graders analyze how a drama's or poem's form or structure contributes to the meaning. Eighth graders compare and contrast the structure of two or more texts and analyze how the structure of each contributes to its meaning and style. Students in grades 9–10 learn to analyze how an author's choices concerning how to structure a text, order events within it, and manipulate time to create different effects. Students in grades 11–12 analyze how an author's choices about how to structure specific parts of a text contribute to its overall structure, meaning, and aesthetic impact. The expectations of Reading Standard 5 for Literature appear in Table 11.1.

For Reading Informational Text Standard 5, students in grade 6 will analyze how a particular sentence, paragraph, chapter, or section fits into the overall structure of the text and contributes to the development of the ideas in the text. Seventh graders analyze the structure an author

Table 11.1 Common Core State Standard 5 for Reading Literature in Grades 6–12

Grade	Standard
6	Analyze how a particular sentence, chapter, scene, or stanza fits into the overall structure of a text and contributes to the development of the theme, setting, or plot.
7	Analyze how a drama's or poem's form or structure (e.g., soliloquy, sonnet) contributes to its meaning.
8	Compare and contrast the structure of two or more texts and analyze how the differing structure of each text contributes to its meaning and style.
9–10	Analyze how an author's choices concerning how to structure a text, order events within it (e.g., parallel plots), and manipulate time (e.g., pacing, flashbacks) create such effects as mystery, tension, or surprise.
11–12	Analyze how an author's choices concerning how to structure specific parts of the text (e.g., the choice of where to begin or end a story, the choice to provide a comedic or tragic resolution) contribute to its overall structure and meaning as well as its aesthetic impact.

Note. The standards are from *Common Core State Standards for English Language Arts and Literacy in History/Social Studies, Science, and Technical Subjects* (pp. 36 and 38), by National Governors Association Center for Best Practices and Council of Chief State School Officers, 2010, Washington, DC: Authors.

uses to organize a text, while eighth graders analyze in detail the structure of the specific paragraphs in a text, including the role of particular sentences in developing and refining a key concept. In grades 9–10, students analyze in detail how an author's ideas or claims are developed and refined by particular sentences, paragraphs, or larger sections of the text. In grades 11–12, students analyze and evaluate the effectiveness of the structure an author uses in his or her exposition or arguments, including whether the structure makes points clear, convincing, and engaging. Reading Standard 5 for Informational Text is shown in Table 11.2.

Reading Standard 5 for Literacy in History/Social Studies also focuses on structure. In grades 6–8, students learn to describe how a text presents information, such as sequentially, comparatively, and causally. In grades 9–10, students analyze how a text uses structure to emphasize key points or advance an explanation or analysis. In grades 11–12, students concentrate on analyzing in detail how complex primary sources are structured. The expectations of Reading Standard 5 for Literacy in History/ Social Studies are delineated in Table 11.3.

As in the former substrands, Reading Standard 5 for Literacy in Science and Technical Subjects focuses on analysis of structure. Students in grades 6–8 analyze the structure an author uses to organize the text, while students in grades 9–10 analyze the structure of relationships among concepts in a text, including relationships among key science terms. In grades 11–12, students analyze how the text structures information or ideas into categories or hierarchies, demonstrating understanding of the information or ideas. The expectations of Reading Standard 5 for Literacy in Science and Technical Subjects are outlined in Table 11.4.

Table 11.2 Common Core State Standard 5 for Reading Informational Text in Grades 6–12

Grade	Standard
6	Analyze how a particular sentence, paragraph, chapter, or section fits into the overall structure of a text and contributes to the development of the ideas.
7	Analyze the structure an author uses to organize a text, including how the major sections contribute to the whole and to the development of the ideas.
8	Analyze in detail the structure of a specific paragraph in a text, including the role of particular sentences and developing and refining a key concept.
9–10	Analyze in detail how an author's ideas or claims are developed and refined by particular sentences, paragraphs, or larger portions of a text (e.g., a section or chapter).
11–12	Analyze and evaluate the effectiveness of the structure an author uses in his or her exposition or argument, including whether the structure makes points clear, convincing, and engaging.

Note. The standards are from *Common Core State Standards for English Language Arts and Literacy in History/Social Studies, Science, and Technical Subjects* (pp. 39 and 40), by National Governors Association Center for Best Practices and Council of Chief State School Officers, 2010, Washington, DC: Authors.

Table 11.3 Common Core Reading Standard 5 for Literacy in History/Social Studies in Grades 6–12

Grade	Standard
6–8	Describe how a text presents information (e.g., sequentially, comparatively, causally).
9–10	Analyze how a text uses structure to emphasize key points or advance an explanation or analysis.
11–12	Analyze in detail how a complex primary source is structured, including how key sentences, paragraphs, and larger portions of the text contribute to the whole.

Note. The standards are from *Common Core State Standards for English Language Arts and Literacy in History/Social Studies, Science, and Technical Subjects* (p. 61), by National Governors Association Center for Best Practices and Council of Chief State School Officers, 2010, Washington, DC: Authors.

Table 11.4 Common Core Reading Standard 5 for Literacy in Science and Technical Subjects in Grades 6–12

Grade	Standard
6–8	Analyze the structure an author uses to organize a text, including how the major sections contribute to the whole and to an understanding of the topic.
9–10	Analyze the structure of the relationships among concepts in a text, including relationships among key terms (e.g., *force, friction, reaction force, energy*).
11–12	Analyze how the text structures information or ideas into categories or hierarchies, demonstrating understanding of the information or ideas.

Note. The standards are from *Common Core State Standards for English Language Arts and Literacy in History/Social Studies, Science, and Technical Subjects* (p. 62), by National Governors Association Center for Best Practices and Council of Chief State School Officers, 2010, Washington, DC: Authors.

What Literacy Skills and Strategies Support Reading Anchor Standard 5?

When we review the literacy skills and strategies in the Common Core State Standards, we can readily determine that gaps exist. As educators, we may find ourselves asking whether we should be teaching a particular concept because it does not appear in the CCSS. However, it is important to note that the Standards are not the determining factor. If the skill or strategy is included in our curriculums, we should teach it. For example, students in grades K–3 are expected to be able to ask and answer questions. Similarly, students in grades 4 and 5 are expected to know and use text structures, such as comparison/contrast and problem/solution. The grade 6–12 CCSS do not address either of these topics, but the students still need to know what they are and how to use them to successfully meet the Standards. That is why we noted in Chapter 1 the importance of our reading the CCSS both vertically (our grade levels) and horizontally (what students are expected to know before they reach our grade levels).

Many of the essential skills that grade 6–12 students need to know, including asking and answering questions and using text structure, are delineated in the grade K–5 Standards. For example, Common Core Reading Standard 1, for both Literature and Informational Text, is associated with Reading Standard 10, which focuses on the expectation that students will read complex text. For students to be able to read, discuss, and write about complex text, they must be able to use the supporting skills and strategies that were introduced in earlier grades. Details of Reading Standard 5, the focus of this chapter, are featured in Table 11.5 for Literature (English Language Arts) and Table 11.6 for Informational Text (ELA, Reading in History/Social Studies, and Reading in Science and Technical Subjects).

How Can We Teach Reading Anchor Standard 5 So Our Students Achieve?

In this section, we discuss the CCSS expectations for students. For example, the fifth College and Career Readiness Standard for Reading requires that students be able to analyze the structure of

Table 11.5 K–5 Reading Standard 5: Supporting Skills and Strategies for Literature in Grades 6–12

Grade	Skills and Strategies
K	Recognize common types of texts (e.g., storybooks, poems).
1	Explain major differences between books that tell stories and books that give information, drawing on a wide reading of a range of text types.
2	Describe the overall structure of a story, including describing how the beginning introduces the story and the ending concludes the action.
3	Refer to parts of stories, dramas, and poems when writing or speaking about a text, using terms such as *chapter*, *scene*, and *stanza*; describe how each successive part builds on earlier sections.
4	Explain major differences between poems, drama, and prose, and refer to the structural elements of poems (e.g., verse, rhythm, meter) and drama (e.g., casts of characters, settings, descriptions, dialogue, stage directions) when writing or speaking about a text.
5	Explain how a series of chapters, scenes, or stanzas fits together to provide the overall structure of a particular story, drama, or poem.

Note. The skills and strategies are from *Common Core State Standards for English Language Arts and Literacy in History/Social Studies, Science, and Technical Subjects* (pp. 11 and 12), by National Governors Association Center for Best Practices and Council of Chief State School Officers, 2010, Washington, DC: Authors.

Table 11.6 K–5 Reading Standard 5: Supporting Skills and Strategies for Informational Text in Grades 6–12

Grade	Skills and Strategies
K	Identify the front cover, back cover, and title page of a book.
1	Know and use various text features (e.g., headings, tables of contents, glossaries, electronic menus, icons) to locate key facts or information in a text.
2	Know and use various text features (e.g., captions, bold print, subheadings, glossaries, indexes, electronic menus, icons) to locate key facts or information in a text efficiently.
3	Use text features and search tools (e.g., key words, sidebars, hyperlinks) to locate information relevant to a given topic efficiently.
4	Describe the overall structure (e.g., chronology, comparison, cause/effect, problem/solution) of events, ideas, concepts, or information in a text or part of a text.
5	Compare and contrast the overall structure (e.g., chronology, comparison, cause/effect, problem/solution) of events, ideas, concepts, or information in two or more texts.

Note. The skills and strategies are from *Common Core State Standards for English Language Arts and Literacy in History/Social Studies, Science, and Technical Subjects* (pp. 13 and 14), by National Governors Association Center for Best Practices and Council of Chief State School Officers, 2010, Washington, DC: Authors.

texts, including how specific sentences, paragraphs, and larger portions of the text (e.g., a section, chapter, scene, or stanza) relate to each other and the whole. We also describe teaching ideas and how they support the Standard. Because technology should be integrated into the curriculum along with the Standards, we embed examples of how to use 21st-century skills in meaningful ways.

Understanding text structure contributes to comprehension. As Duke and Pearson (2002) report, "Research suggests that almost any approach to teaching the structure of informational text improves both comprehension and recall of key text information" (p. 217). Students in earlier grades learn to recognize common types of texts and describe the structure of a story. Students are expected to know about the structures of stories, dramas, and poems. A strong sense of story structure and how to use the appropriate terminology when discussing or writing about literary texts are focuses of Reading Standard 5 for Reading Literature before grade 6.

In Reading Standard 5 for Informational Text in earlier grades, students learn to use various text features and search tools to locate key facts or information in a text efficiently. They also learn informational text structures, such as description, sequence (chronology), comparison/contrast, cause/effect, problem/solution, and of events, ideas, concepts, or information in texts. In the grade 6–12 standards, the expectation is that students will think more deeply to analyze how text structures and their component parts contribute to meaning, style, and aesthetic impact.

Of course, before our students begin addressing these expectations, we first need to ensure that they know how to analyze text. McLaughlin and Fisher (2012) suggest that we begin by examining the definition of the term:

> Most definitions of *analyze* focus on examining the structure of information in detail, particularly for purposes of explanation. *Analyzing* requires a response that demonstrates an ability to see patterns and to classify information into component parts. As teachers, we may also be familiar with *analyze* as a level in Bloom's taxonomy, in which it is defined as taking something learned apart for purposes of thinking about the parts and how they fit together. (p. 12)

They further note that students' abilities to know and use text structures and to generate and respond to questions help them to think about patterns and classify information into component parts. Ciardiello (1998) suggests levels for teaching students about questioning. He focuses on teaching students to generate and respond to questions at four levels: memory, convergent, divergent, and evaluative. He also describes the thinking operations each level requires and provides signal words to help structure questions at each level. (For an overview of Ciardiello's levels of questioning, see Chapter 5, Table 5.2.) "Asking and answering" questions is a standard for reading informational text in grades K–3, but beyond those levels, it is assumed that our students already possess these skills.

Analyzing Literary Text Structures

The eighth-grade student expectation for Reading Standard 5 is "to compare and contrast the structure of two or more texts and analyze how structure contributes to its meaning and style." We know that characters, setting, attempts to resolve a problem, and resolution are the characteristics of narrative text. Prior to summarizing and analyzing the stories, students can engage in retellings of each text. Then they can complete the summaries and analysis. The Comparison/Contrast Story Map (McLaughlin & Overturf, 2013) in Chapter 9, Figure 9.3, focuses on two short stories: "The Lottery" and "The Most Dangerous Game." The organizer contains a brief summary of each story as well as an analysis of the content. The content is discussed in terms of three narrative elements: characters, settings, and themes. Connections are also made to *The Hunger Games*, a book with similar themes but a different writing style.

Analyzing Informational Text Structures

We can also analyze informational text using its structure. In Reading Standard 5 for Informational Text, students are expected to analyze how particular sentences, paragraphs, chapters, or sections fit into the overall structure of a text and contribute to the development of the ideas. Disciplinary texts are classic examples for this expectation. For example, Figure 11.6 shows an Informational Text Chronological Structure Organizer (McLaughlin & Overturf, 2013) that is focused on the Civil War. The text title is "The Civil War," and the sectional subheadings are "The Causes of the War," "The Leaders and the Battles," "General Lee Surrenders," and "Outcomes of the War." When perusing the text, students determined that the structure was chronological. It began with the start of the Civil War and ended with the aftereffects of the war. There are also two areas of the organizer in which to record sectional structures. In one, students noticed that a cause/effect pattern was evident in the section of the text that discussed causes of the war. They also noted a problem/solution pattern in the text, because slavery was a major problem and the passing of the 13th Amendment and the subsequent end of the war might be viewed as solutions.

When analyzing the chapter about the Civil War, students studied its structure and discovered that the author not only shared information chronologically, but also used other text structures. Students contributed additional ideas to their analysis when they noted the use of both cause/effect and problem/solution structures. When discussing the structures, students focused on how they used what they knew about text structures to determine how the ideas in the chapter evolved.

Figure 11.6 Example of Informational Text Chronological Structure Organizer

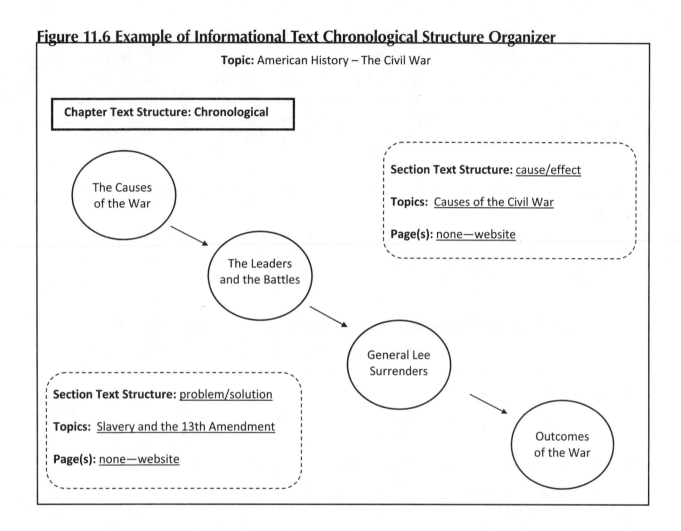

Topic: American History – The Civil War

Chapter Text Structure: Chronological

The Causes of the War

The Leaders and the Battles

General Lee Surrenders

Outcomes of the War

Section Text Structure: <u>cause/effect</u>

Topics: <u>Causes of the Civil War</u>

Page(s): <u>none—website</u>

Section Text Structure: <u>problem/solution</u>

Topics: <u>Slavery and the 13th Amendment</u>

Page(s): <u>none—website</u>

21st-Century Skill Applications for Reading Anchor Standard 5

In this section, we share ideas to help students meet the Reading Standards through the use of 21st-century tools and skills. Although online tools can be used for a variety of purposes, we have chosen to highlight specific tools for use with each particular standard. As teachers, we should select tools we think will work best for our students, using the same tools in multiple ways when possible.

CCR Reading Standard 5 focuses on analyzing the structure of texts, including how specific sentences, paragraphs, and larger portions of the text (e.g., a section, chapter, scene, or stanza) relate to each other and the whole. One way to visually map the ways in which text is structured is to use Popplet (www.popplet.com), a mind-mapping productivity tool that can show how ideas or texts are organized. Popplet is available both as a Web-based tool and a mobile app, and it can be used to organize pictures, video, text, and images found on the Web. Students can organize information into different structures such as cause/effect, sequence, and problem/solution. Students can also demonstrate how ideas found in the text relate to each other. Popplet can be used to organize information for written work and presentations, making it a versatile thinking tool.

Prezi (www.prezi.com) is another tool that can be used to analyze how sections, chapters, scenes, or stanzas are related to each other and the whole. Prezi is a cloud-based presentation and storytelling tool for exploring and sharing ideas on a virtual canvas. A three-dimensional interface helps users to zoom in and out of the presentation. Users often say that the blank canvas causes one to think about the overall structure of the presentation, and the zooming feature makes one think about the hierarchy of ideas. Students can use the blank canvas to create a presentation depicting how an entire text is organized, then zoom in and out of the presentation to discuss particular sections, chapters, scenes, or stanzas and how they relate to the text as a whole. Students can also create pathways to demonstrate how different parts relate to each other.

How Can We Integrate Other ELA Standards With Reading Anchor Standard 5?

When planning to teach College and Career Readiness Reading Anchor Standard 5, we can integrate several other ELA standards to design rich instructional tasks. Examples of ideas to include when creating rich instructional tasks follow.

Integrating Other ELA Standards With Reading Literature Standard 5

- Reading Literature Standard 1 focuses on reading a narrative text closely. *Example:* When students read a narrative text closely, ask students to analyze the structure and form of the text as a clue to deeper meaning.

- Reading Literature Standard 2 focuses on the ability to determine and analyze theme. *Example:* Ask students to use the structure and form of the text to help determine and analyze theme.

- Reading Literature Standard 9 focuses on comparing and contrasting aspects of literary text. *Example:* Encourage students to compare and contrast structure, form, and genre of a literary text.

- Writing Standard 3 describes expectations for students to write narrative to develop real or imagined experiences or events using effective technique, relevant descriptive details, and well-structured event sequences. *Example:* Teach students to use effective form and structure in their writing.

- Writing Standard 9 addresses the expectation that students will be able to draw evidence from texts to support analysis, reflection, and research. *Example*: Ask students to draw evidence from a text to analyze the structure and form.

- Speaking and Listening Standard 2 focuses on students being able to interpret and integrate multiple sources of information presented in diverse formats. *Example:* Encourage students to analyze the structure of multimedia presentations.

Integrating Other ELA Standards With Reading Informational Text Standard 5

- Reading Informational Text Standard 1 refers to closely reading an informational text. *Example:* When reading an informational text closely, ask students to cite textual evidence of the ways in which the structure of the text contributes to the development of ideas in the text.

- Reading Informational Text Standard 2 focuses on the ability to determine central ideas of an informational text and provide an objective summary of the text. *Example:* Ask students to analyze how the structure of the text contributes to the author's explanation of ideas.

- Reading Informational Text Standard 3 focuses on analyzing the connections and relationships among people, events, ideas, or pieces of information in a text. *Example:* Encourage students to analyze various text structures to better understand events or ideas in a text.

- Reading Informational Text Standard 8 addresses reading arguments, including claims, reasons, and evidence to support various points in the text. *Example:* When reading an informational text, teach students to discuss how the author's choice of structure contributes to the way the author supports an argument.

- Writing Standard 2 lays out the expectations for informative/explanatory writing. *Example:* Teach students to write an informative/explanatory essay to analyze the structure and format of informational texts.

- Writing Standard 9 addresses the expectation that students will be able to draw evidence from texts to support analysis, reflection, and research. *Example:* Ask students to write responses that emphasize text structure and format.

- Speaking and Listening Standard 1 describes the expectation that students will engage effectively in a range of collaborative discussions, with specific indicators to demonstrate how to participate in an effective academic conversation. *Example:* Engage students in collaborative academic conversations that include analysis of how authors use text structure to develop ideas.

THE COMMON CORE IN ACTION

In this section, we examine one of the foundational ideas that underpins each of the Common Core's Anchor Standards for Reading. For the fifth standard, "Analyze the structure of texts, including how specific sentences, paragraphs, and larger portions of the text (e.g., a section, chapter, scene, or stanza) relate to each other and the whole" (NGA Center & CCSSO, 2010, p. 10), we have elected to share more detailed information about analyzing informational text structures, which is integral to students' achievement of the Standards for grades 6–12.

Common Core Literacy Task: Informational Text Structures

Understanding and being able to analyze the five informational text structures (description, sequence [chronology], comparison/contrast, cause/effect, and problem/solution) benefit students in multiple ways. We know that research supports the teaching of the text structures and that using such structures supports students' comprehension of text. It is also important to note that each structure should be taught separately through explicit instruction, which includes scaffolding, or the gradual release of responsibility to students. Next, we describe how Alison, a tenth-grade science teacher, explicitly teaches her students about informational text structures. Alison will integrate multiple standards but particularly focus on Standard 5 in the grade 9–10 Reading Standards for Literacy in Science and Technical Subjects 6–12: "Analyze the structure of the relationships among concepts in a text, including relationships among key terms."

Alison is planning a series of lessons that focus on Reading Standard 5 for grades 9–10. Although her primary emphasis is teaching informational text structures, she also wants to ensure that she develops rich tasks that integrate a number of other Common Core State Standards. To prepare to teach her students, Alison knows she will need to have not only multiple examples of interesting text written in each structure, but also graphic organizers or other ideas ready to teach the structures. She also understands that writing and technology will be integrated into her plans.

After determining which text examples she will use for which text structure and how she will use the text structure–based graphic organizers, Alison focuses on how she will explicitly teach the organizational structures. She decides to focus on the five Guided Comprehension steps of explicit instruction: explain, demonstrate, guide, practice, and reflect (McLaughlin & Allen, 2009). Alison plans to teach the problem/solution text structure in this way:

1. *Explain*—Alison will begin by explaining that in the problem/solution text structure, we first need to identify the problem and then ask ourselves how it was resolved. The answer to the question is the solution to the problem. She will remind students about math problems for which they have figured out solutions and explain how, throughout history, society has encountered many problems for which solutions were created. For example, when the shortage of oil caused the price of gasoline to rise, car companies began focusing on developing electric cars, which are much cheaper to use. Students will listen and be prepared to engage in discussion with a partner. (SL.9-10.1)

2. *Demonstrate*—Alison will distribute and explicitly teach the graphic organizer for this text structure. She will introduce the text (an article on climate change) and demonstrate as she reads sections of the article to the class. After reading the first segment, she will think aloud about when climate change did not seem to be an issue and wonder how our current problems came to be. She will invite the students to discuss this. Then, Alison will read more about climate change in the 21st century and pose similar questions. She will note the structure-associated signal words in each segment and ask students to begin thinking about some solutions to the problem of climate change. Students will work with partners to discuss and summarize the information. (SL.9-10.2)

3. *Guide*—Alison will explain that she will read another segment and ask the students to work in partners to determine the solution. They will then verify the solution in the text. Alison will encourage the students to record their thoughts on the Informational Text Problem/Solution Organizer (McLaughlin & Overturf, 2013). Next, she will invite the partners to read a short segment, discuss it, and identify the problem and solution. Again, they will record their thinking on the graphic organizer. She will also ask them to discuss the signal words used in that segment. She will guide the students through this process, offering support as needed. Finally, she will guide the partners to brainstorm problems and select one to write a paragraph about, using the problem/solution text structure. Alison will guide students through this process. (SL.9-10.1; WHST.9-10.2; WHST.9-10.4)

4. *Practice*—Students will practice by working on their own to analyze relationships between and among terms within the problem and solution text structure. Example terms include *climate change* and *global warming*. They will record their thinking on the graphic organizer and discuss the passages with their partners. Then, students will work on their own to write an example of the problem/solution text structure that clearly defines relations between and among terms. (RST.9-10.5; RI.9-10.5; WHST.9-10.2; L.9-10.6; SL.9-10.1)

5. *Reflect*—Students will reflect on the problem/solution text structure and how it differs from others that they have learned. The class will discuss the subject areas in which

students might expect to see this pattern, and how knowing text structures can help them understand what they read. They will also discuss how text structures help them when they write about factual topics. In addition, students will focus on the importance of knowing how various terms in a text are related. (RST.9-10.5; RI.9-10.5; SL.9-10.1)

Reading Standard 5 focuses on ensuring that students are able to read texts that have a variety of organizational structures. It requires students to analyze the structure and relate portions of a text to each other and the whole. Students use text structures to build understanding of a text, just as architects use blueprints to build homes. When they understand text structures, students examine how it is built—they use the blueprints—to understand the texts that they read.

References

ACT. (2006). *Reading between the lines: What the ACT reveals about college readiness in reading.* Iowa City, IA: Author. Retrieved August 22, 2012, from www.act.org/research/policymakers/pdf/reading_report.pdf

Akhondi, M., Malayeri, F., & Samad, A.A. (2011). How to teach expository text structure to facilitate reading comprehension. *The Reading Teacher, 64*(5), 368–372.

Armbruster, B.B. (2004). Considerate texts. In D. Lapp, J. Flood, & N. Farnan (Eds.), *Content area reading and learning: Instructional strategies* (2nd ed., pp. 47–57). Mahwah, NJ: Erlbaum.

Ciardiello, A.V. (1998). Did you ask a good question today? Alternative cognitive and metacognitive strategies. *Journal of Adolescent & Adult Literacy, 42*(3), 210–219.

Duke, N.K., & Pearson, P.D. (2002). Effective practices for developing reading comprehension. In A.E. Farstrup & S.J. Samuels (Eds.), *What research has to say about reading instruction* (3rd ed., pp. 205–242). Newark, DE: International Reading Association.

Gambrell, L.B. (2001). *It's not either/or but more: Balancing narrative and informational text to improve reading comprehension.* Paper presented at the 46th annual convention of the International Reading Association, New Orleans, LA.

Goldman, S.R., & Rakestraw, J.A. (2000). Structural aspects of constructing meaning from text. In M.L. Kamil, P.B. Mosenthal, P.D. Pearson, & R. Barr (Eds.), *Handbook of reading research* (Vol. 3, pp. 311–335). Mahwah, NJ: Erlbaum.

McLaughlin, M. (2010). *Content area reading: Teaching and learning in an age of multiple literacies.* Boston: Allyn & Bacon.

McLaughlin, M., & Allen, M.B. (2009). *Guided Comprehension in grades 3–8* (Combined 2nd ed.). Newark, DE: International Reading Association.

McLaughlin, M., & Fisher, D. (2012, December/January). Teaching students to meet the Common Core Standards in grades 6–12? Analyze this! *Reading Today, 30*(3), 12–13.

McLaughlin, M., & Overturf, B.J. (2013). *The Common Core: Graphic organizers for teaching K–12 students to meet the Reading Standards.* Newark, DE: International Reading Association. Retrieved from www.reading.org/general/Publications/Books/bk021.aspx

Moss, B. (2004). Teaching expository text structures through information trade book retellings. *The Reading Teacher, 57*(8), 710–719.

National Governors Association Center for Best Practices & Council of Chief State School Officers. (2010). *Common Core State Standards for English language arts and literacy in history/social studies, science, and technical subjects.* Washington, DC: Authors. Retrieved August 3, 2012, from www.corestandards.org/assets/CCSSI_ELA%20Standards.pdf

Pressley, M. (2002). *Reading instruction that works: The case for balanced teaching* (2nd ed.). New York: Guilford.

Schwartz, R.M., & Raphael, T.E. (1985). Concept of definition: A key to improving students' vocabulary. *The Reading Teacher, 39*(2), 198–205.

Literature Cited

Lassieur, A. (2004). *The ancient Romans.* New York: Scholastic.

CHAPTER 12

CCR Reading Anchor Standard 6: Point of View

Seeing in Different Ways

College and Career Readiness Reading Anchor Standard 6
Assess how point of view or purpose shapes content and style of a text. (NGA Center & CCSSO, 2010, p. 10)

What Does CCR Reading Anchor Standard 6 Mean?

In College and Career Readiness (CCR) Reading Anchor Standard 6, the emphasis is on point of view and author's purpose. Whether the text is literary or informational, the author writes from a certain point of view so the reader feels a certain way or is persuaded to a certain belief. The goal is for students to understand that stories may be told and text may be written in different ways, depending on who is doing the telling or writing.

Understanding the point of view from which a text is written helps the reader comprehend the text in a deeper way. In English or literature courses, students may be asked to write a Point of View Analysis, which is an essay describing the point of view of the narrator in a literary text and describing how that point of view is used in a text to communicate the author's message. A Point of View Analysis requires students to consider nuances in the text that they might not see otherwise. According to high school Common Core Standard 6 for Reading Literature, by the end of grade 12, students are expected to know how to analyze points of view or cultural experiences in literary works from around the world and to demonstrate knowledge of literary elements, such as satire, sarcasm, irony, and understatement, based on a sophisticated analysis of a narrator's point of view.

When reading informational text, the ability to analyze the author's or narrator's point of view means being able to determine the credibility of the text. The more credible the author, the more credible the information. Not only are students required to determine the author's point of view and purpose for writing the text, but they are also required to analyze how an author uses rhetoric (in this case, style and content) to advance that point of view or purpose. The high school Common Core Standard 6 for Reading Informational Text states that by the end of grade 12, students should be able to "determine an author's point of view or purpose in a text in which the rhetoric is particularly effective, analyzing how style and content contribute to the power, persuasiveness, or beauty of the text" (NGA Center & CCSSO, 2010, p. 40).

Reading Anchor Standard 6 focuses on two college and career readiness reading skills:

1. The ability to assess how point of view shapes the content and style of a text
2. The ability to assess how purpose shapes the content and style of a text

Point of View

A text may be written from one point of view or from a variety of perspectives. A text may be analyzed to determine point of view as a literary device or to determine the author's point of view about a topic. The text may also be analyzed to determine the effectiveness of the author's use of argument in a speech, essay, editorial, or article.

As a literary device, one point of view may be that of a first-person narrator. In first-person narration, the author writes as if he or she were a character in the story who is telling the story. This narrator uses pronouns such as *I* and *my*. Another type of point of view as a literary device, and one that is not often used, is second-person narration. In second-person narration, the author writes as if the reader were in the story. This narrator uses pronouns such as *you* and *your*.

A third type of point of view, and one that is used extensively as a literary device, is that of a third-person narrator. In third-person narration, the author writes the story as an outside voice looking in on the events of the story. In third-person omniscient narration, the author can see inside the minds of all the characters and describe their thoughts. In third-person limited narration, the author tells the story from only one character's point of view. These narrators use pronouns such as *he* and *she*.

Purpose

The author's purpose is the reason the text was written. Literary texts are written to entertain or to convey a message. Even when a text is written to entertain, the author wants the reader to think or feel a certain way and writes from a particular point of view. Informational texts may be written to answer a question, to describe something, or to explain an event, situation, person, or procedure. Students who can determine an author's reasons for writing an informational text are more aware of the text's intended message.

How Do the Common Core Standards Build to CCR Reading Anchor Standard 6?

The Common Core Standards in grades 6–12 build toward College and Career Readiness Anchor Standard 6 by addressing four substrands of reading skills. The Reading Standard 6 substrands addressed in grades 6–12 are as follows:

- Reading Standards for Literature (English Language Arts)
- Reading Standards for Informational Text (English Language Arts)
- Reading Standards for Literacy in History/Social Studies
- Reading Standards for Literacy in Science and Technical Subjects

In Reading Standard 6 for Literature, students are expected to understand and determine the point of view from which the text is written. Whether the text is a story, poem, or drama, either the narrator or the characters tell the story from a certain point of view. In sixth grade, students are

Table 12.1 Common Core State Standard 6 for Reading Literature in Grades 6–12

Grade	Standard
6	Explain how an author develops the point of view of the narrator or speaker in a text.
7	Analyze how an author develops and contrasts the points of view of different characters or narrators in a text.
8	Analyze how differences in the points of view of characters and the audience or reader (e.g., created through the use of dramatic irony) create such effects as suspense or humor.
9–10	Analyze a particular point of view or cultural experience reflected in a work of literature from outside the United States, drawing on a wide reading of world literature.
11–12	Analyze a case in which grasping point of view requires distinguishing what is directly stated in a text from what is really meant (e.g., satire, sarcasm, irony, or understatement).

Note. The standards are from *Common Core State Standards for English Language Arts and Literacy in History/Social Studies, Science, and Technical Subjects* (pp. 36 and 38), by National Governors Association Center for Best Practices and Council of Chief State School Officers, 2010, Washington, DC: Authors.

Table 12.2 Common Core State Standard 6 for Reading Informational Text in Grades 6–12

Grade	Standard
6	Determine an author's point of view or purpose in a text and explain how it is conveyed in the text.
7	Determine an author's point of view or purpose in a text and analyze how the author distinguishes his or her position from that of others.
8	Determine an author's point of view or purpose in a text and analyze how the author acknowledges and responds to conflicting evidence or viewpoints.
9–10	Determine an author's point of view or purpose in a text and analyze how an author uses rhetoric to advance that point of view or purpose.
11–12	Determine an author's point of view or purpose in a text in which the rhetoric is particularly effective, analyzing how style and content contribute to the power, persuasiveness, or beauty of the text.

Note. The standards are from *Common Core State Standards for English Language Arts and Literacy in History/Social Studies, Science, and Technical Subjects* (pp. 39 and 40), by National Governors Association Center for Best Practices and Council of Chief State School Officers, 2010, Washington, DC: Authors.

expected to explain how an author develops point of view of the narrator or speaker in a text. In grade 7, students analyze how an author develops point of view and contrast the points of view of different characters or narrators. In grade 8, students analyze how differences in the points of view of characters and the audience or reader create effects such as suspense or humor. In grades 9–10, students analyze a particular point of view or cultural experience in world literature from outside the United States, and in grades 11–12, students analyze point of view to distinguish elements such as satire, sarcasm, irony, or understatement. Table 12.1 shows the expectations of Common Core State Standard 6 for Reading Literature.

In Reading Informational Text Standard 6, sixth graders are expected to determine an author's point of view or purpose in an informational text and explain how it is conveyed. Students in seventh grade add to this knowledge by analyzing how an author distinguishes his or her position from that of others. In grade 8, students also analyze how the author acknowledges and responds to conflicting evidence or viewpoints. In grades 9–10, students continue to determine an author's point of view or purpose in a text but also analyze how an author uses rhetoric to advance that point of view or purpose. Students in grades 11–12 also analyze how style and content contribute to the power, persuasiveness, or beauty of the text. Common Core Reading Standard 6 for Informational Text is delineated in Table 12.2.

For Reading Standard 6 for Literacy in History/Social Studies in grades 6–8, students identify aspects of the text that reveal an author's point of view or purpose, such as loaded language and inclusion or avoidance of particular facts. In grades 9–10, students compare the point of view of two or more authors for how they treat the same or similar topics, including which details they include and emphasize in their respective accounts. Students in grades 11–12 evaluate authors' differing points of view on the same historical event or issue by assessing the authors' claims, reasoning, and evidence. The expectations for Reading Standard 6 for Literacy in History/Social Studies are shown in Table 12.3.

Reading Standard 6 for Literacy in Science and Technical Subjects also focuses on the author's purpose for writing the text. Students in grades 6–8 analyze the author's purpose in providing an explanation, describing a procedure, or discussing an experiment in a text. In grades 9–10, students build on these skills but also define the question the author seeks to address. In grades 11–12, students continue to analyze the author's purpose, but also identify important issues that remain unresolved. The skills students are expected to achieve in Reading Standard 6 for Literacy in Science and Technical Subjects are outlined in Table 12.4.

What Literacy Skills and Strategies Support Reading Anchor Standard 6?

When we review the literacy skills and strategies in the Common Core State Standards, we can readily determine that gaps exist. As educators, we may find ourselves asking whether we should be teaching a particular concept because it does not appear in the CCSS. However, it is important to note that the Standards are not the determining factor. If the skill or strategy is included in our curriculums, we should teach it. For example, students in grades K–3 are expected to be able to ask and answer questions. Similarly, students in grades 4 and 5 are expected to know and use text structures, such as comparison/contrast and problem/solution. The grade 6–12 CCSS do not address either of these topics, but the students still need to know what they are and how to use them to successfully meet the Standards. That is why we noted in Chapter 1 the importance of our reading the CCSS both vertically (our grade levels) and horizontally (what students are expected to know before they reach our grade levels).

Many of the essential skills that grade 6–12 students need to know, including asking and answering questions and using text structure, are delineated in the grade K–5 Standards. For example, Common Core Reading Standard 1, for both Literature and Informational Text, is

Table 12.3 Common Core Reading Standard 6 for Literacy in History/Social Studies in Grades 6–12

Grade	Standard
6–8	Identify aspects of a text that reveal an author's point of view or purpose (e.g., loaded language, inclusion or avoidance of particular facts).
9–10	Compare the point of view of two or more authors for how they treat the same or similar topics, including which details they include and emphasize in their respective accounts.
11–12	Evaluate authors' differing points of view on the same historical event or issue by assessing the authors' claims, reasoning, and evidence.

Note. The standards are from *Common Core State Standards for English Language Arts and Literacy in History/Social Studies, Science, and Technical Subjects* (pp. 61), by National Governors Association Center for Best Practices and Council of Chief State School Officers, 2010, Washington, DC: Authors.

Table 12.4 Common Core Reading Standard 6 for Literacy in Science and Technical Subjects in Grades 6–12

Grade	Standard
6–8	Analyze the author's purpose in providing an explanation, describing a procedure, or discussing an experiment in a text.
9–10	Analyze the author's purpose in providing an explanation, describing a procedure, or discussing an experiment in a text, defining the question the author seeks to address.
11–12	Analyze the author's purpose in providing an explanation, describing a procedure, or discussing an experiment in a text, identifying important issues that remain unresolved.

Note. The standards are from *Common Core State Standards for English Language Arts and Literacy in History/Social Studies, Science, and Technical Subjects* (p. 62), by National Governors Association Center for Best Practices and Council of Chief State School Officers, 2010, Washington, DC: Authors.

Table 12.5 K–5 Reading Standard 6: Supporting Skills and Strategies for Literature in Grades 6–12

Grade	Skills and Strategies
K	With prompting and support, name the author and illustrator of a story and define the role of each in telling the story.
1	Identify who is telling the story at various points in a text.
2	Acknowledge differences in the points of view of characters, including by speaking in a different voice for each character when reading dialogue aloud.
3	Distinguish their own point of view from that of the narrator or those of the characters.
4	Compare and contrast the point of view from which different stories are narrated, including the difference between first- and third-person narrations.
5	Describe how a narrator's or speaker's point of view influences how events are described.

Note. The standards are from *Common Core State Standards for English Language Arts and Literacy in History/Social Studies, Science, and Technical Subjects* (pp. 11 and 12), by National Governors Association Center for Best Practices and Council of Chief State School Officers, 2010, Washington, DC: Authors.

Table 12.6 K–5 Reading Standard 6: Supporting Skills and Strategies for Informational Text in Grades 6–12

Grade	Skills and Strategies
K	Name the author and illustrator of a text and define the role of each in presenting the ideas or information in a text.
1	Distinguish between information provided by pictures or other illustrations and information provided by the words in a text.
2	Identify the main purpose of a text, including what the author wants to answer, explain, or describe.
3	Distinguish their own point of view from that of the author of a text.
4	Compare and contrast a firsthand and secondhand account of the same event or topic; describe the differences in focus and the information provided.
5	Analyze multiple accounts of the same event or topic, noting important similarities and differences in the point of view they represent.

Note. The standards are from *Common Core State Standards for English Language Arts and Literacy in History/Social Studies, Science, and Technical Subjects* (pp. 13 and 14), by National Governors Association Center for Best Practices and Council of Chief State School Officers, 2010, Washington, DC: Authors.

associated with Reading Standard 10, which focuses on the expectation that students will read complex text. For students to be able to read, discuss, and write about complex text and fulfill the expectations of Reading Standard 1, they must be able to use the supporting skills and strategies that were introduced in earlier grades. Details of Reading Standard 6, the focus of this chapter, are featured in Table 12.5 for Literature (English Language Arts) and Table 12.6 for Informational Text (ELA, Reading in History/Social Studies, and Reading in Science and Technical Subjects).

How Can We Teach Reading Anchor Standard 6 So Our Students Achieve?

In this section, we discuss the CCSS expectations for students at various grade levels. For example, the sixth College and Career Readiness Anchor Standard requires students to assess how point of view or purpose shapes the content and style of the text. To address this, we describe teaching ideas and how they support the Standard. We also share examples of how to embed 21st-century skills in curriculums in meaningful ways.

Determining Points of View

Reading Standard 6 for both literature and informational text has a major emphasis on helping students understand point of view. To address these expectations, we can begin by teaching students how to determine the author's point of view. When selecting text to teach point of view, we should initially use examples in which the author's point of view is pronounced. After students become proficient in identifying the author's point of view, we can teach them how to determine multiple viewpoints within a text. *Talkin' About Bessie: The Story of Aviator Elizabeth Coleman* (Grimes, 2002) is an example of a fictional text about the life of Bessie Coleman, the first female African American pilot. It provides 21 different points of view through poems offered as fictional tributes at Bessie's funeral. Coleman died in a plane accident at the age of 34. A Text-Based Viewpoint Organizer (McLaughlin & Overturf, 2013) based on *Talkin' About Bessie* appears in Figure 12.1.

Analyzing Points of View

We can encourage students to compare and contrast different perspectives by using the Multiple Points of View Organizer. First, we introduce a narrative or informational text by building students' background knowledge. Then, we divide students into small groups to discuss the concept of perspective or point of view. We provide multiple copies of the text so students can read and discuss it with partners.

We can use Jigsaw II (Slavin, 1995), a cooperative learning technique, to help students to think about the different perspectives. Students work in small groups to brainstorm a list of possible points of view. When the perspectives have been determined, students regroup into "expert" groups. The students in each expert group discuss the text from one of the points of view. After the group discussion, students return to their original small groups as an expert on one point of view. The original small group discusses the text, noting what each viewpoint represents. After the discussion, the group records ideas about each viewpoint on the organizer. This helps each student to understand each perspective. Then, they compare and contrast the points of view by discussing the similarities and differences. For example, in Jane Yolen's book *Encounter*, students can use the Multiple Points of View Organizer (McLaughlin & Overturf, 2013) to discuss the points of view of Columbus, the Tainos people, the sailors, and Queen Isabella.

The Multiple Points of View Organizer can also be used to compare and contrast varied perspectives about informational text, such as different accounts of historical events or descriptions of the same scientific concepts written by different authors. For example, it could be used to discuss a variety of perspectives in *Remember Pearl Harbor: American and Japanese Survivors Tell Their Stories* by Thomas B. Allen (2001). When students learn about points of view, they think critically about diverse points of view. In Figure 12.2, the organizer is used to present multiple points of view about dropping the atomic bomb on Hiroshima. The perspectives of Albert Einstein, President Truman, the Japanese, and critics of the United States are examined.

Figure 12.1 Example of a Text-Based Viewpoint Organizer

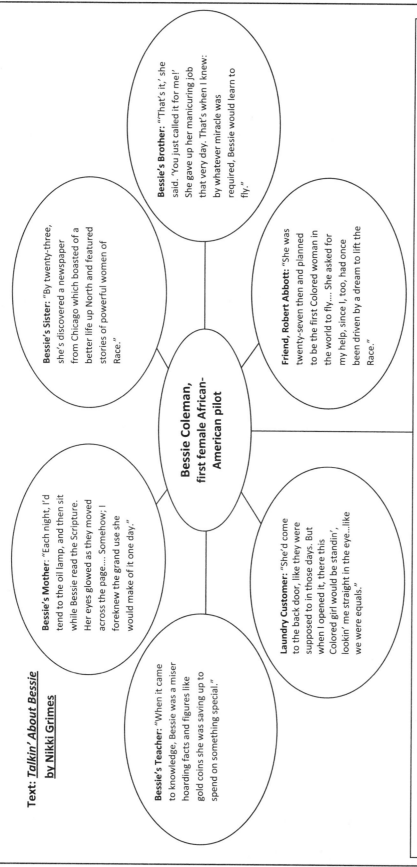

Text: *Talkin' About Bessie* by Nikki Grimes

Bessie's Sister: "By twenty-three, she's discovered a newspaper from Chicago which boasted of a better life up North and featured stories of powerful women of Race."

Bessie's Brother: "That's it,' she said. 'You just called it for me!' She gave up her manicuring job that very day. That's when I knew: by whatever miracle was required, Bessie would learn to fly."

Bessie's Mother: "Each night, I'd tend to the oil lamp, and then sit while Bessie read the Scripture. Her eyes glowed as they moved across the page.... Somehow; I foreknew the grand use she would make of it one day."

Bessie Coleman, first female African-American pilot

Friend, Robert Abbott: "She was twenty-seven then and planned to be the first Colored woman in the world to fly.... She asked for my help, since I, too, had once been driven by a dream to lift the Race."

Bessie's Teacher: "When it came to knowledge, Bessie was a miser hoarding facts and figures like gold coins she was saving up to spend on something special."

Laundry Customer: "She'd come to the back door, like they were supposed to in those days. But when I opened it, there this Colored girl would be standin', lookin' me straight in the eye...like we were equals."

Summary: Bessie Coleman grew up when segregation was a way of life, but she resisted it. When Bessie delivered her laundry to her customers, she went to the back door, because African Americans were not allowed to use the front door at that time. Still, Bessie felt equal to her customers. Even Bessie's teacher knew her student was destined to do great things because she got as much education as she could. Bessie enjoyed reading to her mother, who also saw great things for her daughter. Her sister recognized Bessie's desire to move up north for a better life. When her brother provided information about aviation, Bessie knew it was for her. Her friend Robert Abbott supported her going to aviation school, because at the time, it was not something women or women of color did. Bessie finally fulfilled her dream and became the first African-American female pilot.

Analysis: *Talkin' About Bessie* is told through a series of poems, each supposedly authored by someone who influenced Bessie's life. Nikki Grimes' point of view seems to be that Coleman's life had many rich influences. Each of the characters' viewpoints complements Grimes' thinking. The format is unique and, consequently, a very powerful way to share multiple perspectives of Bessie and the realization of her dream.

Figure 12.2 Example of a Multiple Points of View Organizer

Viewpoint One:
Scientist Albert Einstein

- I had to escape Italy for America.
- There was Nazi persecution in Italy.
- I feared Germany would use atomic powers.
- I am the one who urged President Roosevelt to develop an atomic research program.

Viewpoint Two:
President Harry Truman

- The difficult decision to use the atomic bomb was in my hands.
- I knew the atomic bomb would end the war with Japan.
- I demanded that Japan surrender or face total destruction.
- The bombing saved lives from a prolonged war.

Dropping the atomic bomb on Hiroshima

Viewpoint Three:
Japanese

- We had an army two million strong.
- Surrendering was not an option.
- When the bomb was dropped, 70,000 citizens were vaporized instantly.
- Later, 100,000 of our people died from radiation sickness and burns.
- We finally surrendered.

Viewpoint Four:
Critics of the United States

- Dropping the atomic bomb was barbaric.
- The United States will have negative repercussions.
- Others will now use nuclear weaponry.
- We think the United States' bombing was racist.
- The bomb was a message to the Soviets that the United States is capable of destruction and devastation if pushed.

21st-Century Skill Applications for Reading Anchor Standard 6

In this section, we share ideas to help students meet the Reading Standards through the use of 21st-century tools and skills. Although online tools can be used for a variety of purposes, we have chosen to highlight specific tools for use with each standard. As teachers, we should select tools we feel work best for students, using the same tools in multiple ways when possible.

CCR Reading Standard 6 focuses on assessing how point of view or purpose shapes the content and style of a text. An appealing way for students to focus on point of view or purpose is to use a comic strip generator. There are several free generators available online, such as ToonDoo (www.toondoo.com), Chogger (www.chogger.com), and Make Beliefs Comix! (www.makebeliefscomix.com). ToonDoo has hundreds of characters, scenes, props, and so on, where students can create sophisticated comics. Chogger is another option that makes it easy to draw, import, or use Google images in a comic strip. Make Beliefs Comix! is an educational comic strip creator where students can create comics in English, Spanish, French, German, Italian, Portuguese, and Latin. There is also a tab that discusses the value of comic strip creation for students with disabilities.

Students create comic strips using characters, scenes, props, speech and thought bubbles, and captions to represent the character's point of view or to explain an author's purpose for writing a text. When students create comic panels to represent the retelling of a story or event and include speech and thought bubbles, they decide what the character or individual might think, say, and do. With a teacher's guidance, students can think critically about text by analyzing point of view in order to create comic strips.

How Can We Integrate Other ELA Standards With Reading Anchor Standard 6?

When planning to teach CCR Anchor Standard 6, we can integrate several other ELA standards to design rich instructional tasks. Examples of ideas to include when creating rich instructional tasks follow.

Integrating Other ELA Standards With Reading Literature Standard 6

- Reading Literature Standard 1 focuses on reading a narrative text closely. *Example:* When students engage in close reading of a text, encourage them to determine the point of view of the author and characters.

- Reading Literature Standard 2 focuses on the ability to determine and analyze theme. *Example:* Ask students to analyze the author's or characters' point of view to determine theme.

- Reading Literature Standard 3 focuses on being able to analyze characters, settings, or events in a story or drama, drawing on specific details in the text. *Example:* Ask students to analyze the text by discussing the point of view of various characters.

- Reading Literature Standard 7 focuses on comparing a written version of a text with multimedia or artistic versions of the text. *Example:* When experiencing different versions of a literary text, teach students to analyze point of view in the various versions.

- Writing Standard 9 addresses the expectation that students will be able to draw evidence from texts to support analysis, reflection, and research. *Example:* Ask students to write responses that emphasize text structure and format.

- Speaking and Listening Standard 1 describes the expectation for students to engage effectively in a range of collaborative discussions, with specific indicators to demonstrate how to participate in an effective academic conversation. *Example:* When reading stories, dramas, and poems, engage students in whole-group, small-group, and paired collaborative conversations focused on point of view.

Integrating Other ELA Standards With Reading Informational Text Standard 6

- Reading Informational Text Standard 1 refers to engaging in close reading of an informational text. *Example:* When students read an informational text closely, encourage them to analyze the author's point of view and purpose for writing the text.

- Reading Informational Text Standard 2 focuses on the ability to determine central ideas and purpose of an informational text. *Example:* When students read an informational text, ask them to analyze the author's purpose for writing the text.

- Reading Informational Text Standard 7 focuses on different versions and medium of texts. *Example:* Encourage students to analyze the author's or director's purpose for producing the text.

- Reading Informational Text Standard 8 focuses on the author's arguments, including claims, reasons, and evidence in informational text. *Example:* After students read a text in which the author has stated an opinion, ask students to analyze the author's argument, including point of view.

- Reading Informational Text Standard 9 focuses on comparing and contrasting two or more texts or interpreting or integrating information from several texts on the same topic. *Example:* Encourage students to analyze points of view and purpose when reading multiple perspectives on the same topic.

- Reading Informational Text Standard 10 refers to the expectation that students be able to read complex texts. *Example:* When students engage in reading a complex informational text, encourage them to determine and discuss point of view and the author's purpose for writing the text.

- Writing Standard 1 describes the expectation for students to write arguments to support opinions with reasons and information. *Example:* Encourage students to establish a point of view that will, along with reasons and evidence, support their opinion.

- Speaking and Listening Standard 1 addresses students engaging effectively in a range of collaborative discussions, with specific indicators that demonstrate how to participate in an effective academic conversation. *Example:* Encourage students to engage in a number of collaborative academic conversations to determine an author's point of view and purpose for writing the text.

THE COMMON CORE IN ACTION

In this section of Chapters 7–16, we examine one of the foundational ideas that underpin each of the College and Career Readiness Anchor Standards for Reading. For the sixth Standard, "Assess how point of view or purpose shapes the content and style of a text" (NGA Center & CCSSO, 2010, p. 10), we have elected to share more detailed information about how the author's point of view and purpose shapes the content and style of a text.

Common Core Literacy Task: Assessing an Author's Point of View and Purpose

Troy is a middle school Social Studies teacher who has been teaching a unit on how public opinion is shaped. As part of this unit, he introduced the concept of point of view in the media.

To teach the concept of point of view, Troy began by asking his eighth grade students to analyze famous photographs from history. Troy easily found appropriate photographs that include background explanation on websites such as World's Famous Photos (www.worldsfamousphotos.com) or "13 Photos That Changed the World" (www.neatorama.com/2007/01/02/13-photographs-that-changed-the-world/). He posted the links on his class website and showed them in class, where several of the photographs helped to spur a lively conversation about the content, historical context, and public reaction the pictures may have caused when they were first published. For example, one of the photos was the 1936 photograph of "Migrant Mother" by Dorothea Lange (www.loc.gov/rr/print/list/128_migm.html). This famous newspaper picture shows a young woman who had lost her husband and had to provide for her seven children during the Great Depression by foraging for food in migrant camps in California. Troy asked his students to contemplate several possible points of view when viewing this photo: the separate points of view of the mother, the children, the photographer, and newspaper readers. The students first dramatized the varied perspectives of the photo by participating in a tableau (Wilhelm, 1997). In a tableau, students pose as the people in a painting, photograph, or text, "freeze" the action, and then discuss their thoughts as the character. After the tableau and its resulting discussion, students engaged in critical literacy practice by writing an analysis about the photograph from varied perspectives, including those perspectives that are not immediately obvious, such as the photographer and newspaper readers (McLaughlin & DeVoogd, 2004). After students had explored the photograph through discussion, drama, and writing, Troy revealed that the photograph had actually created a public outcry when it was published in newspapers across the country in 1936, with people demanding that food and supplies be sent to the camp (sadly, the mother and her children had already moved on and did not receive them). Troy then asked students to choose other photographs from a collection he had preselected and write an analysis of the photograph's point of view and possible purposes, including a discussion of reactions the photographer might be hoping to achieve. As students shared their writing, Troy used classroom observation and analysis of student work to determine that his students understood the concept of the photographer's point of view and purpose for taking the picture.

As the next step, Troy is planning to teach point of view and author's purpose in informational text. Troy has chosen to use a literary nonfiction article from *The New York Times* titled "Pro Football's Violent Toll." The author of this article, Frank Bruni (2012), uses expressive language and a facetious approach to state his opinion about problems in the National Football League. Troy knows the article will motivate his students and feels it is a perfect text for them to practice determining an author's point of view and purpose for writing opinions. Troy plans to focus on Reading Standard 6 for Literacy in History/Social Studies in grades 6–8: "Identify aspects of a text that reveal an author's point of view or purpose (e.g., loaded language, inclusion or avoidance of particular facts)" (RH.6-8.6).

To teach this lesson, Troy will do the following:

1. Review the students' experience establishing point of view and purpose using historical photographs.

2. Explain to students that an author of an opinion writes from a certain point of view and has a purpose for writing, often carefully using language to make a point and heighten emotion. This use of language to persuade others is called rhetorical language. An author's bias and purpose is often revealed through use of such language. (RI.8.4)

3. Post the title of the article. Ask students to predict the focus and tone of the article by the language in the title. (RH.6-8.6)

4. Ask students to download the article, and then ask them what they notice about the article. The date of publication (December 3, 2012) and the name of the newspaper should emerge. Briefly discuss the concept of author point of view and credibility. (RH. 6-8.6)

5. Ask students to read the article independently. Encourage them to mark examples of the author's use of loaded language by highlighting or circling words and phrases, either on a hard copy or by using an annotating program for digital text. (RH.6-8.1; RI.8.4)

6. Arrange students into groups of three. Distribute the Determining an Author's Purpose graphic organizer (see Figure 12.3 for a completed example). As students reread the article, they will work in groups of three to discuss each paragraph and add information to their graphic organizers. (RH.6-8.6; SL.8.1; WHST.8.9)

7. Facilitate a class discussion about the article and the author's point of view and purpose for writing. (SL.8.1)

In subsequent lessons, Troy will ask students to read primary and secondary sources about the role of the media and determine the author's point of view and purpose for writing the text (RH.6-8.1; RH.6-8.6). He will then ask students to create a brief research project in order to develop an opinion on the media's role in a social studies issue of interest to the student (WHST.8.7; WHST.8.8). Students will also write an argument supporting their own point of view on the issue they researched while using the criteria outlined in Writing Standard 1 and their research notes (WHST.6-8.1).

Reading Standard 6 focuses on ensuring that students analyze how an author develops and contrasts points of view, determine an author's point of view and how it is conveyed in the text, and examine how style and content contribute to the power and persuasiveness of a text in which the rhetoric is particularly effective. When students see in different ways, they can more deeply comprehend a text.

Figure 12.3 Example of a Determining an Author's Purpose Organizer

Central Idea #1: Football season has been exciting.	
Facts: Many close games	**Language Choices:** <ul><li>Thrillingly down to the wire</li><li>Bleeding into overtime</li><li>Jerking my gaze</li><li>Suffered whiplash from watching</li><li>Seesaw contests</li><li>Last-minute heroics</li><li>Spectacle</li></ul>
Central Idea #2: Football season has also been ugly.	
Facts: <ul><li>Murder-suicide of Kansas City Chiefs player and girlfriend</li><li>Record drug suspensions in the league</li><li>New study shows repeated hits to the head may lead to degenerative brain disease</li><li>Suicide rate is high</li><li>A lot of arrest records</li></ul>	**Language Choices:** <ul><li>Anguished examination</li><li>Something rotten in the NFL</li><li>Dysfunctional culture</li><li>Heightened vigilance</li><li>Physical agony</li><li>Oft-medicated players</li><li>Mood swings, dementia, depression</li><li>Bounty program for knocking players out of the game</li><li>Heartbreaking assessment of his demise</li><li>Alcohol- or drug-addicted</li><li>League is lousy with criminal activity</li></ul>
Central Idea #3: Being an NFL fan is confusing.	
Facts: Not clear how events are connected	**Language Choices:** <ul><li>Morally conflicted</li><li>Supporting something that corrodes lives</li><li>Belcher's bloody end</li><li>Conscience hurt</li></ul>

Based on the author's language, how does the author feel about this subject?
What is the author's purpose for writing this article?

The author uses a lot of violent language, which indicates he thinks the sport has become violent in many ways. The author is conflicted about supporting the NFL because too many players' lives are being hurt. The author wants fans to demand that things be changed.

References

McLaughlin, M., & DeVoogd, G. (2004). *Critical literacy: Enhancing students' comprehension of text*. New York: Scholastic.

McLaughlin, M., & Overturf, B.J. (2013). *The Common Core: Graphic organizers for teaching K–12 students to meet the Reading Standards*. Newark, DE: International Reading Association. Retrieved from www.reading.org/general/Publications/Books/bk021.aspx

National Governors Association Center for Best Practices & Council of Chief State School Officers. (2010). *Common Core State Standards for English language arts and literacy in history/social studies, science, and technical subjects*. Washington, DC: Authors. Retrieved August 3, 2012, from www.corestandards.org/assets/CCSSI_ELA%20Standards.pdf

Slavin, R.E. (1995). *Cooperative learning: Theory, research and practice* (2nd ed.). Boston: Allyn & Bacon.

Wilhelm, J.D. (1997). *You gotta BE the book: Teaching engaged and reflective reading with adolescents*. New York: Teachers College Press.

Literature and Informational Text Cited

Allen, T.B. (2001). *Remember Pearl Harbor: American and Japanese survivors tell their stories*. Washington, DC: National Geographic Society.

Bruni, F. (2012, December 3). Pro football's violent toll. *The New York Times*. Retrieved January 13, 2013, from www.nytimes.com/2012/12/04/opinion/bruni-pro-footballs-violent-toll.html?_r=0

Grimes, N. (2002). *Talkin' about Bessie: The story of aviator Elizabeth Coleman*. New York: Orchard.

CHAPTER 13

CCR Reading Anchor Standard 7: Diverse Media and Formats

 Putting It Together	**College and Career Readiness Reading Anchor Standard 7** Integrate and evaluate content presented in diverse media and formats, including visually and quantitatively, as well as in words. (NGA Center & CCSSO, 2010, p. 10)

What Does CCR Reading Anchor Standard 7 Mean?

College and Career Readiness (CCR) Reading Anchor Standard 7 focuses on the ability to draw on information from multiple sources to address a question or solve a problem. Students need to be able to select appropriate material and evaluate their sources to conduct authentic, credible research and present that research in writing or speaking. They need to be able to integrate information from diverse media (e.g., audio, video, multimedia presentations) and in varied formats (e.g., textbooks, charts, graphs, magazine articles, newspapers) and then put it together to find answers and solve problems.

Reading Anchor Standard 7 focuses on two college and career readiness reading skills:

1. The ability to integrate content presented in diverse media and formats as well as in print

2. The ability to evaluate content presented in diverse media and formats as well as in print

When reading literature, students are expected to analyze multiple interpretations of a story, drama, or poem, such as a recorded or live production of a play or a recorded novel or poem. They may be asked to evaluate how an artist has represented a key scene from literature or evaluate the choices made by a director about how a novel is depicted in film. Technology will play a key role as students search for, review, and analyze online depictions of literary text compared with the written word.

In the disciplines, students need to be able to integrate and analyze sources to develop a coherent understanding of a topic or issue. Students are expected to compare and contrast a written text with an audio, video, or multimedia version of it. An example of this might be a written speech and the recorded version of the speech. Students are expected to use a variety of media to present a particular topic or idea, and they need to be able to evaluate the advantages and disadvantages of using diverse media and formats to present their ideas. Students also need to develop an efficient sense of how to review a number of resources on the same topic or issue, evaluate the sources and information, and choose the resources that are most credible before creating a written or oral presentation.

How Do the Common Core Standards Build to CCR Reading Anchor Standard 7?

The Common Core Standards in grades 6–12 build toward College and Career Readiness Anchor Standard 7 by addressing skills in four substrands of reading. The Reading Standard 7 substrands addressed in grades 6–12 are as follows:

- Reading Standards for Literature (English Language Arts)
- Reading Standards for Informational Text (English Language Arts)
- Reading Standards for Literacy in History/Social Studies
- Reading Standards for Literacy in Science and Technical Subjects

For Reading Standard 7 in Literature, sixth graders are expected to compare and contrast the experience of reading a story, drama, or poem to listening to or viewing an audio, video, or live version of the text. In seventh grade, students compare and contrast a written story, drama, or poem to its audio, filmed, staged, or multimedia version and analyze the effects of techniques unique to each medium. Eighth graders analyze the extent to which a filmed or live production of a story or drama stays faithful to or departs from the text or script. They also evaluate the choices made by the director or actors. In grades 9–10, students analyze the representation of the subject in a key scene in two different artistic mediums, including what is emphasized or absent in each treatment. In grades 11–12, students analyze multiple interpretations of a story, drama, or poem and evaluate how each version interprets the source text. There is a caveat at this level that students analyze interpretations of at least one play by Shakespeare and one play by an American dramatist. Reading Standard 7 for Literature appears in Table 13.1.

For Reading Standard 7 for Informational Text, sixth graders are expected to integrate information in different media or formats as well as in words to develop a coherent understanding of a topic or issue. In seventh

Table 13.1 Common Core State Standard 7 for Reading Literature in Grades 6–12

Grade	Standard
6	Compare and contrast the experience of reading a story, drama, or poem to listening to or viewing an audio, video, or live version of the text, including contrasting what they "see" and "hear" when reading the text to what they perceive when they listen or watch.
7	Compare and contrast a written story, drama, or poem to its audio, filmed, staged, or multimedia version, analyzing the effects of techniques unique to each medium (e.g., lighting, sound, color, or camera focus and angles in a film).
8	Analyze the extent to which a filmed or live production of a story or drama stays faithful to or departs from the text or script, evaluating the choices made by the director or actors.
9–10	Analyze the representation of a subject or a key scene in two different artistic mediums, including what is emphasized or absent in each treatment (e.g., Auden's "Musée des Beaux Arts" and Breughel's *Landscape with the Fall of Icarus*).
11–12	Analyze multiple interpretations of a story, drama, or poem (e.g., recorded or live production of a play or recorded novel or poetry), evaluating how each version interprets the source text. (Include at least one play by Shakespeare and one play by an American dramatist.)

Note. The standards are from *Common Core State Standards for English Language Arts and Literacy in History/Social Studies, Science, and Technical Subjects* (pp. 37 and 38), by National Governors Association Center for Best Practices and Council of Chief State School Officers, 2010, Washington, DC: Authors.

Table 13.2 Common Core State Standard 7 for Reading Informational Text in Grades 6–12

Grade	Standard
6	Integrate information presented in different media or formats (e.g., visually, quantitatively) as well as in words to develop a coherent understanding of a topic or issue.
7	Compare and contrast a text to an audio, video, or multimedia version of the text, analyzing each medium's portrayal of the subject (e.g., how the delivery of a speech affects the impact of the words).
8	Evaluate the advantages and disadvantages of using different mediums (e.g., print or digital text, video, multimedia) to present a particular topic or idea.
9–10	Analyze various accounts of a subject told in different mediums (e.g., a person's life story in both print and multimedia), determining which details are emphasized in each account.
11–12	Integrate and evaluate multiple sources of information presented in different media or formats (e.g., visually, quantitatively) as well as in words in order to address a question or solve a problem.

Note. The standards are from *Common Core State Standards for English Language Arts and Literacy in History/Social Studies, Science, and Technical Subjects* (pp. 39 and 40), by National Governors Association Center for Best Practices and Council of Chief State School Officers, 2010, Washington, DC: Authors.

Table 13.3 Common Core Reading Standard 7 for Literacy in History/Social Studies in Grades 6–12

Grade	Standard
6–8	Integrate visual information (e.g., in charts, graphs, photographs, videos, or maps) with other information in print and digital texts.
9–10	Integrate quantitative or technical analysis (e.g., charts, research data) with qualitative analysis in print or digital text.
11–12	Integrate and evaluate multiple sources of information presented in diverse formats and media (e.g., visually, quantitatively, as well as in words) in order to address a question or solve a problem.

Note. The standards are from *Common Core State Standards for English Language Arts and Literacy in History/Social Studies, Science, and Technical Subjects* (p. 61), by National Governors Association Center for Best Practices and Council of Chief State School Officers, 2010, Washington, DC: Authors.

grade, students compare and contrast a text to an audio, video, or multimedia version of the text and analyze each medium's portrayal of the subject (for example, how the delivery of a speech affects the impact of the words). In eighth grade, students evaluate the advantages and disadvantages of using different mediums, such as print or digital text, video, or multimedia, to present a particular topic or idea. Students in grades 9–10 analyze various accounts of a subject told in different mediums and determine which details are emphasized in each account. In grades 11–12, students integrate and evaluate multiple sources of information presented in different media or formats as well as in words in order to address a question or solve a problem. Table 13.2 shows Reading Informational Text Standard 7.

In Reading Standard 7 for Literacy in History/Social Studies, students in grades 6–8 are expected to integrate visual information (charts, graphs, photographs, video, etc.) with other information in print and digital texts. Students in grades 9–10 are expected to integrate quantitative or technical analysis with qualitative analysis in print or digital text. In grades 11 and 12, students learn to integrate and evaluate multiple sources of information presented in diverse formats and media in order to address a question or solve a problem. Reading Standard 7 for Literacy in History/Social Studies is given in Table 13.3.

For Reading Standard 7 for Literacy in Science and Technical Subjects, in grades 6–8, students learn to integrate quantitative or technical information expressed in words in a text with a version of that information expressed visually, as in a flowchart, diagram, model, graph, or table. Students in grades 9–10 are expected to translate quantitative or technical information expressed in words in a text into visual form, such as a table or chart. They should also be able to translate information expressed visually or mathematically, such as an equation, into words. In grades 11–12, students integrate and evaluate multiple sources of information presented in diverse formats and media, such as quantitative data, video, and multimedia, in order to address a question or solve a problem. Expectations for Reading Standard 7 for Literacy in Science and Technical Subjects are listed in Table 13.4.

What Literacy Skills and Strategies Support Reading Anchor Standard 7?

When we review the literacy skills and strategies in the Common Core State Standards, we can readily determine that gaps exist. As educators, we may find ourselves asking whether we should be teaching a particular concept because it does not appear in the CCSS. However, it is important to note that the Standards are not the determining factor. If the skill or strategy is included in our curriculums, we should teach it. For example, students in grades K–3 are expected to be able to ask and answer questions. Similarly, students in grades 4 and 5 are expected to know and use text structures, such as comparison/contrast and problem/solution. The grade 6–12 CCSS do not address either of these topics, but the students still need to know what they are and how to use them to successfully meet the Standards. That is why we noted in Chapter 1 the importance of our reading the CCSS both vertically (our grade levels) and horizontally (what students are expected to know before they reach our grade levels).

Many of the essential skills that grade 6–12 students need to know, including asking and answering questions and using text structure, are delineated in the grade K–5 Standards. For example, Common Core Reading Standard 1, for both literature and informational text, is associated with Reading Standard 10, which focuses on the expectation that students will read complex text. For students to be able to read, discuss, and write about complex text and fulfill the expectations of Reading Standard 1, they must be able to use the supporting skills and strategies that were introduced in earlier grades. Details of Reading Standard 7, the focus of this chapter, are featured in Table 13.5 for Literature (English Language Arts) and Table 13.6 for Informational Text (ELA, Reading in History/Social Studies, and Reading in Science and Technical Subjects).

Table 13.4 Common Core Reading Standard 7 for Literacy in Science and Technical Subjects in Grades 6–12

Grade	Standard
6–8	Integrate quantitative or technical information expressed in words in a text with a version of that information expressed visually (e.g., in a flowchart, diagram, model, graph, or table).
9–10	Translate quantitative or technical information expressed in words in a text into visual form (e.g., a table or chart) and translate information expressed visually or mathematically (e.g., in an equation) into words.
11–12	Integrate and evaluate multiple sources of information presented in diverse formats and media (e.g., quantitative data, video, multimedia) in order to address a question or solve a problem.

Note. The standards are from *Common Core State Standards for English Language Arts and Literacy in History/Social Studies, Science, and Technical Subjects* (p. 62), by National Governors Association Center for Best Practices and Council of Chief State School Officers, 2010, Washington, DC: Authors.

How Can We Teach Reading Anchor Standard 7 So Our Students Achieve?

In this section, we discuss the Common Core expectations for students at various grade levels. For example, the seventh College and Career Readiness Anchor Standard requires students to integrate and evaluate content presented in diverse formats and media, including visually and quantitatively, as well as in words. To address this, we describe teaching ideas and how they support the Standard. We also share examples of how to embed 21st-century skills in curriculums in meaningful ways.

Table 13.5 K–5 Reading Standard 7: Supporting Skills and Strategies for Literature in Grades 6–12

Grade	Skills and Strategies
K	With prompting and support, describe the relationship between illustrations and the story in which they appear (e.g., what moment in a story an illustration depicts).
1	Use illustrations and details in a story to describe its characters, setting, or events.
2	Use information gained from the illustrations and words in a print or digital text to demonstrate understanding of its characters, setting, or plot.
3	Explain how specific aspects of a text's illustrations contribute to what is conveyed by the words in a story (e.g., create mood, emphasize aspects of a character or setting).
4	Make connections between the text of a story or drama and a visual or oral presentation of the text, identifying where each version reflects specific descriptions and directions in the text.
5	Analyze how visual and multimedia elements contribute to the meaning, tone, or beauty of a text (e.g., graphic novel, multimedia presentation of fiction, folktale, myth, poem).

Note. The skills and strategies are from *Common Core State Standards for English Language Arts and Literacy in History/Social Studies, Science, and Technical Subjects* (pp. 11 and 12), by National Governors Association Center for Best Practices and Council of Chief State School Officers, 2010, Washington, DC: Authors.

Table 13.6 K–5 Reading Standard 7: Supporting Skills and Strategies for Informational Text in Grades 6–12

Grade	Skills and Strategies
K	With prompting and support, describe the relationship between illustrations and the text in which they appear (e.g., what person, place, thing, or idea in the text an illustration depicts).
1	Use the illustrations and details in a text to describe its key ideas.
2	Explain how specific images (e.g., a diagram showing how a machine works) contribute to and clarify a text.
3	Use information gained from illustrations (e.g., maps, photographs) and the words in a text to demonstrate understanding of the text (e.g., where, when, why, and how key events occur).
4	Interpret information presented visually, orally, or quantitatively (e.g., in charts, graphs, diagrams, time lines, animations, or interactive elements on Web pages) and explain how the information contributes to an understanding of the text in which it appears.
5	Draw on information from multiple print or digital sources, demonstrating the ability to locate an answer to a question quickly or to solve a problem efficiently.

Note. The skills and strategies are from *Common Core State Standards for English Language Arts and Literacy in History/Social Studies, Science, and Technical Subjects* (pp. 13 and 14), by National Governors Association Center for Best Practices and Council of Chief State School Officers, 2010, Washington, DC: Authors.

Comparing and Contrasting Text in a Variety of Formats

CCSS expectations for students in grades 6–12 include determining similarities and differences in a variety of text formats. Teaching students to create Transmediations (McLaughlin, 2010) provides learners with essential, first-hand understandings of how various formats impact text. When creating Transmediations, students choose a text in its original format—such as poetry, song lyrics, works of art, and short stories—and transform the text into another medium—a poem into an electronic picture book, song lyrics into a work of art, art into a poem, or short stories into a picture book, work of art, or poem. When teaching students how to engage in this project, a good example to share is Maya Angelou's poem "Life Doesn't Frighten Me." Through the paintings of Jean-Michel Basquiat, the poem has been transmediated into a picturebook with the same title (Angelou, 1993).

Angelou's inspiring words are complemented throughout the book by the bright colors and bold brush strokes Basquiat uses to interpret the poem. After students create their transmediations, they can discuss how the mediums differ and note which transmediations they think represent the original text more effectively. Figure 13.1 features selected slides from a transmediation of Woody Guthrie's song lyrics for "This Land Is Your Land."

Figure 13.1 Sample Slides From a Student's Transmediation

Analyzing Multiple Versions of a Text

To help students meet the CCSS expectation of analyzing multiple versions of a text, we can teach them to reason through the Audio–Print–Film Organizer (McLaughlin & Overturf, 2013). In this framework, students research various versions of the work to compile essential facts and reviews. Then they engage in analysis. Figure 13.2 focuses on the audio, print, and film versions of Doris Kearns Goodwin's (2006) *Team of Rivals: The Political Genius of Abraham Lincoln*. The film *Lincoln* (Spielberg & Kennedy, 2012) is based on a section of the book.

Using Digital Media as Research Sources

In CCR Reading Anchor Standard 7 and the related grade-level standards, students are expected to evaluate information in print and digital media. Internet Inquiry (Leu & Leu, 1999) is a project-based idea we can employ to engage students in evaluating digital sources. As students engage in this research project, they can evaluate the digital sources they use. Questions they might raise include the following:

1. What is the author's expertise on the topic?

2. What is the source of the funds used to support the site?

3. Is the content accurate?

4. Is the site associated with an organization or publication?

5. How reliable are the sites to which the website links? The sites that link to the website?

6. Are the photos/illustration/graphics accurate?

7. How recently was the site updated?

8. Is bias evident in the information presented on the site?

9. Are the format and organization logical?

10. What benefits does the site offer to researchers (e.g., immediacy of information, video streaming)?

When students engage in Internet Inquiry (Leu & Leu, 1999), a discovery-based process, they use digital sources to research a topic. During Internet Inquiry, students identify important questions and then gather information as they seek responses. This is a student-centered approach in which students self-select issues to explore and take responsibility for completing the research. Students can work individually or in groups organized by interest. Internet Inquiry has five phases of student participation:

1. *Generate* research questions about a theme or topic being studied.

2. *Search* for responses to the research questions on the Internet.

3. *Analyze* the information found online.

4. *Choose* a mode to present the findings.

5. *Share* the results with the whole class.

For example, if we were planning to engage our students in Internet Inquiry about major historical figures, such as Dr. Martin Luther King Jr. or Winston Churchill, we might follow these guidelines:

Figure 13.2 Example of an Audio–Print–Film Organizer

AUDIO	PRINT	FILM
Team of Rivals (Goodwin, 2006)	**Team of Rivals** (Goodwin, 2006)	**Lincoln** (Spielberg, 2012)
Essential Facts		
Actor Richard Thomas reads the book.	Doris Kearns Goodwin wrote the book.	Tony Kushner wrote the screenplay.
It is an abridgement, not the entire 944 pages.	The book is 944 pages.	The movie is 150 minutes.
Focus: Lincoln's relationship with his rivals	Focus: Lincoln's relationship with his rivals	Focus: The last four months of Lincoln's life
Reviews: Listeners left wanting to know more about individuals and relationships (abridged version).	"An elegant, incisive study.... Goodwin has brilliantly described how Lincoln forged a team that preserved a nation and freed America from the curse of slavery." (McPherson, *The New York Times Book Review*)	"...took such fascinating and complex source materials and sucked ALL the blood out of it. Film adaptation vampires!" (Steinkellner, 2012)
"A masterful bio, read by a master." (Audiofile)	"...Tells the story of Lincoln's prudent management as a highly personal tale, not a political...one." (Guelzo, *Washington Post*, 2005)	"*Lincoln* is a rough and noble democratic masterpiece—an omen, perhaps, that movies for the people shall not perish from the earth." (Roger Ebert, *Chicago Sun Times*, 11/7/12)

Analysis: *Team of Rivals* in its audio and print versions and *Lincoln*, the movie, provide interesting insights into Lincoln's presidency and his family life. The three formats have similarities and differences. All share information about Lincoln and do so with a great deal of respect for the man and his office. Doris Kearns Goodwin, a well-respected historian and writer, is the author of the book and Tony Kushner is the author of the screenplay, which is partially based on Goodwin's work. The book, which focuses on Lincoln's transitioning his rivals into cabinet members, is lengthy and detailed. The audio version is an abridgement. The movie is far more tightly focused, emphasizing just the last four months of Lincoln's presidency and the passing of the 13th amendment, which abolished slavery. The book and its CD version received excellent reviews. Some reviews offered high praise for the movie; others felt that the film was not well adapted. Although differences do exist in the information presented and the mediums through which it is shared, one thought permeates all: Lincoln may well have been the greatest president of our country. Whether listening, reading, or viewing, we are all left to wonder how our country may have been different if he had not been assassinated.

1. Create an Internet Inquiry about biographies of famous historical figures.

2. Invite students to select a person to research from a list of possibilities.

3. Provide and explain the rubric that will be used to evaluate Internet Inquiries to the students.

4. Encourage students to choose how they will present the biographical information that they locate about the person they chose.

5. Encourage students to generate questions to direct their research. For example, the following are possible questions for a student who chooses to investigate Dr. Martin Luther King Jr.:

   • Who were some of the people who influenced Dr. King, and how did they affect his thinking?

   • What was the message in Dr. King's "I Have a Dream" speech?

   • How did Dr. King change our society?

6. Monitor students' progress as they gather and analyze information.

7. Invite students to participate in periodic conferencing or workshops to ask questions, engage in peer review, and share ideas about the projects they are developing.

8. Use the rubric to evaluate students' Internet Inquiries.

21st-Century Skill Applications for Reading Anchor Standard 7

In this section, we share ideas to help students meet the Reading Standards through the use of 21st-century tools and skills. Although online tools can be used for a variety of purposes, we have chosen to highlight specific tools for use with each standard. As teachers, we should select tools we think work best for our students, using them in multiple ways when possible.

CCR Reading Standard 7 focuses on integrating and evaluating content presented in diverse media and formats, including visually and quantitatively, as well as in words. Writing to build and present knowledge by gathering, assessing, and applying information from print and digital sources is related to Reading Standard 7. Students can access, integrate, and evaluate information from diverse media and formats as they conduct short research projects, and then create their own multimedia posters to present the information they have learned. Glogster (edu.glogster.com) is a free online tool (a premium version is available for a fee) that helps students create their own content presented in diverse media and formats. A glog is another name for a "graphical log." Glogster is a tool for creating an interactive multimedia image that looks like a poster, but glog readers can interact with the elements and content. A glog can contain photos, artwork, video clips, text descriptions, symbols, colors, and graphics. For example, a glog focused on historical fiction about the Holocaust, such as Tatiana de Rosnay's *Sarah's Key*, might include a picture of the cover of the book, descriptions of major events in the book or major characters, charts of Holocaust statistics, photos of the location of the story, video clips of newsreels of the time period, and symbols representing elements in the story. A glog focused on carbohydrates in biology might include text with student-created information, videos of expert explanations, pictures of the molecular structure of carbohydrates, and various facts about the effect of carbohydrates.

Prezi (www.prezi.com) is an online application that acts as a virtual canvas to create presentations that show the "big picture" of a topic. Students can combine text, visual and graphic information, and video to create a presentation that flows from one section to the next. Students can use Prezi to create a presentation based on their research or to integrate and evaluate the ideas presented in a literary or informational text. When mapping the text and creating visual elements to represent ideas, students better understand how content is integrated.

The ability to evaluate content presented in diverse media and formats involves determining the credibility of sources. Students need to be able to conduct online searches effectively, separating high-quality sources from those that are not appropriate. Conducting such online searches requires students to critically think throughout the process. Google Search Education contains lesson plans and search challenges for students (and teachers) to improve online search skills. Google Scholar, another tool that is useful for student research, focuses on scholarly literature across disciplines, including articles, abstracts, and books.

Integrating and evaluating content presented quantitatively is part of Reading Standard 7. The ability to integrate or translate quantitative or technical information expressed in words into visual form is a component of both Literacy in History/Social Studies and Literacy in Science and Technical Subjects. Writing to build and present knowledge by gathering, assessing, and applying information is also related to Reading Standard 7. Easy graphing tools are available online, including Google Docs Spreadsheet (www.docs.google.com/spreadsheet), Create a Graph (nces.ed.gov/nceskids/createagraph), and GraphSketch (www.graphsketch.com).

How Can We Integrate Other ELA Standards With Reading Anchor Standard 7?

When planning to teach CCR Anchor Standard 7, we can integrate several other ELA standards to design rich instructional tasks. Examples of ideas to include when creating rich instructional tasks follow.

Integrating Other ELA Standards With Reading Literature Standard 7

- Reading Literature Standard 1 focuses on reading a narrative text closely. *Example:* Encourage students to cite textual evidence when analyzing written and multimedia versions of literary texts.

- Reading Literature Standard 2 focuses on the ability to determine and analyze theme. *Example:* Invite students to analyze written texts and elements in multimedia presentations to determine theme.

- Reading Literature Standard 3 focuses on being able to analyze interpretations of characters, settings, or events in a story or drama. *Example:* Teach students to analyze interpretations of multiple representations of stories, dramas, and poetry.

- Reading Literature Standard 9 focuses on comparing and contrasting versions and aspects of literary text. *Example:* Ask students to analyze versions of written and multimedia texts.

- Speaking and Listening Standard 1 describes students engaging effectively in a range of collaborative discussions, with specific indicators to demonstrate how to participate in an effective academic conversation. *Example:* When reading and analyzing stories, dramas, and poems, engage students in both whole-group and small-group collaborative conversations about the text that include discussing interpretations of written and multimedia texts.

- Language Standard 5 is the vocabulary standard that refers to the descriptive use of language. *Example:* When students describe visual or multimedia elements of a literary text, invite them to analyze the author's use of descriptive and figurative language.

Integrating Other ELA Standards With Reading Informational Text Standard 7

- Reading Informational Text Standard 1 refers to closely reading an informational text. *Example:* Encourage students to cite textual evidence when analyzing written and multimedia versions of informational texts.

- Reading Informational Text Standard 2 focuses on the ability to determine central ideas and purpose of an informational text. *Example:* Ask students to determine and analyze central ideas of written and multimedia versions of texts.

- Reading Informational Text Standard 5 refers to analysis of text structure and organization of the text. *Example:* Ask students to analyze the structure of both written and multimedia representations of the same text.

- Reading Informational Text Standard 6 refers to point of view or author's purpose. *Example:* Encourage students to analyze representations of written and multimedia informational texts to help them identify or analyze the author's point of view or purpose.

- Writing Standard 7 refers to participating in brief shared or individual research projects that build background knowledge about a topic. *Example:* When students are engaged in shared or individual research projects, teach them to use a variety of sources and formats and integrate the information in order to address a question or solve a problem.

- Writing Standard 8 focuses on gathering relevant information from multiple print and digital sources. *Example:* When searching for answers to questions about a topic, encourage students to explore a variety of informational texts, both print and digital, to answer questions and solve problems related to a specific topic.

- Writing Standard 9 addresses the expectation that students will be able to draw evidence from texts to support analysis, reflection, and research. *Example:* Ask students to write responses that integrate information from print and digital sources.

- Speaking and Listening Standard 1 describes the expectation for students to engage effectively in a range of collaborative discussions, with specific indicators to demonstrate how to participate in an effective academic conversation. *Example:* When engaging in collaborative academic conversations about informational texts, encourage students to analyze written and multimedia versions of the text.

- Speaking and Listening Standard 2 focuses on the expectation that students will interpret information in diverse media and formats. *Example:* Encourage students to interpret diverse informational texts.

- Language Standard 6 is the vocabulary standard that refers to general academic and domain-specific words and phrases. *Example:* When discussing analysis of diverse informational texts, encourage students to use vocabulary that is specific to the discipline.

THE COMMON CORE IN ACTION

In this section, we examine one of the foundational ideas that underpins each of the Common Core's Anchor Standards for Reading. For the seventh standard, "Integrate and evaluate content presented in diverse media and formats, including visually and quantitatively, as well as in words" (NGA Center & CCSSO, 2010, p. 10), we have elected to share more detailed information about integrating content presented in diverse media and formats, which is an explicit part of the standard.

Common Core Literacy Task: Comparing and Contrasting Literary Texts with Alternative Versions

Lydia is an eighth-grade language arts teacher. For several years, she has guided her students to read the short story "Harrison Bergeron" by Kurt Vonnegut Jr. (1961/1968). "Harrison Bergeron" is the story of a gifted teenage boy in a dystopian society where everyone is required to be equal. This story has always resonated with early teens, and after analyzing its text complexity (by reviewing quantitative and qualitative measures and reader and task considerations), Lydia feels this story is still quite appropriate to help her students meet the Common Core Standards. She decides to focus on Standard 7 for Literature to push her students' understanding and abilities to comprehend and critique literary text. Standard 7 for Literature in eighth grade is "Analyze the extent to which a filmed or live production of a story or drama stays faithful to or departs from the text or script, evaluating the choices made by the director or actors" (NGA Center & CCSSO, 2010, p. 37). Lydia searches online and finds a brief video production of "Harrison Bergeron" titled *2081* (Halvorssen & Tuttle, 2009) that she feels is appropriate for her class. Then she plans her lesson sequence.

1. First, Lydia gives each student an index card and a copy of the story. She introduces "Harrison Bergeron" by reading aloud the first paragraph. Lydia encourages students to explore the paragraph by rereading and writing at least three questions about the text on the index card.

2. Lydia arranges the students into groups of four. She schedules about 10 minutes for the groups to discuss their questions and possible answers. The task of each group is to make sure that everyone in the group can discuss possible answers to each question. (SL.8.1)

3. The class reads the text closely as a group. Lydia asks students to read silently to predetermined points, encouraging them to create questions to explore the text and clarify points of confusion, and she engages students in a discussion in which they ask and answer student-generated questions and explore ideas and themes. (RL.8.1; SL.8.1)

4. Lydia explains and demonstrates how to complete the graphic organizer for Comparing and Contrasting Literary Text With an Alternative Version (McLaughlin & Overturf, 2013; see Figure 13.3). She emphasizes capturing the theme and its relationship to the characters, setting, and plot of the written story. She also explains that they will use that information to compare and contrast the print and film versions of "Harrison Bergeron." (RL.8.2)

5. When students are familiar with the story and its theme, characters, setting, and plot, Lydia shows the movie *2081*. She guides students to pay close attention to effects such as lighting, music, and camera angles. Lydia then asks students to complete the graphic organizer by

Figure 13.3 Comparing and Contrasting Literary Text With an Alternative Version

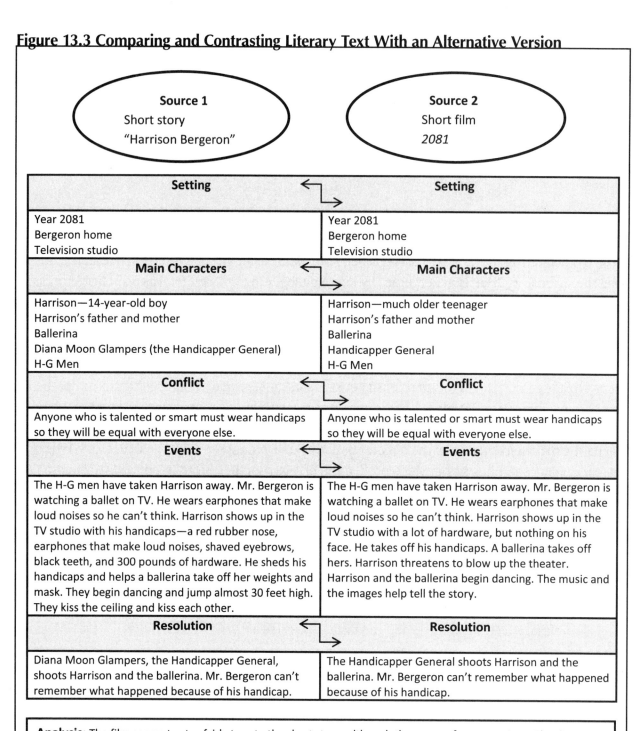

Source 1
Short story
"Harrison Bergeron"

Source 2
Short film
2081

Setting	Setting
Year 2081 Bergeron home Television studio	Year 2081 Bergeron home Television studio

Main Characters	Main Characters
Harrison—14-year-old boy Harrison's father and mother Ballerina Diana Moon Glampers (the Handicapper General) H-G Men	Harrison—much older teenager Harrison's father and mother Ballerina Handicapper General H-G Men

Conflict	Conflict
Anyone who is talented or smart must wear handicaps so they will be equal with everyone else.	Anyone who is talented or smart must wear handicaps so they will be equal with everyone else.

Events	Events
The H-G men have taken Harrison away. Mr. Bergeron is watching a ballet on TV. He wears earphones that make loud noises so he can't think. Harrison shows up in the TV studio with his handicaps—a red rubber nose, earphones that make loud noises, shaved eyebrows, black teeth, and 300 pounds of hardware. He sheds his handicaps and helps a ballerina take off her weights and mask. They begin dancing and jump almost 30 feet high. They kiss the ceiling and kiss each other.	The H-G men have taken Harrison away. Mr. Bergeron is watching a ballet on TV. He wears earphones that make loud noises so he can't think. Harrison shows up in the TV studio with a lot of hardware, but nothing on his face. He takes off his handicaps. A ballerina takes off hers. Harrison threatens to blow up the theater. Harrison and the ballerina begin dancing. The music and the images help tell the story.

Resolution	Resolution
Diana Moon Glampers, the Handicapper General, shoots Harrison and the ballerina. Mr. Bergeron can't remember what happened because of his handicap.	The Handicapper General shoots Harrison and the ballerina. Mr. Bergeron can't remember what happened because of his handicap.

Analysis: The film seems to stay fairly true to the short story, although there are a few exceptions. The director chose to show Harrison as a handsome young man with no "handicaps" on his face, perhaps so viewers can connect with him, see his facial expressions, and notice that he is good-looking. In the film, Harrison threatens to bomb the theater, which he doesn't do in the story. That was probably added for dramatic effect. Also, the ballerina is shown as defiant in the film. She angrily removes her handicaps. In the story, Harrison helps her get the handicaps off, and she seems more as if she is doing what he wants. The director chose to use eerie-sounding music and lots of shadows both in the Bergeron home and in the theater. These effects could represent good and evil. Mr. and Mrs. Bergeron seem to be portrayed in about the same way in both the text and the film versions.

analyzing the extent to which the filmed version of the story stays faithful to or departs from the text. This includes evaluating the choices made by the director. (RL.8.7)

6. Finally, students use the graphic organizer to write an analysis of the ways in which the film compares and contrasts with the written version of "Harrison Bergeron." Emphases include choices made by the author in the print version and the director in the film. (W.8.9a)

Reading Standard 7 focuses on ensuring that students can analyze and integrate information. It requires students to use and analyze visual and multimedia elements in text and use multiple sources to find information. When students put it together, they can evaluate texts and sources and successfully engage in research projects.

References

Leu, D.J., Jr., & Leu, D.D. (1999). *Teaching with the Internet: Lessons from the classroom* (Rev. ed.). Norwood, MA: Christopher-Gordon.

McLaughlin, M. (2010). *Content area reading: Teaching and learning in an age of multiple literacies.* Boston: Allyn & Bacon.

McLaughlin, M., & Overturf, B.J. (2013). *The Common Core: Graphic organizers for teaching K–12 students to meet the Reading Standards.* Newark, DE: International Reading Association. Retrieved from www.reading.org/general/ Publications/Books/bk021.aspx

National Governors Association Center for Best Practices & Council of Chief State School Officers. (2010). *Common Core State Standards for English language arts and literacy in history/social studies, science, and technical subjects.* Washington, DC: Authors. Retrieved August 3, 2012, from www.corestandards.org/assets/CCSSI_ELA%20 Standards.pdf

Literature and Audiovisual Media Cited

Angelou, M. (1993). *Life doesn't frighten me.* New York: Stewart, Tabori and Chang.

Goodwin, D.K. (2006). *Team of rivals: The political genius of Abraham Lincoln.* New York: Simon & Schuster.

Halvorssen, T. (Producer), & Tuttle, C. (Director). (2009). *2081* [Short film]. United States: MPI.

Spielberg, S. (Producer & Director), & Kennedy, K. (Producer). (2012). *Lincoln* [Motion picture]. United States: Touchstone.

Vonnegut, K., Jr. (1968). Harrison Bergeron. In *Welcome to the monkey house.* New York: Dial. (Original work published 1961)

CHAPTER 14

CCR Reading Anchor Standard 8: Claims, Reasons, and Evidence

Hearing the Argument

College and Career Readiness Reading Anchor Standard 8
Delineate and evaluate the argument and specific claims in a text, including the validity of the reasoning as well as the relevance and sufficiency of the evidence. (NGA Center & CCSSO, 2010a, p. 10)

What Does CCR Reading Anchor Standard 8 Mean?

College and Career Readiness (CCR) Reading Anchor Standard 8 focuses on argumentation, a concept that is often misunderstood. When we discuss argumentation in the CCR Anchor Standards, we are referring to formal argumentation, sometimes called rhetoric. Rhetoric, which is typically associated with the teachings of the ancient Greek philosopher Aristotle, is the ability to write or speak in order to inform, persuade, or motivate an audience to support one side of an issue.

Reading Anchor Standard 8 focuses on three college and career readiness reading skills:

1. The ability to delineate and evaluate specific claims

2. The ability to delineate and evaluate the validity of the reasoning of the claim

3. The ability to delineate and evaluate the sufficiency of the evidence for the reasoning

The Difference Between Argument and Persuasion

Although many may believe that *argument* and *persuasion* are synonymous, there is a significant difference between these two terms. In persuasion, a writer or speaker attempts to change the reader's or listener's mind, often by trying to convince the reader to feel a certain way about an issue. In argument, the author attempts to reveal a truth, using facts and/or research to support his or her position.

Persuasive writers and speakers often use techniques that have been developed to affect a reader's or listener's emotions. Such techniques are the foundation of highly expensive advertising campaigns in print and digital media. Common persuasive techniques that may be familiar are bandwagon, slogans, repetition, testimony, expert opinion, and emotional appeal. Writers and speakers often use persuasive techniques when attempting to convince readers or listeners to believe in their position on a political or policy issue or an idea that might affect a certain community.

By contrast, argumentation uses reasons and evidence to convince the reader of one side of an issue regardless of how the writer or speaker actually feels about the issue. In an argument, a writer can argue a position for either side because he or she can prepare to support either side with reasons (facts) and evidence. Logic is the basis of argumentation. Argumentation can be described as "the facts are on my side." This is the type of reading and writing required in CCR Anchor Standard 8.

What Makes a Strong Argument?

A speaker or writer who is developing an argument uses different persuasive strategies to bolster that argument. The basic persuasive strategies in a formal argument are called logos, ethos, and pathos. Logos is the logic that the author uses to develop the text and the facts that the author uses to support the argument. A strong argument is bolstered by a logical organization that outlines what the audience is supposed to believe, the reasons they are supposed to believe it, and the evidence the author presents. An argument includes a claim (the speaker's or author's opinion), grounds for the claim (reasons why the speaker or author believes the opinion is valid), and evidence for the reasons.

Ethos has to do with the source's credibility or the author's authority. For example, an audience tends to trust an author or speaker who has strong credentials and is consistent. Consequently, a person reading a text about how to take care of a pet is more likely to be convinced by a veterinarian than by a person with few or no qualifications.

Pathos is the emotional appeal that some authors and speakers use to prove their point. When an author uses pathos, he or she uses powerful language and facts that relate to the emotions of the audience. For example, if an author is writing against drunk driving, vivid descriptions of people who have been injured or killed in drunk driving accidents will appeal to readers' emotions and make readers more likely to side with the author's proposition. Dr. Martin Luther King Jr.'s familiar "I Have a Dream" speech is an example of an appeal that uses ethos, logos, and pathos.

Students are expected to recognize logical, valid arguments in a text. Students are also expected to argue a point by making a claim in writing or a speech and supporting the claim with logical, valid evidence. Students should be able to recognize plausible data, evaluate whether the author has supported the data, and draw logical conclusions from the data. In the workplace, employees may need to outline an argument for one idea over another and provide valid reasons for their decision. Reading and analyzing an argument means being able to recognize whether an author has actually proved his or her point with sound reasons that are believable and convincing.

How Do the Common Core Standards Build to CCR Reading Anchor Standard 8?

The Common Core Standards in grades 6–12 build toward College and Career Readiness Anchor Standard 8 by addressing skills in three reading substrands. The Reading Standard 8 substrands addressed in grades 6–12 are as follows:

- Reading Standards for Informational Text (English Language Arts)
- Reading Standards for Literacy in History/Social Studies
- Reading Standards for Literacy in Science and Technical Subjects

Table 14.1 Common Core State Standard 8 for Reading Informational Text in Grades 6–12

Grade	Standard
6	Trace and evaluate the argument and specific claims in a text, distinguishing claims that are supported by reasons and evidence from claims that are not.
7	Trace and evaluate the argument and specific claims in a text, assessing whether the reasoning is sound and the evidence is relevant and sufficient to support the claims.
8	Delineate and evaluate the argument and specific claims in a text, assessing whether the reasoning is sound and the evidence is relevant and sufficient; recognize when irrelevant evidence is introduced.
9–10	Delineate and evaluate the argument and specific claims in a text, assessing whether the reasoning is valid and evidence is relevant and sufficient; identify false statements and fallacious reasoning.
11–12	Delineate and evaluate the reasoning in seminal U.S. texts, including the application of constitutional principles and use of legal reasoning (e.g., in U.S. Supreme Court majority opinions and dissents) and the premises, purposes, and arguments in works of public advocacy (e.g., *The Federalist*, presidential addresses).

Note. The standards are from *Common Core State Standards for English Language Arts and Literacy in History/Social Studies, Science, and Technical Subjects* (pp. 39 and 40), by National Governors Association Center for Best Practices and Council of Chief State School Officers, 2010, Washington, DC: Authors.

Table 14.2 Common Core Reading Standard 8 for Literacy in History/Social Studies in Grades 6–12

Grade	Standard
6–8	Distinguish among fact, opinion, and reasoned judgment in a text.
9–10	Assess the extent to which the reasoning and evidence in a text support the author's claims.
11–12	Evaluate an author's premises, claims, and evidence by corroborating or challenging them with other information.

Note. The standards are from *Common Core State Standards for English Language Arts and Literacy in History/Social Studies, Science, and Technical Subjects* (p. 61), by National Governors Association Center for Best Practices and Council of Chief State School Officers, 2010, Washington, DC: Authors.

Reading Standard 8 is only applicable to informational text. In grade 6, students trace and evaluate the argument and specific claims in a text. They distinguish claims that are supported by reasons and evidence from claims that are not. In grade 7, they extend their knowledge by assessing whether the reasoning is sound and the evidence is relevant and sufficient to support the claims. In grade 8, students are expected to delineate and evaluate the argument and specific claims in a text, continuing to assess whether the reasoning is sound and the evidence is sufficient. However, eighth graders also are expected to recognize when irrelevant evidence is introduced. Ninth and tenth graders build on this knowledge to identify false statements and fallacious reasoning. Students in grades 11–12 have specific expectations to delineate and evaluate the reasoning in seminal U.S. texts, including the application of constitutional principles and use of legal reasoning (such as U.S. Supreme Court majority opinions and dissents) and the premises, purposes, and arguments in works of public advocacy (such as *The Federalist* and presidential addresses). Table 14.1 delineates Reading Standard 8 for Informational Text.

Reading Standard 8 for Literacy in History/Social Studies calls for students in grades 6–8 to distinguish among fact, opinion, and reasoned judgment in a text. Students in grades 9–10 are expected to assess the extent to which the reasoning and evidence in a text support the author's claims. In grades 11–12, students evaluate an author's premises, claims, and evidence by corroborating or challenging them with other information. Reading Standard 8 for Literacy in History/Social Studies is featured in Table 14.2.

In Science and Technical Subjects, Reading Standard 8 requires students in grades 6–8 to distinguish among facts, reasoned judgment based on research findings, and speculation in a text. In grades 9–10, students assess the extent to which the reasoning and evidence support the author's claim or a recommendation for solving a scientific or technical problem. By grades 11–12, students are expected to evaluate the hypotheses, data, analysis, and conclusions in a science or technical text. Students at this level also verify the data when possible and corroborate or challenge conclusions with other sources of information. The expectations of Reading Standard 8 for Literacy in Science and Technical Subjects are outlined in Table 14.3.

What Literacy Skills and Strategies Support Reading Anchor Standard 8?

When we review the literacy skills and strategies in the Common Core State Standards, we can readily determine that gaps exist. As educators, we may find ourselves asking whether we should be teaching a particular concept because it does not appear in the CCSS. However, it is important to note that the Standards are not the determining factor. If the skill or strategy is included in our curriculums, we should teach it. For example, students in grades K–3 are expected to be able to ask and answer questions. Similarly, students in grades 4 and 5 are expected to know and use text structures, such as comparison/contrast and problem/solution. The grade 6–12 CCSS do not address either of these topics, but the students still need to know what they are and how to use them to successfully meet the Standards. That is why we noted in Chapter 1 the importance of our reading the CCSS both vertically (our grade levels) and horizontally (what students are expected to know before they reach our grade levels).

Many of the essential skills that grade 6–12 students need, including asking and answering questions and using text structure, are delineated in the grade K–5 Standards. For example, Common Core Reading Standard 1 for both literature and informational text is associated with Reading Anchor Standard 10, which focuses on the expectation that students will read complex text. For students to be able to read, discuss, and write about complex text and fulfill the expectations of Reading Standard 1, they must be able to use the supporting skills and strategies that were introduced in earlier grades. Details of Reading Standard 8, the focus of this chapter, are listed in Table 14.4 for Informational Text (ELA, Reading in History/Social Studies, and Reading in Science and Technical Subjects).

Table 14.3 Common Core Reading Standard 8 for Literacy in Science and Technical Subjects in Grades 6–12

Grade	Standard
6–8	Distinguish among facts, reasoned judgment based on research findings, and speculation in a text.
9–10	Assess the extent to which the reasoning and evidence in a text support the author's claim or a recommendation for solving a scientific or technical problem.
11–12	Evaluate the hypotheses, data, analysis, and conclusions in a science or technical text, verifying the data when possible and corroborating or challenging conclusions with other sources of information.

Note. The standards are from *Common Core State Standards for English Language Arts and Literacy in History/Social Studies, Science, and Technical Subjects* (p. 62), by National Governors Association Center for Best Practices and Council of Chief State School Officers, 2010, Washington, DC: Authors.

How Can We Teach Reading Anchor Standard 8 So Our Students Achieve?

In this section, we discuss the CCSS expectations for students in a variety of grade levels. For example, the eighth Common Core College and Career Anchor Standard for Reading requires that students be able to delineate and evaluate the argument and specific claims in a text, including the validity of the reasoning as well as the relevance and sufficiency of the evidence. To address this, we describe teaching ideas and how they support the Standard. We also share examples of how to embed 21st-century skills in curriculums in meaningful ways.

Table 14.4 K–5 Reading Standard 8: Supporting Skills and Strategies for Informational Text in Grades 6–12

Grade	Skills and Strategies
K	With prompting and support, identify the reasons an author gives to support points in a text.
1	Identify the reasons an author gives to support points in a text.
2	Describe how reasons support specific points the author makes in a text.
3	Describe the logical connection between particular sentences and paragraphs in a text (e.g., comparison, cause/effect, first/second/third in a sequence).
4	Explain how an author uses reasons and evidence to support particular points in a text.
5	Explain how an author uses reasons and evidence to support particular points in a text, identifying which reasons and evidence support which point(s).

Note. The skills and strategies are from *Common Core State Standards for English Language Arts and Literacy in History/Social Studies, Science, and Technical Subjects* (pp. 13 and 14), by National Governors Association Center for Best Practices and Council of Chief State School Officers, 2010, Washington, DC: Authors.

Fact and Opinion

In grades 6–8 in the Reading Standards for Literacy in History/Social Studies, students are expected to distinguish among fact, opinion, and reasoned judgment in a text. To teach our students to discern the difference between fact and opinion, we can use a variety of types of texts including news articles and editorials, which typically contain facts and opinions, respectively. To provide opportunities for students to practice distinguishing fact from opinion, we can use the Fact and Opinion Multimedia Organizer (McLaughlin & Overturf, 2013). A completed organizer that features students' determinations of fact and opinion in an editorial and a play review appears in Figure 14.1.

Identifying Evidence That Supports Reasoning

The CCSS expectations for students in grades 6–12 include identifying evidence that supports reasoning. For example, ninth- and tenth-grade students need to "delineate and evaluate the argument and specific claims in a text, assessing whether the reasoning is valid and the evidence is relevant and sufficient; identify false statements and fallacious reasoning" (NGA Center & CCSSO, 2010a, p. 40). Students can use the What–Why–How? graphic organizer (McLaughlin & Overturf, 2013) to analyze an opinion text. What–Why–How? requires students to raise questions about the text and summarize the key ideas to determine the author's opinion. Students also record how the author supports his or her opinion with reasons and information. This organizer can help students comprehend the author's message and understand the way authors organize opinion-based text. The What–Why–How? framework can be used throughout the grades.

When reading a text that discusses an opinion, ask these questions:

- "What does the author think?" In the first column of the What–Why–How? graphic organizer, ask students to write one sentence that details the author's opinion.

- "Why does the author think this way?" In the second column, invite students to write reasons the author includes in the text for his or her opinion.

- "How do facts in the text support the author's thinking?" In the third column, encourage students to write facts that the author included to support each reason.

Figure 14.1 Example of a Fact and Opinion Multimedia Organizer

Editorial	Fact	Opinion	Excerpt
Hypochondria: An Inside Look Woody Allen, *The New York Times*, January 12, 2013 www.nytimes.com/2013/01/13/opinion/sunday/hypochondria-an-inside-look.html?pagewanted=1&_r=1&ref=general&src=me&		Yes	"What I am is an alarmist, which is in the same ballpark as the hypochondriac or, should I say, the same emergency room."
		Yes	"What distinguishes my hysteria is that at the appearance of the mildest symptom, let's say chapped lips, I instantly leap to the conclusion that the chapped lips indicate a brain tumor. Or maybe lung cancer. In one instance, I thought it was Mad Cow."

Play Review	Fact	Opinion	Excerpt
A Pair of New Witches, Still in Search of the Right Spell Jason Zinoman, *The New York Times*, July 15, 2005 theater.nytimes.com/2005/07/15/theater/reviews/15zino.html	Yes		"But measured by the standard of box-office receipts — these are Broadway musicals, after all — the reigning king of the commercial theater is, inarguably, *Wicked*. Last week it led all Broadway shows with $1.3 million in ticket sales."
		Yes	"The current stars ... seem tentative onstage, devoid of the kind of idiosyncrasies that make a star fun to watch."

Figure 14.2 features a completed What–Why–How? Organizer about the writing of works that have been attributed to William Shakespeare.

The For and Against Organizer (McLaughlin & Overturf, 2013) offers another format to teach students how to analyze arguments. A completed example of this organizer is shown in Figure 14.3.

Writing Standard 1 describes the expectations for students to be able to write an opinion and support it. Appendix C of the Common Core State Standards (NGA Center & CCSSO, 2010b) provides examples of student writing that meets Writing Standard 1 for each grade level. We can use the student examples for opinion writing (argument) and the What–Why–How? graphic organizer to analyze how the writer supported his or her opinion with reasons and information and to provide students with models of writing opinions.

21st-Century Skill Applications for Reading Anchor Standard 8

In this section, we share ideas to help students meet the Reading Standards through the use of 21st-century tools and skills. Although online tools can be used for a variety of purposes, we have chosen to highlight specific tools for use with each particular standard. As teachers, we should select tools we feel work best with our students, using the same tools in multiple ways when possible.

CCR Reading Standard 8 focuses on delineating and evaluating the argument and specific claims in a text, including the validity of the reasoning as well as the relevance and sufficiency of the evidence. Professional blogs are a great source for texts that support a specific argument about a topic (for example, see the *New York Times* Blog Directory at www.nytimes.com/interactive/blogs/directory.html). Writers of blogs usually have a point they are trying to make, and these texts can be used for analysis of the author's argument. Speeches are another source for argumentative text. Some online sources for speeches are American Rhetoric (www.americanrhetoric.com), which offers recorded written transcripts, and The History Place (www.historyplace.com).

A student blog is an innovative way for students to analyze an author's argument and to write their own arguments and share their own opinions with others. Classroom blogs are an excellent way to help students find an equal voice in the classroom (Downes, 2004) and to continue to engage in discussion when not in the physical classroom. Edublogs (www.edublogs.org) and Kidblog (www.kidblog.org) are two excellent tools for classroom blogging. These tools create a safe and secure social environment for students to express their opinions and enhance discussion, whether in the physical classroom or connecting to the blog when away from the classroom. Students can write to support their own opinions about texts and on topics based on texts they have read, and they can comment on classmates' blogs under teacher supervision and guidance.

The ReadWriteThink website contains a student interactive called Persuasion Map (www.readwritethink.org/files/resources/interactives/persuasion_map). Although this student interactive was created to be a template for helping students plan original argumentative writing, it can also be used to analyze an author's arguments. Students read a text containing an argument and map the argument into the Persuasion Map. The completed map can be printed and used to write a discussion of the way in which the author supported his or her claims and supporting evidence.

Figure 14.2 Example of a What–Why–How? Organizer

What does the author think?	Why does the author think this way?	How do facts support the author's thinking?
The author points out that it is possible that William Shakespeare did not write his famous plays.	Documents found related to William Shakespeare point out that he was mainly a businessman and there is no existing evidence of a writing career.	1. Daniel Write, a Shakespeare authorship research professor, stated that only 70 documents of William Shakespeare have been discovered, and not one is literary.
		2. William Shakespeare's signature is only found on legal documents. For example, his signature is found on his ownership in the Globe Theater.
		3. When William Shakespeare died, he left precious possessions, but there are no records of his owning any books.
	There is no evidence to support how William Shakespeare received his education or gained knowledge of rich and famous people.	1. There is no evidence of William Shakespeare learning different languages.
		2. William Shakespeare would have had to know how to fluently use metaphors and intricate puns.
		3. There is no evidence proving how William Shakespeare gained his knowledge of astronomy, medicine, or archery.
The author also provides a point of view focused on why William Shakespeare could have been the writer of his famous plays.	While the level of success is extraordinary, it is possible that William Shakespeare could have been a genius.	1. Anyone can question someone's writing, but there is no strong evidence provided that William Shakespeare did not write his plays.
		2. William Shakespeare's name did appear on some of the plays published during that time period.
		3. Even though there are no manuscripts or letters from William Shakespeare, it was a long time ago.

Figure 14.3 Example of a For and Against Organizer

FOR and AGAINST: Is social networking beneficial to its users?

For			Against		
Write <u>one</u> sentence FOR the issue. Social networking is a communication tool that allows people to contact others from around the world.			Write <u>one</u> sentence AGAINST the issue. Social networking decreases personal interaction and can be dangerous and hurtful.		
Reasons to be FOR the issue	**List at least two facts (evidence) for each reason.**		**Reasons to be AGAINST the issue**	**List at least two facts (evidence) for each reason.**	
Reason Social networking allows communication between friends and family around the world.	**Fact** People find communication via the Internet more comfortable.		**Reason** Social networking diminishes personal social communication.	**Fact** People spend more time online than interacting face to face.	
	Fact Communication can take place 24 hours a day, seven days a week.			**Fact** Students spend several hours each week using social media.	
Reason Social networking provides assistance when engaging in everyday life issues (for example, buying a car or changing jobs).	**Fact** Millions of people receive help with life issues via the Internet.		**Reason** Social networking can be dangerous.	**Fact** Information that users delete can still be retrieved.	
	Fact Experts are available via the Internet.			**Fact** Thousands of sex offenders were identified as having profiles on MySpace.	
Reason Students can use social networking for their education and their careers.	**Fact** More than 50% of students access the Internet.		**Reason** Cyberbullying makes it easier for students to bully, and it makes bullying more public.	**Fact** Too many middle school and high school students have been victims of cyberbullying.	
	Fact 50% of students access the Internet for educational assistance.			**Fact** Because of cyberbullying, victims' grades decrease and victims may get depressed.	

How Can We Integrate Other ELA Standards With Reading Anchor Standard 8?

When planning to teach CCR Anchor Standard 8, we can integrate several other ELA standards to design rich instructional tasks. The following are examples of ideas to include when creating rich instructional tasks for reading informational texts.

- Reading Informational Text Standard 1 refers to closely reading an informational text. *Example:* When closely reading an informational text that includes an argument, teach students to carefully consider the author's opinion, including claims, reasons, and evidence.

- Reading Informational Text Standard 3 focuses on analyzing the connections and relationships among people, events, ideas, or pieces of information in a text. *Example:* When students read an argument, invite them to record ways the author uses reasons and information to support his or her opinion.

- Reading Informational Text Standard 6 refers to point of view or author's purpose. *Example:* Engage students in discussing the author's point of view or purpose for writing an argument.

- Writing Standard 1 addresses the expectations for writing arguments. *Example:* Using the criteria in Writing Standard 1, teach students to write their own arguments with claims, supporting reasons, and evidence.

- Speaking and Listening Standard 3 refers to listening to a speaker. *Example:* As students listen to a presentation, teach them to analyze the reasons and evidence the speaker uses to justify an argument.

- Speaking and Listening Standard 4 refers to reporting on a topic. *Example:* Teach students how to give an oral argument in which they present claims, reasons, evidence, and appropriate speaking skills.

- Language Standard 6 is about the use of grade-appropriate general academic and domain-specific words and phrases. *Example:* Teach students to use appropriate words and phrases, such as *argument*, *claims*, *reasons*, and *evidence*, when speaking and writing about arguments.

THE COMMON CORE IN ACTION

In this section, we examine one of the foundational ideas that underpins each of the Common Core Standards for Reading. For the eighth standard, "Delineate and evaluate the argument and specific claims in a text, including the validity of the reasoning as well as the relevance and sufficiency of the evidence" (NGA Center & CCSSO, 2010a, p. 35), we have elected to share more detailed information about evaluating specific claims in a text, which is an explicit part of the Reading Standards for Informational Text in English Language Arts.

Common Core Literacy Task: Tracing and Evaluating an Argument and Specific Claims

Maria teaches sixth-grade Language Arts on a middle school interdisciplinary team. Maria and her colleagues are planning a brief thematic unit on nutrition choices, with each teacher focusing on appropriate standards for their own discipline. The teachers have decided that the students on the team will read the book *Chew on This: Everything You Don't Want to Know About Fast Food* by Eric

Schlosser and Charles Wilson (2006). Maria will facilitate the reading, writing, and discussion of the book, while other teachers on the sixth-grade team plan lessons that relate to the ideas in the text. For example, in science, students will learn how the body uses food and how a poor diet can affect body systems. In mathematics, students will work on interpreting charts and graphs and practice statistical thinking about food and nutrition. In social studies, students will concentrate on geography and social issues involved in food production. In Language Arts, the sixth graders will focus on Standard 8 for reading informational text: "Trace and evaluate the argument and specific claims in a text, distinguishing claims that are supported by reasons and evidence from claims that are not" (RI.6.8).

To motivate her sixth graders, Maria will read aloud the introduction of *Chew on This*, which discusses how the fast food experience began in California and has grown throughout the world. Maria will do the following:

1. Facilitate a class discussion about the ideas presented in the introduction to *Chew on This*, including the impulse to buy and eat fast foods. (SL.6.1)

2. Review the difference between facts and opinions. Each student will receive four sticky notes. Students will revisit the introduction and write on their sticky notes two facts and two opinions from the information presented. They will then post their sticky notes on wall charts labeled "Facts" and "Opinions." Facilitate a student-led discussion about facts and opinions presented in the introduction. (SL.6.1)

3. Facilitate students in reading the first chapter, "The Pioneers." Students will silently read each section independently, then work with a partner to list three interesting facts they find in each section of the chapter. Together, they will form an opinion about each section. The class will discuss the partners' decisions. (RI.6.1; SL.6.1)

4. Teach the concept of "argument" as an opinion supported by evidence. Include information about the ways in which authors persuade their readers through the use of logic, emotion, and ethics. Demonstrate for students how to form an argument and support the argument with evidence. (RI.6.8)

5. For the remainder of the book, divide students into five groups. Assign each group a chapter of the book (except the last chapter). Each group will read their assigned chapter and create a three-minute multimedia presentation of the argument, facts, and key details presented. (RI.6.8; W.6.6)

6. Ask each group to share its presentation. Students will listen and take notes to form an opinion of the issue. (SL.6.4; SL.6.5; SL.6.2)

7. At the completion of each presentation, ask students to participate in a Pinwheel Debate about the chapter. In a Pinwheel Debate, four chairs are placed facing each other. Students are selected to fill those seats, and the remaining students fill the other chairs in each of the four sections. The chair arrangement then looks like a pinwheel. Each subgroup represents a different perspective on an issue. During the debate, the four lead chairs are the "hot seats." A representative from each perspective sits in a hot seat and states an opinion, with facts from the chapter to support the opinion. Representatives from the subgroups rotate in and out of the hot seats to support their subgroup's perspective. (RI.6.8; SL.6.1)

8. Read aloud the last chapter and facilitate a class discussion on the conclusions of the authors. (SL.6.1)

9. Ask students to write an argument for or against an issue raised in the book, following the criteria of Writing Standard 1 for sixth grade (W.6.1) and the standards for production and distribution of writing. (W.6.4; W.6.5; W.6.7)

Reading Standard 8 focuses on ensuring that students can analyze the way an author supports opinions with reasons and evidence. This standard requires students to analyze arguments, evaluate reasoning, and determine the sufficiency of evidence. When students hear an argument, they can explain how authors support their thinking.

References

Downes, S. (2004, September/October). Educational blogging. *Educause review*. Retrieved December 29, 2012, from net.educause.edu/ir/library/pdf/erm0450.pdf

McLaughlin, M., & Overturf, B.J. (2013). *The Common Core: Graphic organizers for teaching K–12 students to meet the Reading Standards*. Newark, DE: International Reading Association. Retrieved from www.reading.org/general/Publications/Books/bk021.aspx

National Governors Association Center for Best Practices & Council of Chief State School Officers. (2010a). *Common Core State Standards for English language arts and literacy in history/social studies, science, and technical subjects*. Washington, DC: Authors. Retrieved August 3, 2012, from www.corestandards.org/assets/CCSSI_ELA%20Standards.pdf

National Governors Association Center for Best Practices & Council of Chief State School Officers. (2010b). *Common Core State Standards for English language arts and literacy in history/social studies, science, and technical subjects: Appendix C: Samples of student writing*. Washington, DC: Authors. Retrieved August 3, 2012, from www.corestandards.org/assets/Appendix_C.pdf

Informational Text Cited

Schlosser, E., & Wilson, C. (2006). *Chew on this: Everything you don't want to know about fast food*. New York: Houghton Mifflin.

CHAPTER 15

CCR Reading Anchor Standard 9: Compare/Contrast Themes and Topics

 **Weighing the Works**	**College and Career Readiness Reading Anchor Standard 9** Analyze how two or more texts address similar themes or topics to build knowledge or to compare the approaches the authors take. (NGA Center & CCSSO, 2010, p. 10)

What Does CCR Reading Anchor Standard 9 Mean?

The aim of College and Career Readiness (CCR) Reading Anchor Standard 9 is for students to compare and contrast similar themes or topics from a variety of sources. For example, students may be asked to compare and contrast how authors approach issues in texts about similar subjects. Students need to weigh the works to determine and analyze similarities and differences.

Reading Anchor Standard 9 focuses on two college and career readiness reading skills:

1. The ability to analyze how two or more texts address similar themes or topics to build knowledge

2. The ability to analyze how two or more texts address similar themes or topics to compare the authors' approaches

A frequent assignment in many college classes is to write a comparative analysis in which students compare and contrast two or more objects, ideas, or concepts. Students are typically asked to read about and then compare and contrast issues, historical figures, poems, processes, themes in literature and so forth, in classes across the curriculum. In a comparative analysis, the student may discuss two similar things that have significant differences or two things that have obvious differences but also some interesting commonalities. In a comparative analysis, the student observes similarities and differences and then makes raw data into a coherent argument (Walk, 1998).

Comparing and Contrasting in Literature

In English or literature classes, students may be asked to compare and contrast characters, settings, themes, or poetic styles. They may be asked to write a comparative analysis of two works by the same author or two stories with the same basic plot. In this case, students need to understand how to compare and contrast works of literature for similarities and differences and then write a comparison that proves a point or makes an argument. The Common Core expectations require students to analyze how an author draws on and transforms source material in a specific work. An example is how Shakespeare treats a theme or topic from the Bible and how a later author draws on a play by Shakespeare. Students are also expected to demonstrate knowledge of 18th-, 19th-, and early 20th-century foundational works of American literature, including how two or more texts of the same theme treat similar themes or topics.

Comparing and Contrasting in the Disciplines

In the disciplines, students may be asked to write a comparative analysis of issues, topics of information, historical figures, historical documents, or scientific procedures. In this case, students need to understand how to compare (similarities) and contrast (differences) topics and themes in informational texts and write a coherent argument. In the upper grades, students are expected to compare and contrast important documents in U.S. history; integrate information from diverse sources, both primary and secondary, into a coherent understanding of an idea or event; and synthesize information from a range of sources about scientific processes, concepts, or phenomena.

Ways to Compare and Contrast

When authors compare and contrast, there are two basic organizational text structures that they may use: text-by-text (sometimes called whole-to-whole or block) and point-by-point (Walk, 1998). In the text-by-text structure, the author describes one topic in its entirety (A) and then another topic in its entirety (B). In the point-by-point structure, the author writes about one point for both A and B, then moves to a second point about both A and B, etc. Another type of organizational structure is similarities and differences. In this text structure, the author writes about the similarities found in A and B and then about the differences related to A and B. Students choose one of these organizational structures to use when writing comparative essays.

How Do the Common Core Standards Build to CCR Reading Anchor Standard 9?

The Common Core Standards in grades 6–12 build toward College and Career Readiness Anchor Standard 9 by addressing skills in four reading substrands. The Reading Standard 9 substrands addressed in grades 6–12 are as follows:

- Reading Standards for Literature (English Language Arts)
- Reading Standards for Informational Text (English Language Arts)
- Reading Standards for Literacy in History/Social Studies
- Reading Standards for Literacy in Science and Technical Subjects

In Reading Standard 9 for Literature, sixth graders compare and contrast texts in different forms or genres (such as stories and poems or historical novels and fantasy stories) in terms of their approaches to similar themes and topics. Students in seventh grade compare and contrast a fictional portrayal of a time, place, or character and a historical account of the same period to understand how authors of fiction use or alter history. In grade 8, students analyze how a modern work of fiction draws on themes, patterns of events, or character types from myths, traditional stories, or religious

Table 15.1 Common Core State Standard 9 for Reading Literature in Grades 6–12

Grade	Standard
6	Compare and contrast texts in different forms or genres (e.g., stories and poems; historical novels and fantasy stories) in terms of their approaches to similar themes and topics.
7	Compare and contrast a fictional portrayal of the time, place, or character and a historical account of the same period as a means of understanding how authors of fiction use or alter history.
8	Analyze how a modern work of fiction draws on themes, patterns of events, or character types from myths, traditional stories, or religious works such as the Bible, including describing how the material is rendered new.
9–10	Analyze how an author draws on and transform source material in a specific work (e.g., how Shakespeare treats a theme or topic from Ovid or the Bible or how a later author draws on a play by Shakespeare).
11–12	Demonstrate knowledge of eighteenth-, nineteenth-, and early-twentieth-century foundational works of American literature, including how two or more texts from the same period treat similar themes or topics.

Note. The standards are from *Common Core State Standards for English Language Arts and Literacy in History/Social Studies, Science, and Technical Subjects* (pp. 37 and 38), by National Governors Association Center for Best Practices and Council of Chief State School Officers, 2010, Washington, DC: Authors.

Table 15.2 Common Core State Standard 9 for Reading Informational Text in Grades 6–12

Grade	Standard
6	Compare and contrast one author's presentation of events with that of another (e.g., a memoir written by and a biography on the same person).
7	Analyze how two or more authors writing about the same topic shape their presentations of key information by emphasizing different evidence or advancing different interpretations of facts.
8	Analyze a case in which two or more texts provide conflicting information on the same topic and identify where the texts disagree on matters of fact or interpretation.
9–10	Analyze seminal U.S. documents of historical and literary significance (e.g., Washington's Farewell Address, the Gettysburg Address, Roosevelt's Four Freedoms speech, King's "Letter from Birmingham Jail"), including how they address related themes and concepts.
11–12	Analyze seventeenth-, eighteenth-, and nineteenth-century foundational U.S. documents of historical and literary significance (including The Declaration of Independence, the Preamble to the Constitution, the Bill of Rights, and Lincoln's Second Inaugural Address) for their themes, purposes, and rhetorical features.

Note. The standards are from *Common Core State Standards for English Language Arts and Literacy in History/Social Studies, Science, and Technical Subjects* (pp. 39 and 40), by National Governors Association Center for Best Practices and Council of Chief State School Officers, 2010, Washington, DC: Authors.

works such as the Bible. They also describe how the material is rendered new. Students in grades 9–10 analyze how an author draws on and transforms source materials in a specific work. In grades 11–12, students are expected to demonstrate knowledge of foundational works of American literature, including how two or more texts from the same period treat similar themes and topics. Reading Standard 9 for Literature is delineated in Table 15.1.

In Reading Standard 9 for Informational Text, students in grade 6 compare and contrast one author's presentation of events with that of another, such as a memoir and a biography written about the same person. In grade 7, students analyze how different authors writing about the same subject emphasize different evidence or advance different interpretations. Eighth graders analyze ways in which two or more texts provide conflicting information on the same topic. They also identify where the texts disagree on matters of interpretation. Table 15.2 outlines Reading Standard 9 for Informational Text.

In Reading Standard 9 for Literacy in History/Social Studies, students in grades 6–8 are expected to analyze the relationship between a primary and secondary source on the same topic. In grades 9–10, students will compare and contrast treatments of the same topic in several primary and secondary sources. Students in grades 11–12 integrate information from diverse sources, both primary and secondary, into a coherent understanding of an idea or event. They also are expected to note discrepancies among their sources. Reading Standard 9 for Literacy in History/Social Studies is shown in Table 15.3.

In Reading Standard 9 for Literacy in Science and Technical Subjects, students in grades 6–8 compare and contrast information gained from experiments, simulations, video, or multimedia sources with information gained from reading a text on the same topic. Students in grades 9–10 compare and contrast findings presented in a text to those from other sources, including their own experiments. Students at this grade are also expected to note when the findings support or contradict previous explanations or accounts. In grades 11–12, students synthesize information from a range of sources, such as tests, experiments, and simulations, into a coherent understanding of a process, phenomenon, or concept and resolve conflicting information when possible. Reading Standard 9 for Literacy in Science and Technical Subjects is delineated in Table 15.4.

What Literacy Skills and Strategies Support Reading Anchor Standard 9?

When we review the literacy skills and strategies in the Common Core State Standards, we can readily determine that gaps exist. As educators, we may find ourselves asking whether we should be teaching a particular concept because it does not appear in the CCSS. However, it is important to note that the Standards are not the determining factor. If the skill or strategy is included in our curriculums, we should teach it. For example, students in grades K–3 are expected to be able to ask and answer questions. Similarly, students in grades 4 and 5 are expected to know and use text structures, such as comparison/contrast and problem/solution. The grade 6–12 CCSS do not address either of these topics, but the students still need to know what they are and how to use them to successfully meet the Standards. That is why we noted in Chapter 1 the importance of our reading the CCSS both vertically (our grade levels) and horizontally (what students are expected to know before they reach our grade levels).

Many of the essential skills that grade 6–12 students need to know, including asking and answering questions and using text structure, are delineated in the grade K–5 Standards. For example, Common Core Reading Standard 1, for both literature and informational text, is associated with Reading Standard 10, which focuses on the expectation that students will read complex text.

Table 15.3 Common Core Reading Standard 9 for Literacy in History/Social Studies in Grades 6–12

Grade	Standard
6–8	Analyze the relationship between a primary and secondary source on the same topic.
9–10	Compare and contrast treatments of the same topic in several primary and secondary sources.
11–12	Integrate information from diverse sources, both primary and secondary, into a coherent understanding of an idea or event, noting discrepancies among sources.

Note. The standards are from *Common Core State Standards for English Language Arts and Literacy in History/Social Studies, Science, and Technical Subjects* (p. 61), by National Governors Association Center for Best Practices and Council of Chief State School Officers, 2010, Washington, DC: Authors.

Table 15.4 Common Core Reading Standard 9 for Literacy in Science and Technical Subjects in Grades 6–12

Grade	Standard
6–8	Compare and contrast the information gained from experiments, simulations, video, or multimedia sources with that gained from reading a text on the same topic.
9–10	Compare and contrast findings presented in a text to those from other sources (including their own experiments), noting when the findings support or contradict previous explanations or accounts.
11–12	Synthesize information from a range of sources (e.g., texts, experiments, simulations) into a coherent understanding of a process, phenomenon, or concept, resolving conflicting information when possible.

Note. The standards are from *Common Core State Standards for English Language Arts and Literacy in History/Social Studies, Science, and Technical Subjects* (p. 62), by National Governors Association Center for Best Practices and Council of Chief State School Officers, 2010, Washington, DC: Authors.

Table 15.5 K–5 Reading Standard 9: Supporting Skills and Strategies for Literature in Grades 6–12

Grade	Supporting Skills and Strategies
K	With prompting and support, compare and contrast the adventures and experiences of characters in familiar stories.
1	Compare and contrast the adventures and experiences of characters in stories.
2	Compare and contrast two or more versions of the same story (e.g., Cinderella stories) by different authors or from different cultures.
3	Compare and contrast the themes, settings, and plots of stories written by the same author about the same or similar characters (e.g., in books from a series).
4	Compare and contrast the treatment of similar themes and topics (e.g., opposition of good and evil) and patterns of events (e.g., the quest) in stories, myths, and traditional literature from different cultures.
5	Compare and contrast stories in the same genre (e.g., mysteries and adventure stories) on their approaches to similar themes and topics.

Note. The skills and strategies are from *Common Core State Standards for English Language Arts and Literacy in History/Social Studies, Science, and Technical Subjects* (pp. 11 and 12), by National Governors Association Center for Best Practices and Council of Chief State School Officers, 2010, Washington, DC: Authors.

Table 15.6 K–5 Reading Standard 9: Supporting Skills and Strategies for Informational Text in Grades 6–12

Grade	Supporting Skills and Strategies
K	With prompting and support, identify basic similarities in and differences between two texts on the same topic (e.g., in illustrations, descriptions, or procedures).
1	Identify basic similarities in and differences between two texts on the same topic (e.g., in illustrations, descriptions, or procedures).
2	Compare and contrast the most important points presented by two texts on the same topic.
3	Compare and contrast the most important points and key details presented in two texts on the same topic.
4	Integrate information from two texts on the same topic in order to write or speak about the subject knowledgeably.
5	Integrate information from several texts on the same topic in order to write or speak about the subject knowledgeably.

Note. The skills and strategies are from *Common Core State Standards for English Language Arts and Literacy in History/Social Studies, Science, and Technical Subjects* (pp. 13 and 14), by National Governors Association Center for Best Practices and Council of Chief State School Officers, 2010, Washington, DC: Authors.

For students to be able to read, discuss, and write about complex text and fulfill the expectations of Reading Standard 1, they must be able to use the supporting skills and strategies that were introduced in earlier grades. Details of Reading Standard 9, the focus of this chapter, are featured in Table 15.5 for Literature (English Language Arts) and Table 15.6 for Informational Text (ELA, Reading in History/Social Studies, and Reading in Science and Technical Subjects).

How Can We Teach Reading Anchor Standard 9 So Our Students Achieve?

In this section, we discuss Common Core expectations for students at various grade levels. For example, the ninth College and Career Readiness Anchor Standard requires students to compare and contrast texts and integrate information from texts. To address this, we describe teaching ideas and how they support the Standard. We also share examples of how to embed 21st-century skills in curriculums in meaningful ways.

Compare and Contrast Texts

When comparing and contrasting two versions of a literary text, students can address both the content and the mediums. For example, *Romeo and Juliet* is a well-known Shakespearean drama that students often read in high school, but the play has also been adapted to a variety of other mediums. These include the graphic novel *Prince of Cats* and the Broadway play *West Side Story*. When examining these three mediums, similarities and differences quickly emerge. For example, although the story lines are based on Shakespeare's original characters, the setting and the characters are very different in *Prince of Cats* and *West Side Story*. The graphic designs are an integral component of *Prince of Cats*, while music, particularly lively numbers such as "America," "Something's Coming," and "Tonight," play an important role in *West Side Story*. Figure 15.1 shows a Tri-Media Text Organizer (McLaughlin & Overturf, 2013) about the play, the graphic novel, and the musical.

When comparing and contrasting informational texts, students can use graphic organizers such as the Venn Diagram (see Chapter 11, Figure 11.2) and Questions Into Paragraphs (E.M. McLaughlin, 1987) to support their thinking. For example, Questions Into Paragraphs (QuIP) is a graphic organizer in which students generate research questions and record responses from multiple informational text sources. In the extended version of this organizer that appears in Figure 15.2, the nervous system is explored through five questions and three sources: a textbook and two websites. After students respond to each question from all sources, they write a paragraph based on the responses. Students are especially motivated to use Questions Into Paragraphs because they generate the research questions and select the research sources.

Integrate Information From Texts

Press Conference (McLaughlin, 2010) is an inquiry-based activity that promotes oral communication. This process is based on student interest in a particular content-related topic. Students peruse newspapers, magazines, or the Internet to find articles of interest to themselves and their peers. When they find a topic in which they have interest, they discuss it with us. Then, they begin their research. Because the resulting Press Conference presentation lasts only a few minutes, it is the type of inquiry-based activity that each student might present once during each marking period.

When preparing for Press Conference, students use a minimum of three websites as sources. After reading the information that they have researched, focusing on its essential points, synthesizing it, raising additional questions, and reflecting on personal insights, the students share the information through an informal presentation to the class. Members of the audience then raise questions, just as if they were participating in an actual press conference. If the presenter cannot answer the question, he or she joins the questioner in researching a response and reporting back to the class. Press Conference topics are discipline-specific. Possibilities include extreme weather, genetics, novels adapted to films, the economy, and current events.

Figure 15.1 Example of a Tri-Media Text Organizer

Romeo and Juliet

← **Differences** →

1. Arthur Laurents, book
   Leonard Bernstein, music
   Stephen Sondheim, lyrics

2. Musical

3. *West Side Story*

4. New York City

5. Tony, Maria, the Jets,
   the Sharks

1. Ronald Wimberly

2. Graphic novel

3. *Prince of Cats*

4. Early hip-hop days in NYC

5. Tybalt and other
   characters from *Romeo and
   Juliet*

1. William Shakespeare

2. Play

3. *Romeo and Juliet*

4. Verona and Mantua, Italy

5. Romeo, Juliet, other characters
   Shakespeare created

← **Similarities** →

All three versions of the story focus on the characters from *Romeo and Juliet*. The original characters emerge in the Shakespearean play. In *Prince of Cats*, Tybalt is the protagonist, and in *West Side Story*, Jet and Shark gang-based versions of the characters appear. All three works share classic love as their central theme. They also focus on the often senseless nature of life, love, and youth.

Figure 15.2 Example of an Extended Questions Into Paragraphs (QuIP) Organizer

Questions	Answers		
	Source A Miller, K.R., & Levine, J.S. (2008). *Biology*. Boston: Pearson Prentice Hall.	Source B NSTA, "The Nervous System" www.nsta.org/publications/interactive/nerves/basics/nervous_system.html	Source C Kids Health, "Brain and Nervous System" kidshealth.org/parent/general/body_basics/brain_nervous_system.html
1. What is the nervous system?	The nervous system is the body's message system that controls and organizes functions in the body and answers to inner and outer stimuli.	The nervous system is a group of specialized cells working together to send and receive messages.	The nervous system is like a network that sends and receives messages from the brain to different parts of the body.
2. How does the nervous system function?	Neuron cells carry messages for the nervous system. These electrical message signals are called impulses.	Neuron cells pick up messages called dendrites, and axons carry messages to other cells.	Neurons carry messages to and from the brain.
3. How do neurons work?	There are three types of neurons, and they each do something different. The sensory neurons carry impulses away from the sensory organs to the spinal cord and brain. The motor neurons carry impulses from the spinal cord and brain to the muscles and glands. And the interneurons connect sensory and motor neurons and carry impulses between both.	The way a neuron is assembled can tell what function it can perform. A neuron is a lot like a battery. It has the ability to build up a charge. When the neuron is roused, it moves down the axon. The charge moves down the axon until it reaches the end, which stimulates the nerve cell.	Sensory neurons carry information from our sensory organs to the brain. Motor neurons have the job of carrying messages away from the brain and back to the rest of the body.
4. What are the specific parts of the nervous system?	There are two main parts of the nervous system: the central nervous system, which is the brain and spinal cord, and the peripheral nervous system, which is all of the nerves and cells that are not part of the brain and spinal cord.	The brain and the spinal cord make up the central nervous system, and the peripheral nervous system sends signals to the nerves and cells that are not included in the brain and spinal cord.	The brain and the spinal cord are what make up the central nervous system.
5. How does the central nervous system operate?	The brain in the central nervous system receives requests and creates requests for the body. The spinal cord is what carries those requests to the rest of the body. There are 31 pairs of nerves that come from the spinal cord and connect to the brain and different parts of the body.	The central nervous system controls messages for all parts of the body. The spinal cord takes messages from the brain to the rest of the body and gives responses to the brain. The brain controls messages and is where higher-order messages are stored for short- and long-term memory.	The brain stores important information and is what controls the body's function. The spinal cord is made up of nerve tissue and extends down from the brain. It has numerous nerves that branch out to the body, carrying information to the rest of the body.

The nervous system is like a network. It is the body's message system, made up of specialized cells working together. It controls and organizes functions in the body. It also sends and receives messages. The nervous system is made up of cells called neurons that pick up and carry messages. The messages picked up are called dendrites, and axons are what carry messages to other cells. The way a neuron is assembled can tell what function it can perform. A neuron is a lot like a battery. It has the ability to build up a charge. When the neuron is roused, it moves down the axon. The charge moves down the axon until it reaches the end, which stimulates the nerve cell. Sensory neurons carry information from the sensory organs to the brain. Motor neurons have the job of carrying messages away from the brain and back to the rest of the body. There are two main parts of the nervous system: the central nervous system, which is the brain and spinal cord, and the peripheral nervous system, which is all of the nerves and cells that are not part of the brain and spinal cord. The brain stores important information and is what controls the body's function. The spinal cord is made up of nerve tissue, and it extends down from the brain. It has numerous nerves that branch out and carry information to the rest of the body.

21st-Century Skill Applications for Reading Anchor Standard 9

In this section, we share ideas to help students meet the Reading Standards through the use of 21st-century tools and skills. Although online tools can be used for a variety of purposes, we have chosen to highlight specific tools for use with each particular standard. As teachers, we should select tools we think will work best for our students, using the same tools in multiple ways when possible.

CCR Reading Standard 9 focuses on analyzing how two or more texts address similar themes or topics in order to build knowledge or to compare the approaches the authors take. Conducting online research often means integrating and evaluating websites. Diigo (www.diigo.com) is a free online tool or mobile app that can help a student research websites to build knowledge. After downloading Diigo, students can use this tool to bookmark, highlight, and create sticky notes on webpages. When the reader returns to the original website, all the sticky notes and highlights will have been preserved. Students can archive webpages in order to compare and contrast topics and approaches authors take, and they can collaborate with other students to work on a research project in a group. Diigo is an excellent tool for social bookmarking, where students can share webpages and see others' comments.

VoiceThread (www.voicethread.com) is a free online program with an iPad app version that allows participants to post photos, documents, artwork, video, or presentations and create group discussions. Comments can be made by text, video, audio (microphone or telephone), or by audio file. A participant can draw attention to specific points by creating lines on the item or image as he or she comments, with the lines fading after about five seconds. Participant responses are displayed around the image, and can be heard or viewed by clicking on each responder's icon. VoiceThread has the potential to help students to create rich collaborative discussions comparing and contrasting texts, author styles, themes, central ideas, or how different authors approach the same topic.

Subtext (www.subtext.com), described in Chapter 7 of this volume, also provides an excellent format for student analysis of similar themes and topics. Subtext provides a great opportunity to do this kind of analysis within a book.

How Can We Integrate Other ELA Standards With Reading Anchor Standard 9?

When planning to teach CCR Anchor Standard 9, we can integrate several other ELA standards to design rich instructional tasks. Examples of ideas to include when creating rich instructional tasks follow.

Integrating Other ELA Standards With Reading Literature Standard 9

- Reading Literature Standard 1 focuses on reading a narrative text closely. *Example:* Encourage students to read narrative text closely to compare and contrast texts and ideas.

- Reading Informational Text Standard 2 focuses on the ability to determine central ideas and purpose of an informational text. *Example:* Teach students to compare and contrast themes in literature.

- Reading Literature Standard 3 focuses on being able to analyze interpretations of characters, settings, or events in a story or drama. *Example:* Encourage students to use specific information in a story or drama to compare and contrast characters, settings, or events in the text.

- Reading Literature Standard 4 refers to the author's choice and use of words in a literary text. *Example:* When students compare and contrast characters, settings, ideas, or literary texts, encourage them to include the author's use of language, including examples of figurative language.

- Reading Literature Standard 5 refers to analyzing the structure of literary texts. *Example:* Ask students to compare and contrast texts in different forms and genres.

- Reading Literature Standard 6 refers to point of view. *Example:* Explicitly teach students to compare and contrast the points of view of the characters, narrator, or the authors of literary texts.

- Reading Literature Standard 7 focuses on comparing a written version of a text with multimedia or artistic versions of the text. *Example:* Ask students to compare and contrast multimedia versions of literary text.

- Writing Standard 2 lays out the expectations for informative/explanatory writing. *Example:* Following the criteria in Writing Standard 2, teach students to compare and contrast elements of literary texts.

- Speaking and Listening Standard 1 describes students' effective engagement in a range of collaborative discussions, with specific indicators to demonstrate how to participate in an effective academic conversation. *Example:* When engaged in whole-group and small-group collaborative conversations, encourage students to compare and contrast elements of literary texts.

Integrating Other ELA Standards With Reading Informational Text Standard 9

- Reading Informational Text Standard 1 refers to closely reading an informational text. *Example:* When engaging in a close reading of an informational text, teach students to cite textual evidence when comparing and contrasting information in the text.

- Reading Informational Text Standard 2 focuses on the ability to determine central ideas and purpose of an informational text. *Example:* Teach students to compare and contrast authors' presentations of topics.

- Reading Informational Text Standard 3 focuses on analyzing the connections and relationships among people, events, ideas, or pieces of information in a text. *Example:* When students read informational text, encourage them to compare and contrast complex sets of ideas or sequences of events.

- Reading Informational Text Standard 4 focuses on students determining the meanings of unfamiliar words in a text. *Example:* When comparing and contrasting informational texts or integrating information from several texts, teach students to interpret figurative, connotative, and technical meanings of words and phrases found in the texts.

- Reading Informational Text Standard 7 focuses on different versions and mediums of texts. *Example:* Explicitly teach students to compare and contrast authors' interpretations and presentations of key information from multiple texts.

- Writing Standard 1 delineates the expectations for writing arguments. *Example:* Following the criteria in Writing Standard 1, encourage students to write arguments that include supporting ideas from conflicting informational texts.

- Writing Standard 7 refers to conducting research projects to answer questions or solve problems. *Example:* When they are participating in a research project, encourage students to analyze conflicting information from various sources on the same topic.

- Writing Standard 8 focuses on gathering relevant information from multiple print and digital sources. *Example:* Teach students to integrate credible and accurate information from a variety of sources, both print and digital, to answer questions and solve problems about a topic.

- Speaking and Listening Standard 1 describes students engaging effectively in a range of collaborative discussions, with specific indicators to demonstrate how to participate in an effective academic conversation. *Example:* Following the criteria outlined in Speaking and Listening Standard 1, encourage students to participate in academic conversations comparing and contrasting information from various disciplinary texts.

- Speaking and Listening Standard 2 focuses on students integrating and evaluating the credibility of details from multiple sources. *Example:* Encourage students to discuss the credibility and accuracy of key information in multimedia presentations.

- Language Standard 6 is the vocabulary standard that refers to general academic and domain-specific words and phrases. *Example:* When students write or discuss ideas from an informational text, encourage them to use vocabulary specific to the concepts found in the text.

THE COMMON CORE IN ACTION

In this section, we examine one of the foundational ideas that underpins each of the Common Core's College and Career Anchor Standards for Reading. For the ninth standard, "Analyze how two or more texts address similar themes or topics in order to build knowledge or to compare the approaches the authors take" (NGA Center & CCSSO, 2010, p. 35), we have elected to share more detailed information about comparing and contrasting ideas about genetics provided by different sources.

Common Core Literacy Task: Comparing/Contrasting Informational Sources

Olivia is a ninth-grade biology teacher who is planning to teach students to meet Reading Standard 9 for Literacy in Science and Technical Subjects, "Compare and contrast findings presented in a text to those from other sources (including their own experiments), noting when the findings support or contradict previous explanations or accounts" (NGA Center & CCSSO, 2010, p. 62). We have chosen to share more detailed information about comparing and contrasting sources, which is an explicit part of the Reading Standards for Literacy in Science and Technical Subjects as well as English Language Arts.

Olivia teaches from a "hands-on, minds-on" perspective. She believes that students should be actively involved in learning. To motivate her ninth-grade students, Olivia will engage them in a discussion of what they have already learned about genetics from their course textbook. She will then connect the discussion to genetics in real life and introduce examples of how students can apply what they have learned to life situations. Essentially, she will do the following:

1. Facilitate a class discussion about genetics based on what students have already learned from the course text. (SL.9-10.1)

2. Facilitate students' small-group reading and discussion of multiple articles about blood typing from sources, such as the following:

   - Teens Health: "Blood Types," at kidshealth.org/teen/your_body/medical_care/blood_types.html

   - Science in Motion: "Blood Typing," at www.upb.pitt.edu/uploadedFiles/About/Sponsored_Programs/Science_In_Motion/Biology_Labs/Blood%20Typing--%20high%20School%20Student.pdf

   - "Using Blood-Typing to Determine Causes of Death in Surgery Patients," at www.terrificscience.org/lessonpdfs/UsingBloodTyping.pdf

3. Encourage students to contribute to a whole-class academic discussion about using blood types in real life situations. (SL.9-10.1)

4. Introduce several real-life scenarios for which small groups of students will determine solutions. Examples include the use of blood typing in paternity testing, murder case forensics, and determining cause of death for surgical patients. Provide a brief overview of each and encourage students to select a topic of interest. Organize small groups based on students' interests.

5. Teach students how to engage in Inquiring Minds (McLaughlin, 2010), a small-group, discovery-based research approach. Explain and demonstrate. Emphasize the importance of using quality research sources and comparing and contrasting findings. (RST.9-10.9)

6. Encourage students in each small group to develop three research questions, write them on a wall-size sticky note, and hang them. Engage students in a gallery walk, during which each small group will review the posted topics and research questions. Students will also be able to suggest additional research questions to be included on each sticky note. Each research group will review the additional questions the other small groups suggest and discuss whether to pursue them. (WHST.9-10.10; SL.9-10.1)

7. Invite each group to research its issue, using multiple sources including the Internet, and creating a PowerPoint slide show (or technology presentation format of the group's choosing) to share its findings. (WHST.9-10.7, 8, 9; SL.9-10.4)

8. Ask each group to share its presentation and engage in a follow-up discussion in which group members compare and contrast relevant sources. (SL.9-10.1, 4)

9. After all groups have shared their research and solutions, encourage the students to engage in an academic discussion about genetics in everyday life. (SL.9-10.1)

Reading Standard 9 focuses on ensuring that students can compare and contrast texts. It requires students to compare and contrast texts about the same topic written by different authors. When students analyze sources, they weigh the works and are better able to decide not only what information to use but also how to use it.

References

McLaughlin, E.M. (1987). QuIP: A writing strategy to improve comprehension of expository structure. *The Reading Teacher, 40*(7), 650–654.

McLaughlin, M. (2010). *Content area reading: Teaching and learning in an age of multiple literacies.* Boston: Allyn & Bacon.

McLaughlin, M., & Overturf, B.J. (2013). *The Common Core: Graphic organizers for teaching K–12 students to meet the Reading Standards.* Newark, DE: International Reading Association. Retrieved from www.reading.org/general/Publications/Books/bk021.aspx

National Governors Association Center for Best Practices & Council of Chief State School Officers. (2010). *Common Core State Standards for English language arts and literacy in history/social studies, science, and technical subjects.* Washington, DC: Authors. Retrieved August 3, 2012, from www.corestandards.org/assets/CCSSI_ELA%20 Standards.pdf

Walk, K. (1998). *How to write a comparative analysis.* Cambridge, MA: Writing Center, Harvard University. Retrieved July 17, 2012, from www.fas.harvard.edu/~wricntr/documents/CompAnalysis.html

Literature and Informational Text Cited

Houghton, N. (1965). *Romeo and Juliet and West Side Story.* New York: Laurel Leaf.

Shakespeare, W. (2012). *Romeo and Juliet.* New York: Simon & Brown.

Wimberly, R. (2012). *Prince of cats.* New York: Vertigo.

CHAPTER 16

CCR Reading Anchor Standard 10: Text Complexity

 **Stepping Higher**	**College and Career Readiness Reading Anchor Standard 10** Read and comprehend complex literary and informational texts independently and proficiently. (NGA Center & CCSSO, 2010a, p. 10)

What Does CCR Reading Anchor Standard 10 Mean?

According to the Common Core State Standards, our students should be able to read, comprehend, and discuss complex text. College and Career Readiness (CCR) Reading Anchor Standard 10 states the expectation that students should be able to read on grade level and be able to read and comprehend complex literary narratives and informational texts by the end of high school. Students are expected to read and comprehend such texts on their own in classes across the curriculum.

Reading Anchor Standard 10 focuses on two College and Career Readiness reading skills:

1. The ability to read and comprehend complex literary texts independently and proficiently
2. The ability to read and comprehend complex informational texts independently and proficiently

Complex literary narratives have been defined as essays, short stories, and novels that display a number of characteristics: use of ambiguous language in literary devices, complex and subtle interactions among characters, challenging context-dependent vocabulary, and usually messages and or meanings that are not explicit in the text (ACT, 2006). In English and other arts and humanities classes, students will read, analyze, discuss, and write about complex essays, short stories, and novels.

Complex informational texts have been defined as materials that include a sizable amount of data, present difficult concepts that are not explicit in the text, use demanding words and phrases whose meanings must be determined from context, and are likely to include intricate explanations of processes or events (ACT, 2006). Students encounter complex informational texts in every subject area and should be able to read and comprehend such texts independently in every class.

How Do the Common Core Standards Build to CCR Reading Anchor Standard 10?

The Common Core Standards in grades 6–12 build toward College and Career Readiness Anchor Standard 10. The Reading Standard 10 substrands addressed in grades 6–12 are as follows:

- Reading Standards for Literature (stories, dramas, and poems in English language arts)
- Reading Standards for Informational Text (literary nonfiction in English language arts)
- Reading Standards for Literacy in History/Social Studies (informational texts)
- Reading Standards for Literacy in Science and Technical Subjects (informational texts)

The Common Core State Standards are designed with the expectation that students build to understanding more complex texts. In the text complexity band for grades 6–8, some students will need scaffolding to read and comprehend the level of materials suggested. However, by eighth grade, students are expected to read these materials independently and proficiently. The expectations for the text complexity bands for grades 9–10 and 11–12 are similar. Students in the earlier grades may need scaffolding at the high end of the range, but by the end of each text complexity band, students are expected to independently and proficiently read complex text at the recommended level of complexity.

Dimensions of Text Complexity

Appendix A of the CCSS (NGA Center & CCSSO, 2010b) includes a section about text complexity (pp. 2–9). It also contains a discussion of a research base that provides a rationale for increasing text complexity. Appendix A states that text complexity is based on three components:

1. Qualitative dimensions of text complexity can only be measured by an attentive human reader and include concepts such as levels of meaning or purpose, the way the text is structured, how clear the language is, and the types of knowledge demands the text makes on the reader. The qualitative dimension refers to the kinds of background knowledge of text structure, vocabulary, and language any reader must have to be able to comprehend the text. Qualitative rubrics for both literature and informational text that have been approved by the states are provided by the Council of Chief State School Officers (2012; see free PDFs online at programs.ccsso.org/projects/common%20core%20resources).

2. Quantitative dimensions of text complexity are typically measured by computer software and include components such as word length or frequency, sentence length, and text cohesion. The quantitative dimension refers to the measured reading level of a text. The Common Core Standards specifically mention text levels as measured by Lexile, and an addition to CCSS Appendix A (NGA Center & CCSSO, 2010b) contains information on several other leveling systems.

3. Reader and task considerations must be evaluated by a teacher employing his or her professional judgment, experience, and knowledge of the students and the subject. Reader and task considerations refer to knowing an individual student's abilities, experiences, interests, and possible motivation for reading a particular text before making a determination that the text is appropriate for that student. "Suggested Considerations for Reader and Task" (CCSSO, 2012) includes considerations for students' cognitive capabilities, reading skills, motivation and engagement with the task and text, prior knowledge and experience, content and/or theme concerns, and complexity of associated tasks. (Table 16.1 offers a sampling of reflection questions suggested by the CCSSO; the full document is available online at programs.ccsso.org/projects/common%20core%20resources.)

Table 16.1 Sample Questions for Professional Reflection on Reader and Task Considerations

Category	Questions
Cognitive capabilities	• Does the reader possess the necessary attention to read and comprehend this specific text? • Will the reader be able to remember and make connections among the various details presented in this specific text?
Reading skills	• Does the reader possess the necessary comprehension strategies to manage the material in this specific text?
Motivation and engagement with task and text	• Will the reader be interested in the content of this specific text? • Will the text maintain the reader's motivation and engagement throughout the reading experience?
Prior knowledge and experience	• Does the reader possess adequate prior knowledge and/or experience regarding the topic of this specific text to manage the material that is presented?
Content and/or theme concerns	• Does the reader possess the maturity to respond appropriately to any potentially concerning elements of content or theme?
Complexity of associated tasks	• Will the complexity of any before-, during-, or after-reading tasks associated with this specific text interfere with the reading experience?

Note. From "Suggested Considerations for Reader and Task," in *The Common Core State Standards: Supporting Districts and Teachers With Text Complexity* [Webinar], by Council of Chief State School Officers, 2012, Washington, DC: Author.

All three components of determining text complexity are important in the classroom, and all three should be considered when choosing appropriate materials for a particular group of students.

Exemplar Texts

Appendix B of the CCSS (NGA Center & CCSSO, 2010c) includes exemplar texts for each text complexity band. According to McLaughlin and Overturf (2012),

> Exemplar texts are models. They are examples. Some think of them as benchmarks or anchors. They are not mandated texts. They do not comprise all of the literature or informational text that should be taught at a given grade level. (p. 8)

According to the CCSS Appendix B, the titles that were selected should "serve as useful guideposts in helping educators select texts of similar complexity, quality, and range for their own classrooms" (p. 2). Literature includes stories, dramas, and poetry. Informational text for these grades includes literary nonfiction and texts in history/social studies, science, and technical subjects.

Although the Common Core list of exemplar texts features many classic titles, there is a great deal of interest in determining how the complexity of contemporary texts, which students often find to be more motivational, might be evaluated. The Kansas Department of Education (www.ksde.org) suggests the use of what have come to be known as "placemats" when determining the complexity of text.

Placemats are comprised of what the Common Core views as the three components of text complexity: qualitative, quantitative, and reader and task considerations. The Kansas Department of Education (2012) provides completed placemats—text complexity evaluations—for several contemporary young adult novels, including *The Hunger Games* by Suzanne Collins (2008; see Figure 16.1). The

Figure 16.1 Kansas Department of Education Text Complexity Placemat for *The Hunger Games*

Text Complexity Analysis of *The Hunger Games* by Suzanne Collins

Qualitative Measures

Levels of Meaning:
The novel has a multiple levels of meaning. Literally, the story centers around Katniss, who lives in the not-too-distant future in the remains of what was once North America. As her home district's representative to the annual Hunger games, she competes for survival. The book is also a social commentary on reality television and social issues.

Structure:
A simple structure told by a first person narrator with foreshadowing and flashback, the book does require the reader to picture a future world with event and customs that may be unfamiliar.

Language Conventionality and Clarity:
Vivid description, figurative language and imagery are used to help the reader picture this world in the not-too-distant future. The voice of the narrator is conversational, familiar, and contemporary.

Knowledge Demands:
Higher level themes of moral dilemma, social criticism, government control, war and hunger. Events of the novel are unique to Katniss's world of the future and require a deeper level of thinking on the part of the reader.

Quantitative Measures

Various readability measures of The Hunger Games *are largely in agreement that is of appropriate complexity for grades 7–adult.. The ATOS formula (used with the Accelerated Reader program) identifies this title as having a book level of 5.3. A Lexile measure for this novel is 810L .*

Reader–Task Considerations

These are to be determined locally with reference to such variables as a student's motivation, knowledge, and experiences as well as purpose and the complexity of the task assigned and the question posed.

Here in Kansas, educators might want to examine the following elements or issues: the consequences of hunger, people's Constitutional rights, and links to other books such as 1984, The Giver, Fahrenheit 451, and others for student learning differentiation purposes.

Recommended Placement

The Hunger Games is the 2010 Heartland Award winner in Kansas. Both the qualitative and quantitative measures support the novel's placement in the grades 7 and higher text complexity band. This book also ties into social studies and some science standards.

Note. Placemat prepared by Julie Aikins, Royster Middle School, Kansas, Spring 2011. Template and additional placemats available at the ELA and Literacy Resources for the Kansas Common Core Standards webpage of the Kansas State Department of Education, www.ksde.org/Default.aspx?tabid=4778.

placemat for *The Hunger Games* includes comments about qualitative measures, such as levels of meaning, structure, language conventionality and clarity, and knowledge demands. Essential information about quantitative measures such as the ATOS formula and Lexile score are also reported. In the section about reader–task considerations, which relate to students' motivation, knowledge, and experience, it is noted that these factors should be determined locally. In Kansas, for example, teachers may wish to address issues related to hunger, Constitutional rights, and connections to other titles, such as George Orwell's *1984,* Lois Lowry's *The Giver,* and Ray Bradbury's *Fahrenheit 451.* (Blank placemats for planning are available online from the Kansas Department of Education at www.ksde.org/Default.aspx?tabid=4778.)

Determining the complexity of contemporary texts is a meaningful task that functions best when it is collaborative in nature. Working with colleagues provides valuable insights when determining text complexity. Several states, including Kansas, have provided resources to use when engaging in this process.

Supporting Students Reading Below the Text Complexity Expectation

While there is an expectation in the Standards for students to read complex text, there is also a caveat in point 4 of the section headed "What Is Not Covered by the Standards":

> The Standards set grade-specific standards but do not define the intervention methods or materials necessary to support students who are well below or well above grade-level expectations. No set of grade-specific standards can fully reflect the great variety in abilities, needs, learning rates, and achievement levels of students in any given classroom. (NGA Center & CCSSO, 2010a, p. 6)

In the "Readers and Tasks" section of Appendix A (NGA Center & CCSSO, 2010b), three related considerations are discussed:

1. "*Students' ability to read complex text does not always develop in a linear fashion.*" This statement indicates that individual students need opportunities to read complex texts but also should be allowed "to experience the satisfaction and pleasure of easy, fluent reading." Teachers can continue to plan instruction using "particular texts that are easier than those required for a given grade band" as long as students are moving toward texts of higher levels of complexity (p. 9).

2. "*Students reading well above and well below grade-band level need additional support.*" This point focuses on the needs of students who are reading above grade level and gifted readers (see Chapter 4, this volume). It also states that "students who struggle greatly to read texts within (or even below) their text complexity grade band must be given the support needed to enable them to read at a grade-appropriate level of complexity" (p. 9).

3. "*Even many students on course for college and career readiness are likely to need scaffolding as they master higher levels of text complexity.*" This point addresses the fact that most students need scaffolded instruction—the gradual release of responsibility to students—as they learn to tackle complex text. It states that "although such support is educationally necessary and desirable, instruction must move generally toward *decreasing scaffolding* and *increasing independence*" (p. 9). Students need to be taught how to comprehend texts of all types as they learn how to approach more complex texts.

When considering text complexity, we need to think about the needs of our students. Then, we need to collaborate to provide materials that are appropriate to help them build to the text complexity that ensures they can be successful in college and their future careers.

In the Standards, the distribution of literary and informational reading is aligned with the NAEP assessment framework (NGA Center & CCSSO, 2010a, p. 5). According to this framework, in grades 6–8, 45% of instruction should be focused on literary text and 55% should be focused on informational text. In grades 9–12, 30% of texts used for instruction should be literary and 70% should be informational. To reach these percentages, using instructional text for informational purposes should increase in the English language arts classroom as well in the disciplines. As the Standards note,

Table 16.2 Common Core State Standard 10 for Reading Literature in Grades 6–12

Grade	Standard
6	By the end of the year, read and comprehend literature, including stories, dramas, and poems, in the grades 6–8 text complexity band proficiently, with scaffolding as needed at the high end of the range.
7	By the end of the year, read and comprehend literature, including stories, dramas, and poems, in the grades 6–8 text complexity band proficiently, with scaffolding as needed at the high end of the range.
8	By the end of the year, read and comprehend literature, including stories, dramas, and poems, at the high end of grades 6–8 text complexity band independently and proficiently.
9–10	By the end of grade 9, read and comprehend literature, including stories, dramas, and poems, in the grades 9–10 text complexity band proficiently, with scaffolding as needed at the high end of the range. By the end of grade 10, read and comprehend literature, including stories, dramas, and poems, at the high end of the grades 9–10 text complexity band independently and proficiently.
11–12	By the end of grade 11, read and comprehend literature, including stories, dramas, and poems, in the grades 11–CCR text complexity band proficiently, with scaffolding as needed at the high end of the range. By the end of grade 12, read and comprehend literature, including stories, dramas, and poems, at the high end of the grades 11–CCR text complexity band independently and proficiently.

Note. The standards are from *Common Core State Standards for English Language Arts and Literacy in History/Social Studies, Science, and Technical Subjects* (pp. 37 and 38), by National Governors Association Center for Best Practices and Council of Chief State School Officers, 2010, Washington, DC: Authors.

Fulfilling the Standards for 6–12 ELA requires much greater attention to a specific category of informational text—literary nonfiction—than has been traditional. Because the ELA classroom must focus on literature (stories, drama, and poetry) as well as literary nonfiction, a great deal of informational reading in grades 6–12 must take place in other classes if the NAEP assessment framework is to be matched instructionally. (NGA Center & CSSO, 2010a, p. 5)

As delineated in the Standards, much of the text in English classes should consist of literature. Literary nonfiction should be added to the English curriculum, but the bulk of informational text should be required in classes other than English.

Reading Standard 10 for Literature appears in Table 16.2, and Standard 10 for Informational Text is shown in Table 16.3.

Reading Standard 10 for Literacy in History/Social Studies is delineated in Table 16.4, and Standard 10 for Science and Technical Subjects is outlined in Table 16.5.

What Literacy Skills and Strategies Support Reading Anchor Standard 10?

To read and comprehend complex literary text, all the skills and strategies from the College and Career Readiness Anchor Standards 1–9 must be taught and integrated. Supporting skills and strategies for Reading Standard 10 in Literature, Informational Text, History/Social Studies, and Science and Technical Subjects are featured in Table 16.6.

How Can We Teach Reading Anchor Standard 10 So Our Students Achieve?

To be able to read complex literary and informational text at the recommended text complexity band, we need to teach the concepts in Standards 1–9. Students demonstrate their ability to read complex text when engaged in the type of close reading described in Reading Standard 1. Standards 1–9 in Literature, Informational Text, History/Social Studies, and Science and Technical Subjects all come into play when reading complex text. Teaching examples for Standards 1–9 are described in Chapters 7–15.

21st-Century Skill Applications for Reading Anchor Standard 10

In this section, we share ideas for students to meet the Reading Standards through the use of 21st-century tools and skills. Although online tools can be used for a variety of purposes, we have chosen to highlight specific tools for use with each particular standard. In no way do we mean to imply that every standard would require different technology. Teachers should select tools they feel best fit their students, and use the same tools in multiple ways when possible.

CCR Reading Standard 10 focuses on reading and comprehending complex literary and informational texts independently and proficiently. Technology applications described in the previous chapters allow students to explore, analyze, and discuss complex texts. In order to read complex texts, students must have access to them.

Table 16.3 Common Core State Standard 10 for Reading Informational Text in Grades 6–12

Grade	Standard
6	By the end of the year, read and comprehend literary nonfiction in the grades 6–8 text complexity band proficiently, with scaffolding as needed at the high end of the range.
7	By the end of the year, read and comprehend literary nonfiction in the grades 6–8 text complexity band proficiently, with scaffolding as needed at the high end of the range.
8	By the end of the year, read and comprehend literary nonfiction at the high end of the grades 6–8 text complexity band independently and proficiently.
9–10	By the end of grade 9, read and comprehend literary nonfiction in the grades 9–10 text complexity band proficiently, with scaffolding as needed at the high end of the range. By the end of grade 10, read and comprehend literary nonfiction at the high end of the grades 9–10 text complexity band independently and proficiently.
11–12	By the end of grade 11, read and comprehend literary nonfiction in the grades 11–CCR text complexity band proficiently, with scaffolding as needed at the high end of the range. By the end of grade 12, read and comprehend literary nonfiction at the high end of the grades 11–CCR text complexity band independently and proficiently.

Note. The standards are from *Common Core State Standards for English Language Arts and Literacy in History/Social Studies, Science, and Technical Subjects* (pp. 39 and 40), by National Governors Association Center for Best Practices and Council of Chief State School Officers, 2010, Washington, DC: Authors.

Table 16.4 Common Core Reading Standard 10 for Literacy in History/Social Studies in Grades 6–12

Grade	Standard
6–8	By the end of grade 8, read and comprehend history/social studies texts in the grades 6–8 text complexity band independently and proficiently.
9–10	By the end of grade 10, read and comprehend history/social studies texts in the grades 9–10 text complexity band independently and proficiently.
11–12	By the end of grade 12, read and comprehend history/social studies texts in the grades 11–CCR text complexity band independently and proficiently.

Note. The standards are from *Common Core State Standards for English Language Arts and Literacy in History/Social Studies, Science, and Technical Subjects* (p. 61), by National Governors Association Center for Best Practices and Council of Chief State School Officers, 2010, Washington, DC: Authors.

Table 16.5 Common Core Reading Standard 10 for Literacy in Science and Technical Subjects in Grades 6–12

Grade	Standard
6–8	By the end of grade 8, read and comprehend science/technical texts in the grades 6–8 text complexity band independently and proficiently.
9–10	By the end of grade 10, read and comprehend science/technical texts in the grades 9–10 text complexity band independently and proficiently.
11–12	By the end of grade 12, read and comprehend science/technical texts in the grades 11–CCR text complexity band independently and proficiently.

Note. The standards are from *Common Core State Standards for English Language Arts and Literacy in History/Social Studies, Science, and Technical Subjects* (p. 62), by National Governors Association Center for Best Practices and Council of Chief State School Officers, 2010, Washington, DC: Authors.

Table 16.6 Common Core State Standard 10: Supporting Skills and Strategies for Grades 6–12

Grade	Supporting Skills and Strategies for Reading Literature
K–5	All skills and strategies for Reading Literature
6–12	Skills and strategies for Reading Literature Standards 1–9
Grade	**Supporting Skills and Strategies for Reading Informational Text**
K–5	All skills and strategies for Reading Informational Text
6–12	Skills and strategies for Reading Informational Text Standards 1–9
Grade	**Supporting Skills and Strategies for Literacy in History/Social Studies**
K–5	All skills and strategies for Reading Informational Text
6–12	Skills and strategies for Literacy in History/Social Studies Standards 1–9
Grade	**Supporting Skills and Strategies for Literacy in Science Technical Subjects**
K–5	All skills and strategies for Reading Informational Text
6–12	Skills and strategies for Literacy in Science and Technical Subjects Standards 1–9

Note. The skills and strategies can be found in *Common Core State Standards for English Language Arts and Literacy in History/Social Studies, Science, and Technical Subjects*, by National Governors Association Center for Best Practices and Council of Chief State School Officers, 2010, Washington, DC: Authors.

Many complex texts that are appropriate for Common Core instruction, especially classic literature and nonfiction articles, can be found online. However, online resources often contain ads and related links that can prove distracting to readers. The Readability tool (www.readability.com) is a free computer download, also available as a smartphone or tablet app, that enables students to read a webpage without distractions. The tool removes all advertising and related links so that all that the student can see is the story or article. After downloading Readability, students can read the information from the website immediately or save it and read it later. Readability can make it easier for all students, but especially younger or inexperienced readers, to concentrate on the information in a text.

There are a number of free online sources for complex text (Greenstone, 2012). For example, Shakespeare resources include The Complete Works of William Shakespeare (shakespeare.mit.edu), Shakespeare Online (www.shakespeare-online.com), the Shakespeare Resource Center (www.bardweb.net), and Mr. William Shakespeare and the Internet (shakespeare.palomar.edu). There is also a free Shakespeare app by Readdle that contains the complete works of the Bard for mobile phones and tablets (itunes.apple.com/us/app/shakespeare/id285035416?mt=8).

A number of sites offer free classic novels and literature, including poetry, short stories, and essays:

- Planet eBook (www.planetebook.com) provides carefully selected free classic literature in electronic form. The books can be read online or downloaded as a PDF in a one- or two-page format.

- ManyBooks (www.manybooks.net) offers thousands of copyright-free books in an array of formats for readers. Books can be downloaded as a PDF and are available for desktop, mobile, or e-reader formats.

- Open Library (www.openlibrary.org) is a project of the Internet Archive, which is a nonprofit project to preserve our digital heritage by archiving websites and materials found online. More than a million free books have been placed in the Open Library and are available to download or borrow.

- Project Gutenberg (www.gutenberg.org) offers over 40,000 free e-books. Readers can choose among free e-pub books, mobi (Kindle) books, or audiobooks and download them or read them online. A QR code posted on the website allows a reader to immediately download free books to a mobile phone using a QR scanning app.

- PoemHunter (www.poemhunter.com) allows a reader to search for poems from classic and contemporary poets such as Walt Whitman, Robert Frost, or Maya Angelou. The site also includes song lyrics and quotations. However, a note of caution is required. Self-published poems and song lyrics with questionable words and messages may not be suitable for use in the classroom. This site should only be used with teacher guidance.

- Poetry 180 (www.loc.gov/poetry/180/p180-list.html) is a project from the Library of Congress. It provides a poem a day for American high schools.

- The Poetry Foundation (www.poetryfoundation.org) also features a collection of classic and modern poems.

Informational text in the form of magazine and newspaper articles and content-focused websites can be found online. The History Place's Great Speeches Collection (www.historyplace.com/speeches/previous.htm) houses written versions of a selection of famous speeches. American Rhetoric Top 100 Speeches is a collection that includes audio (if available) as well as written transcripts of many speeches (www.americanrhetoric.com/top100speechesall.html). Online textbooks such as Flat World Knowledge (www.flatworldknowledge.com) and FlexBooks (www.ck12.org) are also available.

Kelly Gallagher, author of *Deeper Reading: Comprehending Challenging Texts, 4–12* (2004), has created an online resource of published articles titled "Article of the Week." Gallagher assigns an article from a range of topics to his high school students each Monday in order for students to build background knowledge and practice reading informational text closely. For each article, he asks students to mark their confusion points, show evidence of a close reading by marking up the text with questions and comments, and then write a one-page reflection. "Article of the Week," including archives of articles from the past several years, can be accessed at Gallagher's website (kellygallagher.org/resources/articles.html). These articles can be downloaded onto tablets, and students can use programs such as iAnnotate to highlight, mark up, and make comments on the text.

How Can We Integrate Other ELA Standards With Reading Anchor Standard 10?

When planning to teach CCR Anchor Standard 10, we can integrate several other ELA standards to design rich instructional tasks. Examples of ideas to include when creating rich instructional tasks follow.

Integrating Other ELA Standards With Reading Literature Standard 10

- Reading Literature Standard 1 focuses on reading a narrative text closely. *Example:* When engaging in close reading of a complex text, ask students to cite textual evidence to support explicit and implicit information in the text.

- Reading Literature Standard 2 focuses on the ability to determine and analyze theme. *Example:* When students read a complex literary text, encourage them to infer themes by exploring the characters' actions, dialogue, thoughts, and feelings.

- Reading Literature Standard 3 focuses on being able to analyze interpretations of characters, settings, or events in a story or drama. *Example:* When students read a complex literary text, encourage them to carefully describe the traits of the characters, the significance of the setting, and the manner in which the events take place to support interpretations of the text.

- Reading Literature Standard 4 refers to the author's choice and use of words in a literary text. *Example:* When students read a complex literary text, invite them to discuss the author's choice of particular words and phrases, including examples of figurative language.

- Reading Literature Standard 5 refers analyzing the structure of literary texts. *Example:* When reading a complex literary text, encourage students to analyze the structure and formats of stories, dramas, and poems in order to interpret the text.

- Reading Literature Standard 6 refers to point of view. *Example:* When reading a complex literary text, invite students to analyze an author's or character's point of view in order to interpret the text.

- Reading Literature Standard 9 focuses on comparing and contrasting aspects of literary text. *Example:* Encourage students to compare and contrast two or more complex literary texts.

- Writing Standard 9 addresses the expectation that students will be able to draw evidence from texts to support analysis, reflection, and research. *Example:* Ask students to support written analysis and reflection of literary text with evidence from the text.

- Speaking and Listening Standard 1 describes the expectation for students to engage effectively in a range of collaborative discussions, with specific indicators to demonstrate how to participate in an effective academic conversation. *Example:* When reading complex stories, dramas, and poems, engage students in both whole-group and small-group collaborative conversations.

- Speaking and Listening Standard 2 focuses on students integrating and evaluating the credibility of details from multiple sources. *Example:* Encourage students to read literature in a minimum of three sources, select details, and evaluate each text through discussion.

- Language Standard 4 refers to determining or clarifying the meanings of unknown and multiple-meaning words and phrases. *Example:* When students read a complex literary text, ask them to determine the meanings of unknown words and phrases using context, word roots, affixes, and reference materials.

- Language Standard 5 is the vocabulary standard that refers to the descriptive use of language. *Example:* When students read a complex literary text, encourage them to analyze the way the author used descriptive and figurative language, nuances of meaning, and word relationships.

Integrating Other ELA Standards With Reading Informational Text Standard 10

- Reading Informational Text Standard 1 refers to closely reading an informational text. *Example:* Ask students to cite textual evidence to support conclusions when engaging in close reading of a complex informational text.

- Reading Informational Text Standard 2 focuses on the ability to determine central ideas and purpose of an informational text. *Example:* When students read a complex informational text, ask them to determine the central ideas and purposes of the text.

- Reading Informational Text Standard 3 focuses on analyzing the connections and relationships among people, events, ideas, or pieces of information in a text. *Example:* When students read a complex informational text, encourage them to analyze connections and relationships among people, events, ideas, or pieces of information in a text.

- Reading Informational Text Standard 4 focuses on the use of words and phrases in an informational text. *Example:* When reading a complex informational text, ask students to identify and discuss the domain-specific words and phrases that the author uses.

- Reading Informational Text Standard 5 refers to analysis of text structure and organization of the text. *Example:* When students read a complex informational text, whether in printed or digital form, ask them to analyze the author's use of text structure and organization to increase their understanding of the text.

- Reading Informational Text Standard 6 addresses point of view. *Example:* When reading a complex informational text, invite students to analyze the author's point of view and credibility and purpose for writing the text.

- Reading Informational Text Standard 8 addresses the author's reasons and evidence in informational text. *Example:* When students read a complex text in which the author has stated an argument, teach them to analyze the author's claims, reasons, and evidence.

- Reading Informational Text Standard 9 focuses on comparing and contrasting two or more texts or interpreting or integrating information from several texts on the same topic. *Example:* Teach students to compare and contrast complex informational texts.

- Writing Standard 1 focuses on students writing arguments and supporting their own points of view with claims, reasons and evidence. *Example:* Ask students to write about their opinions on topics introduced in previous readings of complex texts.

- Writing Standard 2 focuses on students writing informative/explanatory texts. *Example:* As students read a complex informational text, encourage them to produce a written analysis of the text.

- Speaking and Listening Standard 1 describes the expectation for students to engage effectively in a range of collaborative discussions, with specific indicators to demonstrate how to participate in an effective academic conversation. *Example:* Engage students in a variety of collaborative academic conversations about complex informational texts.

- Speaking and Listening Standard 3 focuses on evaluating a speaker's point of view, reasoning, and use of rhetoric and reasoning. *Example:* After listening to a speech, encourage students to evaluate the speaker's point of view, reasoning, and use of both rhetoric and reasoning.

- Language Standard 4 refers to determining or clarifying the meanings of unknown and multiple-meaning words and phrases. *Example:* When students read a complex informational text, invite them to determine the meanings of unknown words and phrases using context, affixes, word roots, and reference materials.

- Language Standard 6 is the vocabulary standard that refers to knowledge of general academic and domain-specific words and phrases. *Example:* When students read a complex informational text, ask them to discuss general academic and domain-specific words and phrases used in the text.

THE COMMON CORE IN ACTION

In this section, we examine one of the foundational ideas that underpins each of the Common Core Reading Anchor Standards. For the tenth Standard, "Read and comprehend complex literary and informational texts independently and proficiently" (NGA Center & CCSSO, 2010a, p. 10), we have elected to share another example of close reading of complex text.

Common Core Teaching Task: Close Reading of The Diary of a Young Girl

Examples of close reading tasks have been posted on websites such as that of Student Achievement Partners (www.achievethecore.org). One of the hallmarks of these tasks is that students approach challenging texts with little support from the teacher; in fact, students should read and interpret complex text without the teacher building background for the passage, engaging students in prereading strategies, or teaching reading comprehension minilessons for the text.

During a close reading lesson, the teacher leads students through a step-by-step process, facilitating student discussion and asking text-dependent questions—questions in which students must use and quote the text to provide evidence for their answers. This process prepares students for engaging in close reading on their own, as well as building the ability to analyze complex text as a college and career readiness skill.

Terry, a seventh-grade language arts teacher, is planning a series of lessons to focus on Reading Standard 10. He wants to ensure that his students can read a grade-appropriate complex text closely and independently, so he knows that he will need to facilitate student practice in Reading Standards 1–9. He also knows that he will need to integrate several other ELA standards to create rich instructional tasks that will enhance his students' comprehension of the text, such as vocabulary development, writing, varied opportunities for discussion, and use of digital media.

Terry reviews the text exemplars for grades 6–8 found in Appendix B of the Common Core State Standards (NGA Center & CCSSO, 2010b). He thinks about his students and their abilities and interests before he chooses a text that correlates with the level and complexity of the text exemplars for grades 6–8. The text he selects is Anne Frank's (1952/1993) *The Diary of a Young Girl*. This text has a Lexile level of 1080L, which is well within the "stretch" Lexile band for grades 6–8. The seventh graders have learned about the Holocaust in social studies, so they should have some background knowledge in order to connect the bigger ideas of the text. Of course, Terry knows that some of his students will need support in reading a complex text. He plans to provide learning supports for those students, such as small-group work, partner reading, and listening to recorded text. He also knows that some of his students will be able to move beyond the seventh grade standards, and so he plans for opportunities for these students to extend their learning as well. Along the way, Terry plans for his students to read literary nonfiction such as selected examples from the United States

Holocaust Museum website. This will help students build their background knowledge about the events in Anne Frank's diary and their impact on the human race.

Terry has already taught supporting lessons on applying comprehension strategies when reading complex text, and he continues to plan lessons in which students practice these strategies. However, when planning lessons for *The Diary of a Young Girl*, Terry also plans a series of close reading experiences, including facilitating students asking and answering text-dependent questions. To create text-dependent questions, Terry reviews the expectations of Reading Standards 1–9 for Literature to ensure that he includes some of these concepts in his questions. When writing text-dependent questions, he first analyzes text passages and identifies core understandings and key ideas of the text. He designs opening questions that help orient students to the text and help them build confidence with the passage. He locates key text structures and powerful vocabulary and designs questions that help highlight these. Terry then finds the sections of the text that he thinks will pose the most difficulty for his students, and he carefully designs questions that will help students focus on and work to comprehend these sections. He puts his questions into a sequence that will guide students through the passage and that will help them build a coherent understanding of the text. He does not include questions that students can answer without reading the text. He identifies the Standards he will address in each lesson and additional ELA Standards he can include. Finally, he develops a culminating activity around the key ideas and understandings he has identified that (a) reflects mastery of standards, (b) involves writing, and (c) is structured so students can complete it individually. (For more complete guidelines and access to free professional development modules about creating text-dependent questions, see Student Achievement Partners, 2012a, 2012b, 2012c.)

When Terry teaches these lessons, he will use a whole-group setting so that all of his students are involved. He will follow these steps:

1. He will introduce the text by telling students the title of the text, the name of the author, and the genre. He will introduce a passage of the text with little or no prereading discussion that reveals what is in the passage. He wants his students to experience the text without giving away the secrets of the author. The students must read to find out.

2. *First reading*—Students will read the passage independently without assistance. (Depending on the text and the needs of his students, Terry may reverse the order of the steps and do the next step first.)

3. *Second reading*—Terry will read the text or sections of the text aloud while students read along. This provides a model of fluent reading and allows students to experience the language of the text.

4. *Third reading*—Terry will pose text-dependent question(s) to guide his seventh graders through the text. He will facilitate a discussion of the text in which students ask and answer questions, make logical inferences, and "cite several pieces of textual evidence to support analysis of what the text says explicitly as well as inferences drawn from the text" (NGA Center & CCSSO, 2010a, p. 36) in classroom conversation. To help students better comprehend, Terry may reread sections aloud or do a think-aloud to demonstrate how he approaches the text. He may also ask students to model their thinking about the text.

5. In some lessons, students may use a graphic organizer to help them organize the information. In other lessons, students may engage in art, music, or drama to visualize the

text. Terry decides that he will invite his students to dramatize and illustrate particular passages in order for them to better understand the text.

6. As students read *The Diary of a Young Girl*, Terry plans for them to write analyses of the text that are supported by text-based evidence. He expects his students to cite the text accurately when providing evidence of their conclusions. These analyses will allow him to see the extent to which students can "draw evidence from literary...texts to support analysis, reflection, or research" (NGA Center & CCSSO, 2010a, p. 44).

Students need a great deal of instruction to be able to meet the increased demands of Reading Standard 10. Stepping up the staircase of text complexity means analyzing text selections for grade-level expectations and planning lessons that integrate the ELA Standards. It also means providing instruction in reading comprehension strategies to ensure students have the competencies they need to be able to comprehend more complex text. By combining different types of reading instruction, we can ensure that our students are truly on their way to becoming college and career ready.

References

ACT. (2006). *Reading between the lines: What the ACT reveals about college readiness in reading.* Iowa City, IA: Author. Retrieved August 22, 2012, from www.act.org/research/policymakers/pdf/reading_report.pdf

Council of Chief State School Officers. (2012, January 26). *The Common Core State Standards: Supporting districts and teachers with text complexity.* Webinar retrieved January 22, 2013, from programs.ccsso.org/projects/common%20core%20resources

Gallagher, K. (2004). *Deeper reading: Comprehending challenging texts, 4–12.* Portland, ME: Stenhouse.

Greenstone, B. (2012, February 2). *Strategies for reading digital text.* Maine Learning Technology Initiative webinar retrieved October 23, 2012, from stateofmaine.adobeconnect.com/_a827390218/p5u8jb2u9ke/?launcher=false&fcsContent=true&pbMode=normal

Kansas Department of Education. (2012). Text complexity final recommendation forms (i.e., "placemats"). *ELA and literacy resources for the Kansas Common Core Standards.* Retrieved from www.ksde.org/Default.aspx?tabid=4778

McLaughlin, M., & Overturf, B.J. (2012, December/January). *The Hunger Games* and the Common Core: Determining the complexity of contemporary texts. *Reading Today, 30*(3), 8–9.

National Governors Association Center for Best Practices & Council of Chief State School Officers. (2010a). *Common Core State Standards for English language arts and literacy in history/social studies, science, and technical subjects.* Washington, DC: Authors. Retrieved August 3, 2012, from www.corestandards.org/assets/CCSSI_ELA%20Standards.pdf

National Governors Association Center for Best Practices & Council of Chief State School Officers. (2010b). *Common Core State Standards for English language arts and literacy in history/social studies, science, and technical subjects: Appendix A: Research supporting key elements of the Standards and glossary of key terms.* Washington, DC: Authors. Retrieved August 3, 2012, from www.corestandards.org/assets/Appendix_A.pdf

National Governors Association Center for Best Practices & Council of Chief State School Officers. (2010c). *Common Core State Standards for English language arts and literacy in history/social studies, science, and technical subjects: Appendix B: Text exemplars and sample performance tasks.* Washington, DC: Authors. Retrieved August 3, 2012, from www.corestandards.org/assets/Appendix_B.pdf

Student Achievement Partners. (2012a). *Close reading exemplars.* Retrieved June 27, 2012, from www.achievethecore.org/steal-these-tools/close-reading-exemplars

Student Achievement Partners. (2012b). *Professional development modules.* Retrieved July 15, 2012, from www.achievethecore.org/steal-these-tools/professional-development-modules

Student Achievement Partners. (2012c). *Text dependent questions.* Retrieved July 15, 2012, from www.achievethecore.org/steal-these-tools/text-dependent-questions

Literature Cited

Collins, S. (2008). *The Hunger Games.* New York: Scholastic.

Frank, A. (1993). *The diary of a young girl.* New York: Bantam. (Original work published 1952)

Future Directions

As the Common Core State Standards Initiative unfolds, as teachers, we continue to engage in interpreting the Standards and developing plans that are most appropriate for our students. States are constructing systems for Standards implementation. Districts are designing professional development and district resources. Teachers and administrators are reading the Standards closely and working collaboratively with colleagues to think about the best instructional methods, skills, and strategies that will help their students meet the Standards.

Implementation of the ELA Standards requires us to think in a new way. Phrases such as "staircase of text complexity," "close reading," "text-based evidence," and "writing to sources" are becoming part of our daily speech, and we find ourselves searching for resources and texts to incorporate into our teaching. Designing student-centered lessons based on the Common Core State Standards and constructing Standards-based classrooms takes energy, dedication, and hard work. We know we are up to the task.

Amid all this Standards activity, we have come to a vital realization: We are not alone! There are thousands of teachers across the United States working to determine the best instructional methods and assessment plans for implementing the ELA Standards. As the Common Core Initiative develops, we will share successful plans for helping students meet the Standards, and we will see new teaching ideas and resources emerge. With so many dedicated professionals working together, the goal of all students being college and career ready is far more likely to become a reality.

Index

Note. Page numbers followed by *f* and *t* indicate figures and tables, respectively.

A

academic vocabulary, 138–139, 141–143
accommodations: for English learners, 44; for gifted and talented students, 50–51; for students with disabilities, 46–48
Achieve, 32–33
achievement, CCSS and, 12–15
ACT, 2, 53, 55, 59, 65, 67, 78, 95, 110, 124, 145, 213
action, multiple means of, 47
Adams, D., 50
Ahn, S., 135
Akhondi, M., 146
Allen, M.B., 12–13, 20, 71, 102, 104, 117, 158
Allen, T.B., 165
Allen, W., 193
alliteration, 125
allusions, 96
Almasi, J.F., 21, 68
Alvermann, D.E., 71
Americans with Disabilities Act, 45
analysis: of diction, 124; of explicit meaning, 82–84; of implicit meaning, 84; importance of, 153; of point of view, 160, 164; of text structure, 145–159; of word choice, 126
Anderson, R.C., 53, 128
Angelou, M., 178
archetypes, 96
argument: versus persuasion, 188–189; strong, characteristics of, 189
argumentation, 188–199
Armbruster, B.B., 146
ASCD, 33

assessment: and CCSS, 12, 17–29; resources for, 28
assessment systems, successful, elements of, 23–24
ASSETS, 25–28
Audio-Print-Film Organizer, 180, 181*f*
August, D., 43
AutoRap, 104

B

background knowledge, and inferences, 86
Beach, C., 104
Bear, D.R., 136
Beck, I.L., 87, 129
Berger, G., 148
Berger, M., 148
Berne, J.L., 87
best practices, versus standards, 53
Biancarosa, C., 65
Biemiller, A., 135
Biography, 103
Bio-Pyramid, 102, 103*f*
Blachowicz, C.L.Z., 128, 133
Black, P., 18
Blanton, W.E., 87
blogs: and argumentation, 194; classroom, 89–90, 194
bookmarking, social, 89, 103
Bookmark Technique, 20–21
book structure, 145–146
Borgia, L., 139
Bronger, L.P., 67
Brooks, J.G., 53

Brooks, M.G., 53
Brown, S., 77–78, 92
Bruni, F., 170
Buehl, D., 65, 68

C

Cambourne, B., 53
Cantrell, S.C., 68
Carnegie Mellon University, 134
Carter, J.C., 68
CAST, 46
Catron, R.M., 48
Cause and Effect Text Organizer, 117
cause/effect structure, 147–149, 149*f*
Cazden, C.B., 55
CCR. *See* College and Career Readiness Anchor
   Standards
CCSS. *See* Common Core State Standards
CCSSO. *See* Council of Chief State School
   Officers
Center for K-12 Center & Performance
   Management at ETS, 23–28
central ideas, determining, 95–109
Character, Trait, and Quote Map, 114, 115*f*
characterization, 114, 121–123
charts: Contrast Chart, 117, 117*f*; Semantic
   Feature Analysis, 138, 139*f*
Chogger, 168
chronology, 147; organizer for, 154, 155*f*
Ciardiello, A.V., 61, 154
Clark, K.F., 87
classroom examples: of argumentation,
   197–199; of characterization, 121–123;
   of close reading, 92–93; of comparison/
   contrast, 210–211; of complex text, 224–226;
   of determining central idea, 107–109; of
   diverse media, 185–187; of point of view,
   170–171; of text structure, 157–159; of word
   meanings, 141–143
clipboard, 22
close reading, 55, 77–94; across curriculum, 79;
   term, 55–57, 77–78
Coleman, D., 56, 59

collaboration, 19; and disciplinary literacy,
   65–70
college and career readiness, definition of, 2
College and Career Readiness (CCR) Anchor
   Standards, 2–3, 9*t*, 74; 1, 77–94; 2, 66*t*, 95–
   109; 3, 110–123; 4, 124–144; 5, 145–159;
   6, 160–173; 7, 69*t*, 174–187; 8, 188–199; 9,
   200–212; 10, 213–226; characteristics of, 3;
   organization of, 4, 5*t*; teaching, 73–76
College Entrance Examination Board, 126
College Readiness Partnership, 36
Collins, S., 107, 215
comic strips, tools for, 168
Common Core State Standards (CCSS), 1, 5*t*,
   8*t*; appendixes of, 3; and argumentation,
   189–191, 190*t*–191*t*; and central ideas,
   96–98, 97*t*–98*t*; characteristics of, 3;
   and close reading, 79–81, 80*t*–81*t*; and
   comparison/contrast, 201–203, 202*t*–203*t*;
   continuous improvement teaching loop, 18*f*;
   and development and interaction, 110–112,
   111*t*–112*t*; and diverse media, 175–177,
   175*t*–177*t*; effective use of, 7–16; emergence
   of, 1–2; evolution of, 1–6; implementation of,
   30–41, 31*f*; organization of, 4, 8–11, 8*t*–11*t*;
   and point of view, 161–163, 162*t*–163*t*;
   resources for, 6; and text complexity, 213–
   218, 218*t*–219*t*; and text structure, 150–151,
   150*t*–151*t*; website, 8; and word meanings,
   126–129, 127*t*–129*t*
Common Core State Standards Initiative, 3;
   future directions for, 227; goal of, 2
comparison/contrast, 147, 200–212; alternative
   versions, 185, 186*f*; Story Map, 115, 116*f*
complex text, 213–226; characteristics of, 59,
   59*t*; dimensions of, 214–215, 215*t*; resources
   for, 220–222; standards on, 59–60
comprehension instruction, 13–14; and
   complex texts, 60; constructivists on, 54–55;
   continuing, 57–58; resources for, 15; and text
   structure, 158–159
Concept of Definition Map, 20, 134, 135*f*
Connell, R., 116*f*

connotation, 125, 138

constructivism, 54–55

content area teachers, and disciplinary literacy, 65–70

Context Clue Organizer, 133, 134*f*

continuous improvement, 19, 35; loop, 18*f*

Contrast Chart, 117, 117*f*

Council for Exceptional Children, 46

Council of Chief State School Officers (CCSSO), 2, 9–10, 12–15, 20, 39, 43, 46, 49–50, 55–59, 64–70, 77–82, 86, 92, 95, 97–99, 107, 110–113, 121, 124, 127–129, 131–133, 141, 145, 150–153, 157, 160, 162–164, 170, 174–178, 185, 188, 190–192, 194, 197, 200, 202–204, 210, 213–215, 217–220, 224–226

Creative Commons, 33

critical thinking, 60–61

Cube Creator, 104–105

curriculum: comprehension instruction in, 13–14; standards and, 53–63

D

Dalton, B., 138

Daniels, H., 87

Darling-Hammond, L., 24

Davidson, J.W., 84–85

deep comprehension. *See* close reading

Denner, P.R., 114

denotation, 138

description, 147

details, 126

DeVoogd, G., 170

diction, 124, 126

DIDLS, 126

digital sources, for information, 180–182

Diigo, 89, 208

disabilities, students with, 44–48; resources for, 51

disciplinary literacy, 64–72; close reading and, 79; comparison/contrast in, 201; and diverse media/formats, 174–175; responsibility for, 65–70; standards and, 66–70, 66*t*; strategies

for, 70–71. *See also* domain-specific words; informational text

discussion, 21

Discussion Circles, 87

diverse media and formats, 174–187

Dixon-Krauss, L., 55

Dole, J.A., 58

domain-specific words, 138–139, 141–143; graphic organizer for, 141, 142*f*

Downes, S., 194

Dredger, K., 104

Duffy, G.G., 58

Duke, N., 58, 146–147, 153

Duncan-Andrade, J.M.R., 139

Dynamic Learning Maps, 25, 27*f*

E

Edublogs, 194

Elementary and Secondary Education Act, 48

Empson, W., 56

engagement: and disciplinary literacy, 70; multiple means of, 47–48

English learners (ELs), 42–44; resources for, 51

Environmental Protection Agency, 84

Estes, T.H., 71

ethos, 189

euphemism, 125

event development, 110–123

Evernote, 105

evidence, 188–199; citing, 77–94, 86*f*; identifying, 192–194

exemplar texts, 215–217

Explore-a-Root, 136

expression, multiple means of, 47

F

fact, versus opinion, 192, 193*f*

Fairbanks, M.M., 128

Farr, R., 139

feedback, descriptive, 19

Fielding, L.G., 58

figurative language, 125–126, 137–138

Fisher, D., 153
Fisher, P., 128, 133
Fitzgerald, F.S., 140
Flocabulary, 139
fluency, 60
For and Against graphic organizer, 194, 196f
Forman, E.A., 55
formative assessment: and CCSS, 12, 17–29;
    definition of, 17–19; strategies, 20–23
formats, diverse, 174–187
Foster, T.C., 49
Frank, A., 224

G

Gallagher, K., 220
Gambrell, L.B., 21, 87, 146, 150
genres, 146
Gewetz, C., 56
gifted and talented students, 48–51; and text
    complexity, 217
Glogster, 182
Goldenberg, C., 42
Goldman, S.R., 146
Goodwin, A., 135
Goodwin, D.K., 180–181
Google, 119, 139, 183
Gorman, J., 107–108
Goudvis, A., 13, 86
gradual release of responsibility, 58
Graham, S., 68
graphic organizers: For and Against, 194, 196f;
    Audio-Print-Film, 180, 181f; cause and effect,
    117, 149f; characterization, 121, 122f; for
    citing evidence, 86–87, 86f; for domain-
    specific words, 141, 142f; Fact and Opinion,
    192, 193f; point of view, 165, 166f–167f,
    172f; problem/solution, 149f; Tri-Media,
    205, 206f; What-Why-How?, 192–194, 195f;
    and word meanings, 134, 135f–136f. See also
    maps
Graves, M.F., 128, 133, 135
Greek roots, 134–136
Greenstone, B., 105, 220

Grimes, N., 165
Grisham, D.L., 138

H

Hadaway, N.L., 42, 44
Halvorssen, T., 185
Hammond, H.K., 135
Harris, T.L., 55
Harvey, S., 13, 86
Hebert, M.A., 68
Helman, L., 43–44
Hemingway, E., 87
Henry, O., 100f
Heritage, M., 18
Hiebert, E.H., 53, 58–59
higher education institutions, and
    implementation, 36
higher level thinking, 60–61
Hilden, K., 58
history: argumentation in, 190t; central ideas
    and, 98t; close reading and, 81t; comparison/
    contrast in, 203t; complexity in, 219t; diverse
    media/formats in, 176t; interaction in, 112t;
    point of view in, 163t; text structure in, 151t;
    word meaning in, 128t
Hodges, R.E., 55
Houghton, N., 205
Hunt Institute, 32, 40
hyperbole, 126

I

idea development, 110–123
idiom, 126
Ignite talks, 104
imagery, 126
individual development, 110–123
individualized education plan (IEP), 45
Individuals with Disabilities Act, 45–46
inferences, 86, 86f
informational text, 67; argumentation in, 188–
    199, 190t; book structure in, 146; central
    ideas in, 95, 97t, 102; close reading and, 82t;
    comparison/contrast in, 201, 202t, 204t,

210–211; complexity in, 213, 219t; diverse media/formats in, 174–175, 176t, 178t; interaction in, 110, 111t, 113t; point of view in, 160, 162t, 164t; resources for, 221; text structure in, 145, 147–150, 151t, 157–159; word meaning in, 124, 128t, 133t

Informational Text Map, 84, 84f

integration of standards: with Standard 1, 90–91; with Standard 2, 105–107; with Standard 3, 119–120; with Standard 4, 140–141; with Standard 5, 156–157; with Standard 6, 168–169; with Standard 7, 183–184; with Standard 8, 197; with Standard 9, 208–210; with Standard 10, 221–224

International Reading Association, 12, 17, 19–20, 32, 61, 65

Internet Archive, 221

Internet Inquiry, 180–182

interpretation: of figurative language, 137–138; of words and phrases, 125

Invernizzi, M., 136

J

Jackson, S., 116f

Jacobs, W.W., 101

Jefferson County, KY, 37

Jigsaw II, 165

Johnson, D.D., 10, 12, 138

Johnston, F., 136

K

Kajder, S., 89, 104, 118

Kansas, 35, 35t, 215

Kansas Department of Education, 79, 215, 216f

Kappes, L., 77–78, 92

Kelly, J., 101

Kennedy, K., 180–181

Kentucky, 34–35, 35t, 37, 67–68

Ketch, A., 87

Kidblog, 194

Kober, N., 31

Kucan, L., 87, 129

L

Lassieur, A., 146

Latin roots, 134–136

Learning Forward, 32, 35

Learning Resource Metadata Initiative, 33

Lee, H., 83

LeGuin, U.K., 50

Leu, D.D., 93, 180

Leu, D.J., Jr., 93, 180

Levine, J.S., 102f, 136, 207

Lewin, L., 84

Lipsky, M., 135

Lipson, M.Y., 58

listening, disciplinary literacy and, 69, 70t

Literacy Design Collaborative, 40

literacy practices: for Standard 1, 81, 82t; for Standard 2, 98–99, 99t; for Standard 3, 112–113, 113t; for Standard 4, 130t–132t, 132, 133t; for Standard 5, 152, 152t–153t; for Standard 6, 163–164, 164t; for Standard 7, 177, 178t; for Standard 8, 191, 192t; for Standard 9, 203–204, 204t; for Standard 10, 218–219, 220t

Literary Graffiti, 104, 140

literature, 67; book structure in, 146; close reading and, 82t; comparison/contrast in, 200–201, 202t, 204t; complexity in, 213, 218t; diverse media/formats in, 174, 175t, 178t; interaction in, 110, 111t, 113t; point of view in, 160, 162t, 164t; text structure in, 145, 147, 150t; themes in, 96, 97t, 101, 108f; word meaning in, 124, 127t, 133t

Literature Circles, 87

logical inferences, 78–79

logos, 189

London, J., 114f

Lyric Summary, 21

M

Macon, J.M., 71, 102

Main Idea Table, 102, 102f

Make Beliefs Comix, 168

Malayeri, F., 146

ManyBooks, 220

maps: Character, Trait, and Quote Map, 114, 115*f*; Concept of Definition Map, 134, 135*f*; Informational Text Map, 84, 84*f*; Narrative Text Map, 83, 83*f*; Persuasion Map, 194; Semantic Question Map, 134, 136*f*; Story Map, 115, 116*f*; tools for, 119, 139, 155

McGinley, W.J., 114

McGraw-Hill Education, 33

McKeown, M.G., 129

McLaughlin, E.M., 5, 12–13, 18, 20–22, 44, 53, 58, 65, 70–71, 83–84, 86–87, 100–102, 104, 115, 117, 121, 133–134, 141, 147, 149, 153–154, 158, 165, 170, 178, 180, 192, 194, 205, 215

McLaughlin, M., 211

McTighe, J., 17, 22

media, diverse, 174–187

Menken, K., 18

metaphors, 126

Miller, D., 50

Miller, K.R., 102*f*, 136, 207

Moje, E.B., 64–65

morphemic analysis, 134–136

Morrell, E., 139

Morrow, L.M., 100

Moss, B., 150

Multiple Points of View Organizer, 165, 167*f*

multistate regions, and implementation, 33–34

N

Nagy, W.E., 128, 135, 138

Narrative Text Map, 83, 83*f*

narrative text structure, 147

National Assessment Governing Board, 67–69

National Assessment of Educational Progress (NAEP): communication purposes distribution in, 68, 69*t*; genre distribution in, 67, 67*t*

National Association for Gifted Children, 48, 50

National Association of Elementary School Principals, 33

National Center and State Collaborative, 25–26, 27*f*

National Center on Response to Intervention, 45

National Council of Teachers of English, 33, 40

National Governors Association Center for Best Practices, 2, 9–10, 12–15, 20, 39, 43, 46, 49–50, 55–59, 64–70, 77–82, 86, 92, 95, 97–99, 107, 110–113, 121, 124, 127–129, 131–133, 141, 145, 150–153, 157, 160, 162–164, 170, 174–178, 185, 188, 190–192, 194, 197, 200, 202–204, 210, 213–215, 217–220, 224–226

national organizations, and implementation, 31–33

National PTA, 32, 40

New Mexico, 35, 35*t*

New York, 35, 35*t*

New York City Department of Education, 37

No Child Left Behind Act, 45

NoteShare, 105

note taking, technology for, 88–89, 88*f*, 105, 208

O

observation, and formative assessment, 22–23

O'Connor, J., 17

Ogle, D., 71, 128, 133

Ohio, 35, 35*t*

onomatopoeia, 126

Open Educational Resources, 40

Open Library, 221

opinions, 188–199; versus fact, 192, 193*f*

Osborne, A.G., Jr., 45

Ouellette, J., 141

Overturf, B.J., 5, 34, 67, 71, 83–84, 86, 101, 115, 121, 133, 141, 149, 154, 158, 165, 180, 192, 194, 205, 215

Owles, C., 139

oxymoron, 126

P

Pallangyo, A.A., 67

paradox, 126

Paris, S.G., 58

Partnership for Assessment of Readiness for College and Careers, 17, 19, 23–24

pathos, 189

PDF, annotated, 88, 88f

Pearson, P.D., 10, 12, 53, 58, 138, 146–147, 153

Pearson Education, 33, 40

PechaKucha, 104

peer assessment, 18

Perkins, D.N., 15

personification, 126

persuasion, versus argument, 188–189

Persuasion Map, 194

phrases, meaning of, 124–144

Pilonieta, P., 87

Pimentel, S., 56, 59

placemats, 215–217, 216f

Planet eBook, 220

PLCs. See professional learning communities

Poe, E.A., 114–115

poetry, resources for, 221

point of view, 160–173

Popplet, 155

PowerPoint, 104

Press Conference, 205

Pressley, M., 58, 149

Prezi, 155–156, 183

problem/solution structure, 149, 149f

professional associations, and implementation, 31–33

professional development: higher education institutions and, 36; and implementation of CCSS, 31; school districts and, 36–37; schools and, 37–39; states and, 34–35

professional learning communities (PLCs), 38–39

Project Gutenberg, 221

publishers: and implementation, 31–33; resources for, 40

purpose, 160–173; graphic organizer on, 172f

Q

QR codes, 118, 118f

questioning, levels of, 60–61, 61t, 154

questions: Into Paragraphs, 205, 207f; Thick and Thin, 84, 85f

R

Race to the Top program, 2

Rakestraw, J.A., 146

Raphael, T.E., 20, 70, 134, 147

Rasinski, T.V., 60

reading closely. See close reading

reading comprehension. See comprehension instruction

ReadWriteThink, 118, 194

reasons, 188–199

Reference Scavenger Hunt, 137, 137f

Rehabilitation Act, Section 504, 45

Rentner, D.S., 31

representation, multiple means of, 47

Response to Intervention (RTI), 45

retelling, 100, 100f

rhetoric, 188; resources for, 221

Richardson, V., 58

Rintamaa, M., 68

Roehler, L.R., 58

Rosenblatt, L.M., 56

Russo, C.J., 45

S

Salomon, G., 15

Samad, A.A., 146

Sandburg, C., 125, 138

Sanders, L., 86

scaffolding, 55, 58; and text complexity, 217

Schlosser, E., 198

school districts, and implementation, 36–37

schools, and implementation, 37–39

Schrock, K., 118

Schwartz, R.M., 20, 70, 134, 147

science: argumentation in, 191t; central ideas and, 98t; close reading and, 81t; comparison/contrast in, 203t; complexity in, 220t; diverse media/formats in, 177t; interaction in, 112t; point of view in, 163t; text structure in, 151t; word meaning in, 129t

SDI. *See* specially designed instruction

self-assessment, 18

Semantic Feature Analysis, 138, 139*f*

Semantic Question Map, 134, 136*f*

sequence, 147

Sequence Chain, 117, 148*f*

Shakespeare, W., 205

Shanahan, C., 64–65

Shanahan, T., 43, 64–65

Shankweiler, D., 45

Shaw, J.M., 71

Shepard, L.A., 18

Shoemaker, B.J., 84

similes, 126

Sketch and Label Retelling, 100, 100*f*

Slavin, R.E., 165

Smarter Balanced Assessment Consortium, 17, 19, 23

Snow, C.E., 65

social bookmarking, 89, 103

social-constructivist process, reading as, 54–55

social mediation, 55

social studies: argumentation in, 190*t*; central ideas and, 98*t*; close reading and, 81*t*; comparison/contrast in, 203*t*; complexity in, 219*t*; diverse media/formats in, 176*t*; interaction in, 112*t*; point of view in, 163*t*; text structure in, 151*t*; word meaning in, 128*t*

Songify, 104

speaking, disciplinary literacy and, 69, 70*t*

specially designed instruction (SDI), 45

Spielberg, S., 180–181

Spillane, L.A., 89, 139

Stahl, S.A., 128

states, and implementation, 34–35, 35*t*

Story Impressions, 114, 114*f*

Story Map, 115, 116*f*

struggling readers, and text complexity, 217

Student Achievement Partners, 32, 41, 55, 224–225

subject areas. *See* disciplinary literacy

Subtext, 89, 208

summarizing, and key ideas, 96

summative assessment, definition of, 17, 23

syntax, 126

T

Tag Galaxy, 89

Taylor, B.M., 58

teacher preparation, and implementation, 36

Teaching Channel, 41

teaching strategies: formative assessment and, 20–23; recommendations for, 12–15, 13*t*; resources for, 15; for Standard 1, 82–87; for Standard 2, 100–102; for Standard 3, 113–117; for Standard 4, 132–139; for Standard 5, 152–154; for Standard 6, 164–165; for Standard 7, 177–182; for Standard 8, 191–194; for Standard 9, 204–205; for Standard 10, 219; standards content and, 11–12

technical meaning, 125, 138

technology connections. *See* 21st Century skills

Templeton, S., 135–136

Text-Based Characterization Organizer, 121, 122*f*

Text-Based Viewpoint Organizer, 165, 166*f*

text complexity, 213–226; characteristics of, 59, 59*t*; dimensions of, 214–215, 215*t*; standards on, 59–60

text structure, 145–159

themes: compare/contrast, 200–212; determining, 95–109; development of, 101, 101*f*, 108*f*

Thick and Thin Questions, 84, 85*f*

thinking: levels of, 60–61; through disciplines, 64–72

Tickets Out, 21–22

timeline tools, 119

Tomlinson, C.A., 22

tone, word choice and, 126

ToonDoo, 168

topics, compare/contrast, 200–212

Townsend, D., 138

Trading Card Creator, 118

Transmediations, 178–179, 179*f*

Tri-Media Text Organizer, 205, 206*f*

Tri-State Quality Review Rubric, 33–34, 41

Tuttle, C., 185

21st Century skills: for Standard 1, 88–90; for Standard 2, 102–105; for Standard 3, 117–119; for Standard 4, 139–140; for Standard 5, 155–156; for Standard 6, 168; for Standard 7, 182–183; for Standard 8, 194; for Standard 9, 208; for Standard 10, 219–220

U

Universal Design for Learning (UDL), 46–48

Utah, 35t

V

Vaughn, J.L., 71

Venn Diagram, 117, 148f

Viewpoint Organizer, 165, 166f

vocabulary: academic, 138–139, 141–143; disciplinary literacy and, 69–70; grade-appropriate, 129; Standard 4 and, 130t–132t

VoiceThread, 118, 208

Vonnegut, K., Jr., 185

Vygotsky, L.S., 21, 55, 58

W

Walk, K., 200–201

Watts-Taffe, S., 128, 133

Weber, E., 18

What I Read...What Is in My Head...What the Text Said, 86–87, 86f

What-Why-How? organizer, 192–194, 195f

Wilhelm, J.D., 170

William, D., 18

Wilson, C., 198

Wimberly, R., 205

Wingenbach, N., 48

Wood, K.D., 87

Wood, P.F., 48–49

word accuracy, 60

word choice, and meaning, 126

Wordle, 139–140

Word Museum, 138

words, meaning of, 124–144

WordSift, 103

World-Class Instructional Design and Assessment, 26, 28

writing, disciplinary, 68, 69t

Y

Yep, L., 86

Young, T.A., 42, 44

Z

Zinoman, J., 193

zone of proximal development, 55, 58